Known to millions of people as the witty moderator of such television programs as *The Last Word*, Bergen Evans has always had an extraordinary awareness of English and its usage. He was born in Franklin, Ohio, but spent part of his childhood in England, where his father was assigned by the United States consular service. Back in the United States, he studied at Miami University in Ohio, did graduate work at Harvard, was a Rhodes scholar at Oxford University, and later returned to Harvard for his Ph.D. He is now Professor of English at Northwestern University, where he has been since 1932. In addition to teaching, which he loves, he has written many articles for national magazines and is author of *The Natural History of Nonsense*, *The Spoor of Spooks*, and (with Cornelia Evans) *A Dictionary of Contemporary American Usage*.

Comfortable Words

Also by Bergen Evans:

A DICTIONARY OF CONTEMPORARY AMERICAN USAGE
(*with Cornelia Evans*)

THE NATURAL HISTORY OF NONSENSE

THE SPOOR OF SPOOKS

BOSWELL'S LIFE OF SAMUEL JOHNSON (*edited and abridged edition*)

Comfortable Words

by BERGEN EVANS

ILLUSTRATED BY *Tomi Ungerer*

Random House • New York

FOURTH PRINTING

©Copyright, 1959, 1960, 1961, 1962, by Bergen Evans

© 1959, 1960, 1961, by Esquire, Inc.

All rights reserved under International and Pan-American Copyright Conventions. Published in New York by Random House, Inc., and simultaneously in Toronto, Canada, by Random House of Canada, Limited.

Library of Congress Catalog Card Number: 62-10775

MANUFACTURED IN THE UNITED STATES OF AMERICA
BY THE COLONIAL PRESS INC.

Grateful acknowledgment is made to the editors of the Atlantic Monthly, Vogue, Think, The New York Times, *and* Coronet, *for material in this book previously appearing in these publications.*

U*ncle, for God's sake,*

speak comfortable words!

—RICHARD II *2,ii,76.*

Introduction

IN RESPONSE TO A TELEVISION SHOW that appeared for three years on the CBS network and to a syndicated feature that has appeared in various newspapers and *Coronet* for the past two years, I have received more than a million letters asking questions about the English language. They ranged from such astonishing queries as "Can the longest word in the English language be used in a single sentence?" to searching challenges in etymology, grammar and the philosophic bases of speech. Hundreds of thousands were duplications, but the range of the questions was still enormous and their nature absorbing and revealing.

Aside from specific questions, many of which—with their implications—are dealt with in the following pages, two things of general interest emerged. One was the violence of the intolerance felt for any variation from whatever the writers felt to be "correct." And the other was the extraordinary insecurity that Americans feel about the use of their language. No people can ever have existed as thoroughly cowed and intimidated in the use of its own speech as we seem to be, a situation the more remarkable in that in our everyday use of the language, when for the moment we forget the schoolma'am-induced bogey of "correctness," we speak with great force and vitality, with notable vigor and sparkle.

Perhaps it's part of the price we must pay for having achieved equality by making the middle class universal. In matters of culture, it places us at the mercy of our schoolteachers who, if only because of the rapidity of our educational expansion, are often ill-educated. Yet we have no upper classes to defy them or lower classes to ignore them, and the new semiliteracy which has replaced the old illiteracy timidly accepts their pronouncements as law.

An illustration of this—reflected in tens of thousands of letters—is the belief that pronunciations which don't correspond to spelling are debased. Never has ignorance been more dogmatic and never has timidity been more eager to concur in folly. "Slurred" is the common term for this supposed process, and those who are willing to let what their eyes have seen once overrule what their ears have heard a thousand times have had a wonderfully self-satisfying time with this particular "corruption." At bottom, their attitude probably reflects their nearness to illiteracy, the awestruck respect for the printed page felt by those who have only recently made its acquaintance. Inspired by the humor of Orpheus C. Kerr, they have grown hilarious over such pronunciations as *mare* for *mayor, kloz* for *clothes, wuz* for *was,* and *histri* for *history.*

Unfortunately for the fun, however, these slurred forms happen to be the accepted, standard pronunciations. Though they may not be for long. The emphatic righteousness of the antislurvians is having an immense effect among the half-educated and the insecure. Increasingly words *are* being pronounced as they are spelled. The "l" in *almond, salmon,* and *palm,* for example, is heard more and more of(t)en and we shall probably hear it soon in *psalm* and *alms.* Only the most aristocratic and the most *un*aristocratic now dare say *Saint Looey.*

The letters were rarely concerned with "bad" grammar. That has almost disappeared, along with the rugged individual and genuine independence and cussing and cussedness and the Little Red Schoolhouse. *Had went, them there, they was, knowed* and other sturdy substandards are now so infrequent as to be almost charming. But *A sweet slice of heaven for just you and I, Do you wish some more coffee? Whom were you speaking to?* and such vulgar elegancies are increasing. And *they* are not the faults of ignorance. People don't fall into such errors naturally. They force their way into them by trying to apply rules they don't understand. Those who use such locutions have an uneasy feeling that they once knew the facts of "good" English and the rules governing them, just as they once knew the state capitals, and if they could only remember the facts and apply the rules their speech would be "correct." Then—as many ads, articles and books assure them—they would succeed at the job, win the girl, and be the life of the party.

All of which, of course, is a tissue of sad mistakes. In the first place, one cannot forget the rules of speech and go on talking. One can forget the state capitals and still get on in the world. But if one forgets the significant facts about one's native language, one becomes unintelligible and will probably be locked up. English is the one subject that we all know more about at thirty than we did at twenty.

An even greater mistake is the assumption that English represents a body of facts which we once knew. Nothing that can be said about a language is right or wrong in the way in which a statement about geography or chemistry or the answer to a problem in arithmetic is right or wrong. Three times three is not six, no matter how many children think it is. The only correct answer is nine, and that was true even before men knew how to count. But languages are not like that. What is true about a language one day may be wrong the next. Humpty-Dumpty told Alice: "When I use a word it means just what I choose it to mean—neither more nor less." And if he had only said "we" instead of "I," he would have been absolutely right.

Nice, for example, now a vague term of mild commendation, has at different times meant "stupid," "lascivious," and "shy." *Gossips* were godparents. A *talent* was a weight of silver or gold. Words may change slowly over centuries—as *dizzy* moved from "foolish" to "vertiginous" and now, in slang, back to "foolish" again. Or they may change almost instantaneously as when, in the late spring of 1957 *clean* (which already had fifty meanings) suddenly acquired the additional meaning of "free from strontium 90." *Hobby*, to drive home an important point with added contemporary examples, has shifted within a generation from a term tinged with slight scorn to one rich in approval. *Scan* has completely reversed itself within a generation. Twenty years ago it meant "to peruse with great care." Now, in its most commonly accepted significance, it means "to glance at with superficial haste." Fifty years ago *sophisticated* was a term of condemnation; today it is a term of approbation. And now, just to show what odd things can happen, it has suddenly begun to mean "highly sensitive and responsive to electronic stimuli."

A language is a man-made convention. Its "correctness" is closer to that of style and manners than it is to that of logic or the physical sciences. Modern linguistic scholars, to a man, agree with Puttenham (1598) that a language is simply speech "fashioned to the common understanding and accepted by consent." They believe that the only "rules" that can be stated for a language are codified observations. They hold, that is, that language is the basis of grammar, not the other way round. They do not believe that any language can become "corrupted" by the linguistic habits of those who speak it. They do not believe that anyone who is a native speaker of standard English will get into any linguistic trouble unless he is misled by snobbishness or timidity or vanity.

He may, of course, speak a form of English that marks him as coming from a rural or an unread group. But if he doesn't mind being so marked, there's no reason why he should change. Samuel Johnson kept a Staffordshire burr in his speech all his life. In Burns's mouth the despised lowland Scots dialect served just as well as the "correct" English spoken by ten million of his southern contemporaries. Lincoln's vocabulary and his way of pronouncing certain words were sneered at by many better educated people at the time, but he seemed able to use the English language as effectively as his critics.

The trouble is that in our new Grundyan paradise people are no longer willing to be rustic or provincial. They all want to speak like educated people but they don't want to go to the trouble of becoming truly educated. They want to believe that a special form of socially acceptable and financially valuable speech can be mastered by following a few simple rules. And there is no lack of little books that, preying on their fears and their ignorance and their laziness, offer to supply the rules and promise "correctness" if the rules are adhered to. But these offers are specious. Because you don't speak like an educated person unless you are an educated person; and the little books, if taken seriously, will not only leave the lack of education showing but will expose the pitiful yearning and the basic vulgarity as well, in such sentences as "Whom are you talking about?"

As a matter of fact, the educated man uses at least three languages. With his family and his close friends, on the ordinary, unimportant occasions of daily life, he speaks, much of the time, a monosyllabic sort of shorthand. On more important occasions and when dealing with strangers in his official or business relations, he has a more formal speech that is more complete, less allusive, politely qualified, discreetly reserved. In addition he has some acquaintance with the literary speech of his language. He understands this when he reads it, and often enjoys it, but he hesitates to use it. In times of emotional stress hot fragments of it may come out of him like lava, and in times of feigned emotion, as when giving a pep talk, cold, greasy gobbets of it will be forced out.

The linguist differs from the amateur grammarian in recognizing all of these variations and gradations in the language and accepting them as equally valid in different circumstances. And he differs from the snob in doubting that the speech of any one small group among the language's more than three hundred million daily users constitutes a model for all the rest to imitate.

Those to whom this idea is repugnant—and they are many and vociferous—state that it is the equivalent of saying that anything goes, that whatever anyone happens to say is quite all right. But this is simply their own distortion of something which they are unwilling or unable to understand. The customs and preferences of society are capricious but they are none the less tyrannical. In the United States today, to take a superficial example, one can no more say "I'll set me down and rest for a spell" than one can wear high button shoes. But fashionable people have done both of these things in the past and may do either or both again.

In language, as in dress, the things that are not allowed are fairly obvious. Anyone who cares about the impression he makes knows what these things are and avoids them naturally without giving the matter any thought. What people are really interested in is being elegant rather than dowdy. And this is much harder to achieve. Fine speech, like fine clothes, fine manner, or fine furniture, is basically a matter of good taste, the sense of what is harmonious or fitting. And this is not acquired out of a book or over a weekend.

In order to exercise good taste in English one must know

the full spread of what is allowable, the great variety of forms that are being used by the best speakers and writers. And one learns this not by mastering rules but by paying careful attention to details in the speech or writing of those whose English seems most attractive or compelling. Words are learned only in living contexts. Then, knowing what is allowable, one must have the courage to select the particular forms that are most suitable for a particular occasion and to one's own personality. The best English is easy, simple and individualistic within certain bounds set by the entire English-speaking world.

There is no simple rule about English that does not have so many exceptions that it would be folly to rely on it. For example, one of the best-known rules in English is that a plural subject must have a plural verb. None the less, anyone who has any ear for English knows that "More than one woman *has* changed her mind" is better English than "More than one woman *have* changed their minds." Even though the subject, "more than one," is, by its own statement, plural, the singular verb *has* is required.

No law of grammar is more absolute than that which says that the number of our pronouns must be consistent. Yet Subsection Three of Section Five of Article I of the Constitution of the United States says: "Each House shall keep a journal of its proceedings, and from time to time publish the same, excepting such parts as may in their judgment require secrecy." And this is not bad grammar which must be smilingly excused because of the ignorance of the Founding Fathers. It is good English. It doesn't even prove that things have changed, because such sentences are being written every day and by literate people. It simply proves that the "laws" of grammar are something different from the laws of the land or the laws of the physical sciences.

And just as one can't speak or write good English by applying a set of rules, one can't make poor English better by decorating it. Ornament is a tricky business in any field and if the ornament is tawdry or shopworn or unsuitable, the result may be disastrous.

The cheapest form of decoration is the unfamiliar word, which the speaker thinks must be elegant merely because it is unfamiliar to him. But since no one can use a word effectively unless he is so familiar with it that he has no awareness of its being strange or in any way unusual, the *un*familiarity is the thing that stands out. People who say *luxurious* when they mean *luxuriant* or *methodology* when they mean *method* or *fortuitous* when they mean *fortunate* indicate not only that they are ignorant but that they are vain and slothful as well. They are ambitious to shine but too lazy to consult a dictionary and too little used to good company or good books to know the proper current meaning of the words they use.

The cliché is another form of bad ornamentation. A cliche is not merely a common phrase or an established expression; it is something that once had a dash of cleverness in it, a twist of phrasing that was apt yet unusual, but which has by overuse become stale. Whoever first thought of a cucumber as the type of a particular kind of coolness or conceived that the hinges were likely to be the hottest part of hell or imagined that one part of a brass monkey was more susceptible to cold than the rest had a droll imagination and deserved the applause which his coinage—it is to be hoped—received. But those who repeat such expressions, now that all life has left them, are doubly damned because their use of them shows that they would like to be thought witty yet are actually mere parroters of failing echoes. Their very attempts to be clever show them to be dull.

One of the commonest forms of bad speech is a namby-pambyness where the situation calls for directness. Euphemism ("speaking fair") is a part of every language and is motivated by reverence, kindness, decency, and fear, so that no rules can pertain because every occasion must be decided by itself. But it is in just such circumstances that folly and bad taste exhibit themselves. A hundred years ago the genteel vulgar referred to legs as "limbs" and trousers as "unmentionables" and pregnancy as "being in the family way." To their spiritual descendants today death is "passing away," false teeth are "dentures" and, if they happen to be doctors, a stroke is "a cerebral accident." The same impulse led someone in the Treasury Department to rename the Collector of Internal Revenue the Director of Internal Revenue and someone in many city halls to call the young women who affix tickets for parking offences Meter Maids or Parking Hostesses. But death and taxes remain unsweet by any other names, as do most other human ills. Adultery is adultery even though Billy Graham has improved the seventh commandment to "Thou shalt not commit immorality."

Though they are meant to be soothing, there is something nastily condescending in such expressions. We resent the speaker's superiority to life's unpleasantnesses and his attempt to hoodwink us and lead us past them.

Sometimes, instead of words or phrases, strange grammatical forms are used under the mistaken notion that they add a touch of elegance. Barbarisms of this kind can usually be traced to textbook rules that have been oversimplified or misunderstood. People who try to speak by the rules are especially likely to misuse the subjective pronouns *I, we, he, she* and *they*, as Lorelei Lee does when she says "Life is hard for a girl like I." A common vulgarism that one hears in increasing frequency, and from such high places that the national honor almost demands that we quickly make it standard, is the substitution of *myself* for *me* in such a sentence as "He gave it to John and myself."

Whom is another dangerous word, particularly when it is the first word in a question. As an interrogative, *whom* has not been natural English for more than five hundred years. Of course, anyone who would rather speak like an ill-grounded textbook than like the educated people of his day is free to do so if he can. But the chances are that he won't be able to make it and that what he does say will be wrong from every point of view. For example, *Whom do you want to see?* is correct according to the rules of some textbooks; but *Whom shall I say is calling?* is wrong. And the sort of person who uses the first sentence is very likely to go on and use the second. Most people, to be sure, will not notice the difference. To them, both *whoms* are equally unnatural and therefore equally objectionable. Both sound like a kind of snobbery, an attempt to seem superior to the people one associates with. A few people will perceive the effort and the mistake and be embarrassed for the speaker. No one will be moved to admiration.

False elegance frequently shows in a confusion between adjectives and adverbs. Many English adverbs end in *-ly*, but not all, by any means. And there is no surer mark of uneasy ignorance than to stick an *-ly* onto the end of an adverb that doesn't need it. People who have been terrified into believing that there is something wrong about *drive slow,* in spite of the fact that this is what everybody says, are likely to come up with such oddities as "Write to me really soon" and "I spent some time there, but not an awfully lot." And this is not superior English but intimidated English. Ordinary people, if they hear it at all, probably regard it as finicky. Educated people, cultivated people, the sort of people that presumably it is intended to impress, would regard it as pathetic. But they would sooner accept a leper into their company than someone who talks this way.

Among people who have had at least a high school education (and this will soon be the majority of Americans) and who read at all (and this seems likely to remain a minority of Americans), these pretentious errors are the only kind of grammatical mistake now made. What the linguists call *substandard* is the English of uneducated groups, mountaineers, unskilled laborers, migrant field hands, poor people who have no interest in "book learning" and no wish to change their ways. If a person from such a background should want to become an office worker or a professional man, he would certainly lose his substandard speech in the process of preparing himself for his new life.

Of course not all words that are used with a peculiar meaning, and not all unfamiliar grammatical forms, are mistaken attempts to be elegant. The word may have this peculiar meaning as a technical term or as a piece of jargon in one of the sciences —as *indicated* for "deemed necessary" in medical talk or *destruct* for "destroy" in missile terminology. And the unfamiliar construction may be the accepted way of speaking somewhere else in the world. For example, the British normally say "Give it me" and are likely to regard the American "Give it to me" as a would-be elegance. However, "Give it to me" is the natural, standard form in the United States, where "Give it me" sounds strange.

Similarly, in some parts of the United States *real* is used as an adverb only by the illiterate. But in other parts, principally in the South, even a teacher of English might say "It's real warm today." And the Northerner who condemned this solely because it was not used in his own locality or class would be provincial. So in midwestern America verbs of going are often omitted after verbs of willing. Midwesterners will say "I want off here" or "The cat wants out," speaking the language of Shakespeare,

Masefield, and A. E. Housman, though many Easterners titter when they hear it. Yet these same Easterners reverse *bring* and *take* in a way that arouses the Midwesterner's derision, and out West many say *squoze* for *squeezed,* and for some mysterious reason all over the country people have suddenly started using *any more* in positive contexts ("I shop at the A & P any more; it's nearer"), a construction that affects the blood pressure of aging conservatives.

Grammatical peculiarities may be compared to table manners. Affected gentility is a mark of being ill at ease. But a deviation from the normal may mean any one of a number of things. Suppose—to illustrate—that a hostess notices one of her guests eating her pie with a spoon. She may think that no fork has been put at the woman's disposal and that, being very polite, she preferred to risk ridicule rather than to call attention to her hostess's oversight. Or the guest may belong to some sect that believes God does not want us to eat pie with a fork. Or she may not know any better. Or she may be a real, flat-heeled aristocrat who eats pie any way she damn well pleases and happens that day to damn well please to eat it with a spoon. But certainly if the guest were in all other ways attractive, intelligent, and poised, the hostess would not be warranted, on the basis of this one peculiarity, in assuming that her guest had no knowledge of the ways of cultivated people.

And no matter what she decides, she will *not* try to show that her own manners are superior by pointing out the irregularity to her guest—though many people, not otherwise barbarians, have no compunction about doing this when it's a matter of grammar or pronunciation rather than of spoons or forks.

The belief in a theoretically correct grammar, which still plagues so many Americans and leads them into grotesque and unacceptable forms of speech, began in the eighteenth century. And perhaps the truest thing ever said about the evangelical zeal with which we correct each other's speech was said by Joseph Priestley, the author and chemist, who wrote: "I think that a man cannot give a more certain mark of the narrowness of his mind than to show, either by his vanity with respect to himself, or the acrimony of his censure with respect to others, that this business [of grammar] is of such moment with him. We have infinitely greater things before us."

One of these greater things is *good* English—the English that is most effective in a particular time and place, the English that says most precisely just what we want to say, with the proper emotional overtones and with grace and force and beauty. And nothing does more to prevent a person from acquiring this sort of English than a belief in some theoretically correct forms that are supposed to be superior to any actually in use.

It is hoped that the reader will find in this book not only helpful discussions of many points he may have wondered about but also an introduction to some of the attitudes of modern linguistics and lexicography. And, above all, it is hoped that he will find encouragement to speak his mother tongue, to trust his own needs and passions to find their words from among the wealth which the greatest literature in the world and the daily use and experience of three hundred million people offer.

*a

THE PRONUNCIATION of the indefinite article depends on how emphatic we want to be. In normal, unemphatic speech ("There was a boy here looking for you"), it is always spoken *uh*. Anything else is an affectation. However, if we want to emphasize the idea of singleness ("I did not say *eight* boys; I said *a* boy!"), it is pronounced to rime with "say."

✶ "A Mr. Jones is waiting to see you"

A CORRESPONDENT wants to know if "A Mr. Jones" is rude. Perhaps not intentionally so, but unless the Mr. Jones alluded to were a remarkably humble man he would probably be offended. And if the speaker knew that it would be offensive to Jones, then it was rude to use it.

The *a* here says, in effect, "an obscure individual, calling himself Jones, one Jones out of myriads of undistinguished Joneses, is waiting to see you." Poor Jones, who no doubt sees himself as "*the* Mr. Jones," is crushed.

Of course if you know his first name you may rescue him from Jonesian anonymity by using it: "Mr. Theocritus Jones is waiting to see you." Just "Mr. Jones" is all right. There's dignity in Jones; it could be Inigo, Howard Mumford, or Spike. Should the boss bellow "What Mr. Jones?" into the intercom, you may crush Jones by saying coldly "A Mr. Jones." Or you may attempt to crush the boss by saying warmly "*The* Mr. Jones!" Or you may offer Jones the intercom to establish his own identity.

The is sometimes necessary. It is always necessary when an identifying clause is to follow, as in "The Mr. Jones who is waiting is not John Paul Jones."

✱ abracadabra

As A WORD of mystery, *abracadabra* is very mysterious. We know that it goes back to the second century A.D. Some have conjectured that it is made up from the initials of the Hebrew words *Ab* (Father), *Ben* (Son), and *Ruach ACadsch* (Holy Spirit) and it may well be. Written out in the form of a triangle, the word was hung around the neck to ward off toothache and assorted miseries.

Hocus pocus is much more recent. Appearing sometimes in the fuller form *hokuspokusfiliokus*, it is probably a travesty of the sacrament of the mass—*Hoc est corpus filii* (This is the body of the Son)—and was used by mountebanks to imply some magic in their nostrums. *Hoax* is simply a shortening of *hocus pocus* and the even more recent *hokum* a mixture of *hocus* and *bunkum*. *Prestige* also derives from juggler's jargon, coming ultimately from a Latin word meaning delusion—and still trailing a faint cloud of magic and trickery.

✱ purely *academic*

MANY teachers have written to protest the use of *academic* to mean "theoretical, impractical, speculative, removed from immediate reality, not likely to produce results." But their protests show them to have accepted the very values they ostensibly deplore. It is only to be wished that our academies were more academic, more abandoned to the delights of pure theory. Practical men, with accelerating efficiency, have been getting the most ghastly results of late, each year hatching some new practicality more hideous than the preceding year's.

The *Oxford English Dictionary* recognizes only "belonging to an academy" as the meaning of *academic*. The sneer seems to have crept in, or at least become fixed, during the 1930's. Perhaps it reflected resentment of the Brain Trust.

✱ *accenting* the positive

PEOPLE who write to insist that words have only one "proper" pronunciation have more postage than perception.

If they would only stand in the post office and listen for five minutes before they dropped the letters in the slot, they would be almost certain to hear varying but valid pronunciations. They would note, among other things, that accentuation differs according to grammatical function. The adjective, for example, is *ab'sent* but the verb is *ab sent'*. The noun is *con'flict* but the verb is *con flict'*. The noun is *reb'el* but the verb is *re bel'*. And so on, in scores of words.

And this is no mere prissy pedantry. The Canadian paper that carried a classified ad seeking "UNMARRIED GIRLS to pack fresh fruit and produce at night" had implicit faith in its readers' ability to distinguish between a verb and a noun.

How deft and brilliant we are, right in the middle of some rapidly enunciated sentence—of which the very structure and completion were totally unpremeditated and, in truth, uncertain even as we babble our way through it—to perceive that we are going to use this or that word as an adjective or a verb or a noun and instantaneously to shift the stress!

Or do we merely speak by habit, by usage?

✷ an *Act of God*

Is IT A reflection upon our faith or our arrogance that an *Act of God always* designates some disaster, some overwhelming natural catastrophe, some misfortune so dreadful and unavoidable that even the solemn courts absolve us from our obligations in the face of it? Are there no favorable acts of God? Or do we just ascribe the disasters to Him and the successes to ourselves?

There is on record at least one Act of God that seemed pleasant to at least one person. When the producer Mr. Jed Harris sued Miss Helen Hayes (Mrs. Charles MacArthur) for breach of contract because she became pregnant during the run of a play and claimed that she was thereby relieved of contractual responsibility to continue acting, Miss Hayes claimed that her pregnancy was an Act of God because she did not believe in birth control. And the court upheld her. The angelic hosts must have had an unusual lilt in their songs of praise that evening, after the verdict had appeared in the papers.

✷ Do we say "She's a fine *actor*" or "She's a fine *actress*"?

BOSWELL told Johnson that he had "been at a meeting of the people called Quakers" where he had heard a woman preach. "Sir," said Johnson, "a woman's preaching is like a dog's walking on his hinder legs. It is not done well; but you are surprised to find it done at all."

Woman's place was in the home and our fathers never seemed to get used to finding her elsewhere. If a woman did anything but breed, cook, or sew, it was felt necessary to remark upon it. And since some female has, at one time or another, done almost everything men can do, the language was cluttered with agent nouns with female suffixes. Fifty years ago the dictionaries carried scores of such words as *inventress* (St. Cecilia), *gunneress* (Molly Pitcher), *keeperess* (Mrs. Peachum) and *oratrix* (Mary Yellin Lease).

That time is past, however, and all its dizzy raptures are now no more. Today we rarely stress the sex of a doer where the sex is irrelevant—and the field of relevance has been narrowed practically to the biological. In the 1920's Edna St. Vincent Millay was often called a "poetess." Now she would simply be called a poet. But an *actress* remains an exception: her femininity is essential to her art and no actress objects to having that fact stressed.

✷ *actually*

WHERE some fact is opposed to what seems to be true and the difference, however small, is so important that the speaker feels it should be emphasized, *actually* may be used. It is used correctly in such a statement as this: "If a man looks at the sun, he assumes that he is seeing the sun as it is; but actually he is seeing the sun as it was eight minutes earlier, since it takes eight minutes for its light to reach us." Here the actuality is opposed to the seeming and the word *actually* stresses that fact.

The real trouble with the word is that it has become a vogue word and most of the time its use is not only unnecessary but irritating. When used, as it so commonly is, to introduce a sentence in which the speaker corrects or enlightens a previous speaker, it strikes a note of condescension. When someone says, for instance, "Actually, it's not very mysterious," he is saying, in effect, "You are laboring under a delusion but fortunately for you I am here and will set you straight."

✳ *ad libbing*

Ad lib is short for Latin *ad libitum,* meaning "at pleasure." In theatrical use, to ad lib is to speak off the cuff, to make up something just to give the scene an air of freshness or to cover up some blunder or mischance. In music *ad lib* retains more of its older meaning; it means that the manner of performance of a passage is left to the discretion or pleasure of the performer.

✳ "I wouldn't know him from *Adam's off ox.*"

NOBODY knows quite why this particular animal came to be accepted as the ultimate in indistinguishability, but I'll risk a guess.

There is an older and commoner expression—"I wouldn't know him from Adam"—meaning "I couldn't even distinguish him from the prototype of all men." Humorists have pointed out that Adam did not have a navel and was therefore, especially since he wore only a figleaf, easily distinguishable from other men. But the fact is debatable and is certainly not well enough established to affect the proverb.

My guess about the off ox is that some wit set out to improve "I wouldn't know him from Adam." If strange men look alike to us, oxen look even more alike, and Adam's oxen, the prototypes of all oxen, must have been even less distinguishable than Adam himself. And of the two oxen in the yoke, the off ox, being further from the driver, was even less familiar—and hence less distinguishable—than the near ox.

The image is a little strained, but it has humor and alliteration and *ox* suggests the slight contempt which we all feel for indistinguishable strangers.

※ *adhere* and *cohere*

To *adhere* is to stick to something, to cling to it, to be tightly attached to it. A thing or substance adheres to another thing or substance of a different nature.

Things of the same kind *cohere* when they stick together. A coherent story is consistent throughout; it has a natural and due agreement of parts. Things that cohere form a whole. That which adheres is an addition or an excrescence.

※ When we say "I'm *afraid* I can't come," what are we afraid of?

THEORETICALLY, of the chagrin of the person spoken to. "I'm afraid" in such sentences reflects one of those little fictions of courtesy that imply that the person spoken or written to is very important, so important that his slightest displeasure is grounds for apprehension. Amusingly, it would be unthinkable to use the expression to anyone of whom we might have a genuine fear.

The full expression would be: "I am afraid [of causing you inconvenience or disappointment but] I can't come."

※ *after, afterward* and *afterwards*

Aft means behind in space. In modern use it lingers on only in nautical phrases, such as "fore and aft." *After* is the comparative of *aft*. It's more aft-ish than aft, further behind, more to the rear, at a greater distance—both in space and time.

The suffix *-ward* indicates direction of the action (seaward, onward, upward) and *-wards* is simply *-ward* with the adverbial terminal *-s*. This is the same *-s* that appears in "He works nights" or "It's mine, by rights." But since *afterward* is already an adverb, there is no difference between it and *afterwards*. You may use either, as you choose.

If *aft* means back and *after* means further back, *afterward* or *afterwards* should mean "in the direction of further back." But *after* has lost its comparative force and has come to mean merely behind, either in space or time ("I'll see you after class,"

"And Jill came tumbling after") and *afterward(s)* to mean merely at a later time, subsequently ("Thou canst not follow me now, but thou shalt follow me afterwards").

❋ the *aftermath*

A *math* was a mowing, a harvesting by the scythe. Of the herb Medica, Philemon Holland says you may have "six maths a year." The *aftermath* was the second mowing and the word should not be used without something of this idea in mind.

It is used with pretentious vagueness to mean "result" or "consequence." We read of "a seventeen-year-old youth found dead in the aftermath of a drinking bout." But this wasn't the second but the first harvest. The San Francisco fire was an aftermath of the earthquake, for the first disaster sowed the seeds of the second. But "In the aftermath of long, destructive conflicts great military figures were summoned to lead in peace as they had in war" (Oscar Handlin's preface to Bruce Catton's *U. S. Grant*) is tumid. Peace is not an aftermath of war.

❋ not on the *agendum*

A CORRESPONDENT writes that the chairwoman held in her hand a list of things to be considered. She consulted it repeatedly and referred to it as the "agendum." Shouldn't it, he asks, have been "agenda"?

An *agendum* is a thing to be done. The word has two plural forms, *agendums* and *agenda*. *Agenda* may also be used to mean list of agendums and it is then treated as a singular, as in "The agenda is being prepared." In this sense *agenda* has its own plural *agendas*, meaning several such lists, as in "The chairwomen compared their agendas."

Threading our way through this plurality of plurals, and hoping not to step on the chairwoman's toes, I would say she meant *agenda*. I base this on the fact that the correspondent says she consulted it "repeatedly." If it were an agendum, and hence referred to only one thing, she need not have looked at it again and again. Maybe the handwriting was illegible. But since it was "a list of things to be considered," we must conclude that her grammatical slip was showing and she meant *agenda*.

✳ *ain't* it a shame!

IF OFFICIAL disapproval could kill a word *ain't* wouldn't exist. It's the most-thoroughly-disapproved-of word in the language. In 1925 the General Federation of Women's Clubs had a National Ain't-less Week. In the year 1932 the *English Journal* estimated that over 12 million teacher hours had been spent trying to stop children saying *ain't*. In 1959 the Juvenile Delinquency Project of the National Educational Association listed the use of *ain't* as an indication of potential delinquency.

Yet eighty years ago "Ain't" was not only acceptable but very upper class. Henry James has Sir Claude (in *What Maisie Knew*) say "Ain't I?" all the time and Sir Claude is represented as an elegant gentleman who chooses his words with care. Furthermore Henry James had a very good ear for elegance and vulgarity in speech.

This upper-class "Ain't I?"—which is attested to by a score of good writers—was often represented as "An't I?" (wherein we can perceive a possible telescoping of "Am not I?") and since this "a" was probably pronounced "ah" it could easily be mistaken for "are"—hence explaining the spavined bastard elegance of "Aren't I?" But if it was "ah" (as it probably was), then on the parallel of "t'm*ah*to" versus "t'm*ay*tuh," *ain't* may merely be the poor man's version of the aristocratic "an't."

An educated person is unable to say "Ain't I?" any more. "Am I not?" is ludicrously stiff. You practically have to brush your teeth before you can say it. "Amn't I?" is little improvement. "Aren't I?" is affected and, grammatically, far worse than "Ain't I?" (See amn't I justified?, p. 26.)

Still, *ain't* can't be used now. We've purified ourselves into a position where we can't speak at all. This must be the schoolma'am's supreme triumph.

✳ the wide-wandering *albatross*

AN *albatross* should be hung about the neck of every person who takes the firm, no-nonsense stand that each word has a definite, fixed meaning, a "real" meaning, as they often phrase it.

Surely here we have a fixed meaning. An albatross is an albatross is an albatross, though judging from the hatcheries, no rose. There it is, *Diomedea exulans*, web-footed, tube-nosed, wide-winged, o'er desperate seas long wont to glide till shot by ancient mariners. Under its more prosaic name of *goony bird* its poetic associations drop away, but it's the same creature.

But the word *albatross* is a corruption of the Portuguese *alcatraz* which designated not the albatross but the pelican. The penal island in San Francisco Bay was so called, apparently, because it was infested with pelicans before it was infested with gangsters. None the less, in the speech of America today, *alcatraz* means a prison, not a bird. *Albatross*, by the way, seems to have been corrupted from *alcatraz* because of a mistaken association with *alba*, "white."

Alcatraz itself, however, is a corruption. It's the Portuguese form of the Arabic *al qadus*, the name for a leather water bucket used on a water wheel. The leathery pouch under the pelican's beak probably suggested the name. And the Arabic *qadus* seems to have been a corruption of a Greek word for jar.

Now who shall say what is the "fixed and proper" meaning—goony bird, pelican, prison, leather bucket, or jar?

※ How much is *alimony*?

THE SECOND element of *alimony* certainly suggests *money*, but though ladies have found money in alimony, linguists haven't. The suffix *-mony* merely indicates something resulting or an abstract condition. It is attached to certain nouns derived from Latin, such as *ceremony, matrimony, acrimony*, and *alimony*.

The first part of the word, *ali-*, derives from the Latin verb *alere*, "to nourish." *alimonia* means "nourishment, food, support." It is from the same root that we get our *alimentary* canal.

Some bitter men have claimed that the word is merely a shortening of "all his money." But that isn't true, linguistically.

※ Is the *l* pronounced in *almond, alms, balm, calm, palm, psalm, qualm* and *salmon*?

ALL DICTIONARIES agree that the *l* is not pronounced in any of these words in standard speech, though Kenyon and

Knott (*A Pronouncing Dictionary of American English*) say that it is "frequent" in New England.

Against this may be set the evidence of our ears. The *l* is now heard more often than not in *almond* and *salmon* and frequently in *palm*. In fact many educated people, even, are astonished to hear any questioning of it. I have never heard the *l* pronounced in *psalm* or *calm*.

A decade or so ago Professor Householder, of Allegheny College, found that most of his students pronounced the *l* in most of these words. On further, more extensive investigation, he found it pronounced widely throughout the eastern United States, and almost universally by those under thirty.

It would seem, therefore, that the pronunciation of these words is changing. It is correct at present not to pronounce the *l*, but like many a correctness it may soon be the mark of an old fogy and in time a downright error.

✻ Is *alright* all right?

YES AND NO. It can certainly be distinguished from *all right* as clearly in our speech as *already* can be distinguished from *all ready* or *always* from *all ways*. Yet no dictionary lists *alright* as acceptable—though *alive*, *alarm*, and other parallel elided forms are fully established—and therefore anyone who uses it in writing (everyone uses it in speech) runs the risk of being regarded as slovenly or illiterate.

My own—dissenting—opinion is that most people who write *alright* instead of *all right* (when they mean "alright" and not "all right") are not slovenly. They are simply asking for the privilege of making a distinction in writing which is accepted in speech. And since the tendency of writing for more than a century has been toward approximating speech, the chances are that *alright* will soon be regarded as standard. Certainly Fowler's insistence that "there is no such word" is no longer true and Mencken's damning of it as "a barbaric invention" is absurd. (*Alrighty*, of course, remains a coy abomination.)

Those who feel that in insisting on *all right* they are manning the bastions of purity and defending our language from the corruption of the vulgar may be a little startled to learn that their counterparts across the Atlantic insist with equal firmness on *near by* and regard our defenders as vulgar illiterates because they write *forever* instead of *for ever*.

✳ How low is an *alto*?

Alto means "high." It comes from the Latin *altus*, "high." It's the same word as the first part of *altitude*, "height." We refer to high, veil-like clouds as *alto-stratus*. Why, then, is *alto* the name for the lowest female voice?

Because formerly it described the highest male voice, the countertenor. It was then taken over to describe the lowest female voice, what is properly called *contralto*, the voice intermediate between soprano and tenor.

✳ the demi-breasted *amazon*

UNTIL recently *amazon* indicated a large woman of fairly forbidding mien and manner, aggressive, muscular, tough. But there's been a sudden liking for big women—or, perhaps, a sudden public admission of a liking for big women. The agony columns of disreputable periodicals are replete with demands for oversize females. Choruses now boast of "glamazons."

The original Amazons were a tribe or nation of women warriors who played a part in Greek mythology. One of the labors of Hercules was to obtain the girdle of Hippolyta, the queen of the Amazons. As an undertaking, this was apparently regarded as equal to killing the fifty-headed Hydra, bringing the three-headed dog Cerberus up from the infernal regions, and cleansing the Augean stables. The Amazons fought in the Trojan War, on the side of the Trojans.

The Greeks were fascinated by the ladies and puzzled by their name. They decided it must mean *a*, "without" plus *mazos*, "breast," and said that the Amazons burned off their right breast in order that it should not impede their arrows as they drew back the bowstring. But this assumption of busty amplitude and incisive devotion to duty on the part of the female warriors is what is called "folk etymology"—that is, an attempt to explain a strange word in terms of one's own language. Scholars now believe that *amazon* was a Persian word whose original meaning has been lost.

The Amazon River was so called because an early Spanish explorer was attacked, while descending it, by a tribe of Indians whose women fought alongside their men.

✸ ambulances and the ambulant

AN *ambulant* case is a walking case, yet those unable to walk are carried in an *ambulance*. Why?

Both derive from the Latin verb *ambulare*, "to walk." A walking case is an *ambulant* or an *ambulatory* case.

But walking is a way of moving and, until quite recently, for most people the only way of moving in their entire lifetime. So it is not surprising that the word for walking came to mean just getting there any way at all. Just as we use *go* to mean going in any way, though it used to mean going on foot, as opposed to riding.

During the Crimean War the French established mobile medical units to give first aid immediately behind the lines. Each of these was called a *hôpital ambulant* or "a moving hospital." They had wagons for transporting the wounded to the more permanent hospitals at the rear. The British adopted the term but shortened it by dropping the first word. Our army borrowed it from the British. Civilians took it over from the military.

And so the ambulances go, flashing and wailing through traffic lights, adding one more terror to the fears of poor ambulant pedestrians.

✸ amn't I justified?

REBECCA WEST in one of her novels has an unpleasant, affected American woman say, "I'm just awful, amn't I?" On first reading this I assumed that Miss West assumed that *amn't I?* was an American locution, and I rashly said in print that it had never been heard on land or sea or in the air. But I was soon informed by a host of correspondents, mostly Irish, that "Amn't I?" is not only in wide general use but is definitely preferable to the vulgar "Ain't I?" or the genteel "Aren't I?"

Justly reproved, I have been more alert and have been rewarded by finding "Amn't I" in the writings of Honor Tracy

(*The Straight and Narrow Path* and *Mind You, I've Said Nothing*), Rumer Godden (*An Episode of Sparrows*) and James Joyce (*Dubliners*). That will do for me. "Amn't I?" is in the language and unimpeachable.

✷ *an* F.B.I. man

A CORRESPONDENT wonders why we speak of "*an* F.B.I. man when *F* is a consonant and one doesn't use *an* before a consonant."

The answer is that a consonant cannot be pronounced except in connection with a vowel. The letter *B*, for example, has to be pronounced *bee* or *buh*. One can say "a *B*" because here the consonantal sound precedes the vowel sound that must accompany it. But *F* is pronounced *eff* and in the pronunciation one has to interpose the *n* in "a(n) eff" or else make an unnatural pause.

It is a trifling matter—that one must say "an F.B.I. man"—but it has an interesting signification. Many people claim that a great deal of time is wasted "reading words." They claim that they read "by sight." That is, they say that they have trained themselves to perceive meaning directly from the appearance of print, without going through the process of translating the print into sound and then into meaning.

But this can be claimed only by people who have done very little reading or have given very little thought to the reading process. No eye would pass over "a F" in print without halting—because it wouldn't *sound* right!

Further proof of this fact is furnished by our bewilderment when a word which has to be divided at the end of one line and continued into the next line is improperly divided. Thus if the word *ashamed* were to appear with the *ash-* at the end of one line and the *-amed* at the beginning of the following line, most of us would have to go back to get the meaning and would probably be completely confused for a few seconds.

✷ *and also*

And also is a particular target of those who decry redundancies. They would have us all, like Chaucer's Clerk of

Oxford, speak not one word more than need and that to be "seyd in forme and reverence, And short and quyk and ful of hy sentence."

But *and also* is not, really, a very good place to begin their reform. *Also* means "likewise," "besides," or "in addition" and one can certainly use *and* with any of these without seeming to be repetitious; it merely serves to join an additional thought or comment to what has gone before.

In writing or formal speech one could begin a new sentence and omit the *and,* but in ordinary speech or informal writing the *and* seems to come more naturally. It supplies a momentary beat in the rhythm of the sentence that permits an emphasis on the *also* to be more marked, if one wants it to be.

※ *"And* the Lord spake unto Moses"

MANY people get belligerent over the use of *And* at the beginning of a sentence. They find it offensive and they find it increasing and they demand that something be done about it.

And is a conjunction. It is used to connect grammatically coordinate words, phrases, or clauses. A clause is a group of words containing a subject and a predicate (stated or implied). A clause usually forms a part of a compound or complex sentence, but it can be coextensive with a simple sentence. Where one has a number of such simple sentences or clauses that are connected by *and,* it's a matter of choice whether one clause is terminated by a period and followed by *And* or terminated by a comma (or nothing at all) and followed by *and.* It's purely a matter of punctuation and depends on how closely the writer wishes the reader to associate the two thoughts.

The demand today is for short, clear sentences. "One idea to a sentence," *The New York Times* urges its writers. And this may account for the increasing frequency of the construction.

But it's not as new a thing as most protestors seem to think. Reading the Bible must bring them close to apoplexy, since it must be the commonest form of punctuation therein.

✳ try *and* stop him

MR. THEODORE BERNSTEIN, to whose vigilance *The New York Times* owes much of its clarity, elegance, and precision, feels that "try and get" is "best avoided." He quotes a passage from the *Times:* "Mr. Smart decided to try and get Ernest Hemingway to write for the publication" and admonishes the writer of the passage to substitute "try to get."

"Don't look at the horses, after the bull hits them. . . . Watch the charge and see the picadore try and keep the bull off." —Ernest Hemingway, *The Sun Also Rises* (p. 162, Student Edition).

✳ andiron

"BUT *what* and iron?" wails a puzzled lady.

All we know for sure is that the word *andiron* has nothing to do with *and* or *iron*. A century or two ago some scholars thought it was a corruption of *handiron,* but no one believes this any more.

It's one of those words that grow curiouser and curiouser the more you think about them. It was in the language with its present meaning and almost its present spelling as early as 1300. We know that before that it was *aundire* and that it came from the Old French *andier* which came from the Latin *andena*.

People don't like to use a word that doesn't "make sense" and this word was made to make a certain sense by changing its last element to *iron*. This change was helped along, no doubt, by the fact that there was also an Anglo-Saxon word *brand-iron* which meant the same thing: the iron which supported the brand or burning log.

What is astonishing is that the perfectly sensible, meaningful Anglo Saxon word—brand-iron—should have been lost and the obscure, corrupted Anglo-French *andiron* kept. Maybe the Norman overlords had all the good warm fires and were the only ones that had need of andirons.

✳ anesthetic, anaesthetic and anæsthetic

WHY THESE variant spellings? And what's this strange siamese-twin thing æ?

Æ (from the earliest times also written AE) was a Saxon symbol for a sound halfway between *a* and *e*. This is the sound in Pall Mall which to Americans, when Englishmen pronounce it, sounds like "Pell Mell."

In the thirteenth century this symbol disappeared from the language, but it was brought back in the sixteenth century in words derived from Latin words which were spelled with æ. It didn't affect the pronunciation. It was just a piece of pedantry, and when one of these words became established in the language the tendency was to spell it *e*. The *æther*, or *aether*, is now universally spelled *ether*.

This æ (or *ae*) now remains only in (1) Greek and Latin proper names (*Cæsar, Æneas*), and even these are inclined to change (*Ætna* is often *Etna*); (2) words belonging to Greek or Roman history or art (*ægis*); and (3) scientific or technical terms derived from Greek or Latin. Anæsthetic is one of these. The tendency in America, where a knowledge of Latin is no longer a symbol of prestige, is to use *e* in this group (*anesthetic, hemoglobin*).

✱ high *animal* spirits

WHEN young people are laughing and clowning they are often said to have *high animal spirits*. Why should this be, a correspondent asks, "since very few animals (with the possible exception of otters) are gay or playful?"

To look among animals for "animal spirits" is to go in the wrong direction. This is one of those phrases that have completely changed their meanings.

According to the physiology of the Middle Ages (based on the physiology of antiquity), the arteries were air ducts, carrying not blood but gaseous *spirits*. This theory was based quite reasonably (but erroneously—so much that is reasonable is wrong) on the fact that the arteries were always found to be empty in autopsies.

Of these spirits there were three: the animal, the vital, and the natural. The *animal* was named after the soul, or *anima*. Its seat was the brain which, with the nerves, it controlled. It was the highest of the spirits. The heart was the seat of the vital spirit and the liver was the seat of the natural spirit.

In the seventeenth century, however, the word *animal* acquired its modern restriction to creatures lower than man. "Animal spirits" was affected by this change and the delight in life which was, presumably, the effect of the soul came to mean the exuberance of physical health which we share with young animals.

That gaiety was once a mark of the possession of a soul is a charming thought, scarce credible in these puritan times.

✳ *antipodes*

Antipodes is from the Greek *anti-*, "opposing" and *podes*, "feet."

One of the obstacles in the way of accepting the idea of the rotundity of the earth was concern about how people on the other side—if it were round—managed to live upside down. Why didn't they fall off? That *they* were upside down, from the antipodal point of view, never entered our forefathers' minds. In the blissful times of 600 years ago it wasn't necessary to attempt to see the other fellow's point of view.

And even after the sphericity of the earth was grudgingly conceded, the other people were felt, somehow, to be upside down. Bartholomew the Englishman, in a fourteenth-century encyclopedia, explained *antipodes* about as well as it has ever been explained: "Yonder in Ethiopia," he wrote, "been the Antipodes, men that have theyre feet agenst our feet."

The word was extended to include the countries in which such topsy-turvy people lived, among them Australia, which is "down under."

✳ "I shop there *any more*"

THE EMPLOYMENT of *any more* affirmatively ("I shop at the A&P any more. It's much better.") is one of the most amazing changes in the language. To those who are used to *any more* only in negative statements ("I don't go there any more") the new use is simply unintelligible. Yet hundreds of letters, from every part of the country, attest to the universality and rapidity of this extraordinary development.

But many who regard the negative use as correct but are

aghast at the affirmative might be astonished to know that a number of uses of *any* which seem thoroughly natural to an American sound strange to an Englishman. Thus in the United States *any* is frequently used alone to qualify a verb, as in *Did you sleep any?* But it cannot be so used in England.

Such a sentence as *I'm surprised you come here any more* has long been acceptable in the United States, but the use here is not really affirmative. The principal clause is interpreted as "negative by implication." That is, it means: "I didn't think you would come here any more."

✻ the very possessive *apostrophe*

SIGNS that regulate pedestrian traffic at intersections usually read DONT WALK not DON'T WALK. One would have thought that the omission of the useless apostrophe would have been greeted with cheers by an age that so prides itself on embracing the new and shucking off the past. But no such thing, of course. Rather the invariable laments that "slovenliness" was "corrupting" the language, that the lamp of learning was flickering out, and that the Neanderthals had captured one more bastion of civilization.

But the apostrophe is entirely a printer's problem and has nothing to do with the language itself. It was first used to indicate a genitive singular about 1680 and to indicate a genitive plural about a hundred years later. After perplexing teachers and students alike for less than two hundred years, it is now in the process of disappearing. The Board of Geographic Names, "in the name of uniformity," has dropped apostrophes from place names (Hells Canyon, not Hell's Canyon, is the official name of the gorge of the Snake River on the Idaho–Oregon border). George Bernard Shaw stoutly refused to interrupt the flow of his pen to stick in possessive apostrophes.

If you use an apostrophe where it doesn't belong, it shows that you don't know what you're doing. If you omit an apostrophe where it is usually expected, it may merely indicate that you are a disciple of Shaws.

✳ the *apple* of the eye

"Why *apple*? Why not some other fruit?" a correspondent asks.

Apple in this phrase is a translation into English of the Latin *pupillam*, "the pupil." In *Deuteronomy* (xxxii:10) we are told that the Lord kept Israel "as the apple of his eye" and in *Proverbs* we are enjoined to keep God's law as the apple of our eye.

The pupil of the eye was called the apple in older English because it was thought to be a solid, spherical body. That the "apple of the eye" is one of the most precious things we have but delicate and vulnerable and therefore to be cherished and vigilantly protected does not need to be elaborated.

Why an apple, though, rather than any other fruit? But the older meaning of *apple* was almost any fruit. The old word for pine cone, for instance, was *pineapple*. It was transferred to what we now call a pineapple (*Ananas comosus*) because of the tropical fruit's resemblance to what we now call a pine cone.

By the way, nowhere does the Bible say that the fruit of the forbidden tree which Adam and Eve ate was an apple!

✳ articulation in the *arctic*

How much parental energy has gone into the seemingly hopeless task of trying to get children to pronounce the first *k* sound in *arctic!* What moves the slovenly little devils to leave it out, especially after Papa (who is a mod'l of pr'cise 'nunciation) has pointed it out to them?

It's the nature of the language, Papa, and you might as well give up. Had you consulted a dictionary before the lesson in articulation, you would have noticed that either pronunciation is correct and had you consulted a linguist you might have learned that the concession, in allowing either pronunciation, is not to the slovenly omission but to the meticulous inclusion.

The difficulty is that some scholar inserted the first *c* of the Latin *arcturus* into the established English *artic*, ignoring the fact that the occurrence of two *k* sounds so close together in one word runs counter to ease in speaking. By a process known as dissimilation, we usually eliminate the first of two such bothersome sounds or change it to another. Few people, unless they are of the *prunes-and-prisms* class, pronounce the first *r* in *particular*, for instance, or in *governor* (though we all do in *governess*, where there is not a second *r*). The old word *peregrine* we just changed to *pilgrim*, and dignified Papa when he says "pilgrim" hasn't the faintest idea that he's speaking like a Chinese laundryman with a cleft palate.

The winter overshoes called *arctics* are almost always referred to as *ar' tiks*, even by those who pronounce the first *k* sound in the geographical word. And anyone who puts the first *k* sound into *antarctic* practically has to withdraw from the conversation while he arranges his mouth. A good, clean enunciation of all the consonants in *antarctic* is an impressive performance.

✻ **Do you say "Those who attended the party "*are*" or "*were*"?**

SINCE *attended* makes it plain that the party took place some time in the past, it is better to say *were*. That the guests who then *were* now *are* is not relevant to the statement which is concerned with their attendance, not with their being alive.

✻ *Arkansas*, **The Wonder State**

THE VARYING pronunciations of the name of the Wonder State (possibly so called because of uncertainty in this matter) have keep geographers, linguists, patriots, vaudevillians and sachems of the Arkansea tribes in turmoil for over a century.

In 1881 the legislators of the State of Arkansas, in solemn conclave assembled, decreed that the name of the state "should be pronounced in three syllables, with the final 's' silent, the 'a' in each syllable with the Italian sound, and the accent on the first and last syllables."

The river seemed to have been included in the decree and ever since loyal Arkansans (who sometimes call themselves Arkansawyers) have tried to conform to its dictates. What has emerged, however, as far as most of them are concerned, is *ar' k'n saw'*, which conforms in the matter of accent but manages, somehow, to miss "the Italian sound." Then there's that *w* at the end, dragging along like a hound-dog's tail.

Over in Kansas, next door, many citizens assert States' Rights and call their portion of the river the *ar kan' zus* and Arkansas City, *ar kan' zus* city.

✻ pronunciation of *asthma*

THERE is an increasing tendency to pronounce words as they are spelled, though it might be wiser to spell them as they are pronounced.

Asthma will present a difficulty. If you try to pronounce all the consonants, you'll certainly sound asthmatic. It's better to pronounce it the way everyone else does: *az' muh.*

Asthma derives from a Greek verb *uazein,* "to breathe hard." In its origin it may simply have tried to reproduce in its own sound the sound of the thing it designated. Many words do this— such as *whistle, bang, sigh.*

✻ speaking of *aunts*

THE COUNTRY over—indeed, the language over, and for centuries—the preponderant pronunciation of *aunt* is and has been *ant. Ahnt,* a more recent introduction, is fully acceptable but it is in no way better or more correct. In America the difference is basically regional. One hears the *ahnt* pronunciation more in the Northeast.

The broad *a* is regarded by many people as "more aristocratic," especially by those who feel insecure socially, though the present evidence indicates that until early in the nineteenth century it was a cockney pronunciation. Walker in his pronouncing dictionary (1790) listed the broad *a* as "vulgar" and the flat *a* as "elegant and learned."

Ahnt is far from being universal in England. In John Braine's *Room at the Top,* an English novel about a young man in a hurry shoving his way from the bottom to the top of the heap, the hero-heel has occasion to refer to his father's sister when speaking to one of his new, wealthy acquaintances. "I was going to pronounce Aunt with a broad *a*," he says, "but decided not to attempt it yet."

Some people insist that *ahnt* is necessary to distinguish their kinswoman from an insect. One can only wonder from what crawling kind they come that they think the confusion is possible.

※ **the *avant-garde***

The *avant-garde* is the spearhead of an advancing army. It is the French form of the word which we have slurred down in English to *vanguard*.

Avant-garde is applied to ultra-modern and experimental artists and writers not merely because they are (at least in their own opinion) moving ahead of the main body of contemporary thought and practice, but also because they are usually belligerent about it.

The figure of speech is not perfect, however, because a vanguard is part of the following army. Whereas there is no one the artistic *avant-garde* detests more and feels less a part of than those who are behind them. However, if one thinks of the established and conventional modes as the enemy and artists of the future as the main body of the advancing army, the figure holds.

Avant-garde has had a curious history in English. In its strict military sense it was used in the language from 1470 to 1664, though largely replaced by the English *vanguard*. It reappeared momentarily in the writings of the romantics but disappeared for good in 1800. Its modern figurative use is a twentieth-century reborrowing from the French.

※ ***averse from***

Many people feel that since *averse* means "opposed, antagonistic, hostile," it must be followed by *to*, not *from*. Dr. Johnson, however, condemned the use of *to*.

In practice, either is acceptable. "What female heart can gold despise?/What cat's averse to fish?" (Thomas Gray); "As men averse from war" (*Micah* ii:8); Matthew Arnold wrote of Dido turning "averse from her false friend"; Frank O'Connor speaks of Jane Austen's aversion from poetry and Harold Nicolson of "the male aversion from being a nuisance." The Americans seem to be more averse to things and the British more averse from, but the distinction is not rigidly observed.

✳ *Avuncular* means "uncle-ish." What is the corresponding word for "aunt-ish"?

The correspondent who asked this question has exposed a weakness in the English language, laid bare a reprehensible omission, exposed the insidious workings of the double standard: there isn't any word for things pertaining to an aunt!

Avuncular means, literally, "like a little grandfather," being based on the diminutive of the Latin *avus*, "grandfather." It is applied to such uncle-ish doings and qualities as jocosity, conspicuous beneficence, a semiconspiratorial backing of young rebels and replenishment of young spendthrifts. And, above all, the giving of advice. A pawnbroker is often referred to as "Uncle" and *avuncular* sometimes designates pawnbrokerish doings and attitudes. In Latin, by the way, *avunculus* referred only to a maternal uncle.

Since *amita* is the Latin word for aunt—especially a father's sister—there ought to be a word *amital* or *amitular* to describe auntly actions and qualities. But, alas, there isn't. Aunts, apparently, didn't count. They probably never had enough money to be generous and were too wise to give advice.

✳ some *awful* thoughts

So awful is the present state of the word *awful* ("Gosh, those wieners are awful good. I guess I'll have another!") that we are startled to come on it in its original meaning, as in Richard II's rebuke to the unkneeling Northumberland: "How dare thy joints forget/To pay their awful duty to our presence?" Indeed, so completely is the word debased that it is impossible for a modern to read such a passage as Milton's "Abashed the devil stood,/And felt how awful goodness is" without a smile. We are told in *Oseney Annals* that when Henry I attended the consecration of Christ Church, Canterbury, and the anthem "Terribilis est locus" was sung with a trumpet accompaniment, he was so much moved that he swore aloud that "by God's death the place was indeed awful."

※ *"Axe and it shal be gyven unto you"*

"MY LITTLE boy persists in saying *axe* for *ask*," laments a mother. "What should I do about it?"

Nothing whatever—unless he's deaf.

If you nag him enough, he may take to stammering and then you'll both have a real problem. If you let him alone, he will in time perceive that nowadays most people put the *s* sound before the *k* sound in this word, not after it. And so he will change his pronunciation. At least most people do, for almost all children say *axe* for *ask* but very few adults do.

They used to, though. It's interesting that children make this particular change, because *axe* is the old form—the "correct" form, if you want to call it that. The Anglo-Saxon verb was *acsian*. The modern pronunciation is the result of metathesis—which is a learned way of saying that the *s* slipped out of place. For some reason children feel an urge to put it back. It hasn't been out of place very long, either. Wyclif has: "Axe and it shal be gyven unto you." Caxton (1490) spelled the past tense *axyd*. And as late as 1806 Noah Webster said he preferred *axe*.

There are many words in the language in which a similar sound change has occurred. *Lisp* was formerly *lips*, *tax* was *task*, and *wasp* was *wops*.

※ *axiom, adage* and *proverb*

AN *axiom* is a universally accepted rule or principle. It is stated, usually as the beginning of a chain of reasoning, with the full understanding that everyone assents to it. An axiom is a fact which the speaker, at least, holds to be self-evident. It is an axiom that the whole is greater than any part, that a straight line is the shortest distance between two points, that night follows day, etc.

An *adage* is a saying that has gained authority and credit by long use. It may or may not be self-evident. It may, or indeed it may not, be true. "In vino veritas" and "Where there's smoke there's fire" are typical adages.

A *proverb* is an adage couched, usually, in homely terms, worn smooth, as it were, by generations of speakers. It conveys

—or its users hope it will convey—the idea of practical, earthy wisdom, the fruit of great experience and shrewd observation. Yet this mountain of implication often brings forth a mere mouse of comment ("A penny saved is a penny earned," "Life's not a bed of roses"). Politicians love proverbs because they give their talk a homely flavor and say nothing that anyone disagrees with. Then for almost every proverb there is a counter-proverb. Thus *Proverbs* xxvi:4 advises us to "Answer not a fool according to his folly, lest we be like unto him." But *Proverbs* xxvi:5, the very next verse in the Bible, advises us to "Answer a fool according to his folly, lest he be wise in his own conceit."

An axiom is laid down in an effort to get a basis for logical agreement. An adage is usually spoken to assert a vague authority. A proverb is repeated to gain the reputation of wisdom. Adages and proverbs are sententious and their frequent use marks an empty rather than a full mind.

※ "She *baby-sitted* for us"

Sat is certainly the past tense of *sit*, but *baby-sit* is a new verb and the millions who use it may think of it as something all by itself, not merely an extension of the old verb *sit*. Indeed the ideal baby-sitter doesn't do much sitting; she washes the dishes, tidies up, and in general behaves like Little Orphant Annie.

The tendency to make irregular verbs regular when they acquire new meanings is very strong. New regular verbs are being coined every day, but no new irregular verbs, and the old irregulars are being rapidly abandoned. Thus we think of *wove* as the past of *weave* when we have the ancient art of cloth-making in mind, but when we use the verb figuratively to describe a modern action, the winding of a car in and out of the stream of traffic, *weaved* seems more natural to most people.

So we hear *baby-sitted* ("She baby-sitted for them last week"). We also hear *baby-sat*. But it sounds a little studied and stiff, with too much emphasis on the sitting and not enough on the baby.

Only the public, by its use, can decide which of the two forms will become "correct." And dictionaries, which do not prescribe but describe, will record their choice when usage has settled the matter.

❋ bringing home the *bacon*

THE ALLUSION is to a flitch of bacon which was offered annually at Dunmow, a village in Essex, England, to any married couple that would kneel at the church door and swear that they were happily married. In particular, they had to swear that for a year and a day they had not quarreled and that at no time during the preceding year had either of them wished himself or herself unmarried.

Chaucer (in the fourteenth century) alludes to the custom as already fully established and universally known. Between 1244 and 1772—a period of more than 500 years—the flitch was awarded only eight times.

❋ "I feel *badly*"

"I FEEL badly" can mean that the speaker's sense of touch is impaired. "I feel bad" can only mean that he doesn't feel well, that he may be sick. Since a sense of touch is rarely impaired, "I feel badly" isn't likely to be misunderstood. But it sounds a little affected, as if the speaker thought the adverb more genteel than the adjective.

Until a few generations ago *bad*—an adjective—was required in this construction. *Badly* came to be substituted because some people ignorantly thought than any word following a verb ought to be an adverb and perhaps because some others, guilty as well as ignorant, thought *bad* could only mean wicked. Then the uncertain, the sort of people who say *myself* when they mean *me*, seemed to think that an *-ly* ending added a touch of refinement ("A little money comes in handily," "My, this place smells foully").

Badly is historically and grammatically incorrect in "I feel badly," but it is now so widely used that it has to be accepted as standard. It is one of the many instances of the "corruption" of the language by those who think they are speaking extraly specially finely.

※ *bag and baggage*

There used to be a distinction between *bag* and *baggage*. *Bag and baggage* was a military term denoting the collective property of the army (the baggage) and the property of the individual soldiers. The expression was used chiefly in relation to a besieged garrison that, though compelled to surrender, marched out with honor. There was an established procedure to mark this particular sort of a surrender. The soldiers retained their arms, their drums were beating and their colors flying. Each musketeer carried a bullet in his mouth, bandoliers full of powder, and match lighted at both ends. That is, the army signified that although it was surrendering the city or fortification, it did not regard itself as defeated and was in a posture of defense, ready on the instant to retaliate violence and revenge perfidy. An army that kept its baggage was still a functioning army and soldiers who kept their bags probably kept their morale too.

The modern expression simply means "completely." It is used of ignominious ejections from lodgings, and the like. But what is interesting about the modern use of the phrase—and illustrative of the ways of words—is that although its military significance is forgotten, it retains its former *tone*. There is in it even yet a faint, far-off echo of war, siege, capitulation, and marching out, scorn defying triumph. People are not told to be off *bag and baggage* except after a prolonged to-do, and there is a feeling of something insolent in their departure. We are the victors, but they are not wholly vanquished.

※ a *baker's dozen*

Two explanations are commonly offered for calling thirteen *a baker's dozen*.

One is that under certain laws bakers were formerly punished severely if their loaves were less than a prescribed weight and that, to protect themselves, they always threw in an extra loaf with each dozen. But this explanation raises doubts. There is not much likelihood that many people would buy a dozen loaves at a time and, surely, if the baker were to be punished he could be punished for making a single loaf underweight.

The more likely explanation (which is supported by a number of quotations) is that retailers were privileged by law to receive a thirteenth loaf free every time they bought a dozen, the extra loaf to be their profit.

There was formerly a term *in-bread*, the extra loaf "thrown in" by the baker. It was sometimes called *vantage bread* and this was defined in a dictionary published in 1611 as "the thirteenth loaf given by bakers unto the dozen."

※ **the *banged* girl**

Bang(s), the straight fringe of hair across the forehead, is a shortening of *bangtail*, a word first applied in America (1770) to the docking of a horse's tail in a similar fringe. This tail-do became very popular. Several bangtails won much-publicized races and by 1880 the term was applied to the hair-do. William Dean Howells (1880) referred to "a young lady's bang" and the *Evening Standard* in the same year mentioned "the present style of banged girl." Why the plural only is now used is uncertain. Maybe it is thought of as a series of fringes.

In our own day horses have supplied us with another coiffure: the pony-tail.

Bangtail, by the way, is not to be confused with *bob-tail*, in which the whole tail, bone and all, was cut short. It was a bob-tail that added to the joy in "Jingle Bells" and a bob-tail that did so well at the Camptown Races. Bob-tailing was very cruel, though, because the horse was unable thereafter to whisk away flies.

※ **Why "called to the *bar*"?**

WHEN we say that a lawyer who has been qualified to practice has been *called to the bar* we are alluding to an arrangement in the Inns of Court in London many centuries ago. The Inns of Court served as the law schools and in their halls was a barrier or partition which separated the seats of the readers and benchers, who were lawyers of a recognizedly superior rank, from the rest of the hall. When a student had attained a certain standing he was "called" from the body of the hall and permitted to take a place among the worthies on the other side of the bar or barrier.

The English *barrister* originally indicated one who had been so called.

✵ *basement* and *cellar*

ALTHOUGH *basement* and *cellar* are used loosely as synonyms, they describe different things.

Cellar is the much older word. It meant originally a storage place, usually underground, for foodstuffs and the like. We retain this meaning in *wine cellar* and *coal cellar*. The Authorized Version of the Bible (1611) says (*Luke* xii:24): "Consider the ravens . . . which neither have storehouse nor barn." In Wyclif's version (1382) this is rendered: "Behold the crows . . . to which is no cellar neither barn."

Basement, which first appeared in 1793, designates properly the foundation or lower part of a wall. A basement apartment (shortened to *basement*) is thus the lowest story of a building, wholly or in part below the level of the ground. It may furnish wretched habitation, but it's not a cellar.

A cyclone cellar is properly a cellar. It is a safe place to be during a cyclone, whereas a basement would be a dangerous place to be.

✵ to *baste*

Baste seems to be a very versatile word, since it can mean "to sew," "to cook," and "to beat." But, actually, there are two words here and possibly three. They just happen to sound and be spelled alike.

The word meaning "to sew with temporary stitches" derives from *bast*, the inner bark of certain trees which was made into a coarse thread. The word meaning "to moisten meat while cooking with drippings or butter" derives from Old French *basser,* to soak or moisten. *Baste* meaning "to beat" may be a humorous application of the idea of "soaking" or it may derive from an Icelandic word *beysta,* meaning "to beat or thresh."

The colloquial *lambaste* is simply a duplication for emphasis. *Lam* also means "to beat" ("I'll lam you kids when I get my hands on you!"). Both words are strong words and when combined are slightly comic.

※ "Will you *bath* the baby?"

A CORRESPONDENT writes from Philadelphia and another from California to ask whether a mother can *bath* a baby. Doesn't she have to *bathe* it? they ask. Both have heard *bath.*

Not necessarily. *Bath* as a verb is a standard English word of great antiquity. It is recognized in the dictionaries and is not described as archaic, colloquial, or dialectal. It is in widespread use in England where they bath in a tub and bathe in the sea. The Knights of the Bath used to bath ceremonially. John Evelyn saw their bath-ing in 1660.

Here's a word that was in use in 1483 and has been in continuous, daily use ever since, in England and in America, in London in 1660 and in Philadelphia and Santa Barbara in 1960. Yet very few educated people have ever heard it.

※ pronunciation of *bayou*

WHENEVER life becomes insupportably dull, you can start an argument with someone over the pronunciation of *bayou.*

The pronunciation seems to vary as widely as the spelling, which has been variously *bayou, bayoue, bayoe, bayeau, bayau* and other assorted forms. Originally it was a Choctaw word for a river or creek. The Choctaw word was represented as *bayuk*— but, of course, that was English spelling, probably by an untrained phonologist, and may have conveyed only the vaguest idea of how the Choctaws pronounced it.

The dictionaries recommend *By′ oo.* Many Northerners, not greatly concerned with Choctaw, Creole French, or the topography of Louisiana, pronounce it *Bay′ oo* and get on about their business. Those who live in them call them *By′ oes*. It's a swampy subject.

✱ *beat* it

WHAT is it you're expected to beat when you're told to "*Beat it!*"? The street with your feet as you hurry away. *On the lam* probably has the same meaning.

✱ *beating the Devil around the bush*

THE EXPRESSION occurs in many forms, "Beat the Devil around the gooseberry bush" and "Whip the Devil around the post" being the most common. In America, where it seems to have been more popular in the South than in the North, it was "Whip the Devil round the stump."

It meant "to get around a difficulty by means of some fabricated excuse." A newspaper, in 1841, said that many legislators, after having run their constituents into debt by lavish appropriations, "want to whip the Devil round the stump" and let somebody else levy the necessary taxes.

The meaning is vaguely but not precisely clear. To whip the Devil round a bush or stump would reflect great credit on the whipper, would show him to be a man of the highest virtue, the most unbounded courage and one who acted vigorously in the cause of righteousness. It would occasion an enormous uproar and draw a great deal of attention. But it would be highly unlikely to happen and anyone who professed to have done it could expect to be believed only by the credulous.

✱ the *Beatitudes*

Beatitude means "supreme blessedness, exalted happiness." *The* Beatitudes are the sayings of Jesus Christ (*Matt.* v:3-12; *Luke* vi:20 23) prefacing the Sermon on the Mount. In the Beatitudes Jesus speaks of the happiness or blessedness of those who possess certain qualities. To the shorter form, as given in *Luke*, are added certain contrasting "woes."

A student in an examination paper once referred to these

sayings as "the B attitudes." I have always wondered what he thought the "A attitudes" were, what superior moral injunctions he thought were being concealed from him.

Attitude has no connection with *beatitude*. It is, rather, a slurred form of *aptitude*. And certainly our moral attitudes are often determined by our aptitudes—those sins we have no mind to.

✻ the beatified *beatniks*

IT WAS one of their prophets, Mr. Jack Kerouac, who named them—or at least popularized them as—"the beat generation." Old fogys ("squares") assumed that this meant that they felt they were a beaten, beat-up, battered generation and wondered why (since they are all post-World War II) they thought they had taken any worse beating than anybody else. But Mr. Kerouac and their other seers scornfully repudiated this etymology. They said that *beat* was related to *beatified*—that they were blissful and blessed, not beaten.

It may be. Certainly many of their utterances resemble the peace of God "that passeth all understanding."

The *-nik* is a Russian agent-suffix. Like our *-er* (as in *performer, dancer*), it indicates one who is involved in the action of the verb. The suffix had already come into facetious use in America, possibly through Jewish comedians ("He's a real nogoodnik," i.e., one involved in actions from which no good need be expected), and was attached to the beats in good-humored waggery.

✻ *been, bin,* and *ben*

AMERICANS pronounce the word *been* as *bin* or *ben*. Some British—but not all, by a long shot—pronounce it *bean*.

Bin is a very old pronunciation. And so is *ben*. *Bean* is fairly recent. Our pronunciation, which is sometimes derided by Britishers who know very little about the history of their own language, is simply the older English pronunciation which the early settlers brought over. *Bean* is not proper in the United States; it's affected.

Many Americans are just as silly about *ben* as some English are about *bin*. There are still sections of the United States where *ben* is the only form heard and we know that formerly it was widespread. Whittier, for one, pronounced it that way:

   For of all sad words of tongue or pen,/
   The saddest are these: "It might have been."

We have Emerson's assurance that this was not a pronunciation adopted for the rime's sake, that it was Whittier's regular pronunciation. As it was of millions of his contemporaries—and is of ours.

✻ beeves, beefs, and beefings

THE RAPID increase in the use of the once slang, now colloquial, *beef*, meaning "a complaint" or "to complain" (probably from the idea of bellowing, with that note of indignation which can be so plainly distinguished in the bovine voice), has raised certain problems about plurals.

The standard plural of *beef*, referring to cattle, is *beeves*, though *beefs* is also acceptable. However, "Four roast beefs" would mean four individual servings of roast beef while "Four roast beeves" would mean four oxen or steers roasted whole. The plural for the complaint is *beefs* ("I never start beefs with waiters," said Mr. Mickey Cohen, denying that he had slugged a waiter) or *beefings*, for those who prefer the gerund.

To *beef-up* is to infuse vigor. The English beef themselves up mightily with Bovril, the very essence of bovinity. The expression is a virile one. *Time* is very fond of it: the Indonesians seek Communist arms "to beef up their obsolete arsenal" (Jan. 6, 1958, p. 24); the Reverend Dr. Fred S. Buschmeyer has been selected to beef up *Memo*, a Protestant publication (Jan. 13, 1958, p. 71). There's a fine suggestion of snorting and pawing the ground.

✻ beg to advise

A STENOGRAPHER writes (discreetly asking that her name be withheld) to question her boss's prose style. It seems that the tycoon (who must wear a stovepipe hat and use a quill pen) is fond of the time-honored expression "beg to advise." The stenographer said that people didn't like unsolicited advice (or even solicited) and urged deletion of the phrase. The boss said that *advise* here doesn't mean to give advice but to give information and *beg* is just a polite expression to take the curse off giving information.

I think the stenographer has the stylistic, psychological, and commercial advantages in the argument, but in the sheer matter of language the boss is right.

One of the meanings of *advice* is information. The word was formerly used a great deal in this sense ("We have received advices from Portugal. . . .") and still is occasionally. Attached every month to my paycheck is a document entitled *Remittance Advice*—and the English of a paycheck is impeccable! And *advise* can mean to convey information. But because of the more common meaning, it is certainly open to the misconstruction of seeming to recommend a course of conduct. And since such a suggestion must imply that whatever course of conduct was being followed was inadequate or wrong, the suggestion will probably be resented. Unless, of course, the boss's correspondents are all of his own tastes and vintage. Then they will simply feel that he writes a good, solid letter.

✻ *begging the question*

Begging the question is commonly used as if it meant evading the question, weaseling out of it.

But that's not its exact and proper meaning. It means, rather, to take your own position for granted at the beginning of an argument, to assume a premise which your opponent will not admit. It is the *petitio principii* of the logicians. For example, the afflictions of Job, as told in the Bible, led him to question whether there was a moral order in the universe. His comforters began all of their arguments by assuming that there was such an order. But that was the very thing he was questioning and he found them not a comfort but an added affliction.

The expression means literally: "You—like a shameless beggar—are asking me, your opponent, to *give* you the whole argument at the outset!"

❋ begin, began, and begun

A MOTHER appeals pathetically from the tyrannous dictates of her high-school daughter. The daughter had used *begun* as the past of *begin* and when the mother had recommended *began* had stated that her teacher said it was *begun*.

The teacher is either a duocentenarian or some wretched graduate student who hasn't yet worked his way out of the eighteenth century. Though it may be that the daughter is deaf, dishonest, or just fed up with Mama.

The standard past tense of the verb *begin* is now *began*. *Begun* was once literary English (Byron used it as the preterite) but it hasn't been used as the past tense for almost a century.

The participle is now *begun*, though once it could have been *began* as well. But "had began" would sound strange today.

❋ "I believe I will"

MANY people get agitated about the use of *believe* to mean *think*. But it is so used by educated people every day and most dictionaries recognize it as standard.

This seeming laxness is due to the fact that *believe* is a general term and covers a wide range of credulity, from the most solemn conviction to the vaguest meanderings of thought or desire. When a man says that he believes in God or in the honesty of his brother, he makes an affirmation of great solemnity and profound (though in the latter instance perhaps misplaced) confidence. But when he says that he believes he'll have another piece of pie, he is merely stating, half apologetically, that his belly is about to triumph over his good sense.

To *think* is merely to form a notion in the mind ("I think it will rain before dark").

Since usage has long ago established *think* and *believe* as interchangeable at certain levels of meaning, the careful speaker or writer can only watch them and make sure that they are not used interchangeably where their meanings are not interchangeable. Otherwise he may sound pompous or flippant

✳ Is "Believe you me" bad English?

It isn't bad English, but it's bad rhetoric and certainly bad conversational strategy.

The Psalmist admits that he was a little hasty when he said in his heart that all men are liars. But even if he had stopped and thought it over, he could have made only a few exceptions. Men have lied so long, so ingeniously, so convincingly, and so persistently that scarcely any assertion beyond the order of the alphabet or the facts of the multiplication tables can hope to be received without a measure of incredulity.

As a result all languages are full of protestations of veracity and, of course, the more the protestation the more the suspicion. Among such expressions in our language is "Believe me." But no one believes someone else merely because he demands to be believed and the phrase soon grew weak. Then somebody tried to give it fresh force by inserting "you" and inverting the word order.

But it doesn't work. The excess of protestation stimulates an excess of doubt. And the contrived word order leads one to suspect that the statement it prefaces will be equally contrived.

✳ I read of someone that he sat *below the salt*. What did this mean?

It meant that he was of an inferior social position or else that in genuine or assumed humility he took an inferior place.

In former times, when social distinctions were outwardly marked and great importance attached to them, a large salt-cellar at the middle of the table marked the seating line that distinguished the honored guests from the less important ones. To sit *below the salt* was like living on the wrong side of the tracks.

Unless one were a nobleman or an ambassador or someone whose position would have made such a gesture ludicrous, it was always good breeding to take a seat below the salt and wait to have the host insist that one move one's seat and sit above it.

✳ *beside* himself

WHEN we say that someone is *beside himself*, we mean that he is so completely removed from his normal self that he is able to stand alongside himself.

The underlying idea is a common one. We say that so-and-so was "out of his mind" with grief or worry or "out of his senses" when he did something foolish. We say that a piece of music "sends" us (away from our ordinary selves) and that we are "carried away" or "gone, man, gone." The more dignified might prefer "enraptured," but *enraptured* is merely Latin for "seized and carried away." Hotspur (in Shakespeare's *I Henry IV*) was so annoyed with himself on one occasion that he said he could "divide" himself and "go to buffets." Festus said to St. Paul (*Acts* xxvi:24): "thou art beside thyself; much learning doth make thee mad."

Beside was formerly used in this sense more than it is now. Men could be beside their patience, or their gravity, or their wits. But such expressions are now archaic and today a man can be beside himself only.

✳ best *bib and tucker*

A *tucker* was a piece of lace or other material worn by women around the neck or tucked into the top of the bodice. Children also wore something like it. Among them may have been Little Tommy Tucker who sang for his supper.

Bib is related to *imbibe* and *bibulous* and other drinking terms. It is not certain whether a child's bib is so called because it is put on when the child is given something to drink (it was formerly called a *feeder*) or because by the time the child is finished the bib itself is so sloppy.

An adult's bib is the top part of an apron. *Best bib and tucker* was first used (two centuries ago and principally of women—men had *best bib and band*) with some seriousness. But it is now wholly humorous, with an affectionate overtone, suggesting that we think of the expression solely in relation to children.

✻ *best* foot forward

MANY correspondents are disturbed by the fact that they were taught never to use a superlative when a comparison involves only two things and yet are encountering such superlatives, in quite respectable places, every day. "People always say 'Which of the two do you like best?' Shouldn't they say 'like better'?"

Logically one should not use a superlative with two, but in idiomatic English we often do. Everyone says "Put your best foot forward," yet we've only two feet and they know it. Anyone who said "your better foot" would be laughed at. I once heard a sports announcer, poor bewildered creature, say "And may the better man win!" Whereas Shakespeare said, "whose blood is reddest, his or mine." Milton said, "Then thou shalt see . . . whose God is strongest, thine or mine." Jane Austen wrote of "the youngest of two daughters" and DeQuincey of "much the least of two evils." The list could be extended clear to the other side of the Hall of Fame.

And not only the great, but everybody else. Of two cars battered in a collision, surely everyone would say "the blue car got the worst of it." Anyone who said "worse of it" would be speaking pretentious, unidiomatic, nonstandard—just plain bad —English.

Logic is often a helpful guide, but that which people "always say" is, in the last analysis, good English.

✻ *between each* stroke

THERE's a great to-do about the expression *between each*. The logic of the objection to it, which is vociferous, seems to be that since *each* obviously refers to one thing and you can only be *between* two things, it's an impossibility.

This is one of those assertions that seem so irrefutable to those who assert them that after giving them utterance they flush with triumph, look around the assembled company with benign satisfaction, and with a slight nod accept the murmured gratulations of their adherents.

But, actually, *each* is what is called a "distributive." That is, it refers to an individual but only in its quality as a member of a group. There is always a plural idea in mind when we say *each*. We can't use *each* when there is only one; we can't say "each Europe" or "each China."

When we say "between each," as in "He rested between each stroke," we are saying by elision, "He rested between each stroke and the next one." And the language permits elision.

The expression has been used by almost every distinguished writer of English from Shakespeare to John Mason Brown and must be accepted as idiomatic English. It cannot even be regarded as an innovation and the objections to it are more ingenious than warranted.

✱ **Do you capitalize *biblical*?**

CERTAIN words, such as proper names, are invariably capitalized. But there are other words where capitalization is not obligatory but is used to show respect. And here you have to let your conscience be your guide. It's like a man's taking his hat off in an elevator. Some men do, some men don't. In some buildings, you would be a boor not to do it; in other buildings, you would be a boob to do it. Some take their hats off only when a pretty woman gets in, thus showing they are worshippers of beauty. And whichever a man does, he will be admired by some of his fellow passengers and despised by others.

In the old days, when scholars strove to be Christian gentlemen and gave much thought to the sacred and profane implications of punctuation, the words *devil* and *hell* were not capitalized, lest one seemed to pay respect where disrespect was due. Today they are as likely to be capitalized as *bible* or *Biblical*—not out of increased respect for them but out of increased respect for consistency in capitalization.

Among the idiosyncrasies of current capitalization is the fact that *Negro* is always capitalized, *white* never. The motivation here seems guilt and uneasiness.

James Thurber makes a very nice distinction in capitalization in his quotation of Harold Ross's emotional farewell to John McNulty who, against Ross's wishes, was leaving *The New Yorker* to go to Hollywood: "Well, God bless you, McNulty, goddam it."

✳ *bicker* and *dicker*

Despite the frequent confusion arising from the similarity of their sounds, *bicker* and *dicker* are not synonyms. Dickering often leads to bickering, but the two activities are not identical.

To *bicker* is "to quarrel," especially petulantly, "to squabble," "to wrangle." It characterizes more a sort of reciprocal nagging than any slam-bang, knock-down-and-drag-out affair. It once meant "to skirmish in battle." It comes from an old Teutonic word meaning to hack or stab and was probably weakened by the influence (due to the close similarity of sound) of the French *piquer*, "to peck." (We say that someone is *piqued* when he has been irritated by some sting or some peck at his vanity.)

Dicker now means "to haggle, to trade by petty bargaining." It is chiefly used in the United States, but it is a very old word. It goes back to *decuria*, the Latin word for the bundle of ten hides which the Roman legionaries made the basic unit of trade with the barbarians at the frontier. Apparently the barbarians didn't accept the Roman evaluation of their hides without a great deal of chafing and chaffering.

✳ "Ne se, *bigot!*"

Bigot, which is enjoying quite a vogue at the moment, is applied in contemporary usage to almost anyone who obstinately refuses to share our prejudices. In its history it has meant a hypocrite or someone unreasonably devoted to a particular creed of which the speaker does not happen to approve. If the speaker approves, the bigot is, of course, anything from "a man of high principles" to a saint.

The origin of the word is uncertain but it seems to have been an early pronunciation of "by God." It was first applied to the Normans who were, apparently, either very devout or very profane. Probably the latter. For centuries the English were known in France as "goddams."

The story (told by Wace, a twelfth-century chronicler) is that when Rollo, a Norman baron, was required to kiss the foot of King Charles the Simple, as an act of homage, he roared "Ne se, bi got" ["Not I, by God!"] and the phrase was applied to all his mutinous, truculent, blasphemous countrymen.

✻ a *bill* of lading

A *bill* was originally a written document, formal and sealed. Linguistically the word *bill* is related to a papal bull at one extreme of dignity and a billet-doux at the other. It got its name from the *bulla*, or seal, with which formal documents were sealed. In commonest contemporary use *bill* means a statement of money owed. But there are many remnants of the older meaning in such terms as *bill of fare, playbill, true bill, dollar bill, bill of particulars,* and *a clean bill of health.*

Lading simply means "loading." We are familiar with this vowel in the verb *to load* in the poetic form of its participle: *laden.*

The *bill of lading* was the official receipt which the master of a ship gave to the consigner, making himself responsible for safe delivery to the consignee. Such a document constituted legal proof of ownership and was often used as security for a loan. Modern bills of lading are strictly business, but the old bills of lading ended with: "And so God bring the good ship to her desired port in safety."

✻ Does *biweekly* mean every two weeks or twice a week?

To OUR eternal confusion *biweekly* can, with equal propriety, mean "every two weeks" or "twice a week."

We speak a language rich in poetic splendor, magnificent in its possible rhythms, admirable in its sonorities, ancient in its lineage and glorious in its achievement—but a bit spotty in the matter of precision.

✷ *blacklist* and *blackball*

Blacklisting and *blackballing* are different procedures. Both indicate a man isn't wanted, but there are so many who are not wanted in so many ways!

A man is *blacklisted* when his name is placed on a list of persons who, because of suspicion or as a form of punishment or retaliation, are not to be employed. Such lists are almost always kept a secret and their very existence denied.

A man is *blackballed* when he is denied membership in a club. Many clubs require unanimous acceptance by their members of any new member and many other clubs grant every member the right to exclude from membership any outsider for whom he has a strong dislike. Voting was customarily by white and black balls, to preserve anonymity. (*Ballot*, by the way, is a diminutive of *ball*.) One black ball was sufficient to deny membership to a candidate.

The verb *to blackball* has been extended to mean "to exclude" or "to ostracize."

✷ *blasé* or *bored*?

To BE blasé is to be bored, but to be bored in a particular way—to be bored with the pleasures which simpler, less world-weary people still find delightful.

Blasé is a French word meaning "worn out." It derives from an older word meaning "blown" (which, of course, is what *exhausted* means). That is, all the breath's out of you. But what a difference between being blasé and being breathless in the face of some delight!

It is interesting that the word was introduced into English by Lord Byron in *Don Juan*. Byron was blasé and his hero was meant to be more so.

✷ *bluestocking* ladies

Bluestocking was first used, to describe a lady with literary tastes, in the middle of the eighteenth century. This was the time of the salon, of sedan chairs, of elaborate costumes, of enormous gambling, fantastic drinking, and forced and frothy gaiety in high society. Among the leading London hostesses of the day was Mrs. Edward Montagu who sought distinction by having intellectual parties. At her salon, to show their disdain for the fripperies of rival salons, the guests ate sparingly and did not dance or play cards but talked of high and learned matters and wore the plainest clothes. Plainest of all was a Mr. Benjamin Stillingfleet who went so far as to wear the homely blue-gray woolen stockings that tradesmen wore instead of the white silk stockings which a gentleman was then expected to wear on formal occasions. This was too much for the rest of society which at once dubbed the eggheads "bluestockings" and the name stuck. It stuck to the ladies, however, though they didn't wear the stockings. Maybe it just seemed more outrageous to think of ladies wearing them.

The word is a literary term. It's not in common use. It's a bluestocking word.

※ it's all *bluff*

Bluff, in one sense, was originally a seaman's word to describe the perpendicular prow of a boat: "If her stem be upright, she is called bluff or bluffheaded." Then it came to be used to describe a perpendicular, broad, bold cliff at the shoreline. This word (as John Wesley noted in 1737) was used by the American colonists to describe similar formations along river banks and remains in this application an Americanism.

It is tempting to assume that *bluff*, "to pretend," consists of putting a broad, bold face on some matter. But the authorities say no. This meaning of *bluff*, they say, is derived from a dialectal word for a horse's blinkers, that its basic meaning is "to deceive" and that the bluff heartiness with which this is done (when bluffing) is only incidental. This meaning too, by the way, is of American origin.

Bluff, when applied to a person, meant "surly, blustering, domineering," a development of the prow and cliff meanings. Its change to the modern meaning of "roughly but good-naturedly frank" was the work of Sir Walter Scott.

※ the bare *bodkin*

A *bodkin* is now chiefly thought of as a blunt needlelike instrument by means of which one can rethread the tape that holds up one's pajamas. Not quite the thing one would reach for to make one's quietus.

In Hamlet's day it was a small dagger and, apparently, a common object. Women wore them as hairpins. Bodkins must have been lying around everywhere in an Elizabethan palace. Otherwise the famous lines don't make much sense:

> For who would bear the whips and scorns of time,
> Th' oppressor's wrong, the proud man's contumely,
> The pangs of despis'd love, the law's delay,
> The insolence of office, and the spurns
> That patient merit of th' unworthy takes,
> When he himself might his quietus make
> With a bare bodkin?

Even in my college days I had a confused idea, somehow, that a bodkin was a bodice and *bare* meant "naked." In my mind's eye (Horatio) I saw John Barrymore, tearing open his ruffled shirt preparing to mar that whiter skin of his than monumental alabaster. And I find that many others still have some such confused notion. But *bare* here doesn't mean "naked"; it means "mere." Hamlet says "Why should a man put up with all this when he can put an end to it with a mere bodkin?"

Dr. Johnson, in his grumbling way, pointed out that except, perhaps, for the pangs of despis'd love, there were few things in the catalog that a prince would have to put up with.

※ the new *bohemia*

Bohemian has had a revival, largely a literary revival and chiefly due to Mr. Russell Lynes's description of a new social class "the Upper Bohemians." In its earlier meaning of someone with artistic tendencies who acts with a disregard for conventional behavior, *bohemian* suggested gypsies and was based on the erroneous assumption that gypsies came from Bohemia. Just as *gypsy* itself is based on the erroneous assumption that they came from Egypt. Much of what *bohemian* conveyed in the 1890's is now conveyed by *beatnik*.

The modern word carries more envy and admiration than

contempt. The Corporation Man peers wistfully at Bohemia across the cyclone fence that surrounds the plant, and modern bohemians are above rather than below respectability.

Bohemians differ from nonconformists in the bases of their nonconformity and in the degree of it. Their approach is much lighter, more complacent, and is not likely to go so far as to reach discomfort. If the modern bohemians had to conform, they would mockingly conform. While, of course, a true nonconformist would not.

The modern bohemian isn't a *radical*. He has no desire to change things from the root up. And, then, today *radical* has largely political connotations and the bohemian isn't concerned with politics. He would regard such concern as naive or vulgar.

✳ a *bon(e)fire*

THE JOLLY associations of *bonfire* ill prepare us for the real grimness of the word.

Originally it was spelled *bone fire* and a definition in a Latin dictionary of 1483 leaves no doubt that it was a fire "wherein men's bodyes were burned."

A bonfire may have been a fire in which the dead were burned after a victory and it may be from that fact that we think of it as a part of a celebration. By now the festive associations have so completely overshadowed the gruesome ones that when we read in an Elizabethan book that Queen Dido burned herself up "in a bonfire," our first thought is that some gaieties had had an unexpectedly tragic ending.

✳ "make no *bones about it!*"

To *make no bones about* now means to speak frankly. Originally it meant to make no objections to, to find nothing against. It is a very old expression and its early forms were "to find no bones in" or "to make no bones in."

It referred, apparently, to finding bones in soup as an obstacle to swallowing the soup. It is now semihumorous but was formerly serious. Thus a serious work, in 1548, says that Abraham when commanded to sacrifice Isaac "made no manner [of] bones . . . but went to offer up his son."

There are many terms in the language wherein acceptability is spoken of in terms of eating, such as "That won't go down with him," "That sticks in my craw," "I won't swallow that," "I can't stomach it."

✻ so much *to boot*

THE WORD *boot* in the phrase *to boot* has nothing to do with the thing we wear on our feet. It's a totally different word, being related far off to the word *better*. And it means— and has meant for a thousand years—just what it means in this phrase: "to the good, into the bargain, extra, besides."

From this it came to mean a way of mending matters by making a gift to an injured party, giving him something to boot. Such amends was a regular part of Old English law, and tables of reparation—the proper "boot" to meet various injuries and slights—were drawn up. Certain crimes, however, were regarded as too serious to be so expiated. They were known as "bootless" crimes and were to be punished by death. This meaning of *bootless* has been lost, but we still use the word (though it is slightly archaic and poetic) to mean unavailing, unprofitable, useless ("It's bootless to argue with him; his mind's made up").

✻ *both of them*

MANY correspondents have timidly asked if it is permissible to say *both of them* and many more have roundly asserted that it is not permissible "Since *both*, when speaking of two, means *all;* whereas *of* implies only a part of."

Educated people in America use *both* and *of* together in this way all of the time. They have been so used for centuries. Shakespeare uses the expression ("Good day to both of you") and so does the Bible ("The eyes of both of them were opened"). The fact that a construction is used by Shakespeare and the Bible does not, of course, mean that the construction is necessarily acceptable in contemporary American English. But if it can be shown that a construction is used today (as this one is) and was used 350 years ago, it's pretty hard to argue that it's not an established idiom.

One wonders how long the first person who devised this tortured objection to "both of them" stayed awake until he thought of it.

✻ Can milk be said to be *bottled* when it's put into a waxed-paper carton?

WE THINK of *bottles* as something made of glass, but that's a very recent conception, a thing of a few hundred years at the most, and one that may even now be obsolescent.

For countless thousands of years before glass came into common use, bottles were made of leather or skins. That's the whole point of the biblical parable about not putting new wine in old bottles. If the bottles had been made of glass, it wouldn't have mattered. But old leather bottles or wineskins are dry and brittle and would burst if there were any fermentation left in the new wine—as there most likely would be. But new bottles, still supple and pliant, could stretch a little and absorb the pressure. There is a reference in the Bible (*Jeremiah* xix:1) to "a potter's earthen bottle." But the necessity of so describing it makes it plain that it was less usual than a wineskin.

So if a *bottle* was once skin or leather and then became glass, there is no reason why it should not now be waxed paper and in the future, maybe, plastic or DuPont knows what, and why the act of filling it, whatever it is made of, should not remain *bottling*.

✻ *boughten* goods

AS A PARTICIPIAL adjective, *boughten* was once widely used in the United States. By the middle of the nineteenth century, however, it was becoming rustic, and highly "correct" writers and publications were setting it off with quotation marks or including it only in passages whose spelling indicated that it was uneducated. But the common people, who did not read such authors or subscribe to such publications, went right on using it up until a generation or so ago.

The *Oxford English Dictionary* lists it as poetic (it was originally a corruption, on the analogy of the archaic *foughten*), dialect, or an Americanism.

It has been revived in the pseudo-rusticity of suburban speech to suggest that manufactured things are rare and expensive, prized above the familiar, homemade ones. As such, it is an affectation. Should there still be anyone, however, to whose lips the word comes naturally, there's no reason why he should not continue to use it.

✱ Is *bowdlerizing* a synonym for censoring?

Bowdlerizing is not quite a synonym for censoring. It is a particular form of censoring—censoring solely to remove the morally objectionable.

The word derives from Dr. Thomas Bowdler who, in 1818, published an edition of Shakespeare from which he had removed "all words and expressions which cannot with propriety be read aloud in a family." Apparently the Bard was felt to be in need of purification, for Bowdler's version was enormously popular, many editions being called for. Gratified by this response, he then castrated Gibbon, removing from the *Decline and Fall* "all passages of an irreligious or immoral tendency," a labor which can only be compared to re-writing *Hamlet* in such a way as to remove all trace of the Prince of Denmark. In the preface Dr. Bowdler blandly assured the reader that Gibbon himself would have approved the deletions.

On our own side of the Atlantic, Noah Webster, not to be outdone by the British, in 1833 published a bowdlerized edition of the Bible, "Many words and phrases" of which, he said, were so offensive to young females as to make them "reluctant to attend Bible classes."

Bowdlerization's masterpiece was a minute but brilliant emendation in the passionate, plaintive sixteenth-century lyric "O Western wind, when wilt thou blow." The original is:

> O western wind, when wilt thou blow
> That the small rain down can rain?
> Christ, that my love were in my arms,
> And I in my bed again!

In a mid-nineteenth-century anthology this appeared practically intact, except that *Christ* had been changed to *Ah* and the first word of the last line had been changed from *And* to *Or*. Never has so little done so much.

✻ the *boy friend*

A CORRESPONDENT writes that she is a successful business woman in her early thirties, unmarried and with no intention of getting married. She has, she says, a devoted admirer who is constantly with her. Her question is, how shall she refer to him? "He's not my fiancé. 'Boy friend' is vulgar and teen-age-ish. 'Mr.' seems stuffy. What can I call him?"

She has a real problem, though the difficulty lies in the realm of mores rather than of language. An attractive woman in the early thirties who has a devoted male attendant but does not intend to get married is something so new in the world that we haven't got around to finding words to fit her case.

Boy friend is not only vulgar but arch and, sometimes, startlingly inadequate ("Dear Miss Landers: I'm 17, unmarried and have a 2-month-old baby. Before my boy friend went into the Army he passed out cigars but that's as far as it went . . ."). *Fiancé* is formal and, anyway, unsuitable here. *Steady* is slang and vulgar. *Swain* won't do. *Sweetheart* would startle any modern gathering. *Sweetie* is mawkish. *Lover*, improper and perhaps unwarranted.

Nothing remains but the obvious. Refer to him informally by his first or full name and formally (stuffily) as *Mr.* If his status must be defined, why not "my friend"? I assume he is a friend, though the letter does not make it clear.

✻ *brainwashing* or brainmuddying?

I AM TOLD that *brainwashing* is a Chinese term which we have translated literally. But in taking it over we have been dupes of their propaganda. It may be brain*washing* from their point of view but surely from ours it is brain*muddying*. We've neglected our own resources. There's that wonderful old English word *addled* which means both "to confuse" and "to make rotten."

However, we don't really think of brainwashing as *washing*. A literal use of *brainwashing* to signify a cleansing strikes us as improper. I recently read a testimonial from a police officer who said that a short course he had taken (on juvenile delinquency) had completely changed his ideas for the better. He said, "I got a brainwashing, learned some new ideas."

Most Americans would feel that this use of *brainwashing* wasn't quite right. The term, despite its literal implications, means, rather, confusing, misleading, insidious perversion of truth, making the worse appear the better reason.

So it may be that in the wonderful way language sometimes has, we have put our true feelings into the word even though its plain meaning seems to be opposed to our feelings.

✻ bran(d)new

Brand-new doesn't mean "with the brand still on it." Many a brand remains on a product as long as the product exists. It certainly remains on cattle. And no one would think it absurd to refer to a newborn calf as "brand-new" even though it had not yet been branded.

Brand in the expression *brand-new* means "burning." Though the word is now archaic and poetic, we still recognize the meaning of "a brand on the hearth," i.e., a burning log. One of the older variations of *brand-new* was "fire-new" ("Despite thy victor sword and fire-new fortune"—Shakespeare). The term as a whole means as new as if fresh and glowing from the furnace.

Bran-new is just as acceptable as *brand-new*, and is not merely a slovenly omission of the *d*. Of the two forms, the English prefer *bran-new*, Americans *brand-new*.

✻ getting down to *brass tacks*

SOME say that *brass tacks* were formerly tacked onto the counters in dry-goods stores and were used to measure yard goods. So that "to get down to brass tacks" means "let's stop all this vague talk and measure it accurately."

Others say that the brass tacks are, properly, the copper bolts of a ship or the rivets in the hull. When, in scraping a hull, you got down to the bolts or rivets, you had cleared away all barnacles. But this seems very far-fetched and no one has been able to show proof that bolts or rivets were ever called "brass tacks."

Still others believe it is simply a rime for "crass facts." The tendency to rime is a strong formative element in speech and a whole species of slang is based on it. This explanation, though it may seem to the layman least probable of all, is the one that has most scholarly support. It explains, at least better than the other theories, the slight touch of menace that so often accompanies the suggestion that we "get down to brass tacks."

The expression has a homely, folksy flavor that suggests it is very old. But this isn't so. The first recorded instance of its use was in 1903.

※ the *breadwinner*

OUR WORD *win* comes from the Anglo-Saxon word *winnan,* meaning "to toil." Naturally, if you toil enough you acquire something, if only a stiff back. This is the meaning still retained in *breadwinner.*

Of course other people were out toiling and aquiring, too, and there was bound to be conflict. *Win* came to mean to strive or fight. A thirteenth-century Bestiary says that in the equinox "summer and winter win," meaning that they strive together.

The modern meaning of "to gain a victory in contest" was probably the result of optimism and Darwinism. If you just equated struggle with victory you might strengthen your nerve a bit. And those who were defeated probably had very little effect on the language thereafter.

So a breadwinner is one who toils and suffers to get bread, and the other meanings fit in too: he has to struggle competitively for it and only the victorious get it.

✻ bring, take, and fetch

ONE WOULD have thought that *bring* and *take* were like *bread* and *water*, so clear in their meaning, so indispensable to all expression, so rooted in the language and so constantly in use that there could not be the slightest doubt in anyone's mind as to their exact significance. But this isn't so. Hundreds upon hundreds of letters attest to some uncertainty and confusion about these words and the only inference one can make is that a change is taking place.

As far as the person performing the action is concerned, there's no difference between taking and bringing. It all depends on whether he is coming or going from the viewpoint of an observer. If you *bring*, you approach the observer (who is the speaker). If you *take*, you go from him.

At least that's the way the words have been used in English since the beginning of the language. Within the past few years, however, and especially in the vicinity of New York City, the two words are frequently reversed. One will occasionally hear even an educated man say such a thing as "I won't be in tomorrow; I've got to bring my boy down to Princeton." This would seem an astonishing illiteracy were it not so widely used. As it is, it must be accepted as a puzzling and sudden shift of meaning.

Fetch, meaning to go get and bring to, has fallen into disfavor in contemporary American speech—though it is a fine old word ("Let us fetch the ark of the covenant"). It seems to have suffered from being used in the training of dogs by people who in their secret hearts must despise dogs.

✻ Isn't *broker* an unfortunate name for a man who sells stocks?

THERE's an old gag that a *broker* is called a broker because he breaks the news to you that you're broke. Certainly on the surface the word does have unfortunate connotations.

Originally, however, it was *broacher* and was applied to the retailer of wine who merely broached (that is, tapped) wineskins or casks. He didn't grow the grapes or make the wine or put it into the wineskins. He just bought it wholesale and sold it retail. Wine was one of the few things the peasant bought, rather than made for himself, and *broacher* or *broker* became a generalized term for a middleman. In its most common use today it means a middleman in financial transactions. But there are still marriage brokers and commodity brokers and pawnbrokers.

❉ a fine *broth* of a boy

Broth has no esoteric meaning here. The phrase is simply colloquial Irish-English for "the very essence of what a boy ought to be." Broths were formerly thought to be exceedingly nourishing because it was assumed that since the nutritive value had been boiled out of the meat it must have gone into the broth.

❉ *brouhaha*

Brouhaha is a French word, the equivalent of the English *hurlyburly* and *hubbub* and, like them, an attempt to reproduce that confused sound of an agitated crowd. It is interesting that the Gallic ear catches an echo of laughter or excited exclamation in the sound; where the English is rougher, more surly and grumbling.

It is too recent and too rare a borrowing to have yet been recorded in our dictionaries. I have encountered it chiefly in the writing of S. J. Perelman and in the conversation of his admirers (of whom I am one), who wear it as a badge of minor distinction.

Modern French borrows from English, by the way, even more freely that we borrow from it. And sometimes we don't recognize a word which we have lent them and, mistaking it for one of theirs, borrow it back with their spelling and an approximation of their pronunciation. An example is *redingote*, which is simply the French form of *riding-coat*. They do the same thing. French *rosbif* is simply the *roast beef* which Old English borrowed from French in the first place.

※ *buffet* and boo fay′

A *buff* was originally a blow. The word sought, apparently, to echo or suggest the sound of a muffled blow. A *buffet* (the *-et* marks a diminutive, as in *owlet, islet,* etc.) was a small blow or a light blow, a blow as with the fist or open palm that might hurt but wouldn't inflict the injury that a club or sword would. This is a very old word.

The other *buffet* is also old but nowhere near as old as the first one and is in no way connected with it. Originally it meant a low stool. In some early versions of the famous nursery rime Miss Muffet sat on a buffet. It then came to mean a sideboard or side table on which china and plate were displayed. As servants became rarer, it became increasingly common to place food on such a sideboard and allow the guests to serve themselves.

The English still pronounce the two *buffets* alike, to rime with Muffet. But in the United States one rarely hears the second of the two pronounced any way but *buh fay′* or *boo fay′*.

※ an Irish *bull*

LUDICROUS incongruities were called *bulls* long before they were called *Irish bulls*. The origin of the term is unknown, but it is probably related to the Old French *boule*, "deceit." There was a Middle English *bull* meaning "falsehood" and there is a modern Icelandic *bull* meaning "nonsense."

An Irish bull is a statement that on the first hearing seems to make sense but that on a second's reflection is seen to be absurd but which none the less has meaning and often a very profound one. Good examples are the man who said, "I'm an atheist, God help me" and the banner which is said to have been displayed at the Eucharistic Congress of 1932 in Dublin: "GOD BLESS THE TRINITY."

I suspect that such statements came to be called "Irish bulls" because the Irish peasant, under the English occupation, had, like our Negro slaves, to play the role of a clown and could loose his shafts of resentment only when they were deeply hidden in a joke or made to seem utterly stupid. There was often impertinence under the ludicrousness. It was this that led Maria Edgeworth to say drily that you could tell an Irish bull from the fact that its horns were tipped with brass.

Yet there was often serious meaning, too. And it was that that led Professor Tyrrell to say that an Irish bull differed from other bulls in that it was always pregnant.

✷ bully for you!

"BULLY!" an exclamation meaning "excellent," "splendid!" is as much a part of our picture of Theodore Roosevelt as the glasses and the teeth.

It's an old English word which originally meant *lover* (cf. modern German *Buhle*). In time it was diluted to mean "a great guy" or "old pal." This is its meaning in relation to Bully Bottom, the Weaver, in Shakespeare's *A Midsummer Night's Dream*, and it was used in this sense among miners and rivermen into the middle of the nineteenth century.

It also became an underworld term and in the lingo of the underworld came to mean a pimp and a tyrannical coward, one who made himself a terror to the weak. In this sense it was colored by the idea of the animal bull. So colored it rose from the underworld and it is this version that has survived long after T.R.'s exclamation has become ludicrous.

✷ a lot of bunk

WHEN the Missouri Compromise (1820) was being debated in Congress, Representative Felix Walker, from Buncombe County, North Carolina, delivered a speech so utterly irrelevant, so completely unrelated to the matter in hand, that even his fellow congressmen were startled. When one of them asked him later just what connection his remarks had with the issue before the House, he confessed cheerfully that they had none at all. He wasn't attempting to impress his colleagues, he said, but his constituents. He was talking "only for Buncombe."

The innocence of the reply, rather than the unusualness of the performance, singled him out from other congressmen and gained him an immortality of absurdity. Until a few years ago, the word was spelled *bunkum* or even *buncombe* though today only the shortened form *bunk* is used.

✳ buoy

IN ENGLAND it is pronounced *boy* and it seems to be *boy* here among many of those who work with buoys. The famous soap is pronounced "Lifeboy" and its extensive radio advertising may have helped to give this pronunciation dominance.

But *boo′ i* is not incorrect. It is not only acceptable but strongly preferred by many, especially yachtsmen and some navy men, who regard *boy* with exuberant contempt.

Buoy derives ultimately from a word meaning "chained" or "fettered." However, the chain that anchors a buoy, though vital, is unperceived, and to the landlubber the significant thing about a buoy is that it floats. So that, by one of those fascinating associative changes of meaning within a word, *buoyancy* and *buoyant* convey a meaning of lightness and freedom almost diametrically opposed to the basic idea of being chained or fastened.

✳ the ubiquitous -burger

HAVING detached itself from *hamburger*—probably because the first syllable seemed to be the edible *ham*— *-burger*, like an escaped balloon, has soared into the wild blue yonder. A diner at University Place and 12th Street in New York City offers the pious *lentburgers*. Just outside the Minneapolis–St. Paul Airport, the traveler may purchase *spaceburgers* [and see *-orama*].

✳ Is there a verb *to burgle*?

THE VERB *to burgle* is a fairly recent back formation from *burglar*. Many quite reputable words have come into the language by back formation—that is, the formation of a word from one that looks like its derivative. By this process we got *diagnose* from *diagnosis, peddle* from *peddler, donate* from *donation, typewrite* from *typewriter,* and many others. But *burgle* seems to lack dignity and remains colloquial at the best. Maybe the undignified *gurgle* is too prominently suggested. But it certainly is a better word than the prompous *burglarize* which may very well become standard.

Burglar itself is a mixed-up word. It's the old Teutonic word *burg*, "dwelling," with the Latin ending *-ator*. A *burgator* was a "houser," one who got into your house. Then *burgator* got scrambled up with the Latin word *latro*, "thief," and the *l* and the second *r* jumped across. Then there was a fourteenth-century *burgulare*.

To *burgle* seems a natural. It appears in Gilbert and Sullivan's *The Pirates of Penzance:* "When the enterprising burglar's not a-burgling."

✻ busted or bursted?

THE PAST of the verb *to burst* is *burst* ("The dam burst yesterday"). *Bursted* is an attempt to give a more elegant pronunciation to the vulgar but vigorous *busted.*

Bust, a pronunciation more old-fashioned than downright vulgar, sometimes used *bust* as its past. Both forms are merely *burst* with the *r* not pronounced. But it was used so widely in America during the nineteenth century that it was felt, apparently, to be a different verb and coined its own regular past *busted* ("Here a poor captive's heart busted"). This was always nonstandard, but certain uses of *bust* became so fixed in the language that it would be ludicrous to attempt to replace them with forms of *burst*. It is *broncho-buster* and *trust-busting,* and banks and speculators go busted.

The other *bust*, with its adjective *busted,* is an entirely different word. When we say, a little pompously, that a lady is "fullbusted," we don't mean that she's bankrupt. Quite the contrary.

✻ pronunciation of butter

THE DICTIONARIES say it is pronounced *but' er*, but the sound one usually hears in America is much closer to *bud' er*.

And when an American hears an Englishman enunciate the double *t*, clearly and distinctly, it sounds affected to him.

If you call the ordinary educated person's attention to his actual pronunciation of the word, he's likely to be annoyed and, unless he is of a scientific turn of mind or of a moral strength far above the average, he'll simply deny it and insist that he said and always has said *but' er*.

This insistence may be due to the alphabet which, like the atlas, exercises a hidden tyranny over our minds. *D* and *t* are the same sound except that *d* is voiced. But because the letters representing the voiced and unvoiced forms of this sound are far apart in the alphabet, the ordinary speaker, when questioned, thinks you are accusing him of great ignorance, of an inability to distinguish things as widely separated as the fourth and twentieth letters of the alphabet.

The descriptive linguist merely remarks, however, that in contemporary American usage the *t* in *butter* is usually voiced.

✻ "butter wouldn't melt in her mouth"

IT'S ALWAYS a feminine mouth that butter won't melt in. The expression was formerly applied to men and women, but for more than two hundred years it has been used only of women, and young women at that. It is spoken of one who seems demure and proper but is (in the speaker's opinion) nowhere near so demure as she looks. It is always followed by a *but*. We say: "She looks so cold that you would imagine that even butter wouldn't melt in her mouth. But . . . !" And then we proceed to dish out the dirt.

The saying once had a fuller form: "She looks as if butter wouldn't melt in her mouth, but [actually] cheese won't choke her." That is, she appears to be cold and fastidious but, in reality, nothing's too strong or gross for her.

✻ Is *buxom* a synonym for "fat"?

EVEN yet, *buxom* doesn't mean merely "fat." Not in entire forgetfulness of its past does it come to our lips, but trails a few wispy clouds of its former glories. It means "delightfully plump, full-bosomed, radiant in health." It describes an ideal of womanly attractiveness that prevailed before the gaunt but glamorous gargoyles of today exerted their witchery over us.

Originally *buxom* meant "yielding." *Unbuxom* in *Piers Plowman* (1362) did not mean "gaunt" but "disobedient." Spenser (1590) says that it is a joy to see a wild beast tamed "and buxom to his bands." Milton's angels (1667 for the writing; 4004 B.C. for the doing) winged their way through "the buxom air."

In its application to a woman, it first meant yielding to her husband's will, being obedient. How it came from that to mean plump can only be conjectured. Perhaps only the well-fed, their nerves padded, can be good-naturedly obedient. Perhaps (some men would say) obedience in a wife leads to happiness and happiness leads to health and plumpness. Perhaps (some women might say) only corn-fed rustics, who have not yet heard of women's rights, would obey a man.

※ *buy* or *purchase?*

To *purchase* originally meant "to procure, to obtain by pursuit." In the sense of acquiring by a payment of money, there is no difference between *buy* and *purchase* except the obvious one that purchase is the more formal and pompous word. It applies to large-scale transactions, like the Louisiana Purchase. Anyone who said he was going to *purchase* a toothpick or offered to *purchase* a friend a soft drink would seem to have delusions of grandeur.

What we call "installment buying" the British call "the hire-purchase system." Their expression is the better of the two. It lures the buyer on. Ours has the ominous sound of "stall" right in the middle of it.

※ *by and large*

By means "close." When we say "He got by" we mean that he passed, but with a strikingly narrow margin of safety. *Large* means "broad, wide, liberal, free." We say that an escaped convict is "at large," meaning that he is free from the confines of the prison. When a man bestows *largess*, he gives liberal gratuities; he is open-handed, free with his money.

By and large is a nautical expression. It means to sail as close to the wind as possible and to sail with the wind full in the sail, under as favorable conditions as possible. That is, the expression includes all ways of sailing, from the least favorable to the most favorable. Hence it came to mean "in general," "over-all," "in all aspects."

But since we are rarely asked to consider anything in general except when minor discrepancies are to be disregarded, the phrase, in its most common use, has come to mean "Considered in all aspects, overlooking minor exceptions and regarding only the substantial truth."

✻ can not or cannot?

THE DICTIONARIES list *can not* and *cannot* as merely variant forms. But I feel that *cannot* represents the written form of *can't*, whereas *can not*, by compelling—as it does—a clearer pronunciation of the *not*, is a more emphatic negation.

✻ "*Can* you tell me?" "*Could* you tell me?"

Could is the courteous form because, being the subjunctive, it removes the question from facts to ideas. It isn't a question of whether the person addressed is physically able to tell you; it's a question of his inclination. When we use *could* we are saying, "Considering that I have interrupted you and bothered you with a question which you are under no obligation to answer, could you find it in your generous heart, drawing on the plenitude of your knowledge, to tell me?"

Could is a mighty economical way of saying all that!

Then *can* to literal-minded people (and the world is full of them) means solely physical ability. I have twice in my lifetime had the disconcerting experience of asking a stranger "Can you tell me, please, how to get . . . ?" and having him say "Yes" and then glare at me. His meaning was plainly, "I can, but I see no reason why I should."

✻ they *canceled out*

"ISN'T *out* unnecessary in *canceled out?*" hundreds demand. With what hot breathing do they pursue the "unnecessary" word.

They are right, of course. It is unnecessary, and in reference to the crossing out of some one thing seems awkward as well. But in reference to two things that cancel each other, it is a well-established idiom.

When we have all become robots feeding tape into IBM machines we may have eliminated all such unnecessary words. But until that dreadful time, as long as we are human beings—gabby, sociable, preferring rhythm to exact meaning and dawdling our inefficient lives away—we will continue to use idiomatic rather than precise or logical speech.

* Is there such a word as *cannibalize*?

To *cannibalize*, to take usable parts from a discarded plane with which to repair another, is as established in the maintenance shops as "wrench" or "piston."

When Columbus asked the Caribs their name, they said, or he thought they said, they were *Canibals*. In their own tongue the word meant "strong men." Columbus thought it marked them as subjects of the Great Khan and hence proved that he had reached Asia. The Spanish populace heard the Spanish *can*, "dog," in the name and decided they were very fierce, a decision that was reinforced by the further knowledge that they sometimes ate each other.

My, how meanings do slip around in words, and what a Partingtonian task the purists have set themselves in trying to stop it!

* "I'll see if I *can't*"

THIS means, of course, "I'll see if I can." The contradiction bothers many worthy people. In S. N. Behrman's comedy *The Cold Wind and the Warm*, a young lady says to a young man "I love you so. I'm going to ask Dan if I can't take you along on the honeymoon." A correspondent feels that *can* "would sound better" here and thinks we would always do better to "accentuate the positive" in our speech.

But I'm afraid that I don't think *can* would be better here. In fact, it would utterly destroy the joke.

The joke carries an indirect question. "I'm going to ask if I can" would mean that she would say to Dan "Can I take him along?" "If I can't" means she will say "Can't I take him along?" "Can I?" would be a simple, straightforward question which would get the simple answer "No." "Can't I?" is an involved question, implying "Why can't I?" And that is the joke.

It's unfair to Mr. Behrman to spell out his joke in detail, but the point is "Can't I?" *does* accentuate the positive. It implies that she sees no reason against it. "Can I?" represents total uncertainty. If she had said "if I can," she would have had no opinion one way or the other; she would be totally negative.

Such an analysis is certainly breaking a butterfly on the wheel, but the elfin tinkle of its crunching bones* reminds us how extraordinarily delicate a good joke is, how subtly our wonderful language paces every shift and turn of thought—and how sad it is to be earnest and bewildered, outside the fun, accentuating the positive.

✷ cantankerous

Cantankerous is a mighty expressive word. It carries a wonderful suggestion of someone all cankered and tanked up with rancor. Its very sound suggests its meaning: the ill-natured snarling of some cross old man.

It's a humorous word and so remains colloquial, the sort of word we would use freely in speech but would feel was out of place in a formal address or a solemn piece of writing.

It first appeared in Oliver Goldsmith's *She Stoops to Conquer* (1772). It was probably a dialect word Goldsmith had picked up, more likely an elaboration of the medieval English word *contek,* meaning "strife." *Contek,* once a very common word, had last appeared in writing in the works of Chaucer, in the fourteenth century, but it had apparently been living on, as words do, in the speech of some out-of-the-way place.

✷ pronunciation of *caramel*

Of the standard acceptable pronunciations, *kar' uh m'l* is the most often heard, with the first syllable pronounced as

---

* I know that a butterfly doesn't have any bones. Please don't write me pointing this out.

77 · *careening* and *careering*

in "carry." *Kar′ uh mell* is also acceptable. *Kahr′ m'l* (first syllable as in "cart") is now used by so many well-educated Americans that it must be accepted as a permissible alternative.

This is one of those words to whose "proper" pronunciation many people attach great importance, regarding it, apparently, as an indication of status. But it is peculiarly unsuited for this, since the "proper" pronunciation, if anyone wants to insist there is a proper one, used to be *calamele*, a French word derived from the Latin *calamus*, cane. The *-el* marked a diminutive, a little cane. But it got confused with *canna mellis*, sugar cane. The *r* was substituted for the first *l* because of the tendency in our language to avoid the repetition of a consonant at too close intervals in a word.

So that *caramel*, however pronounced, was pretty well "corrupted" to begin with.

※ *careening* and *careering*

THE VERB *to career* comes from a Latin word meaning "chariot." To *career* is to move at full speed, as a chariot.

To *careen* comes from a Latin word for "keel." It means to keel over, to cause a ship to lie on its side. Pirates careened their ships on lonely beaches in order to scrape their hulls. By extension, the verb has come to mean "to lean, sway, or tip to one side; to heel over, as a ship in rough sea."

In the United States today there is a widespread use of *careen* where *career* would seem to be the intended word. But it's not always easy to know what is intended, because when something is careering along it is very likely to careen. Honor Tracy speaks of men careering from one bar to another, but it would not be long before they would be careening. James Joyce speaks clearly of automobiles "careering homeward" from the races. But the reader is not quite certain what Bruce Catton means when he writes in *Grant Moves South* (p. 380) of "the first steamboat careening through" Yazoo Pass.

The problem is further complicated by the fact that *career* could also mean to lie over on the side. Lord Howard of Effingham in one of his dispatches during the fight with the Spanish Armada, wrote that one of the Spanish galleasses "was fain to be carried away upon the career." And Professor Mattingly, in *The Armada* (p. 306), glosses this as "listing."

However, in contemporary use, *careen* must be regarded as incorrect unless there is a marked tipping from side to side. But the universality of the error is very likely to establish the "corrupt" meaning as standard.

※ **"bell the *cat*"?**

THE EXPRESSION alludes to one of the many fables ascribed to Aesop, though this one first appeared in European literature in *The Vision of Piers Plowman* (written between 1362 and 1399). The fable says the mice met in council to protect themselves, once and for all, from the cat menace. A mouse suggested that since the cat's attacks were successful because of its stealth it would never catch them if they could hear it coming. The remedy was simple: let a bell be tied around the cat's neck to warn them of her approach. This idea was greeted with applause. Then an old mouse arose and asked who was going to bell the cat? There was a prolonged silence. The story is alluded to today as if its moral were that heroism conquers all difficulties. But our ancestors were no such fools. The moral: It's easy to propose impossible remedies.

※ *catchup? catsup? ketchup?*

THE WORD, however spelled, is an attempt to present in English the Malayan word *kechap* (sauce), which, in turn, seems to have been an attempt to present a Chinese phrase in Malayan.

The older dictionaries regarded *ketchup* as correct and *catchup* a permissible variant. *Catsup* they labeled as incorrect. But the public seemed to prefer *catsup* to the other forms and no contemporary dictionary lists it as anything less than a permissible variant. It is a very common form—perhaps the most common—on the labels on the bottles of the stuff.

In England ketchup can be made from mushrooms or walnuts and various other things, and it used to be so here. But in America now *ketchup, catchup,* or *catsup* is practically synonymous with tomato catchup. So firmly so that many manufacturers no longer bother to put "tomato" on their label.

✻ **Can one properly speak of a** *cavalcade* **of boats or automobiles?**

Certainly. It is true that the word originally meant a procession on horseback, that *caval-*, the root, means "horse" (as in *cavalry*), but the idea of the procession came to dominate the idea of the horses and now we use the word of many processions. The idea of the horses lingers enough, however, to prevent us from using it to describe just plain marchers; they have to be on or in something.

This shifting of the meaning of a word from one of its aspects to another is very common, especially when the word is foreign or has become archaic. The word *matinee,* for instance, means "morning," but we use it to designate an afternoon performance. A *serenade* is, properly, an evening song, but the common reader wouldn't be agitated if he read of someone being serenaded in the morning, and even the uncommon reader, whose objections are more often designed to show off than to show up, wouldn't dare squawk at "a serene morning." An *audience* is properly a group which hears (from *audire,* "to hear"), but the silent films drew large audiences. *Dilapidated* means that the stones have fallen off, but he would be more foolish than learned who objected to a reference to a dilapidated frame house or log cabin.

✻ ***center in* or *center around?***

Those who thank God daily that in matters of speech they are not as other men assert that since a center is a point, things can only gather towards or converge upon it. They insist that things can only center *in*.

But although in mathematical theory a true center, like a true line, has no breadth or area, in the functioning everyday world sane people don't speak in such abstractions. *Center*, as a verb, doesn't necessarily mean "to reach the center." It can mean "converging in the direction of a center." And where the object regarded as the center is circular, the converging may very well be in a form that can be described as *around*. Surely no violence is done the language if one says that the spokes of a wheel center around the hub.

The Oxford English Dictionary defines the intransitive use of *center* as: "to gather or collect as round a center."

Centered *in* is, of course, equally correct and more common. But there are places in which it would be confusing. If one said, for instance, that a herd of cattle centered in a water hole, one might assume that the cattle were actually in the water. Whereas *around* would suggest that they had converged upon the hole from all directions but were not in it.

✶ Is there a *chaise lounge* in the house?

Is THERE such a thing as a *chaise lounge*, I am asked.

Well, an elongated chair is sold under that name by hundreds of manufacturers and dealers throughout America. A score of dealers in New York City were questioned and not one sold the object under any other name. So there certainly is such a thing.

But is the name "proper"? Shouldn't it be *chaise longue*, the French for "elongated chair"? Not if the American people decide they prefer a "corrupt" English word to a correct French word. And a glance at the furniture ads in any newspaper ought to convince the most obdurate that the people have so decided. The dictionaries haven't recorded the change yet, but they will; they are not concerned with "should be's" but with "are's." And the process that has effected this particular change is a recognized shaping force that has added hundreds of now-quite-legitimate words to the language.

An enterprising Chicago dealer, no linguist but probably a

successful salesman, has carried the thing a notch further and offers the weary public: FOLDING CHAISE CHAIRS.

✷ "I say, old *chap!*"

Chap is an abbreviation of *chapman* and a chapman was a buyer and seller. Burns called peddlers "chapman billies." *Chap's* present sense of "man," especially in its plural form in direct address to mean "pals" or "buddies," stems from a particular use of *chapman* to mean "customers," and keeps a tincture of the ingratiation of salesmanship. It came into use in the eighteenth century when the Industrial Revolution was beginning to turn England into a nation of shopkeepers.

Chapman is related to the word *cheap* which (in the verb form *to cheapen*) originally mean "to do business, to buy and sell." A twelfth-century version of *Luke* xix:13 (which in the Revised Standard Version is "Trade till I come. . . .") says "Cheapen until I come." It goes back to a Latin word meaning "a wine seller."

The modern meaning of *cheap* or *cheapen* merely reflects the transaction from the buyer's point of view before the time of fixed prices. Beating the price down has been an indispensable part of purchasing until very recently, and still is in most countries.

✷ Has *cheap* become a dirty word?

A WOMAN writes of an exasperating experience: "The other day in a pet shop I asked, 'Is that the cheapest dog leash you have?' The proprietor replied, 'It's the lowest-priced leash; we don't carry anything "cheap."'" She asks, "Has cheap become a dirty word?"

Cheap is not yet of necessity a dirty word, though only the rich dare use it with dignity any more. But it has acquired evil connotations in some contexts ("She looked cheap in all that makeup and those high heels"), especially among the poor and the vulgar. And whoever uses it must bear in mind that it conveys the ideas of "shoddy" and "contemptible" to many people.

[And I think I would go to another pet shop. A man doesn't

have to be a linguist to run a pet shop, but he ought to have some manners. The ordinary person so rarely has the courage to ask for anything cheaper any more that the proprietor probably perceived at once that his questioner was a superior person and hated her.]

※ **On what thin ice does a *cheapskate* skate?**

Cheapskate is a very strange term for a tightwad.
The *cheap-* part is plain enough. Among the common people (where it ought to be a term of highest praise) *cheap* is an expression of contempt.

The *-skate* part doesn't refer to ice skates or to roller skates but to the fish, the skate. We have the same word in *blatherskite* which has the older forms of *bletherskate* and *bladderskate*. It was a humorously scornful term for a gabby person, comparing him to one of those fish that inflate themselves and try to look ferocious when taken out of the water but are actually harmless and merely swelled up with wind and alarm.

This word—*blatherskate*—occurred in the chorus of a Scotch song "Maggie Lauder" which was very popular among the American soldiers during the Revolutionary War. The *blather-* was plain enough and the *-skate* got detached as a mere suffix of contempt and was later attached to *cheap-*.

※ **the shifting *chemise***

WHEN the *chemise* was the height of fashion several years ago an indignant male besought me to expose "the impropriety of at least the name of this detestable, dangling drape." The use of *chemise* he regarded as "a deliberate affront to decency and common sense" which could have been bestowed upon the garment "only in cynicism."

Alas, 'tis a pity that one who speaks so well should speak in vain, but there is no impropriety in words. The impropriety can lie only in our associations with the words and few words illustrate this better than *chemise*. It has been used at various times to designate the outer garment of a priest and the undershirt of a layman. It has changed sex and positions with dizzying confusion. It named a woman's undershirt, then a female outer garment, then her undershirt again, and at the time of the indignant letter an outer garment again. And under a different pronunciation it has described a dance and a defect in the steering mechanism of an automobile. (See *shimmy*.)

✻ Why is a stale joke called a *chestnut*?

IN *The Broken Sword* (1816), a play by William Dimond, there is a certain Captain Xavier, a tedious blowhard who is always repeating himself. He starts to tell a yarn that involves a cork tree when another character, Pablo, corrects him. Pablo says it was a chestnut tree. The captain is enraged at the interruption and says emphatically that it was a cork tree. Pablo is just as insistent that it was a chestnut. The captain said he ought to know: it's his story. Pablo says he ought to know: he's heard it twenty-seven times before and it was always a chestnut!

Fame is an unpredictable thing. How pleased the poor playwright would have been to have been told that his writing would enrich the language. How depressed he would have been to have been told that only this one word, and that out of context, would be remembered, while all else—characters, situations, plot, wit, dialog, the author himself and all about him—would be utterly forgotten.

✻ a *Chinaman's chance*

THE PHRASE is always used with a negative implication: "He hasn't got a Chinaman's chance." But why has a Chinaman so slight a chance that it's practically no chance at all?

The expression seems to have originated in California in the years following the gold rush of 1849. Thousands of Chinese coolies were imported to work on the railroads and thousands more managed to get themselves smuggled in. They were willing to work harder and longer and for less pay than the native whites and intense feeling was aroused against them. They were cruelly mistreated and in any conflict with an American stood very little chance of receiving justice. Lucius Beebe and Charles Clegg in their compilation *The American West* reproduce a dozen contemporary drawings and illustrations of the lot of the Chinese coolie in the West in the early days, and these leave no doubt of the slimness of his chance.

Among the ways in which these Chinese earned their meager livings was working over the tailings, or refuse earth or leavings, of the white goldminers. Naturally, there was little likelihood of their finding any considerable amount of gold in this residue, and this may have been the *Chinaman's chance*—a very poor one!

✹ It's become a *chore*

A *chore* is a light odd job around a house or farm, usually something routine, like burning trash, chopping firewood, or collecting the eggs.

It is interesting that our ancestors always used the word in the plural and stressed, in its use, the lightness of such tasks. Chores were mere turns of the hand compared to the real work of threshing or clearing land or, for the women, raising a dozen children. Today the word has acquired an overtone of whining protest. We speak of a single chore and of that, commonly, as something burdensome ("It's becoming quite a chore").

Chore was an English dialectal pronunciation of *chare* or *char*. It got fixed in America but never became standard in English usage. We recognize one of its phonetic cousins in *charwoman*, but some of its more distant relatives are surprising. It derives from an Anglo-Saxon word meaning to turn (a *chore* was a turn of work). From the same root comes Charing Cross, a place where the Thames turned. (It is true that Edward I erected a cross here in memory of his queen, Eleanor of Castile; but that Charing comes from Chere Reine, "dear queen," is no longer held.) The word *ajar* also comes from this root. A door is ajar when it is turned slightly on its hinges.

✹ under the *circumstances*

SOME people, knowing that *circum* is Latin for "around," have insisted that it must be *in the circumstances* and will not hear of *under* under any circumstances. Among these were Professor-President Woodrow Wilson and the Terrible-Tempered Mr. Harold Ickes. Mr. Ickes when Secretary of the Interior refused to sign any letter in which the phrase "under the circumstances" occurred and notified the employees of the department to that effect.

But *under the circumstances* is the older of the two phrasings, much the older. It has been used by the most respectable writers and we hear it every day from educated men and women. Those who object seem to think that we can be surrounded only on a plane. But "round," as H. W. Fowler points out, applies to vertical as well as to horizontal relationships. Fowler says that a threatening sky is no less a circumstance than a threatening bulldog, and we are certainly under the sky.

The distinction is not established in the language. Meaning, logic, past and contemporary usage all support *under the circumstances*. Those who insist that it must be *in* show an elementary knowledge of Latin and a profound ignorance of English.

※ a traffic *citation*

A NUMBER of correspondents have been disturbed to see the word *citation,* which they connect with some great honor, like the Congressional Medal of Honor, used of traffic tickets. They feel this use degrades the word.

But it doesn't. *Citation* simply means a summons to appear or a mention in a report. It can be for good or bad conduct.

Its use in relation to bad conduct is much the older. The *Oxford English Dictionary* quotes the summons meaning as early as 1297. Whereas the special military use—a citation with a decoration—doesn't appear until 1918 (so given in Mathews' *Dictionary of Americanisms*).

The fact that so many find the earlier use startling is a definite sign that the word is changing its meaning. But it is being elevated, not degraded.

※ the *Civil War*

MANY people have asked what is the official name of the war fought in this country from 1861 to 1865.

Wars don't have official names. They are often given different names by different participants. For instance, the war that we call King William's War is called in Europe the War of the League of Augsburg and what we call Queen Anne's War, the War of the Spanish Succession. Our War of 1812 was a remote salient of the Napoleonic Wars. And so on.

The war fought in this country from 1861 to 1865 has never been given an official name. Two Acts of Congress (1874, 1880), directing the compilation of official records, designated it the War of the Rebellion. "The rebel yell" is still referred to and "Johnny Reb" turns up in fiction once in a while, but any allusion to "the late unpleasantness between the states" as a rebellion would be improper today. Public Law 85–305 (1957) establishing a commission to commemorate the hundredth anniversary of the conflict designated it as the Civil War. In the South it is most often referred to as the War Between the States.

Time and the victor usually determine a war's name and this particular one seems to be settling down to the Civil War here and the American Civil War in Europe.

Every war is called "*the* war" by the generation that endures it. Or used to be so called. They're coming so fast now that we have to number them to keep tab on them.

* *claptrap*

THE MODERN American term is more often "grandstand play." But *claptrap*—something without real merit, designed solely to catch applause—is the better word. Its very sound—of something flimsy flapping about—expresses contempt.

* "*clean* from Pittsburgh"

Clean as an adverb, meaning "wholly, completely, quite thoroughly," is good standard English and has been in use as long as the language has existed. Shakespeare used it ("though not clean past your youth"; "it is clean out of the way," etc.). King Charles I used it, on the scaffold while the headsman waited ("A subject and a sovereign are clean different things"). And the author of *Anatomy of a Murder,* who is a judge, uses it ("The line of people stretched . . . clean down the marble stairs").

Many people prefer *clear,* which is also correct but came into this use many centuries after *clean,* and regard *clean* as rustic and humorous ("I come clean from Pittsburgh in one day"). As an adverb *clean* does seem to be fading from use, but it is not incorrect.

✹ *"cleansed* for your personal use"

A WOMAN writes to say that she was annoyed when she read on its cellophane wrapper that the drinking glass in her hotel room had been "cleansed" for her use.

Her annoyance is understandable. She was entitled to a clean drinking glass and this was a pretentious to-do on the management's part. A statement that the glass had been scientifically cleaned might in these germ-phobic days have been reassuring, but "cleanse" and "just for you" is too much. Another notice might have told her that the bed had been "re-linen-ated," and so on. There need be no end to it.

But in addition to the public-relations impertinence, *cleanse*, the older form of "to make clean," has certain semantic associations that make it unsuitable on a hotel drinking glass. It's a much stronger word than *clean*. It means to free from filth, pollution, and offensive matter—and a guest might dislike the thought that this had been necessary. It might incite him to wonder what depraved, infected monsters had previously occupied the room. Into what lazarette had he strayed?

Then *cleanse* has religious association. It means to free from moral impurity or guilt ("Cleanse thou me from secret faults"— *Psalms* xix:12). And the use of the word to "sell" the amenities of a bathroom might be offensive at the other end of the aesthetic scale.

Hotels would do well to clean the glasses as a part of their job and say nothing about it.

✹ "a *clerk* ther was of Oxenford"

THE FIRST meaning of *clerk* in English was "a clergyman." In British legal language that is still its meaning. *Cleric* is simply a later spelling.

In the Middle Ages literacy was largely confined to the clergy, so much so, indeed, that if a man could read but one verse from the Bible (the first verse of the 51st Psalm was usually selected) he could plead benefit of clergy and save his neck from the gallows. So *clerk* became a synonym for anyone who could write and was applied to notaries, recorders, accountants, and so on. This became the word's chief meaning up until well into this century and it is this that leads us to refer to office work as clerical work and office assistants as clerks. Bob Cratchit, in Dickens' *A Christmas Carol,* was Ebenezer Scrooge's clerk.

Then the term—which always had a tinge of contempt in it, the contempt of the feudal warrior for any man so unmanly as to spend his life scratching with a pen—was applied to store or shop assistants, its commonest contemporary application.

And an interesting thing is that once the word had thus been disassociated from the idea of learning and literacy, it was purged of the contempt. A stenographer would be offended to be called a clerk, but a check-out girl in a grocery wouldn't.

※ Why is the decoration on men's socks called a *clock?*

THE ORIGINAL meaning of *clock* was "bell," and the design on hosiery that we call a clock was at first bell-shaped. The term, which is very old in this meaning, used to be applied to the design on other garments but—such are the odd ways in which words develop—it has become fixed solely on the side of a sock.

※ pronunciation of *clothes*

NO DICTIONARY recommends the pronunciation of the *th* in *clothes,* though some admit it, because more and more people are coming to feel that it is "correct" to pronounce words the way they are spelled. And, of course, in time, if enough are convinced of this, it will be correct, though spelling pronunciations of *Psalms, caught, pneumonia, listen,* and scores of other words, would sound strange to us. Still, no more strange than many of our pronunciations would sound to an Elizabethan.

For the present, however, most people, educated and uneducated, pronounce *clothes* as *klohz'*—just like "*close* the door." And no one, however genteel, can pronounce the *th* in *clothespin* or *clothes closet.*

※ why *clubs?*

"DIAMONDS and hearts on cards are plainly diamonds and hearts. Spades look something like a spade. But clubs don't look remotely like a club. Why are they so called?" asks a correspondent.

Because we borrowed the designs from one country and the names from another.

In Spain in the sixteenth century *spades* were swords (Sp. *espados*), *clubs* were clubs or cudgels (Sp. *bastos*), *diamonds* were square pieces of money (Sp. *dineros*), and *hearts* were chalices (Sp. *copas*).

In France the suits were *pique* (a soldier's pike), *trèfle* (trefoil or cloverleaf), *carreaux* (a building tile, lozenge or diamond-shaped), and *coeur* (heart).

So it is plain that we have taken over the French symbols, translated the names of two (hearts, diamonds) into English, and applied to the other two English translations of Spanish names for different symbols.

It just shows, once again, how utterly illogical and unmethodical the language is.

✳ coals to Newcastle

WHY, a correspondent asks, when someone does something unnecessary do we say that he is "carrying coals to Newcastle"?

It isn't merely something unnecessary. It has to be absurdly superfluous, a waste of effort, especially the taking of something to the very source of supply. The Newcastle in the proverb is Newcastle-on-Tyne, the chief port city in England's coal district, and has been famous for its export of coal since the thirteenth century. Almost all the mineral coal that the South of England knew for centuries came from Newcastle. Indeed, what we call "coal" was distinguished from charcoal by being called *sea-coal* because it came (from Newcastle) by sea.

So that to have taken coal (or "coals," as they were then called and are still named in the saying) *to* Newcastle would have been as superfluous an effort as could be imagined. If we were making up the saying today we might say "automobiles to Detroit" or "beer to Milwaukee." Or, as Ring Lardner put it, "coals to Newcastle, Pa."

※ "the *Coast*"

A PECULIAR trifle in our speech has been the common agreement during the past ten years or so that *the Coast* shall mean the West Coast—indeed shall mean more specifically Los Angeles. TEAMSTER LOCAL INDICTED ON COAST says *The New York Times* and, although there is an Atlantic Coast and a Gulf Coast and a Maine Coast and fifty other coasts the world over, there is no need to be more specific. It's Los Angeles.

The thing seems to have been taken over from the speech of migrating movie moguls and performers who used to shuttle between New York and Hollywood. TV and advertising adopted it and hence it became chic and, in time, standard.

To some there is, apparently, nothing in between. I was once reached on the telephone in Nashville, Tennessee, by a TV executive. He said, "How are things on the Coast?" I don't know to this day whether he thought Nashville was on the Coast or whether, with consummate tact, he was ignoring so gauche a proceeding as my going to Tennessee.

※ Why is a spiderweb called a *cobweb*?

A SPIDERWEB is called a *cobweb* because *cob* is a form of *cop* which is an old word for "spider." Modern Flemish and Westphalian still have *coppe* and *cobbe* for spider and Dutch has *spinnekop*.

※ Why when someone says something absurd do we say he's *cockeyed*?

ONE OF the meanings of the verb *to cock* is "to set or to turn up to one side," especially in an assertive or jaunty manner. This meaning is probably derived from the rooster who carries his head and comb so challengingly.

Thus *cock* meant "set to one side" and *cockeyed* meant "asquint." So that when we tell someone he's cockeyed, we are saying that he has a distorted view of whatever it is that's being discussed. And in addition we are implying that, like a rooster, he's showing off and is a trifle ridiculous.

✻ the *cockles* of the heart

A *cockle* is a bivalve mollusk of the genus *Cardium*. Viewed from one position, the heart resembles a cockle shell and this may have led to both the expression "the cockles of the heart" and the scientific name for the mollusk, since *Cardium* derives, through Latin, from the Greek word for heart.

Some have sought the derivation of the phrase in a resemblance between the valves of the mollusk and the valves of the heart. Others insist it derives from *corculum*, the Latin diminutive for "heart" (which might be translated "heart of my heart").

Though references to the mollusk and its shell are very old, *cockles of the heart* is fairly recent, making its first appearance in the late seventeenth century. The heart was then seriously—as now poetically—conceived to be the seat of the emotions.

Formerly the cockles of the heart could be terrified or delighted or made to rejoice. But now they can only be warmed.

✻ Why are Londoners called *cockneys?*

MANY Americans seem to assume that all Londoners are cockneys, but this is a misapprehension. Formerly the term *cockney* was confined to those "born within the sound of Bow Bells." Today it is confined to those from the East End (the slums) who speak a certain—now rapidly disappearing—dialect. This dialect is now thought to be very funny (though some of its most striking features can be shown to be in standard English where they go unrecognized simply because we use them every day).

The word *cockney* is one of the oddest in the language. At first it meant a delicate, pampered person, a spoiled child. From this it came to mean a townsman (who probably seemed delicate and pampered to the countryman), then a Londoner, and finally a particular kind of Londoner.

It may be related to the French *coquin*, "rascal." Or it may refer to the diminutive eggs that hens sometimes lay and which were formerly thought to be produced by roosters (*cock + ei*, the old word for "egg"). That is, the countryman may have thought the citizen as worthless as one of these eggs—or as unnatural.

And, perhaps, as dangerous—something from which you need expect no good. For one of these cock's eggs if hatched out by a toad produced (in popular lore) the dreaded cockatrice whose very look caused death.

✳ Why is the pilot's section of an airplane called the *cockpit*?

ORIGINALLY the name for the pit or enclosed area in which game cocks were set to fight, *cockpit* was extended in the late seventeenth or early eighteenth century to the cramped quarters on the lowest deck of a man-of-war, the quarters to which the junior officers were assigned. The designation may have been humorous, because the young men fought so much in this crowded space. Or it may have been grim, because it was here that the wounded were received and cared for during an engagement.

Aviation has taken many of its terms from ships. In World War I the fighter pilots chose to call their narrow section of the plane the *cockpit* and the name carried over into peacetime. There is now, however, a tendency to get away from the dangerous implications of the name and pilots on the huge airliners, in those chatty communiqués they issue to the uneasy passengers, seem to prefer the more sonorous "flight deck."

✳ "*cocksure* for evermore"

ONE WOULD assume that *cocksure*, dogmatic self-confidence, had something to do with the strutting aplomb of a rooster, but the history of the word makes this unlikely.

Originally *cocksure* meant security, not certainty, and was used seriously. Foxe, in his *Book of Martyrs* (1596), says, "Who so dwelleth under . . . the help of the Lord, shall be cock-sure for evermore." It was not until the middle of the eighteenth century, two hundred years later, and several centuries after its first appearance, that our meaning came into the word.

Several conjectures have been made concerning its origin, all supported by textual evidence. One is that *cock* here is a stopcock or spigot, one type of which could be locked, thus making the wine secure.

We know that for five hundred years *Cock* was used for *God* in oaths (as we use *gosh* and *golly*) and there is the possibility that it originally referred to the security of God.

✻ why *cocktail*?

H. L. MENCKEN, in his first *Supplement* to *The American Language*, records many theories of the origin of *cocktail*. But the fact that he finally lists seven as having some plausibility shows that nobody really knows.

The earliest mention of the mixed drink under this name was in the Dutch settlements in New York. Washington Irving refers to it by name in his *Knickerbocker History* (1809) and says it was a Dutch invention. But others ascribe its origin to New Orleans and say it is from French *coquetier*, "an egg cup," or *coquetel*, "a mixed drink." Some think it's the English *cock-ale*. Some think it was so called because it was first served in glasses with a rooster painted on them. Some think it was a toast, after a cockfight, to the winning cock.

One man's guess, like one man's cocktail, is just about as good or poor as another's.

✻ Is one a *cohort*?

The New York Times still stoutly insists that no news that refers to an individual as a *cohort* is fit to print without a little editing, but they are fighting one of their splendid rearguard actions in this. To be sure, it originally meant one of the ten divisions of a Roman legion and all dictionaries give its meaning as a group or company. But, possibly under the influence of *co-worker*, it has come to be used so widely to designate an assistant or associate (usually with humorous or resentful overtones) that this meaning cannot be dismissed any longer as a mere blunder. Elizabeth Janeway so uses it (*The Third Choice*, p. 284): "one of Charlie's cohorts was waiting with the car." And Mary McCarthy (*The Groves of Academe*, p. 276): "The old poet had left, accompanied by two of his cohorts." The dictionaries will have to be revised.

✳ *cold slaw*

IT'S PROPERLY *coleslaw* and in the more expensive restaurants is so designated, but most of the populace now gets it as *cold slaw*.

Cole is Dutch for "cabbage" (the German form of the same word appears in *kohlrabi*) and *slaw* means "salad." However, it is served cold and, as word changes go, *cold slaw* is accurate and moderate.

The distortion of strange words to make them fit a known meaning is one of the formative processes of language and has given us such now-quite-respectable words a *isinglass, crayfish, primrose, hangnail,* and hundreds of others.

✳ the *collect* and the *collection*

A CHURCHGOING correspondent is puzzled by the *collect* which he rightly surmises, has nothing to do with the *collection*.

His bewilderment about the word has been shared from the year 1100 on by theologians and linguists. Their conclusions add up to two possibilities: (1) that the prayer was originally a summing up or *collecting* of the thoughts expressed in a preceding discourse; (2) that it was a short prayer delivered at a place in which the people *collected* before proceeding to the church where mass was to be said.

The preponderance of the evidence is in favor of the second of these explanations.

✳ *colloquial* and formal

MANY people think that words marked *colloquial* in the dictionary should be avoided. Perhaps they think *colloquial* is related to *local* and hence indicates that the word is provincial and not in general reputable use. But, actually, it is related to *colloquy* and *elocution* and simply means the language people use in talking with each other, as distinct from the language in which they would write a formal document.

One might, for instance, write the word "serpent," but one

would always say "snake." One might write "Make a note of this, lest you forget it." But one would say "so you won't forget it" or "So's you won't forget." Educated people say "I worked good and hard at it," using "good and" as an intensive. But they wouldn't so write it.

There are thousands of such differences between speech and writing—in vocabulary, grammar, and sentence structure. But the colloquial is in no way inferior. It's not to be confused with *dialectal* speech, though they are sometimes related. It can, on rare occasions, even be more formal than written language, or at least more often polysyllabic. Thus *knowledgeable* is listed as colloquial, though it's a word that is heard only in the speech of the highly educated.

The tendency in modern writing is to move closer to the colloquial. Dictionaries might perform a more useful service to those who consult them if they would indicate certain words as *formal*.

✻ the strange pronunciation of *colonel*

BREATHES there a man with mind so dead that he never to himself hath said, "Why is there such an extraordinary divergence between the orthography and the pronunciation of *colonel?*"

The answer is that it's an olla-podrida of error, confusion's masterpiece.

Colonel is the French form of the Italian *colonello*. The officer was so called because he led a little column (Latin *colonna*) of soldiers. That's where it got its spelling.

The pronunciation is due to the dissimilation in Spanish of the word into *coronel*. Dissimilation is the tendency in speech to change a sound in a word because it is similar to a sound in a neighboring syllable. It isn't that we mind saying the same sound over. We love to repeat vowels ("choo-choo," "hopscotch," "slambang"), but we hate to go to all the trouble of enunciating a consonant and then two seconds later have to go back and do it all over. We're lazy—or efficient. Thus the Latin *peregrinus* became *pelegrino* in Italian and *pilgrim* in English.

For a long time the spelling *coronel* was used in England, supported by the erroneous belief that the officer was so called because he served the crown (as the *coroner* did). But eventually, for no reason that anyone knows of, the French spelling and the Spanish pronunciation were fixed on.

✻ "Uncle, for God's sake, speak *comfortable* words"

Comfort derives from a Latin word meaning "to strengthen." It could once mean a physical strengthening and supporting, though it now seems quaint to read in Wyclif's translation of the Bible (1382) that the carpenter "comforted" the wall with nails and that God "comforted the locks of the gates." In the best-known of all uses of the word in the Bible—"thy rod and thy staff they comfort me"—the strengthening and support is, plainly, moral and spiritual, though the metaphor is close to its physical basis and assumes an awareness of it in the reader.

But once secure, we give ourselves up to tranquil enjoyment, ignoble ease, and peaceful sloth, and *comfortable* ceased to mean sustaining, inspiring, spiritually strengthening or even consoling and, one of civilization's triumphs, achieved its present meaning of foam rubber pillows with the thermostat turned 'way up. The British have carried the word (but not the process; their comfort seems austerity to an American) to perfection as *comfy*.

The comfortable words that Richard's queen besought from Edmund, Duke of York, were, of course, meant to be words of sustenance and encouragement, strengthening words, hopeful words, not soothing words that our meaning might lead us to expect.

✻ *common* and *vulgar*

Vulgar formerly meant "pertaining to the common people" and there was nothing necessarily condescending or disapproving in it. We retain this older sense in the now-strange-seeming term *vulgar fractions*, i.e., common fractions, and in *The Vulgate*, the Latin version of the scriptures. *The Vulgate* is so called because it is St. Jerome's translation of the scriptures from Greek and Hebrew, in the fourth century, into the then common or vulgar tongue—Latin.

However, the word *vulgar* now definitely reflects the scorn and dislike of the educated for the masses. It suggests ignorance, lack of breeding and refinement and, in its commonest use (its most vulgar use), ribaldry and coarse indecency. One cannot now substitute *vulgar* for *common* in, say, Lincoln's statement that "God must have loved the common people, He made so many of them," without affecting the meaning.

Common has acquired some of this meaning ("Don't scratch your head at the table; it's so common") but it has at the same time retained a dignity now impossible in *vulgar* ("Suffering is the common lot of man").

※ **componentry**

I AM SENT an advertisement of a phonograph that boasts of the machine's "custom componentry" and asked if "there is such a word as *componentry*?"

Plainly there is such a word. There it is, black on white, boldly emblazoned to sock us in the eye. The questions are: (1) Is it standard (i.e., "good English," acceptable, recognized, listed in the dictionaries)? (2) If not, is it a good coinage? (3) Is it suited to its purposes?

(1) It is not listed in any dictionary. That, however, doesn't mean that it's bad English. Our language would never have become the wonderful thing it is if people had not felt free to make up words whenever they wanted to.

(2) It doesn't seem a good coinage to me. In the hi-fi world *components* is much used for *parts*, and the suffix *-ry* (a shortening of *-ery*) does mean "the product of" (*pottery, millinery*) or "a collection of" (*jewelry, crockery*). But "a collection of parts" doesn't induce me to want to buy the phonograph. It's too much like the one I already have.

(3) We can't judge if a word is suited to its purposes until we know the purposes. One of the purposes of this ad may have been to make a great clatter of announcement, to suggest—with a drumroll of syllables—that something mighty important was happening. If so, *componentry* seems suitable.

※ **Is there a suggestion of sacrifice of principle in the word *compromise*?**

ORIGINALLY it meant "to promise together." That is, the disputants both promised to accept the decision of a referee. There was, in their so doing, a mutual surrender, and if the matter involved principle there must have been some surrender of principle, because a man just doesn't yield his principles to the judgment of another. In a matter that touches clearly upon basic principle a man of honor will not *compromise*.

However, we are no longer as certain of basic principles as we were. Practical matters demand most of our effort and attention and in practical matters compromise is the very soul of action and peaceful co-existence. Edmund Burke (when urging the British to compromise with their American colonies) said that "All Government . . . every human benefit . . . every virtue . . . is founded on compromise."

The English-speaking peoples are eminently practical, so that in English *compromise* is for the most part an honorable term. In French the word has the same two meanings that it has in English, but in French the idea of a shameful surrender of principle predominates. This illustrates the difficulties and dangers in translating. The English and the French have the same word with the same two meanings, yet in each country the emphasis falls on a different meaning, so there would be a great deal of talk at cross purposes.

We still retain certain principles, however, in regard to which we are not willing to give way in the least. And in relation to these the word is condemnatory, as when we speak of a woman who has "compromised her honor." Here it certainly does not mean to anyone (except, perhaps, herself) that she has merely made a reasonable concession in a practical spirit of cooperation.

✳ *comptroller* or *controller?*

Comptroller is an erroneous spelling of *controller*, introduced about the year 1500 by some zealous pedant who had found out that the French word for *account* was *compte*.

This absurd spelling became established in the titles of certain positions and in these titles it remains. Thus it is the Comptroller General of the United States, so fixed by law. But it is still pronounced *controller*—though one hears *comp-troller* every now and then from some earnest soul who just can't believe that *mp* is ever pronounced *n*.

Except where *comptroller* is fixed as part of a title, *controller* may always be used in its place. But the process is not reversible: *comptroller* cannot always be used for *controller*. The "controller of our destinies" cannot be called "the comptroller of our destinies."

✷ *congratulations!*

AMONG the many doubts that the ordinary wedding inspires in the guests is a feeling that saying "Congratulations!" to the father of the bride may sound as if you were praising him for having got her off his hands.

But this uneasiness is based on a misunderstanding of the word.

There is a word, now very rare, to *gratulate*, meaning "to rejoice." And to *con*gratulate someone is to rejoice with him. On occasions of receiving honor—such as graduating from college, receiving an award, and so on—it is assumed that the one accepting the honor is happy. To avert the evil eye, courtesy requires us to assure the recipient that we, too, are happy: we are happy for him, we rejoice *with* him, we congratulate.

Under these circumstances *congratulate* has taken on a great deal of the meaning of *praise*. But there are other occasions, such as weddings, where the word retains its more literal meaning. There's no praise in it. It is taken for granted that the bride is happy and further for granted that her father is happy because she is happy. Then you come in and tell him you're happy, too, just because he's happy. You rejoice with him. This may be a fiction, but you're not under oath, and if your rejoicing doesn't come spontaneously there is usually champagne to stimulate it.

✷ *conned* into it

MERELY being cheated isn't being *conned*. To be conned, you have to be cheated in a certain way. Being shortchanged is being cheated, but it's not being conned.

To be conned you must first yield to flattering persuasion. You must be a victim of the *confidence game*. You must have been bamboozled into being confident that somehow or other you were going to make wonderful gains.

✱ **Is one *continually* or *continuously* interrupted by the ringing of the telephone?**

CONTINUALLY. *Continually* and *continuously* overlap in many meanings, but there are places, and this is one of them, where one cannot be used for the other. That is done *continually* which is done at short intervals over a long period of time. That is done *continuously* which is done uninterruptedly. Now the telephone rings and stops. A large part of the irritation which its ring causes is due to the frustrated hope that each stop is the beginning of a period in which one can get on with other things. But one can't be interrupted by that which is uninterrupted.

Continuously means uninterrupted in time or space. But of the two words, it alone can apply to space. *Continually* can apply only to time. A hedge, for example, can be *continuous* with a fence. That is, it can go on without a break from where the fence stops. But it can't be *continual*. The Great Wall of China is continually (repeatedly) mentioned among the wonders of the world. It extends continuously (without a break) for 1500 miles.

✱ ***constructive*, as construed**

Constructive is rapidly taking its place, along with *leadership,* among the argle-bargle of the higher idiocy. I advance two instances:

(1) Mr. Jack Pearl, the dialect comedian, in an interview with Bob Lichello of the *National Enquirer* (Aug. 11, 1957, p. 5), commenting on an adverse criticism of his act by John Crosby, said: "The trouble with criticism is that unless it's constructive, it becomes personal. Then a man has no right to say it."

Well, at least, that brought "constructive criticism" right out in the open; it has to be praise or nothing!

(2) A famous givestress of advice to the lovelost had defended the practice of a fifteen-year-old chick of sitting on her uncle's lap and fondling him. She felt that family affection was a sacred thing and should not be discouraged. An excited reader wrote to say that such goings on "showed unconstructive signs of affection."

※ *convince* or *persuade?*

To MANY, *convince* is the stronger word of the two. To them it suggests that the mind has been overwhelmed, conquered, brought by force to agreement; whereas *persuade* seems to indicate more of an inclining of the judgment by working on the emotions.

But these are only seemings. The actual difference between the words is that there are certain idiomatic constructions in which one can be used and the other can't. *Persuade*, for instance, may be followed by an infinitive; *convince* may not. And it is probably the sense of strangeness when *convince* is used with an infinitive that leads people to feel that the wrong word is being used—though, actually, it is the wrong construction.

Of course, if this error persists, *convince* will take an infinitive. Indeed, it is almost inevitable that it will, in order to conform to *persuade*, now that their meanings have come so close. But this is not yet standard usage, a fact established not by the fiat of grammarians but simply because it "doesn't sound right" to educated ears.

※ "a man *convinced against his will*"

"WE SAY, 'He that is convinced against his will/Is of the same opinion still.' How can a man be convinced against his will?"

The proverb, in the form in which the correspondent gives it—which is the form in which one generally hears it—doesn't make strict sense. The original, in Samuel Butler's *Hudibras* (1678), runs: "He that complies against his will/Is of his own opinion still." And that's different.

In a sense, however, I think a man could be convinced against his will if "will" is interpreted as "desire." Many an honest man has been convinced, by irrefutable evidence, against his deepest wishes to believe otherwise.

※ If a *coolant* cools, what heats?

A COOLING agent is called a *coolant*. But there doesn't seem to be a parallel word for a heating agent.

There are some specialized ones in medicine: *pyrogen* for a hypothetical fever-producing substance; *calefacient* for a heat-producing remedy; and *calorifacient* for a heat-producing food.

But there is no general term and we need one. I can't find *thermant* in any dictionary, but since Merriam-Webster's *New International Unabridged* lists *thermantic* ("capable of heating"), I see no reason why *thermant* should not exist. Or *heatant* or *warmant*. The letters of the alphabet are at every man's disposal and if a coinage catches on the dictionaries will record it in time.

✻ the *cop* on the beat

MR. J. EDGAR HOOVER believes that use of the word *cop* casts disrespect on the police and appeals to the public not to use the word. But he is fighting for a lost cause: the word is as essential to headlines as "nab," "flay," "slay," and "rape" and there is not the faintest chance that considerations of space will ever yield in the newspapers to so trivial a matter as respect. The word is undignified and even, perhaps, a little contemptuous, compared to *policeman,* as is attested by the fact that no one would use the word to a policeman in the course of receiving a ticket. But the disrespect may have encouraged the word as much as the word the disrespect. Sixty years ago not one in a hundred respectable, ordinary middle-class people had anything to do with the police in their whole lives. But the crowding of urbanization, Prohibition, the income tax, rationing during the war years and, above all, the automobile—all these things combined have changed us into a nation of petty criminals. Now it is scarcely one in a hundred who has *not* been fined or has not cheated or evaded in some way, trifling but enough to give one a slightly apprehensive and therefore slightly resentful view of the police. The universal use of *cop* is not unrelated to eternal uneasiness about overparking or speeding or not seeing a stop sign.

For *cop* is an underworld word, as Mr. Hoover says. It is a shortening of *copper,* indicating a policeman as one who would "cop" or catch you. Or at least that is one theory of the word's origin. Another is that the police were called "coppers" because they wore copper buttons on their uniforms. We know that during labor troubles in Manchester, England, in 1864, the workers would hold up copper coins to the police as a sign of contempt. Linguists think the first of the two theories is the correct one. The implied derisive pun of the coins was probably a later thought.

The London *bobby* is so called after Sir Robert Peel who in 1828 remodeled the Metropolitan Police Force. Peel has a double fame in this particular field. From 1812-1818 he was Chief Secretary for Ireland and among his duties founded the Irish Constabulary who were called *peelers,* a name later extended to the English police.

❋ Can you hate someone *cordially* or devoutly?

Cordially means "with the whole heart." *Cor* is the Latin word for heart and the heart was thought to be the seat of the emotions. The first syllable of *courage* is the same word. *Cordially* is now generally restricted to the more pleasant emotions, especially those of social amity. But people hate as well as love with their whole hearts and *cordially* may still be used with an unfavorable meaning. Indeed, the very rarity of such a use nowadays may give it an added effectiveness.

Devoutly means "with the fervor of a vow." Perhaps one should not vow to hate, but men do and there must be a word for it. The youthful Hannibal vowed eternal hatred of Rome, a truly devout hatred to which he firmly adhered.

❋ the *coresponding correspondent*

"WHY ARE people in divorce cases called corespondents?" several correspondents ask.

They aren't. The person who brings the suit is called the plaintiff. The person against whom the suit is brought is called the defendant or, since he or she is required to answer the charges brought, the respondent. Sometimes, as in cases charging adultery, a third person is named. And this person is called the *corespondent*. Note that there is only one *r*. The word is pronounced *coe ri spon' dunt.*

One who writes letters to another is a *correspondent*. Here there are two *r*'s and the word is pronounced *core ess pond' d'nt.*

Letters are often produced in divorce suits as evidence, and since the conventions of love, particularly of illicit love, seem to require a heated and mawkish style, the reading of such letters in court often enlivens the proceedings. Many an ardent correspondent has found himself a reluctant corespondent and has wished that he had learned earlier the value of restraint in love and language.

✻ whence *corny?*

Corny seems to be derived from *cornfed,* a term used in America for 150 years to mean (when applied, as it usually was, to women) countrified, plump (". . . a hardy race of strapping, corn-fed wenches"—Washington Irving). Country people were formerly unsophisticated and seemed, at least to hardhearted city slickers, unrestrainedly sentimental.

✻ the *corporate* personality

"Is A CORPORATION singular or plural? What about those that have half a dozen names in their title?"

The mixture of singular and plural in the correspondent's questions is an answer in itself. A *corporation* can be treated as either singular or plural, depending on whether you regard it as a whole or have the individual partners or stockholders in mind.

Firms usually employ the plural in their brochures and correspondence. They have to say "Write to us" or "Send for our catalog." "Write to me" or "Send for my catalog" would be confusing and "Write to it" or "Send for its catalog" would be repellent.

But it is equally correct to say "U. S. Steel have revised their catalog" or "U. S. Steel has revised their catalog." Some grammarians claim that the second of these is incorrect because it combines a singular verb and a plural pronoun. But this mixed form is used by many of our greatest writers, including the Founding Fathers, who wrote in the Constitution (Article I, Section 5): "Each house shall keep a journal of *its* proceedings, and from time to time publish the same, excepting such parts as may in *their* judgment require secrecy." [Italics mine.]

✳︎ "studded with *corposants*"

A *corposant* is a light, usually in the form of a ball, due to atmospheric electricity, sometimes seen during storms on the mastheads and yardarms of sailing ships and occasionally on church spires or in tree tops. It moves with a gliding motion.

The name is a development (or a slurring, if it makes you unhappy to believe that the language is being "corrupted") of the Latin *corpus sanctum*, holy body, these lights being thought by sailors to mark the presence of good spirits. They are also referred to as "St. Elmo's Fire."

Dampier, the great navigator, records (1697) that as a storm abated he saw "a *Corpus sant* at our Main-top-mast head." Richard Dana in *Two Years Before the Mast* (1840) felt it necessary, after mentioning a corposant, to add "corpus sancti" in parentheses. But forty-eight years later, in his account of the eruption of Krakatoa, Captain Watson felt no such need, or perhaps no such relationship, and merely said that the mastheads and yardarms of his ship were "studded with corposants."

✳︎ "Lend me a *couple* dollars"

One hears this construction in common speech all the time ("Lend me a *couple* dollars, will you?" "He had a *couple* dogs up in the woods last night") but it is definitely substandard. We have to say "a couple of dollars," though in speaking *of* is almost always reduced to *uh*.

The omission is simply following the pattern of *dozen*. People used to say "a dozen of eggs," but that would now sound strange. But usage is tyrannical. Though we are not only permitted but required to omit the *of* with *dozen*, we may not omit it with *couple*.

✳︎ pronunciation of *coupon*

Most of those to whom *coupon* means a detachable statement on a bond specifying interest due, pronounce it koo' pon.

Most of those to whom it means a printed slip, often imitating the appearance of paper money, entitling the holder to a free cake of soap or a reduction in price of some commodity, pronounce it *kew' pon*.

Since familiarity with one of these pieces of paper rather than the other is a pretty sure indication of social status, this difference in pronunciation, slight as it is, has been made much of as an indication of the degree of one's culture. The dictionaries support the bondholders' pronunciation, even the boldest of them admitting the free-cake-of-soapers' pronunciation only as secondary. But since there are far more *kew' pons* than *koo' pons*, and since the disparity is likely to increase rather than to decline, *kew' pon* will probably win out.

✹ the *Court of St. James's*

A MAN is permitted to pronounce and punctuate his own name as he chooses, and institutions and places have the same privilege. Courtesy requires the use of the established form. This varies beyond all conception and no rule applies. There's nothing for it but to find out what the proper form is in each case. It's Teachers College, the Court of St. James's and Harpers Ferry. If something important is involved, don't trust gumption, commonsense, rules, or learning. Look it up.

✹ "the soul of *couthness*"

". . . his nubile daughter (Joanne Woodward), who is the soul of couthness. . . ."—*Newsweek*, April 7, 1958, p. 96.

Newsweek was, no doubt, laboring to be gay in thus contrasting Miss Woodward's role with that portrayed by Mr. Orson Welles—"a feudal Big Daddy . . . whose lifelong uncouthness denies him the respectability he now seeks."

Couth no longer exists as a word, and when it did exist, it did not mean smooth or courteous or anything else opposed to *uncouth*. It meant "known." Chaucer speaks of "far-off holy places couth in sundry lands." And when Spenser says "Uncouth, unkissed," he does not mean (as we would) that a rough, unmannerly boy or girl remains unkissed, but that if nobody knows you nobody will kiss you. He is saying, in fact, what any Hollywood star will support: that there's nothing like publicity for making a commonplace young man or woman seem glamorous and attractive.

The manner in which *uncouth* acquired its present meaning is plain. Anything unknown is strange. The strange seems odd, frightening, rough. And conversely, the odd, frightening and rough seems strange. Hence the word which meant "unknown" came to mean "rough and unmannerly." But it did not become fixed in this meaning until *couth*, "known," had been utterly lost from our speech. So *couthness* is a joke in limbo.

※ **creeping** *crap*

Crap, unprintable forty years ago, is now fairly common in print. Through the ages it has been applied to every conceivable kind of excrement, offal, and refuse and in the process became too unsavory for polite use. It has never quite descended to the level of the genuine sturdy unmentionables, however. Its voltage has been shocking but not lethal. Its use marks rather plain, rough honesty carried away by indignation than foul-mouthed indecency. When used for feces or defecation, it is a euphemism sufficiently close to a more common and coarser word to avoid the imputation of sissiness. But most of the time it is used metaphorically to mean nonsense, insincerity, lying, bluffing. And even here it is a sort of euphemism. Though contemptuous and condemnatory, it is saved by its jocularity from being as offensive as a plain statement in standard English. "That's a lotta crap" will be allowed to pass, or will be parried with a blustering reaffirmation, where "You are lying" will create tension and enmity.

It is solely in the metaphorical sense that it has begun to appear in print: "I never heard so much crap in my life" (John O'Hara, 1939); "I'm not interested in stories . . . or any crap" (Arthur Miller, 1949); "rumors . . . small-town crap" (William Styron, 1957); "no psychological crap . . . just plain, honest business" (Alexander King, 1958); "any of that crap" (Garson Kanin, 1959).

✸ It's not *cricket*

THE EXPRESSION—which is purely English; only fools or humorists use it in America—is based on the fact that cricket is a gentleman's game. Its rules are so ill-defined, says author George Orwell, "that their interpretation is partly an ethical business." It is a game in which form and style are more valued than success. So to say that something "is not cricket" does not mean that it's dishonest but that it doesn't measure up to the exacting requirements of the highest ethical standards.

✸ *crocodile tears*

IT WAS formerly believed—or at least asserted (God knows how much, then as now, of what was asserted was believed)—that the crocodile wept and moaned to attract the sympathetic and helpful, whom he then devoured, weeping as he ate. "It is the nature of crocodiles," we are told in Hakluyt's *Voyages* (1600), "when he would have his prey, to cry and sob . . . to provoke them to come to him, and then he snatcheth at them." That *snatcheth* restores our faith in humanity slightly; it suggests that at least some of the helpful had sense enough to be a little wary.

So the crocodile became a symbol of dangerous hypocrisy that plays on our pity. In particular, it reminded men not to be moved to forgiveness by the feigned tears of women.

✻ to come a *cropper*

TODAY's youngsters who are familiar only with the comparatively quiet and decorous destructiveness of the automobile can form no conception of the violence and horror of accidents with horses.

A *cropper* was originally "neck and crop." The *crop* or croup or crup was the rump. So that a horse that fell "neck and crop" fell completely, all together, front and back, in one lunging, lashing, shuddering heap. And that's what it is to *come a cropper:* to have a severe fall, headlong and furious, as a horse falls when galloping at full speed.

✻ an unholy *crusade*

The American College Dictionary, The Oxford English Dictionary, Webster's New International, and *Webster's New World Dictionary* all define a *jihad* (a Mohammedan Holy War of extermination against infidels—i.e., chiefly Christians and Jews) as "a crusade." In its extended sense of "any aggressive movement for the defence or advancement of an idea or cause," *crusade*, I suppose, can include *jihad*. It is true that one has to stop and think for a moment to recollect that the Crusades were directed against the Mohammedans and that *crusade* contains the word "cross," but the use of the word to describe its opposite seems questionable. It probably depends on how living, and hence intrusive, the basic idea of a word remains. No one would say that Jove was jovial or that Socrates asked socratic questions. But few ears would be offended by "knavish boy" or "boorish farmer."

I am told that St. Boniface's church in San Francisco advertises itself as "a mecca of devotion." They're going to find a muezzin in there one of these days calling the faithful to prayer.

✻ Can a man or woman be *cultured* without an education? Are uneducated people uncultured?

SUCH questions are almost impossible to answer because the words they seek to clarify have several relevant meanings. One of the meanings of *culture*, for instance, is the sum total ways of a people's living—their art, values, knowledge, customs, and techniques. A more limited meaning is the development or improvement of individuals within this civilization and their resulting enlightenment. This process, in its broadest sense, could be defined as *education*.

If it were so defined, the answer to the first question would have to be "No" and the answer to the second question "Yes."

However, if *culture* is defined in the much narrower—and much commoner—sense of an aspiration toward and an appreciation of high aesthetic and intellectual ideals, and if *education* is defined in the much narrower and much commoner meaning of schooling, then the answer to the first question would be "Yes" and the answer to the second question "No." All *cultured* people are *educated*, but they are not necessarily educated in school. The author of the Gettysburg Address was not an uncultured man, never mind how few days he had actually spent in classrooms.

✳ some *curious* meanings

Curious sometimes means "strange" and sometimes "inquiring" ("it is curious that the child should be so curious"). It derives from a Latin word meaning "full of care or pains." One of Chaucer's characters, about to set out on a journey, begs his wife to be "curious" in watching over their property while he is away.

Then it was applied to one who exercised care or expended pains to learn things, one who was minute in inquiry. And in this application, at first and for centuries to follow, it was chiefly derogatory—much like our *inquisitive* or *prying*—because our ancestors strongly disapproved of what we call "scientific investigation." They felt it was meddling, that God would let us know whatever He thought we ought to know and the rest was none of our business. It's only very recently that curiosity has been regarded as a virtue. Even in our grandfathers' time it was felt to be contemptible at best. "Go, wretch!" the youthful William Cullen Bryant sneered at Thomas Jefferson, "Resign the Presidential chair!/Go search with curious eyes for horned frogs." Plainly an interest in amphibia was regarded as reprehensible.

The other meaning of *curious*, "strange," simply means that which arouses curiosity, that which excites close attention because of its novelty. They would have to be the opposite of commonplace or we wouldn't be curious about them: they are odd, queer, bizarre, remarkable in some unusual way.

✱ the unknown *curmudgeon*

Curmudgeon's origins are completely unknown. The dictionaries don't even risk a guess—not since 1775, at any rate. But it's a marvellously expressive word, with its suggestion of currishness, and grudging and begrudging, and dudgeon. Just the word for a snarling, avaricious, crabbed old man.

The word is dear to lexicographers for having been the occasion of the most wonderful boner in the whole history of plagiary. When Dr. Johnson was preparing his dictionary he received a letter suggesting that the word was derived from the French words *coeur* (heart) and *méchant* (evil). Either the letter was unsigned or Johnson lost it and forgot who wrote it. The suggestion, though unsupported, was interesting and plausible and in his dictionary (1755) Johnson set it down for what it was worth: "a vitious manner of pronouncing *coeur méchant,* Fr. an unknown correspondent." In his *New and Complete Dictionary of the English Language* (1775), Dr. John Ash, cribbing from Johnson but, unfortunately, knowing no French, entered it as "from the French *coeur* unknown, *méchant* correspondent."

✱ to *curry favor*

To curry favor is a corruption of an earlier expression, *to curry favel*. Favel, or Fauvel, was the name of a horse in the once-famous French *Roman de Fauvel*. This was a fourteenth-century satirical poem in which the horse Favel, who symbolized worldly vanity, was soothed and lovingly tended by all classes of society. So that *to curry favel* was to seek to advance yourself in the things of this world. And since men have always believed—with some justification—that the best way to do this was to ingratiate yourself with the powerful, to gain their favor ("It ain't what you know; it's who you know"), the corruption of the phrase was as logical as it was inevitable.

✳ "too old to *cut the mustard* any more"

Mustard ("hot stuff") appeared in a number of slang phrases sixty years ago. *To be the mustard* or *to be the proper mustard* was to be the genuine article, the main attraction. To be *all to the mustard* was to be very important ("Why don't you invite him if he's so much to the mustard?"—O. Henry, 1907).

Of the many meanings of *cut*, one was frolicsomely showing off, being frisky (*cutting up, cutting capers, cutting a dash*). So that to *cut the mustard* was to show that you were the genuine article, to show you were important, by a frolicsome excess of energy. Something like the guest of honor being also the life of the party.

The very vagueness of the expression left a considerable margin for interpretation, proper and improper. No one who has not heard Rosemary Clooney and Marlene Dietrich sing "Too Old to Cut the Mustard" has a complete knowledge of the full scope of innuendo.

✳ *Dan Cupid*

Like the Spanish *Don* and the Portuguese *Dom*, *Dan* was a title of respect derived from the Latin *dominus*. It meant "Master" or "Lord" and was applied chiefly to the more impressive members of the clergy. Chaucer's Monk ("a manly man, to been an abbot able") was addressed as "Dan Piers." The poet Spenser, who lived a couple of centuries after *Dan* in this sense had fallen into disuse but who loved archaic words, revived it in reference to Chaucer himself whom he called "Dan Chaucer." Spenser was much imitated and there was quite a vogue of calling old poets "Dan."

Shakespeare in *Love's Labour's Lost* (III,i,181) called Cupid "Dan Cupid." This may have been intended in humorous respect to Cupid or humorous disrespect to Spenser. But it is what fixed the title (which some mistake for a first name) on the god of love. In *Romeo and Juliet* (II.i.13) Mercutio calls him "Abraham Cupid." Scholars were so bewildered by this that all modern editions change it to "Adam Cupid" and, where they bother to explain, say that it was a reference to Adam Bell, a famous archer. That's drawing the longbow for you!

✻ get his *dander up*

THERE are two possibilities as to what happens when you get your dander up. *Dander* is a dialectal form of *dandruff*. So that to get one's dander up may have been to raise one's hair (as on the backs of many animals when they are roused to fight) with the dandruff on it.

However, there is another word *dander* which means "ferment." So getting one's dander up may be a sort of rising ferment of anger.

The *up* is as interesting as the *dander*. For some reason anger is thought of as something rising. See a *Towering rage* (page 346).

✻ these *data*

Data may be treated as a singular or a plural. Most Americans find the real singular of the word strange—as in Aldous Huxley's reference to "an unpleasant datum."

Social scientists commonly use *data* as a singular. They say "the data shows" and refer to their data as "it." They talk about "much data" and "very little data." These are singular constructions and they are quite all right if they are not followed by a plural verb.

In the physical sciences, on the other hand, *data* is more often treated as a plural. This too is quite all right. But it must be consistent. It's not enough merely to use a plural verb. If one is going to say "the data are," then he must refer to "they" and say "these data" and "many data." He cannot use *much* or *little* with *data* and then use a plural verb. He can't say "much of the data are now outmoded" or "little data are available."

Standard Rate and Data, one of the most distinguished advertising services, uses the word consistently in the plural.

✱ Who was *Davy Jones?*

Davy Jones first appeared, with his grim locker, in a sea story by Tobias Smollett in 1751. Smollett, who had served in the British Navy, said that Davy Jones was an apparition much feared by sailors.

How did a spook get so jolly a name? There is a West Indian word *duppa, duppy,* or *duffy,* which means a malevolent ghost and students of folklore believe that Davy is an Anglicization of this word and that *Jones* is Jonah. So Davy Jones may well be Duffy Jonah, our old friend out of the whale, whose chief task now is to preside over horseplay on ships crossing the equator.

✱ *dead right*

BEING dead is one of the most absolute, unchangeable conditions there is. In a number of ways *dead,* expressing inertness, came to signify "absolute" and "complete." A dead silence is utterly devoid of sound. Dead water is motionless. A dead stop is a full stop. Hence it is not surprising that the idea of absoluteness got detached from the specific instances of it and came to stand alone in some uses of the word. *Dead right* is absolutely right, as *dead level* is absolutely level.

✱ a *dead ringer*

A *dead ringer* is not a defunct sexton but someone who bears a startling resemblance to someone else.

A *ringer* was a slang term for counterfeit. It may have derived from the sale of brass rings as gold at country fairs. One of the meanings of *dead* is "absolute" (*a dead loss, dead certain*). So that a dead ringer is an absolute counterfeit, a complete imitation.

❋ a *dear* of corn

Dear is related to *dearth,* meaning "scarcity." Indeed, they were once the same word and men spoke in times of famine of "a dear of corn."

What is scarce, if it be necessary to life, will be competitively bid for and its price will rise until it is very expensive. And what is expensive will be cherished and will be "dear" to us in another sense. These three ideas—scarcity, cost, desirability—have circled around in the word *dear* since the beginning of the language.

❋ Is it a *deck* or a *pack* of cards?

WHETHER you say a *deck* of cards or a *pack* of cards depends on whether you prefer to speak American English or British English, or, to be more exact, whether you choose to speak the English of Shakespeare and Mark Twain or the English of Dickens and Tennyson.

Deck is the old word ("The King was slyly finger'd from the deck"—Shakespeare). *Deck* continued in use in Scotland and America but has not been used in England (in this sense) for more than two hundred years.

Pack is now widely used in America and is fully acceptable, but it has certainly not yet displaced the old *deck.*

❋ "*deliver* us from evil"

To *deliver* something, a correspondent writes, is to bring it to you. She is puzzled by "deliver us from evil."

To *deliver* was, originally, "to set free." *B* and *v* are closely related sounds (compare *Havana* and *Habana*) and *deliver* and *liberate* are simply variants. *To deliver* meant especially to set free from restraint, danger, or evil. And this is the meaning in the Lord's Prayer.

The old meaning is kept in the phrase "jail delivery" which was a clearing of the jail of its prisoners in order to bring them to trial at the assizes.

In a like manner a woman was *delivered* of her child at term. We now often say that the doctor delivered the child, though our fathers would have said that he delivered the mother. Modern parents who wish even fiction to be correctly expressed must insist that while the stork delivers the baby to the mother, the doctor delivers the mother of the baby.

The modern meaning of *deliver* grew from the fact that the carrier, who has assumed a responsibility in accepting goods, is freed of his burden when he reaches the consignee.

※ Is *demean* a synonym for *debase*?

THE VERB *demean* is related to the noun *demeanor*, meaning "conduct" or "behavior." Any kind of conduct or behavior, good or bad. It used to be that a man could demean himself ill or he could demean himself with dignity and honor. But he couldn't just demean himself—not and convey any idea to the listener or reader. The word isn't—or formerly wasn't—connected with the adjective *mean,* meaning "base."

But the adjective *mean* is so much better known than the noun *demeanor* that most people hear it in *demean* and assume that the word is a synonym for *debase*. And so many have heard it so often and assumed this erroneous meaning so long that it must now be accepted not only as a standard meaning but as the principal meaning. Some dictionaries try to meet the problem by listing the two *demeans* as separate verbs.

※ *destruct*

A SCORE of indignant letters want to know if there is such a word as *destruct*.

Apparently there is. And not only a verb *to destruct* but a noun *destruct,* the acting of destructing, and a *destructor,* that which destructs, and a *command destruct* and a *command destruct signal* and a *destruct line,* the boundary line beyond which a missile cannot fly without being destroyed under destruct procedures.* *Destruct,* it would seem, is as common a word at missile bases as *rocket* or *fuel.* That the word isn't in any ordinary dictionary is irrelevant. Dictionaries are far behind rockets.

Among the urgencies of firing missiles none is more dramatic and critical, I gather, than the necessity of destroying in space a missile that is malfunctioning. There had to be a word for this. *Destroy,* seemingly, wouldn't do. Perhaps it is used for destroying a missile while it is still on the ground or for dealing with the enemy. The new word had to be something that would be instantly understood but could not be confused with *destroy.* If so, *destruct* seems a satisfactory coinage.

I am told by other correspondents that around missile bases *destruct* is coming to be used in more general, nontechnical senses ("You ought to destruct that old stuff in the attic"). This —to an earthbound outsider—seems clumsy, unnecessary and, perhaps, affected. But in the age of missiles it may very well replace *destroy.*

※ Why is the word *"deuce"* used for "devil"?

THE DEUCE is the lowest throw at dice, and the disgust that the thrower has in his voice as he states "deuce" or "the deuce" has made it an expression of exasperation and impatience ever since the middle ages. It was first used as a euphemism for the devil in the time of Cromwell. Cromwell forbade swearing and "the devil" was either regarded as swearing or feared to be so dangerously close to it that it was advisable to find some other

* From *Aerospace Glossary,* Research Studies Institute, Air University, United States Air Force, 1959. Dr. Woodford Heflin, ed.

name. And here was "the deuce," conveniently beginning with the same letter and already charged with fury and disapproval.

❋ Does the doctor *diagnose* the disease or the patient?

"HE WAS diagnosed as having cancer." Shocking, cry the purists. The man was not diagnosed at all; the disease was diagnosed. And in the strictest sense, they are right. *To diagnose* is to identify, to tell apart from others, to recognize. But there is bitter wisdom in the popular usage, for a man and his sickness are one. *Disease* would be meaningless, were it not for a sentient organism to be dis-eased. It is a soothing fiction that the man "has" the malady; too often the malady has him.

Curious that the purists don't balk at *diagnose* itself, a recent back formation from *diagnosis*. They rarely seem to mind that.

❋ changing *diaper*

Diaper means "double white." It was originally—and until very recently—used to describe a simple geometric pattern woven into cotton or linen cloth, especially one consisting of diamond-shaped reticulations so woven that the light was reflected differently in the alternating rows.

Application to a baby's breechcloth is an Americanism and dates (seemingly) from the beginning of this century. The extension may have come about through the use of the diapered pattern of napkins. In non-U British, the word is *nappie*.

In relation to the breechcloth, the plural is almost always used. Possibly because all things connected with the legs run to plurals (pants, trousers, shorts). Possibly because you have to have a number of them; one alone isn't much good.

In the Midwest, at least, the common pronunciation, even among the educated, is *die′ p′r*. The *a* is pronounced, however, when the reference is to the pattern in linen.

✳ "What the *dickens?*"

Poor Dickens! The expressions "I'll give him the very dickens" or "There'll be the dickens to pay" and the like have nothing to do with the novelist. They were in use centuries before he was born. In Shakespeare's *The Merry Wives of Windsor* (1598) Mistress Page, trying to call Falstaff's name to mind, says "I cannot tell what the dickens his name is." And there are many other uses of the word in this sense in our literature.

It is used as a euphemism for *devil* because it begins with the same consonant, as *gosh* is used for *God*. It may have been a worn-down form of *devilkin*, "little devil."

✳ our *diffident* millionaires

To be *diffident* is to be shy, modest, retiring, self-effacing. But it's a little more than that. It is to be such because of lack of confidence in one's own ability, worth, or fitness. It is to be self-mistrustful.

The word has been impressed on our consciousness in the past few years by the adroitness of its use in a series of stately, full-page advertisements for the Rolls-Royce. After pointing out in a quiet, almost embarrassed manner, that the Rolls-Royce is the utmost of perfection in automobiles, the advertisement concludes by pointing out that "Except for the radiators," the Rolls-Royce and the Bentley "are identical motor cars." The Bentley is for "people who feel diffident about driving a Rolls-Royce."

A number of things combine to make this statement one of the most inspired pieces of advertising copy of our times. In the first place, it makes it fantastically easy to be one of the cognoscenti and furnishes mountains of brushwood fuel for the fires of automobile enthusiasm. Every Rolls-Royce that passes can be identified as not being a Bentley and every Bentley as being secretly a Rolls. Then there is the idea—uproariously funny to an American—of being able to afford a Rolls-Royce but being too shy to drive it.

These are but superficialities, however. The real virtue is as hidden behind *diffident* as a Rolls motor and chassis behind a Bentley radiator. The advertisement is for the Rolls-Royce, not for the Bentley. And this particular sentence in it is brilliant not because it says that those who drive a Bentley lack confidence in themselves, but because it implies that those who drive a Rolls-Royce have full self-confidence and are the glorious masters of their own destiny that we all would like to be. It's really saying, "Come on—be your better self—cease to restrict your glorious potential—dare to live—buy a Rolls-Royce!"

✱ all *diked* out

Diked in "all diked out" is an American dialectical word. It may be a form of *decked*. One of the oldest meanings of *deck* is "to clothe with rich or ornamental garments, to adorn, to beautify" ("Deck the halls with boughs of holly"). It could once be so used seriously, even solemnly. The second verse of the 104th Psalm, which in the Authorized Version reads "Who coverest thyself with light as with a garment," in the Coverdale version (1535) reads: "Thou deckest thyself with light." But *deck* is now used in this sense only in humor and usually with a slight touch of scorn. *Dike* suggests false finery, over-ornamentation with showy cheapness. "Dike the halls with Woolworth tinsel, tralalala-la-tra-la, la, la."

There is an old English word *dight,* meaning "to put in order, to array, to make ready." And *diked* may be this word. Or it may be a mixture of the two.

✻ a *dirigible*

A DIRIGIBLE is an airship which can be directed (*dirige*), in contrast to a balloon which merely drifts with the wind. The improper emphasis on the second syllable, which is often heard, seems to be the result of a belief that the word *rigid* is a part of dirigible, as though the name were derived from the rigidity of the structural framework. But blimps, which are not rigid, are dirigibles—because they can be directed in flight.

The standard pronunciation is *dir′ ij ub′l*.

✻ the *disc jockey*

Jockey is the diminutive of the Scottish pronunciation of the name Jack. It's the word we spell *Jackie*.

It was originally used in Scotland and Northern England as a familiar or contemptuous name for a common soldier, a helper, or an errand boy. In Dickens' *Dombey and Son* (1848) a man says to Mr. Dombey's young assistant, "You're Dombey's jockey, a'nt you?"

It was particularly applied to stable boys and postilions and became fixed as the special name for professional riders in horse races, most of whom were boys or tiny men.

It was the idea of their riding the *discs* (with some idea of competition and a race) that led the word to be humorously transferred in slang to the professional players of records. And thence, having acquired the meaning of a man's occupation, it has been extended to clerks or stenographers ("desk jockeys"), soda jerkers ("juice jockeys"), and so on.

✻ *disjointed* and *unjointed*

IN THE sense of having the joints or connections separated, there is now no difference between *disjointed* and *unjointed*.

However, *disjointed* alone retains the metaphorical meaning of incoherent ("His talk was all disjointed"). *Unjointed* used also to have this meaning, but it sounds strange to a modern ear when Hotspur, in Shakespeare's *I Henry IV* (1596) refers scornfully to the "bald, unjointed chat" of a silly, garrulous noble.

✳ "the *distaff* side"

"Mrs. William G. Stratton adds an attractive distaff note to Republican party judicial campaign rally," says the caption under a picture of Governor and Mrs. Stratton.

Unless used to belabor caption writers, a *distaff* emits no perceptible note. It is a short stick formerly used to hold the wool or flax from which a thread was drawn in spinning. Visitors to Latin America may have noticed that as the peasant women trot along the road with huge burdens on their heads and backs they are busy twirling a short stick in their hands. They are spinning and the stick is a distaff. It was once so associated with women that it came to stand as a symbol. When they got married they had to take a little time off from spinning to cook and suckle and plow and weave. But an unmarried woman remained a *spinster*.

Dis-, the first part of *distaff*, means "a bunch of flax." It occurs also in the word *bedizen* which originally meant "to put flax on a distaff" and since has come to mean to adorn oneself gaudily so that one looks like a distaff with its fluffy bunch of unspun flax.

The reference to women as distaffs and, above all, to one's mother's family as "the distaff side," apart from being a cliché, betrays a peculiar uneasiness about the mention of such basic facts of life as *woman* and *mother* that is characteristic of journalism and especially of society columns. Perhaps it is a characteristic of the middle class which in its upper reaches always refers to a man's wife as his "bride" and in the lower as his "better half."

The companion phrase for the male side is "on the sword side." But this sounds frightfully Wardour Street.

✳ "a conventional *dither*"

Nellie Forbush, in *South Pacific*, contemplating her wonderful guy, found herself in "a conventional dither."

Dither is a phonetic variation of a very old word *didder*, which meant "to tremble or quake" ("chill wretches that didder with the cold"—1375). It's akin to *dodder* which was to didder on your pins and was used seriously up into the middle of the 19th century ("the dither of the engine").

In contemporary use, however, *dither* has been specialized to mean to hesitate and waver in irritating uncertainty, the hesitancy being due to anxiety and ineptitude. It's a humorous word with slight overtones of scorn.

✻ pronunciation of *divorcee*

THE PRONUNCIATION of *divorcee* bothers those who make a point of being bothered. The masses, including most divorcees, have no trouble with it.

The dictionaries used to insist on the French, or partly French, pronunciation: *d'vor say'*. But more recently they have accepted the only pronunciations that one hears from most Americans: *di vor see'* and *di vor' see*. Anything else now sounds a little affectedly elegant. Having far more divorcees than the French, we can assimilate the word for our own.

✻ *Dixie* Land

ALTHOUGH the existence of the Mason-Dixon Line may have helped the word *Dixie* catch on, it is highly doubtful that the word actually came from the line. The weight of evidence is also against the theory that the word derives from bank notes issued in New Orleans bearing the French word for ten, *dix*.

The most incredible explanation seems the most probable. A man by the name of Dixie once kept slaves on Manhattan Island until forced by hostile Northern sentiment to move south. The slaves were not happy in the South and longed for the old place, Dixieland. Soon the term came to represent a Negro paradise which was assumed by Northern sentimentality to be in the sunny Southland.

The word *Dixie* first appeared in Daniel Decatur Emmet's famous song "Dixie" (1859) which was certainly not regarded during the Civil War (as it is now often assumed to be) as the "national anthem" of the Confederacy. After Grant's successful skirmish at Belmont, Missouri, in 1861, his regimental band played "Yankee Doodle," "The Star-Spangled Banner," and "Dixie"—

and Grant was not inclined to regard the Confederacy with sentimental, tear-misted eyes.

✱ *dizzy*

Dizzy is a dizzy word. It's come around in a complete circle.

The modern slang use of *dizzy* to mean "foolish," especially in a featherheaded, improvident way ("Some dizzy broad . . ." —Jerome Weidman) is exactly the word's original meaning. A ninth-century West Saxon version of the Gospel of St. Matthew says of the ten virgins which took lamps and went forth to meet the bridegroom: "Five of them were dizzy, and five prudent./ And the five dizzy [ones] took lamps, but they didn't take no oil with them."

One can hear the exact words and rhythm in contemporary vulgate: "This dizzy blond, she took a flashlight but didn't take no battery!"

The moral is not that Holy Writ is ungrammatical, for it isn't. Or that slang is grammatical, for it doesn't care. Or that dizzy had been "corrupted" and then recorrupted to its pristine purity, for that is nonsense. But that the speech men actually use is wonderfully alive.

✱ "till death us *do part*"

THE ORIGINAL wording of the marriage service in *The Book of Common Prayer* was "till death us depart." *Depart* is now an intransitive verb, but formerly it meant to divide something into parts, to separate. In 1400 an author spoke of "a great hill that departeth Macedonia and Thrace," and in the Arthurian legends we are told that King Arthur tried to *depart* two knights who were fighting.

So the phrase meant "till death separates us." *Depart* was kept in the marriage service until 1662, nearly a hundred years after it had disappeared, in the meaning of *separate*, from common speech and writing. It was then changed to *do part*, still being kept in the subjunctive to preserve the beautiful rhythm. "Till death parts us" would have been prosaic in comparison.

A slave preacher in Kentucky in the days before the Civil

War met the exigencies of the peculiar institution by uniting Negro couples in wedlock "until death or distance do you part."

❋ Why "as dead as a *dodo*"?

WHY "as dead as a dodo" or "as dull as a dodo"?

The *dodo* is extinct, and you can't be deader or duller than that.

And even when alive, it wasn't much. It was a pigeon about the size of a goose, with huge feet and short legs, stubby useless wings, an immense skull, a heavily plated hooked bill and a ludicrous poodlelike tail. It lived on the island of Mauritius in the Indian Ocean. The Portuguese discovered the creature in 1507 and called it *doudo*, "simpleton," because it was absurd and seemed to have so little sense of self-preservation. The Portuguese introduced pigs to the island and the pigs ate the dodo's eggs. The last dodo seen alive was in 1681. Its misfortunes are fixed, as a sort of epitaph, in its scientific name: *Didus ineptus*.

As a term of good-humored contempt, *dodo* is applied chiefly to elderly gentlemen. Perhaps it is felt that they are really extinct but too obtuse to perceive it. Or maybe they remind people of the confused and pompous dodo in *Alice in Wonderland*.

❋ *does* or *doesn't?*

"PEOPLE say, 'Don't be surprised if he *doesn't* visit you one of these days.' But they mean 'if he *does* visit you.' Aren't they saying the opposite of what they mean?"

One would think that *yes* and *no* were the clearest words in the language. But they are the most confusing. It's so often uncertain, when a question has been put, just what is to be assented to or denied. It was, in part, a recognition of the commonness of this perplexity that made the song "Yes, We Have No Bananas" so popular.

"Don't be surprised if he doesn't," meaning "Don't be surprised if he does," must be accepted as an idiom, a construction peculiar to the language that defies grammar and logic and yet is in daily use and is fully understood.

We are not the only ones who have this difficulty. The French say *n'est ce pas?* ("isn't it not so?") and the Germans say *nicht wahr?* ("is it not true?"). And in each case they, as we, expect the answer to the unnecessarily negative question to be "Yes."

❋ putting on the *dog*

THE EXPRESSION *putting on the dog* to describe dressing up with unusual splendor originated about 1870 as a piece of college slang.

The most likely explanation of its origin is that it was a reference to the high stiff collar (which was called a "dog collar") then indispensable to formal wear. Ladies' diamond chokers were also called "dog collars" as were the heavily-braided collars of officers' uniforms. And since stiff collars, diamond chokers, and dress uniforms were all ornamental and all used on highly formal occasions (when our grandfathers went in for a great deal of fuss and feathers), *putting on the dog* would mean preparing for such an occasion.

There was a humorous derivative "doggy," meaning spiffy or ornamental. One still hears it once in a while but it's outmoded.

❋ Why are *dog days* so called?

THE HOT days of August are called *dog days* not, as is often asserted, because they are the days when dogs go mad, but because they occur at the time (July 3 to August 11) of the rising in conjunction with the sun of one of the Dog Stars, Sirius or Procyon. These are hot, dry days, and when rabies was thought to be an expression of insatiable thirst combined with a fear of water (*hydro*, "water" + *phobia*, "fear"), the association was natural.

✸ in the *doldrums*

THE WORD was originally (early nineteenth century) slang. It was formed from *dull* on an analogy with *tantrum* to mean a fit of low spirits. Sailors applied the expression to a becalmed sailing ship, and since ships were most often becalmed in the equatorial regions between the trade winds, the word came to be applied to those regions. But they constitute a vague and shifting zone and cartographers have left the word to poets and novelists. Webster's *Geographical Dictionary*, which names more than 40,000 places on the face of the earth, does not list the *doldrums*.

In common—particularly journalistic—use, *doldrums* is often used to mean vacuity, inactivity ("A tip that Moskovitz . . . had been kidnapped . . . reached the city desk of the *Chronicle* in the doldrums of a late Saturday afternoon").

The most famous description of the geographical doldrums is in Coleridge's *The Ancient Mariner*. It was there, "under a hot and copper sky," that the ill-fated vessel lay motionless, with "Water, water everywhere . . . Nor any drop to drink."

✸ "tame" or "*domesticated*"

THOUGH the two words are loosely used interchangeably, there is a distinction between them. That animal which has lost the timidity or savagery of its wild state is tame, but that which has been reduced to domestic use is domesticated. A pig is domesticated, but we would not speak of it as tame. A deer might be accustomed, by gentle treatment, to come to a house for food. It would be considered tame, but not domesticated. *Domesticated* always means "reduced to use or habituated to living in or around a house." Most husbands are domesticated. *Tame* is often extended to mean no more than *mild* (as in "This was mighty tame abuse.") Few husbands are tame.

✻ Can a man *dominate* at *dominoes?*

Dominate and *dominoes* derive from the Latin word *dominus* meaning "master." The name for the game is generally thought to derive from the Latin through the French phrase *faire domino,* i.e., to make oneself master, to win the game by placing the last man. Some scholars, however, doubt this explanation.

The use of two words of similar sound in one sentence is not a question of grammar but of style. If it states the facts, you could say "The dominie in the domino dominated at dominoes," but you would startle the hearer or reader and must expect his attention to be diverted from the meaning by the expression of it. And this is almost always a bad thing.

✻ Just what is a *donnybrook?*

A *donnybrook* has become a term for a brawl because of the cheerful violence, the open-hearted pugnacity, the sociable clouting of skulls by shillelaghs, that for centuries distinguished the annual fair held at Donnybrook, in Ireland, now a peaceful suburb of Dublin.

✻ the *donor*

". . . it turned out the strange comas of Bernadette and Venita Fratantonio had been caused all along by large doses of barbiturates. The confessed donor: their mother."—*Life,* August 22, 1960, p. 33.

A *donor* is a *giver,* but *to donate* and *to give* cannot always be equated. Misgivings and misdonations would not be the same. Historically a donor is one who grants an estate and a donation has always been expected to be considerably more than a gift—though a gift is sometimes pompously or flatteringly called a donation and a donation sometimes in humble simplicity is called a gift. Possibly because it has until recently been a legal word, *donate* seems stilted.

A giver can give many things. He can give you a present and he can give you bubonic plague. A donor has hitherto conferred only benefits, but the word is no more sacred than any other and can be extended unfavorably as well as favorably. *Life's* new meaning may have been influenced by the very common use of *donor* for one who contributes blood in a transfusion. *Blood* has so many historical, literary, and religious associations and is so necessary to the maintenance of life that the solemn *donor* seemed fitting, rather than *giver*. In the age of the tranquilizer the same solemnity may carry over to the barbiturates.

* "I *don't think*"

THOUSANDS have written to insist that one cannot say "I don't think it's true." For, say they, incontinent in an ecstasy of superiority, if one says "I don't think," he cannot go on to state the thought he admittedly has not thought! Hundreds add that they were so taught in school, leaving one appalled at the revelation of what is done with the taxpayers' money.

Whence came this whiff and whimsy within the circumference of their figmentitious fancies? By what zeal of perversity did they arrive at such fatuity?

Insofar as one can make any sense of it, the belief that "I don't think" nullifies any idea that follows it in a sentence is based on the mistaken assumption that an adverb modifies only the word immediately following it—that the elided *not* in "I don't think it's true" must modify *think* and only *think*. But this is unwarranted. An adverb can modify a single word in a sentence and when it does it usually stands directly before that word. But more often an adverb qualifies an entire statement, as it does here.

"I never saw a purple cow" doesn't mean that the speaker was born blind, that he never saw. And no one with even a rudimentary acquaintance with English would assume for a second that it did.

✱ What is a *doppelganger?*

Doppelganger is a German form of a word that is sometimes anglicized as *doubleganger*. It means "a spook, a wraith, an apparition which is the exact double of a living person." It's a silly word for a silly thing.

✱ the double negative

IN ALGEBRA always and in Latin usually (though not invariably), two negatives make a positive. But not in English or any other Teutonic language. The only place in English where two negations make an affirmation is where one negative directly qualifies the other, as in "It's not bad" or "I'm not unhappy." This construction is thoroughly respectable. And even here the two negatives don't completely cancel each other: this form of the double negative expresses the weakest possible positive attitude.

Multiple negatives were formerly used freely. In the oldest English translation of the Gospels it says that the foolish virgins "took lamps, but didn't take no oil." This strikes the modern educated ear as improper. But separate two negatives a little in a sentence and we don't mind at all. When, for instance, someone says, "He couldn't sleep, not even with a sedative," he is using a double negative, since his meaning is "even with a sedative."

✱ Why were our soldiers called *doughboys?*

THERE are a number of explanations of why American soldiers in World War I were called *doughboys*, but the only thing certain is that the word was applied to U. S. infantrymen long before World War I, probably during the Civil War or even the Mexican War.

Some say that it is a corruption of *(a)dobe* which was derisively applied to soldiers in the Southwest and meant "mud spattered." To support this is the fact that *'dobe* was sometimes spelled *doughboy*.

Some say that *doughboy* was a term for a small, solid doughnut and that this word was applied to the buttons on the uniforms of the infantry in the Civil War and then to the soldiers themselves. This explanation can be dated pretty close to the Civil War.

Some say that it simply means that the marching soldiers mulched the mud of the roads into dough. This may be, but a marching army usually reduced dirt roads to something more like gruel than dough.

✻ Had *drank* or *drunk?*

THE STANDARD past form of the verb *to drink* is now *drank* ("He drank his milk"). The participle is *drunk*, but there is enough divergence in practice to make many of the foremost scholars insist that *drank* must be accepted as a permissible variant (". . . as if too much whiskey had been drank in it"—Frederick Law Olmsted; "After having drank each placed his bottle on the mantelpiece . . ."—James Joyce). *The Linguistic Atlas of the United States and Canada* shows that over large areas of the United States, especially in New England and the northern sections of the Midwest, *had drank* is almost as common as *had drunk* among people of all degrees of education. In some places one hears *had drinked* but this, while not without charm, is certainly nonstandard.

Drunk was formerly a fully acceptable past. It may have been discontinued because of the bad associations of *drunk* meaning "intoxicated." And it may be this same repugnance that makes people use *drank* for the participle.

✻ the *drawingroom*

THE NAME has nothing to do with drawing. It's a shortening of *withdrawing-room* and at first (sixteenth and seventeenth centuries) designated a private chamber attached to the public rooms, a chamber into which a monarch or other great person might withdraw when he wanted privacy. In the eighteenth century the term was applied to the room to which the ladies withdrew from the table, leaving the gentlemen to their port and pornography. It was in this shift that it acquired its connotation of elegance.

Today it is best known as the most spacious of pullman accommodations.

✻ DRIVE SLOW(LY)

DRIVE SLOW is perfectly good English. DRIVE SLOWLY is equally good, but since it requires a little more of the taxpayer's paint and the driver's attention, the shorter form is preferable.

Many people object to DRIVE SLOW, apparently on the assumption that *slow* is an adjective and *slowly* the adverb. But slow has been used as an adverb (that is, has been an adverb) —as well as an adjective—for almost five hundred years. "How slow this old moon wanes," Shakespeare wrote. Milton spoke of the curfew bell "swinging slow with sullen roar," and Byron of a ship that "glided slow."

So that when you have Shakespeare, Milton, Byron, a hundred and fifty million or so Americans *and* the County Road Commissioners arrayed against you, you might as well give in. And when you realize that a form which you see on every roadside every day has been in universal use for more than five centuries, it's a little late to start getting upset about it.

✻ How can a liquid be dry, like a *dry martini*?

FROM its basic sense of "free of moisture," the word *dry* branched out into a number of meanings, all having to do with some lack (like "dry bread" for bread without butter). Among these meanings was that of wine free from sweetness and the flavor of the fruit. In a sweet wine some of the grape sugar remains as sugar, but in a dry wine all of the sugar has been converted to alcohol. When we speak of a dry martini, we mean one in which there is little or no sweetness.

The French word for dry is *sec* which appeared in Elizabethan English as *sack*. The sack that Falstaff drank so freely was dry sherry. He liked to add a little sugar to it. If he really did drink two gallons of it at a sitting, as his tavern reckoning showed, he was indeed a "huge bombard of sack," a "stuff'd cloakbag of guts."

✷ high *dudgeon*

High dudgeon is a cliché so worn that it has almost acquired the status of a specimen. Our hearts leap up when we hear someone use it seriously; it comforts us to know that corn still flourishes. Like many clichés, it also has a value to the wits. S. J. Perelman speaks of a man who went off "in low dudgeon."

"High dudgeon" is now the only place where *dudgeon* appears and it has been petrified in that phrase for a hundred years. Before that people sometimes referred to "deep dudgeon" and most often to taking something "in dudgeon," that is, being offended by it. A character in one of Trollope's novels says, "You must not be in dudgeon with me."

The origin of the word is not known for sure, but it is probably derived from an Italian word meaning "to overshadow." If so, it is parallel to another old phrase "to take umbrage," which also means to be overshadowed. Shakespeare speaks of surly, resentful men as "cloudy" men, and a generation ago there was a slang expression "to put someone in the shade," meaning to surpass him and hence to incur his ire. Apparently, we are resentful if we don't have a place in the sun.

✷ "Put up your *dukes*"

Dukes, a common slang term for fists ("Put up your dukes"), is puzzling. But, then, all slang is puzzling; it's meant to be. Let squares sluggishly tread the track of the alphabet and timidly appeal to dictionaries to warrant their words; the coiners of slang prefer to gambol, turn somersaults, walk on their hands, leap and cavort along untrodden ways. Unless they startle the staid and bewilder the solemn, they have labored in vain.

Wentworth and Flexner in their *Dictionary of American Slang* have a quotation to show that *dukes* was originally "Duke of Yorks," that this, by riming slang (a common form of cockney slang) stood for *forks* and that *forks* was common slang for fingers. Could be.

※ Why is a stupid person called a *dunce?*

WORDS reflect prejudices as well as facts.

John Duns Scotus—presumably a Scotsman born in the town of Dunse—was a Franciscan who achieved fame as a teacher at Oxford and was later (1307) appointed head of the theological school in Paris.

He opposed the teachings of Thomas Aquinas and for two hundred years after his death his followers triumphed over the followers of Aquinas. But with the Renaissance the Scotists were attacked with renewed fury as hairsplitting obstructionists of the new learning and the new theology. Scorn and ridicule were heaped on them and they were charged with impenetrable stupidity. *Dunsman* or *dunce* became a synonym for a stupid fool and this scorn lives on in the word. Logicians may be rich in faith and hope but they are notoriously limited in their charity. So far as the language is concerned, the learning, the precision, and reach of mind of the Subtle Doctor count for nothing.

※ *durst*

Durst is not only quite acceptable English, it is much older than the now generally preferred *dared*. It's also more literary. Shakespeare uses *durst* 48 times and *dared* 9 times. The Bible uses *durst* 7 times but doesn't use *dared* at all. *Dared* was just coming into use in Southern England the century before the King James Version (1611) was translated, but the translators obviously regarded the old form as the better. The King James Version has (*Mark* xiii:34): "And no man after that durst ask him any question." The Revised Standard Version (1952) changes this to "dared."

W. S. Gilbert preferred *durst:*

> The bravest names for fire and flames
> And all that mortal durst,
> Were General John and Private James,
> Of the Sixty-seventy-first.

The *ur* sound in English is often pronounced *ar*. We know that the British, for example, pronounce *Derby* as though it were spelled *Darby*, and there are scores of other illustrations.

Now *durst not* was often pronounced *darsn't* and this, with the *a* flattened and the *r* not pronounced gave us the form *dassent* which up to fifty years ago was a very common pronunciation. *Durst* is now a little archaic and is more likely to be heard in a negative statement than a positive one. We are more likely to hear *durst not* than *durst.*

✻ *dyed-in-the-wool*

"Died-in-the-wool," as a number of correspondents spelled it, may be, for aught I know, an expression in use among sheep to signify a peaceful departure from the vale of bleats.

"Dyed-in-the-wool" is a very old English term for something deeply ingrained. It is based on the fact that dyes applied to raw wool are more lasting than those that are applied after the wool has been spun into thread and woven into cloth. So that anything that is "dyed-in-the-wool" is basic, fixed, unremovable.

Ingrained means "dyed in grain." And this means dyed with kermes, a scarlet dye that was strikingly fast. We now know that kermes (the word is related to *carmine* and *crimson*) is made from the dried bodies of insects which are found on an oak. They were formerly, however, thought to be plants, not animals, and were assumed to be grains.

✻ Is "*each* and *every*" redundant?

Each means "all, taken separately." It is used when the members of a group are thought of individually ("You must pick up each leaf"). *Every* is used when the members of a group are thought of as a unit ("England expects every man to do his duty").

At one time *each* was used in speaking about a countable number of individuals and *every* in making a universal statement. A feeling for this distinction survives in such phrases as "what every woman knows," but it is not felt very strongly and we often interchange *each* and *every* merely for variety.

Each and every is now repetitious, since the old distinction has faded. But there is a difference between being repetitious and being wrong. Repetition is a way of emphasizing and emphasis is very important in expressing our meanings. Then "each and every" has a rhythm that is missing from "each" and "every" when they are used separately, and rhythm is also very important in expression.

✱ Why do we say that something set aside has been *earmarked*?

Earmarked now means that something has been set aside and distinguished in some way (as, perhaps, by being put into a special account) so that it can't be used for any other purpose.

It derives from a mark in the ear of a sheep or other animal which served as an indication of ownership. As cattle are branded, sheep and pigs were identified by daubs of tar or red ochre or by slits or other cuttings of the ear.

✱ within *earshot*

ONE OF the meanings of *shot* is "the range of a shot." Tennyson speaks of Sir Lancelot riding "a bowshot" from the bower of the Lady of Shalott. *Earshot* was coined in analogy to this and means "within the range of hearing."

✱ Why is confessing an error called *eating crow*?

THE FLESH of a crow must be nauseous. To eat one would be a disgusting experience and to have to eat one in public would be humiliating.

Beyond these obvious assumptions and the facts that the expression was at first "to eat boiled crow," that it was originally applied to political prognosticators who had guessed wrong, that it came into use in the United States and first appeared in print in the 1870's, nothing is known.

There is a yarn that the expression originated during the war of 1812. The story is that during a truce on the Canadian border an American soldier shot a crow in Canadian territory. A British officer demanded that he surrender his gun and then, to teach him a lesson, compelled him at gun's point to eat a mouthful of the crow. He then returned the gun and the American, holding the gun on his former captor, made him eat all the crow.

The story is of fairly recent date and is highly improbable. It is not likely that after subjecting an enemy to a humiliation you would blandly hand him a loaded gun. And why did sixty years pass before anyone heard of the phrase?

✱ **Why is listening in called *eavesdropping*?**

THE *eaves* (originally a singular noun) was the overhanging edge of a roof. Under this was a space—usually about two feet—which received the rain from the roof and this was called the *eavesdrop*.

The space between the edge of the eaves and the wall of the house was an excellent place for snoopers and peepers to crouch. They were called *eavesdroppers*, and there must have been quite a few of them because the law went out of its way to define them as "Such as listen under windows or the eaves of a house to hearken after discourse, and thereon to frame slanderous and mischievous tales." Sir William Blackstone, the great jurist, said they were "a common nuisance" and should be haled into court.

From the noun *eavesdrop*, the place of the eaves' dripping, thus came another noun *eavesdropper* and from that, by back formation, a verb to *eavesdrop*. In this word the sense of snooping has so overpowered the idea of either *eaves* or *drop* that we can now speak of somebody eavesdropping indoors, and on a dry day too, without exciting the most rigorous purist. *Eavesdropping* has recently been applied to wiretapping, with the most extraordinary linguistic consequences. *Science News Letter*, for instance, refers (Dec. 5, 1959, p. 384) to "eavesdrop equipment that works on the induction principle" and speaks of a special device invented by the telephone company that catches "the eavesdropper with his receiver down."

✱ **Does the word *effigy* necessarily imply scorn?**

No. An *effigy* is a likeness or image of any kind, whether painted or sculptured ("Hanze Albein hath taken th'effigies of my Lady Anne"—1539; "the Effigies and Representations of Martyrs"—1611).

The word has acquired a bad meaning from the phrase

"burning in effigy." Since the image of someone so detested that his likeness is publicly insulted and burned would hardly be a noble likeness, but rather a grotesque caricature, the word acquired, in this particular use, the suggestion of a ludicrous scarecrow or dummy. And this use is tainting the word. If one were to refer to the statue of Abraham Lincoln in the Lincoln Memorial in Washington, for instance, as an "effigy," most hearers would be offended. It wouldn't matter that they were "wrong" and the speaker "right." If he offended without intending to be offensive, then he failed to express his proper meaning. The tainting of words cannot be ignored.

Effigy is a corruption, by the way. The "proper" word was *effigies*. But this was mistaken for a plural and the *s* dropped.

※ **egging on**

"TO EGG ON" has puzzled many people who feel that the throwing of eggs can hardly be regarded as encouragement.

The explanation is that there are two entirely different words—spelled alike and pronounced alike but unrelated in origin and meaning.

One *egg* is a Norse word that came into English about the year 1200. And it meant then just what it means now—"to incite, to urge on."

The commoner word *egg* is also Norse, though there is no connection between it and the other *egg*. The old English word for a hen's egg was *ei* with the plural *eyren* (the *-r* plural that we have in the archaic *childer,* plus the *-n* plural that we retain in *oxen*). *Egg* now seems so "natural" an English word that it is hard to believe it was a borrowing. But it was, and the old *ei* remained in use in some parts of England until the end of the fifteenth century. We know this because William Caxton, in the preface to a book which he published in 1490, told, from his own knowledge, of a merchant whose ship was held in the estuary of the Thames for several days by adverse winds. The merchant (who, by the way, was a Northcountry man) went ashore to get some provisions and was angry when he asked for some *eggs* and was told by a farmer's wife that she didn't understand French. But the eggs were procured when another in the company asked her if she had any *eyren*.

✣ "I'm not, *either!*"

SOMEBODY says, "You're late." The person spoken to, denying that he's late, says, "I'm not, *either!*" *Either* what?

Either is used here as an intensifier in a statement that is simple contradiction of a preceding positive statement. If the statement had been negative, *too* is often used as an intensifier in contradiction. ("You're not late." "I am, *too!*") Neither word is used as an intensifier in any other situation.

This use of *either* and *too* is familiar to every American and must be classed as an American idiom.

As for its standing, it seems as good as any other intensive form. We hear it too often from people of all walks of life and all degrees of education to insist that it must be regarded as substandard. It's quite respectable spoken English and its fault is not in itself but in its too frequent use. But that's a matter of style, not grammar.

✣ Can "*either side* of the street" mean both sides or must it mean one side or the other?

Either here can mean "each" and it can also mean "both of the two." It did not acquire the meaning "only one of two" until fairly late and even after acquiring this meaning it has continued to be used in both senses.

It has the meaning of "each, or both, of two" in the Bible: *And the king of Israel and Jehoshaphat king of Judah sat either of them on his throne* (II Chronicles 18:9). This plainly does not mean that they took turns, sitting one at a time, but that they both sat on separate thrones at the same time. Tennyson uses *either* in this way in the opening lines of *The Lady of Shalott* (1852): "On either side the river lie/Long fields of barley and of rye . . ."

So it is clear that this is not a new development in English.

It would certainly be tidier and more practical if *either* were limited to one meaning or the other. But it isn't.

✷ What is *elegant*?

Elegant is an elegant word. It means tastefully fine or luxurious, gracefully refined, pleasingly superior. In aesthetic matters it is a word of the highest commendation ("The elegant Miss McCarthy," the London *Times* admiringly calls Miss Mary McCarthy). Hazlitt said that *elegance* "implies a precision, a polish and a sparkling." It is being blunted by being used merely as a synonym for "expensive" or "luxurious" or even "exclusive" ("Frankie Laine said he stopped in a Hilton hotel that was so elegant 'Room Service' had an unlisted number").

It derives from a Latin word which originally meant "to pick out"—hence to be choosy, fastidious.

The word itself is a little old-fashioned now, which enhances its meaning of fastidiousness. The days when *elegant* was fashionable were the days of reaction against the heavy ornateness of Victorian splendor. Hence it acquired overtones of graceful slenderness, severe simplicity, unadorned richness. "An elegant woman" would suggest to most imaginations today someone gracefully thin, exquisitely gowned, with a minimum of jewelry, perhaps a little jaded and droopy. It would certainly not suggest the ripe, corseted, bustled, bosomed, beruffled and befeathered object of the Victorian lecher's longings.

✷ Why *eleven* rather than "*one-teen*"?

Eleven and *twelve* are very strange words. Why aren't they "one-teen" and "two-teen" like the other respectable numerals that follow them?

The first part of *twelve* is plainly *two* and the first part of *eleven*, though not so plainly, is *one*. Eleven used to be spelled *endlufen, endleofan, onlevene,* and many other different ways, but ways that showed that the first element was *one*.

But what's the second element, *-lve* in *twelve* and *-leven* in *eleven*? There's been a great deal of study, speculation, and argument about it and most scholars are now convinced that it means "left," "remaining." That is, *eleven* means "one left (over)" and *twelve* means "two left (over)." This would imply that ten was the basic maximum and that counting in the Stone Age, as now, was based on the fingers.

❋ Do only lovers *elope*?

To *elope* is to lope out or away from. It is related to an Old English word for the escaping of a jailbird. Originally only married ladies eloped—and from their husbands. Modern slang and colloquial English have re-created the idea in the phrase "run out on." Eloping is now restricted almost entirely to the running away from home of a young woman with her lover for the purpose of being married. If they lack this honorable purpose, they just "run away with."

Elopements most often occur when the parents do not approve of the young man, and where they disapprove they often do so because they feel he does not belong to their social class. He is an *interloper*. He runs in where he doesn't belong—and then has a run-in with Papa.

❋ emerita

It was a nice touch for *The New York Times* (November 25, 1959, p. 27) to caption the picture of Mrs. Agassiz as "President Emerita of Radcliffe." At first glance it seemed a contradiction, since her life work had been towards removing the distinctions between men and women in education. But this was a special case; her femininity deserved to be stressed.

Linguistically it was interesting, too. You could scour Latin literature without finding the form *emerita* and there may have been a little snorting in various Classics Departments. But there should have been rejoicing: like the invention a year or so ago at the Vatican of a Latin word for *helicopter*, it showed that Latin is not yet a completely dead language. As long as a language is living it will change, and as long as it can be changed it has at least a spark of life.

✳︎ *empty* indignation

"Rivers do not *empty* into the sea," a lady writes, quivering with excitement at the greatness of her discovery, "they *flow* into the sea." "It annoys me," she adds.

I assume it is not the movement of the water that annoys her but the lighthearted indifference to accuracy of the slovenly millions who, knowing quite well that rivers are rarely empty at their mouths, go right on speaking as if they were.

She has many to be annoyed at. This meaning of *empty* as a verb—the discharging of a river into another river or into the sea—is one of its oldest meanings, antedating almost every other. It goes back for more than 400 years and among those who must endure her displeasure are the philosopher Hobbes and the novelist Defoe and, in modern times, the Merriam-Webster Company who publish not only a number of general dictionaries that recognize this meaning but a special *Geographical Dictionary* which actually employs it.

Some rivers run dry; and if any do this right into their estuaries (and one or two may), they may perhaps be said to *empty* themselves. So lofty a dedication to strict accuracy as this correspondent's, involving as it does the condemnation of more than a billion people, many of them learned in this particular field, surely requires that she compile a list of all such rivers and keep it pasted on her writing desk so that she may be sure, before she gives way to annoyance, that in each case her condemnation is warranted.

An easier course would be to accept the language as it is spoken and written, especially where it has been so spoken and written for five centuries; to recognize that many words have many meanings and that among these some are inaccurate, some mere approximations, some exaggerations, some figures of speech not to be taken literally, and some downright errors. And surely among the crimes and follies of mankind there is something more worthy of this splendid annoyance than a poor old poetic trope.

※ **Can one *enhance* by taking away?**

"ENHANCE your figure by dieting," the advertisement urged. "But doesn't *enhance* mean 'to add to'?" an apprehensive woman inquired.

"To add to" is only one meaning of *enhance* and a vague, derivative meaning at that. The original meaning was "to lift up." Knights enhanced their swords in battle and monks enhanced their voices in prayer. Then the word acquired the metaphorical ideas of raising in degree, heightening, intensifying, magnifying. And one way to magnify is to become larger physically, to add to your bulk.

However the chief modern meaning—the one intended in the advertisement, I am sure—is to increase in attractiveness or value. Some men think a little plumpness does this to a woman, but the beauty salons don't agree.

※ **"I *enjoyed* myself"**

IT IS astounding how many people regard the common, innocent expression "I enjoyed myself" as improper. Many seem to regard it as indecent, suggesting that they assume it can allude only to onanism. And a few appear to have even more extravagant illusions in mind. "Only an insane cannibal could enjoy himself!" one indignant matron cries.

Under the circumstances the question of sanity was an unfortunate one to raise. People have strange ways of enjoying themselves and one of the strangest is twisting a plain expression to find a fault that has passed unnoticed by others for centuries.

"I enjoyed myself" means that the speaker had a good time. For three hundred years this idea has been expressed by these words. The earliest meaning of *enjoy* was to be put in a state of joy, just as *to enrage* is to put into a state of rage. Luke i:14, which now reads "and many shall rejoice at his birth," used to read (1382) "and many shall enjoy in his nativity."

It is true that enjoy also has a second meaning, to get joy from, as in *I enjoyed the movie*, and this is the usual sense of the word today. But one meaning doesn't disappear or become wrong just because a new one has been acquired.

✳ *enthuse*

ALL CURRENT dictionaries list *to enthuse* but describe it as an Americanism and a colloquialism. A colloquialism is the sort of thing we use in informal speech but not in formal writing. So that classification doesn't quite fit *enthuse* because we find it with increasing frequency in fairly formal writing.

It's a back formation from *enthusiasm,* and a recent popular book on the language states that "as such it is classed as a colloquialism." But that isn't so, either. If back formations were all to be regarded as colloquialisms, we couldn't make any formal use of such standard nouns as *pea, minnow, goiter, gloom, cherry,* or *hush* or of such verbs as *to preach, to grovel, to diagnose,* or *to beg.* For all of them—and hundreds more—are back formations.

The real trouble with *enthuse* is that it is overworked and is used to mean merely "to become excited" rather than to mean "to become excited because of an obsession." In such a sentence as "Daly wasn't enthused when the network hired Wallace," *pleased* would have been a better word. But there's no grammatical fault in *enthuse* and it seems to be moving relentlessly toward becoming a standard, fully accepted term.

✳ pronunciation of *envelope*

Envelope is an amusing word in that a strange, ignorant mispronunciation of it has come to be regarded as an indication of cultural superiority and has been adopted by so many eager strivers that it has finally gained acceptance.

The old American pronunciation, by the way, the one that historically has the best claim to suggest that your family not only came over on the *Mayflower* but were literate enough to write back, is *en vel' up*, the same as the verb. It is still heard in remote places but is now considered dialectal.

Every dictionary now gives *en' vuh lope* as the standard contemporary American pronunciation. Most have thrown in the sponge and accept the bastard *on' vuhlope* as well. Several, however, go out of their way to condemn it. Kenyon and Knott's *Pronouncing Dictionary of American English* (a very scholarly work) labels it "pseudo-French." Colby's *The American Pronouncing Dictionary* says it is "un-English" and is "a recent corruption" introduced by someone who thought he was speaking French but wasn't.

What all this means is that *en' vuh lope* is the standard American pronunciation and that *on' vuh lope* was once an affected and ignorant mispronunciation but has been affected by so many so often and so long that it, too, must be accepted.

✻ Is there such a word as *epizootic?*

Though many think it a comic coinage, *epizootic* is a standard word. It means "a disease temporarily prevalent among animals." Rabies could be epizootic (for *epizootic* can be either a noun or an adjective); so could hoof-and-mouth disease. When such a condition prevails among human beings, we call it an *epidemic* (*epi-*, "upon or among," + *demos*, "the people"). *Epizootic* is sometimes used humorously for a mild infection that's "going around" among people.

✻ *erstwhile* thoughts

"The dictionary lists *erstwhile* as archaic," writes a stouthearted correspondent, "but who decides? I use it. Am I wrong?"

The dictionary doesn't decide; it merely records what people say and write. And *archaic* doesn't mean "not in use" but "antiquated" or "characteristic of an earlier period." *Obsolete* is the word for "definitely not in use any more." If you use an obsolete word (such as *swink*, "hard work," or *rathe*, "early," or *sweven*, "dream") you simply won't be understood. But if you use an archaic word, you may be thought quaint or affected—or, perhaps, three hundred years old.

Erst is definitely archaic. Anyone who said "We lived erst in Chicago before we moved out here" would certainly be regarded as peculiar. *Erstwhile*, as an adjective meaning "former" ("erstwhile friends"), is still used often enough to be received without uneasiness. But as an adverb, meaning "formerly," it is too old-fashioned to be acceptable in ordinary speech or writing. We don't say, "Erstwhile, local phone calls were only a nickel."

All the dictionaries do is to call our attention to these facts. They tell us that 1662 was the last time, so far as is known, that *erstwhile* was written as an adverb in a serious piece of writing. If, knowing that, you want to go ahead and use it, you are as free to do so as to wear a basket-hilted rapier or knee breeches with bunched lace at the knees. They, too, were in style in 1662. It's no vellum off the dictionary's spine.

✳ *esquire*

An *esquire* was a young man of good family who attended upon a knight, in particular being his shield-bearer (the doublet *squire*, by the way, is a much older word). Then the term was transferred to a man belonging to the higher English gentry, just below a knight. But in the general inflation in honorifics that has marked the progress of democracy this distinction has been lost and the word, now in widespread though declining use in England (sustained in large part by its value in limericks), has the same meaning as *Mr.*

In the United States it is not used except by those who ape English ways. With one exception, however: lawyers use it a great deal in the formal salutation of letters addressed to other lawyers. This use is increasing and *Esquire* may come to designate a lawyer here as surely as *Doc* designates a physician. Even women lawyers may become esquires. Certainly there's nothing in the nature of the language to forbid it. Nobody's bothered any more when young ladies are declared *Bachelors* of Arts.

In written addresses, *Esquire* always follows the surname, as: Richard Roe, Esquire. Where it or its abbreviation is used, no title should be prefixed. That is *Dr.* (or *Mr.*) *Richard Roe, Esq.* is incorrect. But titles may be suffixed: *Richard Roe, Esq., LL.D.,* or *Richard Roe, Esq., Professor of Jurisprudence.*

✳ "*evacuate* the scene"

Evacuate (originally a medical term) is an endless trial and triumph to the purists. The trial is other people's use and the triumph their own. They never tire of insisting that people cannot be evacuated from a place, the place can only be evacuated of the people.

The military early took over *evacuate* as a word for withdrawing from a fortified place. It was the place that was evacuated, but in nonmilitary use, almost from the beginning, it was the people who were evacuated. To civilians, the troops—their sons, fathers, brothers, husbands—were the focus of interest. They didn't give a damn about the position. And this shift of meaning, later extended to designate the removal of masses of civilians from a threatened area, did no more violence to the language than many another idiom.

The word retains, however, a flavor of the military, an aura of grim emergency. It can properly apply only to fairly large bodies of people and to situations of danger. In times of armed tension, such as our own, when all prose must be "horribly stuff'd with epithets of war" to seem brisk, it has become a much-overworked word, used for everything from digging a hole to changing your seat on a plane. The following instances, all taken from current books and newspapers, seem improper to me: "The cabin immediately filled with thick vapor and all passengers were evacuated into the rear"; "Degerby was evacuating [digging a foundation] for Dunbar Builders Corporation"; "Yeoman Conner abandoned his efforts to evacuate some files"; "The two ghouls fled at the sound of the first pistol and evacuated the scene swiftly."

✻ When is *evening*?

IN THE narrowest sense *evening* is twilight, when the light is evening from daylight to dark. But there is no record of its ever having been restricted to this limited sense. In *Genesis* i:5 ("And the evening and the morning were the first day") it seems to indicate all of the day except the morning, as it still does over most of the southern United States. In the North it is usually restricted to the period from late afternoon to bedtime.

Evening is thought by many to be more elegant than *night*, more upper-class. Joe Lampton, a rising young heel in John Braine's *Room at the Top*, telephones Susan Brown, a young lady far above him socially. "I've got two tickets for the ballet on Saturday night," he says, "I wondered if you'd care to see it."

" 'Saturday night?'

" 'I mean evening,' I said, cursing myself."

The time intended was 7:00 P.M. It might have comforted the

resentful Mr. Lampton to know that his lower-class speech was here (as it is in so much) much nearer upper-class speech than Miss Brown's middle-class.

Evening has a number of idiomatic peculiarities. "Good evening" serves as a common greeting, but it is rarely heard at parting. One thanks a hostess for a pleasant evening, never (with discretion) for a pleasant night. And there's quite a difference between an evening gown and a nightgown. In "The Dead," James Joyce has the servant maid Lily greet Mrs. Conroy with the salutation "Good night." This is, apparently, established usage in Ireland, but it would sound strange to American ears.

Eve has come to designate the evening before an important day and *evening* the conclusion of the day itself. Christmas Eve is December 24. Christmas evening is late December 25. The eve of battle is the night before the battle. The evening of battle is the twilight succeeding the battle.

✷ What is *every other?*

IF WE say, "Every other man wore a black tie," do we mean that every man except one wore a black tie or that each alternate man wore a black tie?

Such questions stream in, usually with the expectation that there will be some little trick that makes it "good English" and unequivocal or some slur or slovenliness that marks it at once as bad English.

But it's quite good English and at the same time equivocal. Only the context would make the meaning definite. Speech is not mathematics; it abounds in confusions and uncertainties, as do our minds that created and shape it. The speaker or writer must make an effort to make himself clear—though if he fails he may comfort himself with the thought that so, at one time or another, has every other human being. And I don't mean each alternate human being. We can't blame others for misunderstanding us; we must blame ourselves for being misunderstood.

✷ "*every so often*" or "*ever so often*"?

Ever means "at all times," "continuously." *Every* means "each" and "every so often" means at each of a number of frequently repeated occasions. Since frequent repetition comes close to being continuous action, it is easy to see how *ever* and *every* have become confused in this expression.

The matter is complicated by the fact that over a large area of the United States *every* is pronounced like *ever* ("He hit ever man in the crowd"). This was recorded as a peculiarity of uneducated Southern speech as early as 1893, and if we may trust the dialog in some of Robert Penn Warren's novels (and Warren has a very good ear for speech), it is in widespread use today. Before anyone who does not use it gets too scornful about it, however, he should remember that *every* is a similar eliding of *ever each*.

✳ *Fabian* tactics

IN THE year 217 B.C. the Romans had been crushingly defeated by Hannibal in the great battle of Lake Trasimene. Several other defeats had preceded this and Rome lay almost at Hannibal's mercy. The people, thoroughly frightened, chose as Dictator Quintus Fabius Maximus, a slow-moving, prudent, unemotional man who was called "Cunctator" or "the delayer" because he would not risk an open engagement with Hannibal but, despite the reproaches and demands of the populace and many of his own officers, fought only delaying actions, skirmishes and raids. Fabius realized that the Romans could not afford another defeat and that Hannibal could not afford not to have a final victory, since his army, though victorious, was gradually wasting away. He therefore adopted and insisted on the tactics which gave him his name, put an adjective in the language and, eventually, destroyed Hannibal.

It was because they thought socialism should adopt the same tactics that the British Fabian Society took that name.

✳ *façade*

Façade (pronounced *f' sahd'* or *fa sahd'*), after disappearing for many years, is very popular.

Originally a French word meaning "the face of a building," the term was formerly used widely in America because so many of our buildings then had pretentious faces that belied their miserable actuality. They went in for tin cornices, unconvincing cupolas, imitation-brick facings, and the like. This gave the word its suggestion of falseness, of a misleading front, and it is this meaning that has brought it back to meet the needs of our times.

❋ *fag*

Fag for cigarette was British pre-World War I slang. The origins of slang are almost always obscure. The best guess on this is that fags were so called because they sapped the smoker's strength and left him fagged or exhausted. Though the word may simply have been an abbreviation of *faggot*. Most parents have inveighed against cigarettes, dwelling especially on their harmfulness. Young smokers have not only been unimpressed but have—with a shocking disregard of the Fifth Commandment—made a joke of their parents' wisdom. A common name for cigarettes used to be "coffin nails."

The verb *to fag* meant "to droop" and may be related to *flag* (as we speak of "flagging energies"), also meaning "to droop." The *fag* of British public school terminology is the same word. Apparently the fag was made to work by the older boys until he was worn out.

Fag for a homosexual is an abbreviation of *faggot* (which is used a good deal by male homosexuals, scornfully, of their own kind). Two hundred years ago there was a dialectal word *faggot* used in scorn in relation to women and this may be a transference of that. Or it may mean heretic. Heretics had close associations with faggots and those who recanted were obliged to wear the representation of a faggot embroidered on their sleeves—as a reminder to them of what they had had coming and to all true believers, no doubt, to continue to persecute them.

❋ Should *father* be capitalized?

NOT IF it refers merely to any male parent ("There are ludicrous moments for the father of the bride").

Yes, however, if it is used in direct address ("Please, Father, send me some money") or in reference to one's own father ("I told Father I would be home by eight").

Of course all references to God as Father are capitalized.

✻ **"The child *favors* his father"**

ONE OF the very old meanings of *favor* (going back to 1450) is "features" or "appearance." When, for example, Iago, in Shakespeare's *Othello*, urges Roderigo to assume a disguise, he says: "Defeat thy favor with a usurped beard." The original meaning of *favor* was "goodwill." The commonest meaning of the word today is "something conceded out of good will." The meaning of features grew out of the idea of "that which conciliates good will."

So that when someone says that a child *favors* his father or mother, there is no suggestion of favoritism. It just means that the child has the features or favors of that parent. Plainly at first the features must have been favorable, but the word became fixed and designated unfavorable features as well.

Favor in this sense is now regarded as colloquial. That is, it is the sort of word that educated people would say but not write.

Honor Tracy combines the two meanings, or rather uses the modern meaning with an echo of the other: "The younger, Thomas O'Driscoll, was less favored, with his red curls and narrow shoulders" (*The Prospects Are Pleasing*, p. 4). These are the touches that make good writing.

✻ *featherbedding*

THERE is a story that the use of the word *featherbedding* for holding down an unnecessary job or being paid for work not performed, began on the Rock Island Railroad. It is said that when the men complained of cornshuck mattresses in the caboose they were asked by a scornful trainmaster, "What do you want, featherbeds?"

But the chances are that the railroads picked it up from the army. A *featherbed soldier,* as a term for one who shirked, who had it soft while others did the work, was used in the United States Army as early as 1848.

❋ Why when a pilot stops a propellor in flight is it called *feathering* the propellor?

IT ISN'T the stopping of the propellor that constitutes *feathering;* it's the changing of the angle of the blades to bring them as near parallel as possible to the line of flight. This reduces wind pressure on the blades, a pressure which might otherwise tear the engine out of the wing.

Feathering in this sense is taken over from rowing, where an oar is said to be feathered when it is turned as it leaves the water in such a way as to pass through the air edgeways. As it is so turned, to lessen the resistance of the air upon it, the water runs off it in a feathery form.

All meanings of *feather* derive in some way from a bird's feather—resembling it in appearance or use. This particular one is a fascinating instance of how language develops. It is an image derived from an image. Since *feather* derives from a word meaning "to fly," *feathering* a propellor went from a pinion to foaming water to an oar and then back into the sky again!

❋ pronunciation of *February*

NINE out of ten educated Americans if asked directly how they pronounce the name of the second month in the year will say *Feb' roo eri.* And they will have the support of most dictionaries.

Nine out of ten educated Americans, however, when inveigled into using a sentence in which the word occurs in some inconspicuous way—and are hence concerned with saying something and not with impressing others by the way they say it—will say *Feb′ yoo eri*. And they will have the support of most scholarly pronouncing dictionaries.

Either form is acceptable. The first is precise, the second is natural. By "natural" I mean that it is in accord with the English language, one trait of which is a reluctance to pronounce two *r*'s when they occur too close to each other in the same word. Most people, even highly educated people (indeed, chiefly highly educated people) omit the first *r* in *Cante(r)bury, the(r)mometer, su(r)prise*, and the like. And in the case of *Feb(r)uary* this natural tendency is strengthened by its continual pronunciation in conjunction with *January*.

✳ "*Feed* a cold and starve a fever"

THERE is much argument as to exactly what "Feed a cold and starve a fever" means. Grammatically, the question is whether *feed* is in the subjunctive or in the imperative. That is, whether the proverb advises us to feed a cold and to starve a fever or whether it says "If you feed a cold, you will, in consequence, have to starve a fever later." But since the imperative and the subjunctive forms are identical, there's no way of telling.

Doctors say the whole thing is nonsense anyway. Doctors Levine and Cohen, of the Medical Research Institute of Michael Reese Hospital in Chicago, state, in special reference to this proverb, that a patient with a fever must eat and drink at least the normal amount to replace the loss of water and repair the breakdown of body tissues caused by the fever. Overeating, with or without a cold, is always inadvisable.

One form of the proverb went "Stuff a cold and starve a fever."

Whatever its form or medical value, the saying is very old because there is a Spanish proverb in answer to it that is at least 400 years old. It says, "It is better to feed a fever than weakness."

✳ *feet of clay*

NEBUCHADNEZZAR, the king of Assyria, dreamed that he had seen a great image with a head of gold but with feet of iron and clay mixed. A stone struck the image on the clay feet. They crumbled and the whole thing collapsed.

Nebuchadnezzar demanded that his wise men interpret the dream. He had forgotten the dream and couldn't tell them what it was, but he demanded that they interpret it anyway and told them they would be put to death if they didn't (*Daniel* ii:1-5). This seems a little unreasonable to us, but, then, oriental potentates were notoriously unreasonable and, anyway, these wise men were court magicians and surely knowing what the dream was should have been simple compared to interpreting it.

The prophet Daniel, by means of a vision, knew the dream and its significance: the destruction of Assyria (which though golden on top—a subtle compliment to Nebuchadnezzar—had weak foundations) by another kingdom that would then last forever. Nebuchadnezzar who, unlike most other despots, seemed to prefer bad news to uncertainty, immediately made Daniel Chief Wise Man.

In modern metaphor *feet of clay* represent some base and vulnerable trait in an otherwise admirable person.

※ **Why is a receiver of stolen goods called a *fence*?**

A RECEIVER of stolen goods is called a *fence* for the same reason that an enclosure or barrier along the boundary of a field or yard—whether of bushes or of stone or wood or iron—is called a fence. For the same reason that swordplay is called *fencing*. For the same reason that an elephant's tusk and God himself used to be called a *fence*. Namely, that the word in all its many uses is a shortening of *defence*.

We think of the receiver of stolen goods solely as a middleman between the thief and the purchaser of his loot. But he is usually more and formerly was much more. He was the trainer, master, arch and patron of the thieves and—until such time as he found it more lucrative to betray them to the gallows—their defender.

※ *ferry*

Ferry boats go back beyond history. Crossing rivers by boat was until not very long ago an indispensable part of going almost anywhere. Even the dead, in Greek mythology, had to be ferried over the Styx to the underworld. The Greeks put a small coin under the tongue of a corpse to pay his *fare* on this last voyage. I italicized *fare* because *ferry* is related to it. Both are connected with the old word *fare* (now chiefly poetic) meaning "to go." It remains in many uses, however, from the romantic "Farewell!" to the prosaic "How much is the fare?"

✷ a *fey* assertion

MR. JEROME BEATTY, JR., writing in *The Saturday Review* (March 8, 1958) offers: "Words that Intelligent People Use All the Time and Get Wrong because They Don't Really Know the Meaning Of." Number 8 in this forced but fascinating series was *fey*. Intelligent people, said Mr. Beatty, use *fey* all the time as if it meant "fairylike in a sort of daft way." But they get it wrong, he avers, because the real meaning is "fated to die."

Mr. Beatty arrived at this conclusion, which puts him one up on intelligent people, by either consulting a dictionary at least a hundred years old or reading only a part of what he would have found in a contemporary dictionary. He may have faulty vision. He may be fey.

The first recorded meaning of *fey* was "a foe" or "an outlaw." From that it developed into the meaning Mr. Beatty was so pleased with himself to have discovered: "doomed to die." People who were under spells and doomed to die were thought to have sudden insights, visions, and fits of irrational high spirits and gaiety. So that when someone had an unexpected attack of the giggles or behaved in some other odd, gay way, it was common in Scotland to say, "I wish the body be na fey." That is, I hope this doesn't presage death. It probably wasn't said solemnly but more like our "He's gone nuts" or "He's crazy."

But it was still an odd craziness—"daft" was the word for it—and this is the modern American meaning, for the intelligent and the nonintelligent. All dictionaries recognize the "doomed to die" meaning. But had Mr. Beatty read on in Merriam-Webster's *New International*, he would have found "otherworldly, elfin, visionary"; in *The American College Dictionary:* "appearing to be under a spell"; in *Webster's New World Dictionary:* "in an unusually excited or gay state"; in Funk and Wagnalls *Standard Dictionary:* "Affected by association with the fairies; enchanted, under a spell; hence out of touch with reality. Visionary; touched in the head"; in Chambers's *Twentieth Century Dictionary:* "marked by extravagantly high spirits."

The older meaning of a word is not its "real" meaning at all. When the public ceases to attach a meaning to a word (no matter how long that may have been the meaning), that isn't the word's meaning any more. There's no use saying that the "real" meaning of *silly,* for example, is "blessed," or that *prevent* means "to go before," or that *dicker* means "ten hides," or that a *fiasco* is a bottle or a *junket* a reed or a wicker basket. Such assertations would not display superior intelligence but merely the extraordinary lengths to which vanity will go to secure attention.

Incidentally, the arrangements of the various definitions of *fey* in the dictionaries afford a clear illustration of the fact that the first definition in a dictionary is not always the preferred meaning.

✻ What is a *fifth columnist?*

WHEN in 1936 General Emilio Mola, second in command to Franco, was leading four columns to attack Madrid, he told reporters and the defenders of the city that he had a *fifth column* of sympathizers within the city who were only waiting for his attack to join him. The pronouncement led to a great many innocent people being rounded up and shot.

The phrase was helped into our vocabularies by Hemingway's employing it as a title for a melodrama in 1938. Hemingway's sympathies were with the defenders of Madrid, so to him the fifth columnists were secret enemies. To Mola they were, of course, secret friends.

The phrase created a new conception of treachery. It suggested that the spy and the traitor was not a bearded stranger in dark glasses but your friendly neighbor. Field Marshal Lord Ironside warned the British public in 1940 that the really dangerous people "are the best behaved." Had not the public had considerably more sense than the Chief of Imperial General Staff such an assertion would have destroyed morale at once. It didn't, but the idea of a *fifth column* had a tremendous psychological effect. In an era of treachery and violence it increased mistrust and shook, as few phrases ever have, the stability of men's minds.

Our feeling about words and expressions is strongly affected by other words and phrases of similar sound. Part of our attitude towards those who, with full Constitutional justification, claim the protection of the Fifth Amendment may be due to an irrational echo of "fifth column."

✻ *fill in* or *fill out* a form

It seems as if there ought to be a difference between *filling in* a form and *filling it out*, but there isn't. English has a great many verbs that can be used with either of two apparently opposite adverbs. We can *drink it up* or *drink it down* without affecting the fact that we drink it all and it all goes in the same direction.

Perhaps when we think of filling *in* a form, we're thinking of the individual blank spaces and when we fill it *out*, we're thinking of the whole form. But if we do, the thought is certainly not very strong or clear.

When, however, someone says "Fill me in," meaning give me the necessary information, there may be an idea of the in-ness of secrecy.

We *fill in* when we take someone's place and are needed. We *fill out* when we serve merely as a supernumerary to swell a number.

✻ Is there such a word as *finalize?*

"Is there such a word as *finalize?*" correspondents demand, and the tone of their letters implies: "You know damn well there isn't!"

But there is. One hears it frequently and sees it in formal as well as informal documents. It is listed as a standard English word in Funk and Wagnalls *Standard Dictionary*. A President of the United States used it in a formal speech.

Many have attacked the word as "gobbledygook" and "pretentious polysyllabry"—though *generalize, minimize, neutralize, formalize, verbalize,* and hundreds of other similarly formed words don't seem to bother them. It is, indeed, almost a classic example of the use of the *-ize* suffix on adjectives derived from Latin ending in *-al, -ar,* or *-an.* Of its legitimacy, in the sense of being in accord with established formative processes of the language, there can be no doubt.

When questioned further, those who object to *finalize* usually say, "It doesn't say anything that *complete* doesn't say, so why have it?" But in bureaucratic use (and all livable parts of the modern world are now bureaucratic) it does have a meaning more than *complete*. It means to put into a final form a set of conclusions which has been agreed upon roughly through a preceding series of discussions or actions. Maybe things shouldn't be done that way, but they are and there has to be a name for it.

❋ Why is a man who loses his job said to be *fired*?

Fired for "dismissed from a job" is an American term dating back only about seventy-five years. It seems originally to have been a pun on *discharge*. It's in universal use today but has never been accepted as standard—perhaps because it involves a pun.

Discharge is a very old word, far antedating firearms. To charge was to load or burden, a sense we retain when we say that some utterance is "charged with meaning." A man was charged with a certain responsibility when he was given a job. When he was discharged of the responsibility, he was relieved of the job. Formerly a man was discharged *of* his job, not *from* it. A weapon that is discharged is freed of its charge or load. In a gun the discharge is accompanied by a flash of fire. Hence *fired*.

The British slang equivalent is "to get the sack" or to be "sacked." This is a grimly humorous reference to the old practice of sewing certain unwanted folk into sacks and having them thrown in the river.

❋ *first* and *firstly*

First, second, third, and so on, are adverbs as well as adjectives and may be used interchangeably with the other adverbial forms: *firstly, secondly, thirdly*. It makes no difference which is used. As adverbs, of course. The adverb *firstly* cannot be used in place of the adjective *first*, but no one thinks it can; no one ever thought of saying "The firstly man I saw was Joe."

Many people feel that *firstly* is an affectation. They will begin with *first* and then shift and go on with *secondly, thirdly* and the other forms ending in *-ly*. But *firstly* has been in the language for more than four hundred years and has been used by scores of distinguished writers. It was not until the nineteenth century that certain finicky folk began to think there was something wrong with it. "I detest the ridiculous and pedantic *firstly*," DeQuincey wrote. But he was ridiculous and pedantic to say so.

✳ "When we were *first* married"

A MAN is exasperated with his wife because she continually says, "When we were first married." "Both of us have been married only once," he writes. "I tell her she should say, 'Soon after we were married.'"

If I were the wife there might well be a second marriage, or at least a termination of the first. The husband's error (other than giving his wife lessons in English) is the common one of assuming that a word has only one meaning. Had he looked in a good unabridged dictionary, he would have seen that *first* has at least eighteen meanings.

Originally *first* meant "most outstanding" or "earliest." Its commonest current meaning (which the husband assumes to be the sole meaning) is "the one that begins a series." But this is a later development that became widespread but did not drive out all the older meanings. "The First Lady of the Land," as it refers to the President's wife, means the outstanding lady. The husband would insist that it means Martha Washington only, or maybe Priscilla Alden (née Mullens), or even Pocahontas.

When *first* stands immediately before a simple verb or inside a verb phrase, it always means "the early period," as in "I was surprised when you first spoke about it." When it follows the full verb, it has the meaning "the beginning of a series," as in "I was surprised when you spoke about it first."

✳ Is there such a word as *flabbergast*?

Flabbergast first appeared in 1772 in a list of new slang words. Among them, by the way, was *bored*, which has now become thoroughly respectable. But *flabbergast*, possibly because of its absurd sound, remains colloquial. As with most slang, its origin is obscure. It seems to be a mixture of *flabby*, or *flap*, and *aghast*. Presumably it describes a state in which one is so aghast as to be limp or flabby. There is also a noun *flabbergastation*.

✳ "The batter *flied* out to left field"

The term *flied* as the past for batting a fly ball ("The batter flied out to left field") is recognized by every up-to-date lexicon of our language. The term has been in respectable and continuous use since 1893.

It seems a sensible coinage. *Flew* would be misleading. When the announcer says that so-and-so "flied into right field," everyone interested in baseball (and no one else is listening) knows that he hit a fly. If you say he *flew*, God and Dizzy Dean alone know what he did.

See also *baby-sitted* and *spinned*.

✳ gone *for good*

"Why when someone's not coming back do we say he's gone *for good?* What's good about it?"

It all depends on who he is. Some permanent departures would look mighty good.

The expression *for good,* however, in this sense is a shortening of "for good and all." This at first meant "as a valid conclusion." When one desired something or proposed a course of action "for good and all" he did so, presumably, after due consideration and under the impression that he had fixed upon the best thing to do under the circumstances. This then came to mean "finally," "as a final act." And it is this thought we now express in *for good.*

But one is rarely certain of the wisdom of one's conclusions. There is something alarming in irrevocable decisions and ultimate partings. All endings—except of things definitely painful—have a melancholy hint of our own end and are tinged with sadness. There's often very little feeling of good in the phrase *for good.*

✷ Is *forgotten* vulgar?

"Years ago I was taught in school never to use the word *forgotten*," writes a misguided matron. "I cringe every time I hear it!"

As the past particple of the verb *forget*, *forgotten* is the standard American form. Every dictionary so lists it. Every mouth so speaks it. Every hand so writes it. Every ear so hears it. The British now prefer *forgot* but such a sentence as Goldsmith's "I had almost forgot the wedding ring" would sound strange to an American. And formerly even the British used *forgotten* ("The wicked in his pride . . . hath said in his heart, God hath forgotten"—Psalm 10).

That one should cringe throughout a lifetime at such a plain, common, established, universally accepted word is a striking instance of the harm that teachers do.

✷ *founder* and *flounder*

"I read of sailors 'foundering around in the ocean.' Shouldn't it have been 'floundering'? Doesn't *foundering* apply to cattle that have eaten too much alfalfa?"

The word *founder* comes from the Latin *fundus*, "bottom" (whence also *foundation* and *fundamental*). When a ship founders she fills with water and goes to the bottom.

Flounder, "to struggle awkwardly and impotently," may be related to *flounce* or *flutter*. Or it may be a mixture of *founder* and *blunder*.

The "around" in the quotation makes it plain that the word should have been *floundering*, as the correspondent suggests. Had the sailors *foundered* (though the word is practically never applied to persons), they would have gone to the bottom.

A horse founders when it trips, stumbles and goes lame. Overeating of certain foods causes laminitis, an inflammation of the fleshy laminae of the feet of horses and cattle. Laminitis is called *the founder* and an animal so afflicted is said to be *foundered*.

❋ a *four-in-hand* tie

Four-in-hand originally referred to two teams of matched horses driven tandem by one person. It was an expensive, aristocratic, and showy way of driving, much affected by the young bloods. Washington Irving alludes to the boastfulness of "four-in-hand gentlemen."

In the nineteenth century there was in England a very swank club called the *Four-in-Hand* and the necktie seems to have come from that. Whether the members wore this particular kind of a tie or whether the tie was so called merely to reflect some of the distinction of the club is not certain.

Horsy elegance and neckwear seem to go together. Only horsemen and horsewomen still wear a stock. And, of course, there's the *ascot*.

❋ the *fourth estate*

ONE MEANING of *estate* is an order or class regarded as a part of the political body. In early English parliaments there were three estates: the Clergy, the Barons and Knights, and the Commons. In France the Three Estates were: the Clergy, the Nobles, and the well-to-do townsmen, the Bourgeoisie. It was these that met in 1798 at the Estates General.

Macaulay said that the gallery of the House of Commons, in which reporters sat, "has become a fourth estate of the realm." Carlyle picked up the phrase (and incorrectly attributed it to Burke) and it passed into the language. Reporters, delighted to find others taking them at their own evaluation, have cherished the expression and repeated it until it has become a very tired cliché.

The term was not wholly new with Macaulay. Rabelais (1548) had called lawyers "a fourth estate" and Henry Fielding, two hundred years later, had more justly termed the mob "the fourth estate."

❋ pronunciation of *foyer*

MANY people, knowing that *foyer* is French, get all Gallicized about it and try *fwa yay′* or compromise with *foy yay′*.

But although the word is a fairly recent borrowing, its pronunciation has been completely anglicized to *foy' yer*.

✷ *Frankenstein*

IN MARY SHELLEY's novel *Frankenstein, or the Modern Prometheus* (1818), Victor Frankenstein was a young student who accidentally stumbled on "the secret of life" and created another being. This being—the monster—was bad only because he was unloved. The novel was written not primarily as a horror story but as a treatise to show the necessity for love in the proper upbringing of children.

So that, strictly speaking, *Frankenstein* is the creator and the creature is *Frankenstein's monster*. But the name of the creator has been transferred to the thing created (as with *guillotine*, *derrick*, and a hundred other words) and all dictionaries now recognize "a Frankenstein" as any monstrous creation that threatens to destroy its creator.

Such a transference is common in many languages. What is more interesting is that up until the second decade of this century the dictionaries did not recognize the word. Only the twentieth century has felt the need for a word to describe things which threaten to destroy their inventors.

✷ Why *French leave* for a surreptitious departure?

ALTHOUGH the prejudice which assumes that anything French must, in some way, be wicked, has led us to use *French leave* to designate surreptitious departures, desertions, abscondings, and the like, the origin of the term was not only innocuous but admirable.

In eighteenth-century France it was permissible to leave a party quietly without taking leave of the hostess or of any of your fellow guests ("He went out of the drawing-room without saying good-bye, a la française"—Tolstoy, *War and Peace*, Ch. 5, part 6). No one who has lingered for dreary hours at social gatherings simply because he couldn't bring himself to go through the business of formal farewells (or feared to offend the hostess by starting an avalanche of departures) can regard the custom as anything but civilized and enviable.

Lest we assume that life was once perfect, though, it is well to be reminded that *entering* the French salons in the eighteenth-century was an extremely formal and fussy business, however merciful the getaway.

✻ Must *fulsome* mean disgusting?

Fulsome once meant "exceedingly full." The "seven plenteous years" of Joseph's administration in Egypt (Genesis xli:47, Authorized Version) appeared in a thirteenth-century translation as "seven fulsome years." But gradually the word acquired the meaning of "surfeit," an excess of something which in moderation might even be pleasing but which in gross excess is offensive. It may have been helped to this meaning by association with the word *foul* which (like the first syllable of *fulsome*) was pronounced more like *fool* than *fowl* or *full*. In this meaning it became specially associated with praise, flattery, and compliments which were felt to exceed the bounds of good taste and to be lacking in truth and sincerity.

This is now the word's most common meaning, but either it is reverting to its original meaning or the old meaning has never wholly died out, though the last use recorded in the *Oxford English Dictionary* is 1678. None the less *Life* (May 19, 1958, p. 2) referred to Miss Margaret O'Brien as "a fulsome 20-year-old" with "sinuous curves" and later (June 9, p. 12) the editors explained that they meant she was "full or copious." Russell Lynes (*A Surfeit of Honey*, p. 80) says of certain foppish young men that their coats "drape fulsomely." Here excess is meant, but merely an excess of fullness, not disgust. *Fulsome* in the sense of full, with no implied condemnation, appeared in the *New York Times* (Dec. 2, 1957), but the author of the piece was chided by their grammatical watchdog, Mr. Theodore Bernstein. Mr. Douglas Edwards, of CBS News closing his Christmas newscast (1957) hoped that his viewers would have a fulsome Christmas. Here it may have been ambiguous; it all depends on how you feel about Christmas. The list could go on and on. I find *fulsome* used in the sense of abundant, copious, plentiful in the *New York Times Book Review Section,* Elizabeth Burton's *The Pageant of Elizabethan England,* and in so many other places and by writers of such skill and precision and sensitivity to words that I do not believe the old meaning can properly be regarded as obsolete.

✱ Can *fun* be used as an adjective?

CAN *fun* be used as an adjective ("We had a fun time") or as an adverb ("Fun drive the Lark today")?

Not in my hearing without inducing nausea.

However, it is only fair to add that hundreds of nouns have become adjectives and hundreds of words from all parts of speech have become adverbs and there is no reason why *fun* should not so be used if the people who speak the language want to so use it. For centuries *fun* was used as a verb ("Do you think to fun me out of it?") and the participle was used as a noun ("Cease your funning") and while both of these forms now strike our ears as offensive, they didn't bother the distinguished writers who used them.

As often with what is posed as a grammatical problem, the real question is one of taste or style. One reason, perhaps, that *fun* as an adjective is offensive is that its use in this way doesn't seem natural. It is so used almost entirely by affected, shrill young people striving a little too hard to be gay and breezy.

✱ What's funny about the *funnybone*?

THE TINGLING feeling that we experience when we "hit our funnybone" does have something ludicrous in it. At least to observers, who usually find it amusing when somebody strikes that particular nerve against that particular bone and claws and clutches and swears and jigs in irritation and anger.

It isn't the bone—as a matter of fact—that hurts. The bone (the medial condyle of the humerus) simply serves as an anvil on which we strike the ulnar nerve which lies above it.

Some linguists believe that *funnybone* was originally a pun on *humerus*. It first appeared in *The Ingoldsby Legends* (1840) by the Reverend Richard Harris Barham, a mighty punner.

The furcula in birds that we call the *wishbone* used to be called the *merrythought* because of the gaiety attendant upon breaking it between two people.

✻ fussbudget

A *budget* was originally a bag or wallet, usually of leather. Large water containers were called budgets and a leather purse was a budget. When the British Chancellor of the Exchequer made his annual statement of probable revenues and expenditures for the ensuing year, he was formerly said to *open the budget*. Every magazine now urges every housewife to keep a budget, but it is interesting that the *Oxford English Dictionary* as late as 1933 designated the use of *budget* to describe an individual's financial plans as "humorous."

One who fussed a great deal used to be called a *fuss*. Then someone thought of such a person as nothing but a container full of fuss. The English, by 1915, had the terms *fuss-box* and *fusspot*. But *fussbudget* was American, coined at about the same time.

It was a clever coinage, better than its British equivalents. The repetition of the same vowel is always good in a scornfully humorous term (*namby-pamby, hill-billy, claptrap, tommyrot*) and *budget* not only conveys the idea of a bag but suggests *fidget* and someone who, for all his fussy fidgeting, won't or can't *budge*.

✻ "He has his *gall*"

When various organs were thought to be the seats of various emotional qualities—as the heart of courage, the intestines of stamina, the spleen of irritability—the gall bladder was thought to be the seat of bitterness. And bitter men are inclined to be impudent. *Gall* is the insolence of despair, the disregard of convention of a desperate man. Though the word has weakened a little, it's still pretty strong. "He has his gall" is a stronger statement than "He has his nerve."

Doves, by the way, were thought not to have a gall bladder and it was felt that this explained their gentle nature.

✻ Why are things knocked *galley west?*

Things are knocked *galley west* when they are smashed or totally disordered by the force of the blow. But why the *galley* rather than any other part of the ship? And why *west* rather than any other point of the compass? And, above all, why the combination?

The word, apparently, hasn't anything to do with ships or the compass. It came into American use through Mark Twain who used it—in its present meaning of "to knock into smithereens"—in one of his letters in 1875, and then has Aunt Sally Phelps use it in *Huckleberry Finn* (1884). Chances are that he heard it on the river or knew it as an old family expression.

Scholars are pretty certain that it is a corruption of an English dialect term *collyweston*. There is, or was, a place in Northamptonshire called *Collyweston*. Henry VII's mother lived there. Maybe the inhabitants were given to excessive violence. Then there was a saying, when things had gone unusually and perversely wrong, "It's all because of Colly Weston." But no one knows who Colly Weston was. Some local trouble maker? Or, more likely, some minor spook, like Rumpelstiltskin or Robin Goodfellow or Lob-Lie-by-the-Fire who came at night and mischievously rumpled and disordered things.

✷ ten-*gallon* hats

THE STRANGE name for the broad-brimmed hats with the high, conical crown so common in the Southwest isn't related to their liquid capacity, or even caused by Texas exaggeration. It's the product of folk etymology.

The Spaniards in the old days of the Southwest used to ornament their large-brimmed hats with braid, often silver braid. Very fine hats might have had as many as five or seven or even ten of these braids. And the Spanish word for braid of this kind was *galón*.

✷ The meanings of *garnish*

THOSE who insist that a word "must" have a certain and fixed meaning should temper their absolutism by considering the word *garnish* which formerly meant "to warn" and now means "to sprinkle parsley" and "to estop wages."

Initial *g* and *w* are interchangeable in a number of teutonic words (*guaranty, warranty; guard, ward*) and the first part of *garnish* is, historically, the same word as *warn*. But it didn't do much good just to warn a fortress, say, that it was going to be attacked. Along with the warning the overlord usually sent food and arms and reinforcements. One meaning of *garnish* used to be "to garrison." And furthermore he put the fort in good condition. He adorned and embellished it. And this is the meaning that has sunk (in these belligerent but unwarlike times) to meaning sprinkling parsley on steaks or putting paper frillies on the ends of lamb chops.

From the point of view of the man whose wages are attached or *garnished* (or *garnisheed*, either form is correct), they are seized and he is deprived of them. From the point of view of the law, however, the action is a warning to the employer in whose hands the money reposes. He is warned not to pay it to the employee but to the creditor to whom the employee owes it and who has taken action to recover it.

✱ two *gauntlets*

There are two *gauntlet*'s in the English language. They are spelled and pronounced alike but are totally unrelated.

The *gauntlet* which means a glove is the French *gantelet*, "a little glove."

The *gauntlet* which means a military punishment, wherein a man was made to run between two rows of men who struck at him with ropes and even weapons, was originally *gantlope*. It was spelled this way up until a hundred years or so ago and is still sometimes spelled and pronounced *gantlet*. *Gantlope* was a nasalized pronunciation of a Swedish word *gatlopp* from *gat-*, "a lane or narrow path" and *-lopp*, "run" (akin to our *lope* and the second part of *gallop*).

✱ What is a *gazebo*?

Originally a gazebo was a windowed turret in the roof of a house in which one could sit and gaze out over the landscape. Similar structures were erected in gardens and the name was extended to any summer house with a view.

The word was probably a humorous invention. *Videbo* is the first person singular, future tense, of the Latin verb *video*. It means "I shall see." So *gazebo* may have been a fanciful elaboration of the English verb *to gaze,* suggesting "I shall gaze out." However the humorous inventor, if there was one, is unknown and there is the possibility that it is a corruption of some oriental word.

It is pronounced *guh zay' boh.*

✱ Who was then the *gentleman?*

SOME years ago *The New York Times* ran a charming photograph of one of the more delightful moments in the history of the United Nations. In the course of some remarks Mr. Henry Cabot Lodge had referred to Mr. Andrei Vishinsky as "the gentleman from Russia." Mr. Vishinsky had immediately interrupted to demand a retraction of this insulting epithet, the use of which, he felt, was wholly unbecoming the dignity and courtesy that should prevail in such an assembly. The picture shows Mr. Lodge laughing heartily and his laughter dutifully mirrored in the faces of the American delegation. The British ambassador has taken evasive action in doodling. His immediate assistant has a deadpan expression that must have earned him promotion in the Foreign Office, though two lesser figures have so far forgotten themselves as to snicker. The only other Russian visible is either reading *Izvestia* or hastily scribbling a secret report on the matter. Mr. Vishinsky himself has assumed a pixyish air of pseudo-resentment and is pounding the table in well simulated indignation.

Was this mere Muscovite merriment or has the word *gentleman* in its descent actually reached the place where it may be regarded as an insult?

If Mr. Vishinsky had the British idea of *gentleman* in mind (and he may well have, for it is more common than the American which is a very vague and confused concept), he may have been quite sincere in his protest. To be called one who disdains labor and scorns commerce and lives in idle elegance off inherited wealth would not seem complimentary to a Bolshevik. *Gentleman* in England is still a term for a member of a definite social class. The last day of one of the vacations at Oxford the porter of my college warned me as I left my bicycle in the lodge that I had better lock it thereafter. For, said he, in explanation, "The gentlemen are coming back today, sir." Here "gentlemen" (undergraduates) was plainly equated with "thieves." Yet he was not being ironical. Now Vishinsky, as a member of a militantly classless society, could not allow himself to seem to be beguiled by capitalist hirelings into regarding himself as one of them. Stalin was then in the Kremlin and the comrade behind Vishinsky may have been scribbling for a reservation at the Lubianka.

Though Americans are democratically profuse in their use of *gentleman* to describe any adult male not actually at that moment cleaning a cesspool or doing time, most of them would back away from any application of the British meaning. Chesterfield's warning to his son that "a gentleman never laughs out loud" or Oscar Wilde's remark, when someone cried to him to look out of the window, that "a gentleman never looks out of a window" would certainly be regarded over most of the United States as typical of that despised species.

Since the Americans did not recognize a nobility, and yet since every sturdy colonial was one of nature's noblemen, the word *gentleman* came to have in America a different meaning from what it commonly had in England. Or, rather, it took one of the British meanings and elaborated on it to the disregard of all others.

Theoretically in the United States, at least by the time of the Jacksonian revolution, *gentleman* meant a man of refinement and good manners, not necessarily a man of good family. But since it was exceedingly dangerous to suggest that anyone might be lacking in either refinement or good manners, it became polite—and safe—to call every male a gentleman. Finicky theorists like Emerson tried to include truthfulness and clean linen in the general concept, but these were too subtle attributes for the masses to grasp or care about.

The simple fact is that the Americans, at the highest, were bourgeois. And the gentleman, in the European sense, is not bourgeois. There is a Spanish proverb that a gentleman will wear rags but not patches. This would have been incomprehensible to the nineteenth-century American who would have thought of an impoverished gentleman as wearing very neat patches. The title of Moliere's famous play—*The Citizen Gentleman*—would have been totally lost on an American audience.

Moliere meant it as a paradox; to them it would have seemed quite natural.

Today the word has become more tarnished than Mr. Lodge, in his gentlemanly way, perhaps realizes. Part of its decadence may be due to resentment of the overworked term "a Southern gentleman." Clare Boothe Luce's statement that "If you can shoot like a South Carolinian, ride like a Virginian, make love like a Georgian, and be proud of it as an Episcopalian, you're a Southern gentleman" (*Kiss the Boys Goodbye*, II.ii) would elicit more nausea than applause anywhere in America today except a few country clubs. Whereas the rival definition of a Southern gentleman as one "who rises to his feet as his wife comes in bearing the firewood" would be applauded.

Perhaps *gentlemen* is associated too much with toilet doors. It is, apparently, in some quarters, acquiring slight shades of indecency. I was once scoffing at such euphemisms as *His* and *Hers* and *Adam* and *Eve* and *Pointers* and *Setters* when an angry proprietor of a New York night club told me that it was all very well for eggheads to talk smartalecky like that but that "decent people" were offended by "gentlemen" on a door in a restaurant.

In summation, I would say that *gentleman* doesn't have the glory it once had, in either Great Britain or America. Among provincial and older people it might still be regarded as a compliment, or at least a courtesy. But among city dwellers and sophisticates it would probably be felt to be stilted, hence insincere, hence insulting. Many would cringe and attempt to laugh it off. A few, but only a very few, would resent it. It's not yet a dirty or a ridiculous word, but it may become one— and Russia may merely be a few steps ahead of us in the dank descending corridor of time.

✻ "*a gentleman and a scholar*"

CAN A MAN be a gentleman *and* a scholar? The phrase is peculiarly American, a piece of old-fashioned, orotund, rustic blarney. But was it meant to suggest the felicitous combination of two admirable accomplishments, or did the flattery intend to go further and suggest that the recipient combined in himself virtues elsewhere irreconcilable?

Probably the first. *Gentlemen* and *scholars* were alike alien to the experience of most who employed the phrase, and there is little likelihood that they even guessed at their fundamental opposition.

For if *gentleman* be interpreted in the American sense, as designating a man endowed with natural kindness, marked by delicate consideration for others, and graced with polished manners, nothing could be more opposed to it than *scholar*. A scholar is interested solely in the pursuit and publication of facts and no one is more ruthless, less considerate, more devoid of kindness. And few occupations have been marked by manners as consistently bad as those shown by scholars. They are not interested in making a good impression—and they shouldn't be. Dr. Johnson, who with some justice regarded himself as an adept in complimentation, once said in praise of the author of *Philological Inquiries*, "Sir, Harris is a sound sullen scholar."

Of course if *gentleman* is interpreted in the British sense, as designating one of good family, with some education and not in trade, the combination is possible. Indeed, it has been made many times. Newton was a gentleman and a scholar. So was Darwin. So were Lecky, Buckle, and dozens of others. The supreme example of a gentleman (in this sense) and scholar must be Henry Cavendish (1731-1810), great-grandson of the first duke of Devonshire, one of the greatest chemists and physicists that ever lived, but so gentlemanly (and, fortunately, so wealthy) that he spent his entire life in seclusion and seemed to regard the publication of his discoveries as vulgar.

But the British sense of *gentleman* won't do; the phrase is used only in America.

※ **"Let *George* do it"**

FAME is utterly unpredictable. It sometimes lights even on men of merit. Among these must be reckoned Georges d'Amboise (1460-1510), Cardinal, First Minister of State and Lieutenant-General of the Army under the French king Louis XII, who has been immortalized in the phrase "Let George do it."

D'Amboise was one of those incredible Renaissance figures—like Cellini and Leonardo—who seemed able to do everything and do it well. And do it soon, too. He was a bishop when he was fourteen, though that was not as remarkable then as it would be today. His contemporary, Cesare Borgia, was a canon when *he* was seven and a bishop seven years later. And the record for either pull or piety must be held by Frederick Augustus, George III's second son, who became Bishop of Osnaburg when he was six months old.

The phrase "Let George do it" was originally King Louis' and was satirically intended. In its first form it was "Let George do it; he's the man of the Age." Louis admired the Cardinal and trusted him and was well and faithfully served, but there's something about perfection that annoys us a little.

✳ Geo. Wash. Bridge

THE Daughters of the American Revolution protested against the indignity of the abbreviation. The authorities replied that no offense was intended to the Father of His Country but "the fast-moving motorist must assimilate sign information quickly." The D.A.R. said that the speed limit at this point was 35 miles an hour and that wasn't too fast to understand GEORGE WASHINGTON.

Aesthetic tastes make strange bedfellows. I find myself in agreement with the D.A.R. There are some names so well known in their entirety that an abbreviation doesn't simplify but confuses. They're right about the indignity, too. To be sure, Washington himself sometimes abbreviated the George to *Geo.* and sometimes even to *Go.*, but that was his privilege and one he didn't extend to others. He demanded respect. When General Howe addressed a letter to him as "George Washington, Esq., etc. etc.," he preferred to let war go on rather than to open the missive; he said he didn't know what improprieties were veiled under those "etc's."

Some things lend themselves to abbreviation; others don't. Addison and Swift were both horrified at the use of *mob* for *mobile vulgus* and feared that unless something were done it might in time become a part of the language. And it's only been in the past generation that the preliminary apostrophe has been finally omitted from *bus*. It was generally '*bus* to show that it was not a "real" word but only a clipping of *omnibus*.

※ *getting* to know better

"MY MOTHER says that in her youth *get* plus the infinitive, as in 'get to know' was not used. Yet in an article in *The New York Times* I read: 'I did not get to know him.' Is this now acceptable?" So writes a woman who is finally, apparently, beginning to get suspicious about her mother's dogmatism. She encloses the article from *The New York Times*.

All I can say is that if her mother's youth antedates the use of this construction she is to be congratulated on a longevity exceeded only by Methuselah's. *Get* followed by the infinitive with *to* has been used in literary English for four or five hundred years to mean "to attain, reach, or secure an opportunity of doing something." This use is recognized in every major dictionary and heard every day. It's not only acceptable, it's accepted.

The author of the piece in the *Times*, by the way, is Mr. John Mason Brown. That settles it as far as I'm concerned; "get to know" is *in!*

※ "Each contestant will be *gifted* with a prize"

"ON A TV program the MC says 'Each contestant will be *gifted* with a prize.' I find this shocking English. Surely they could say given!" So writes "Indignant Mother."

I share the mother's provincialism but not her indignation. "Will be given" would certainly sound better to me, but that merely shows how limited my reading and conversation are, because there's nothing wrong, grammatically or historically, with *gifted with*. *To gift* is a regular verb formed from the noun *gift*. It has been in fairly wide use for a least 400 years and is recognized as standard by every dictionary. The participle, as an adjective, doesn't bother anyone ("He was a very gifted man"). The verb *to gift* stresses the desirability of what is given rather than the generosity of the giving (which for the TV program's purposes is very good). *Give* has many shades of meaning and all that is given is not a gift ("He gave her a black eye").

Perhaps it's the frequently mawkish associations of the word that annoy us ("Gypsy Rose Lee gifted Billy Rose with an Afghan hound, and their romance is in full cry"—*Hollywood Chatter*, Dec. 29, 1959). It's much used by the chatter columnists, probably because it has two letters more than *gave*.

The strange in language is always slightly shocking, but it is encouraging to see how quickly we get over these shocks and how well insulated we are from high-voltage innovations in our own vocabularies. In "Indignant Mother's" letter, for instance, *TV* and *MC* are far more "shocking"—that is, they are newer, stranger, more radical departures from the established nature of the language—than is the venerable *gifted*.

✳ the *gift horse*'s mouth

Two PROVERBS are concerned with looking *gift horses* in the mouth and they are diametrically opposed, as proverbial sayings so often are. One says "always look a gift horse in the mouth." The other says "never look a gift horse in the mouth."

Both are based on the fact that a horse's value depends to a large extent on its age and its age can be determined by examining its teeth. So that to look a gift horse in the mouth is to attempt to appraise its value.

The one form of the proverb, then, says: "Examine all gifts with care. You never get anything for nothing. There are always strings attached and sometimes what appears a gift is in reality a snare." Like the Trojan horse. There was a gift horse that should have been looked into at both ends!

The other form of the proverb, now the more common form but fairly wishy-washy compared to the first, says, "It's bad manners to examine a gift with the intent to see what it's worth." Maybe it is, but bad manners and good sense sometimes go together.

✳ *ginger* and *gingerly*

Ginger and *gingerly* are not related.

Ginger, the pungent, spicy, rootlike part of a plant, was imported into Greece from India and its name derives from a word in Sanskrit (though probably not a Sanskrit word) meaning "shaped like an antler."

Gingerly first appeared in the sixteenth century in reference to a mincingly effeminate way of dancing ("mincing it full gingerly, tripping like goats, that an egg would not break under their feet," snarled a disapproving pamphleteer). It was formed from a French word meaning "dainty," a word related to *genteel*. From this it came to its modern meaning of handling something with extreme caution for fear of being hurt in some way.

❋ *good and* mad

HOWEVER illogical it may be, *good and* is certainly used to mean "very" in spoken English in the United States when it qualifies an adjective or an adjective-like adverb that follows a verb. No American, of any level of education or in any part of the country, would feel "I'm good and mad" or "It's good and cold out" to be strange, or even substandard, locutions, though some grammarians condemn the construction. *Nice and* is used in much the same way, except that it always implies approval, as in *nice and cold*. This is not similarly condemned, however, because the grammarians can at least pretend that the words are meant separately and independently and the speaker might equally well have said *cold and nice*.

❋ *good-bye*

Good-bye is a slurred contraction of "God be with you." It appears in English literature, from the late sixteenth century on, in every conceivable form: *god b'uy, god buy you, god be wi' ye, good-buy, good b'w'y, good bwit'ye,* and so on. *Good* may have been substituted for *God* because of such expressions as *good day* and *good night*.

There was a much older expression *God buy you*, meaning "God redeem you (from sin)," and it is thought by some that this may have been the origin of *good-bye*. But almost all early representations of *good-bye* show an awareness that it was clipped, which would not have been the case had the *bye* been *buy* and the *you* merely dropped.

Time and elision have squeezed all precise meaning out of

the expression, but it serves as an amiable sound at parting and, even more usefully, it indicates that a parting or the termination of a conversation is necessary or desired. Many phrases have more meaning but few have more value.

✻ good riddance

THE HOMELY vigor of *good riddance* has led many to wonder if it is "good English," their teachers, apparently, having left them with the idea that if English is forceful or easy it can't be good.

The verb *to rid* has been in the language ever since it could be called English. Originally it meant to clear a way or space, especially to clear the land of trees or undergrowth. Then it developed the more general meaning of clearing out, freeing from rubbish or encumbrances. This meaning survives in the dialectal phrase "to redd up" a room or house.

The suffix *-ance* conveys the general sense of action or process, as in *assistance, resistance, conveyance*. So that *riddance* is the act of getting rid of, or a general chucking out of, unwanted clutter. From the earliest meaning of clearing land, the word carries a suggestion of energetic violence. "*Good* riddance," of course, merely reflects the speaker's opinion of the clearing out.

Riddance is quite good English. It's been in reputable and even dignified use for over four hundred years. The Authorized Version of the Bible says (*Zephaniah* 1:18) that the Lord in his wrath will make "a speedy riddance" of those who have sinned against him. The Revised Standard Version wishy-washys this down to "a sudden end."

✻ the Good Samaritan

THE *Good Samaritan* is now the accepted designation for the "certain Samaritan" who in the parable (*Luke* x:30-35) was kind to the man who had fallen among thieves. But nowhere in the Bible is he called the *good* Samaritan and some feel that the adjective is an interpolated redundancy and should be omitted.

Long usage, however, has fixed the word *good* in the phrase.

It emphasizes the significance of the parable. At the time of Jesus, hatred between the Jews and the Samaritans was intense. Yet it was a Samaritan who helped the injured Jew, while those upon whose mercy he had a better claim "passed by on the other side." It is that fact which lends such force to the question that concludes the parable: "Which now . . . was neighbor unto him?" The adjective *good* underlines the great moral teaching that no nation or people has a monopoly of virtue.

✳ "Good wine needs no bush"

Good wine needs no bush means that a good product doesn't need to be advertised: its merits alone will attract attention and customers. It's an earlier version of the "better mousetrap" theory of distribution and is regarded with disapproval and scorn by the advertising profession.

The actual meaning of the expression has been obscured not by linguistic but by social changes. In the days when most people could not read, shops were identified by signs: a hatter would have a large wooden hat above his door, a glover a gloved hand, and so on. Wineshops were marked by a protruding pole on which was hung an ivy wreath (ivy being sacred to Bacchus) or, sometimes, a wisp of hay. This was called a *bush*. The proverb merely says that if the wine is good men will know about it and no such identification will be needed.

The Spanish say "Good wine needs no trumpeter" and the Germans say "Good wine sells itself."

✳ the growing respectability of *goose*

ON THE dust jacket of Theodore Bernstein's *Watch Your Language* we are told that Mr. Bernstein, who among other editorial duties is guardian of the linguistic purity of *The New York Times*, "goaded, goosed, and jollied . . . more than six hundred reporters . . . in the direction of better writing."

An author is not responsible for what is written on the outside of his book, but the juxtaposition of the verb *to goose* and Mr. Bernstein's conservatism in style at least puts the verb closer to respectability than it has yet been.

Once unusable in polite company, it's been creeping up,

from the privy to the sanctum, and is fairly common in print now. ("in the dark foyer, she goosed him and laughed"—Nathanael West; "Our young people would be goosing one another"—H. Allen Smith.) In metaphorical senses, it is very common ("You finally goosed the police into action"), especially as a term for choking a car. Many who so use it probably have no idea that it has improper connotations.

To goose, "to jab sharply with the thumb in the anus, with the intention of startling or stimulating," is, as H. L. Mencken characterized it, "one of the most mysterious American verbs." It is a fairly recent coinage, of the last fifty years at the most (in Victorian slang, to be *goosed* was to be hissed, to get the bird), yet it is now in almost universal use in the United States. Some think it derives from a Southern expression *to goose* meaning to attack in the manner of a goose. Some think it may come from poolroom horseplay in which, it seems, a receptacle called "the goose" was frequently jabbed into the posterior of a player just about to make a shot. A correspondent, who claims to have been a goose breeder, assures me that a thrust of this nature is an established procedure in the art of distinguishing between geese and ganders, especially in the varieties of the *toulouse* and the *white emden*. In these, the two most common varieties, he says, the male and female are indistinguishable except when so jabbed. He had earlier submitted this etymology to Mencken who found it "reasonable." Most other linguists are inclined to the first of the suggestions given above.

✻ "his goose is cooked"

THAT "his goose is cooked" is usually said of someone whose good fortune has run out, someone who has been enjoying an advantage but is now disgraced or ruined.

Some attribute the origin of the expression to a Swedish king, Eric the Mad. It is said that he was besieging a city which derisively hung out a goose over the walls—either for his men to shoot at or as a sign that the garrison was so well victualled they could hold out interminably. Eric said grimly that he had come to "cook their goose" by burning the city.

If he did this, he was probably merely quoting an established saying. It is more likely a reference to the goose that laid the golden eggs, or any goose, for that matter, which, once cooked, would lay no more eggs.

✻ "I've *got* plenty of nothing"

MANY people who feel they must leave the earth a little better place than they found it have chosen as their modest contribution the replacing of "I've got" by "I have." But all is vanity, in several senses of the word.

Have got may mean *have* in the sense of "to possess." This is a perfectly natural extension of the meaning "to acquire" which is the basic meaning of *to get*. If you've acquired something, you have it. This use of *got* is at least 400 years old. It is used by hundreds of millions of people every day—especially, by the way, in England, where they also say "had got" ("The boy had got an apple in his hand"—meaning merely that he held it there).

Have got is also used to mean *must*, equivalent to *have to*, as in "We've got to hurry." Some think "have to hurry" is better, but there is no more reason why *have* should mean *must* than why *got to* should. It's all a matter of idiom. This use of *got*, by the way, is no more than a hundred years old. It is more acceptable in the United States than in Great Britain. And in this construction the past form *had got* is sometimes heard in America but not in England.

* Why is New York called *Gotham*?

LEGEND has it that King John (1167-1216) planned to build a castle in the English town of Gotham. But when he came to look the town over, he noticed that the villagers acted very strangely. Some were trying to rake the moon's reflection out of a pond; others were trying to drown an eel; still others had linked hands in a ring around a bush in a vain effort to keep a cuckoo prisoner. Loath to settle a garrison in the midst of such a flock of dizzards, the king decided to build his castle elsewhere —to the delight of the villagers whose behavior had been a deliberate scheme to avoid the burden of supporting the castle.

There is little plausibility in the story. John was a brilliantly brutal man and not likely to be diverted from his purposes by rustic antics. Still, the story tickled men's fancy and as time passed the wits embroidered it until the jokes filled a whole book, *Merie Tales of the Mad Men of Gotham*.

The name was applied to New York by Washington Irving (in the *Salmagundi Papers*, 1807) because, in his opinion, the inhabitants thereof were so foolishly wise and wisely foolish.

* Should we say a student *graduated* or *was graduated*?

COME Commencement time and diffident parents, more uneasy than ever in their children's company and anxious not to shame them any more than can be helped, get all riled up as to whether it's *graduated* or *was graduated*.

In colleges, where the word is most used, one hears only *graduated*.

In English a transitive verb is frequently used intransitively with a passive sense. Thus we say "The boat upset," "The door closed," "The hot cakes sold fast." It all depends on whether we want to stress the act or the agent. If we say "The boat was upset," we stress the fact that something upset it.

Graduated means "raised to another grade." To say "Johnny graduated" implies that he raised himself. To say "Johnny was graduated" implies that the faculty did the raising.

Now the faculty may have done the upgrading, but the important thing to Johnny and his family is that Johnny got through! And since, today, Johnny's education may well have cost his parents ten thousand dollars, they are surely entitled to the mild grammatical indulgence of assuming that Johnny did it. However, for the same sum, they are also entitled to the little extra elegance of "was graduated," since it often seems to them a little more learned and hence befitting.

✲ "with a *grain of salt*"

When we say of some statement that it must be *taken with a grain of salt*, we are saying that it must be seasoned a little in order to be "swallowed." It's a humorously blunted way of saying that in our opinion the statement is a lie or unfounded or grossly exaggerated.

It comes from Pliny the Elder's (A.D. 23-79) account of Mithridates, King of Pontus (120-63 B.C.). Mithridates, Pliny says, guarded against being poisoned by accustoming his body to poison by small daily doses. However, he overdid it, because later when he tried to commit suicide by taking poison he found that he was totally immune and had to have a soldier stab him.

Pliny adds that after Mithridates's death a prescription for an antidote against all poison was found among the king's possessions. Unfortunately, Pliny doesn't give the prescription, but he says that the last line was "to be taken with a grain of salt."

Pliny was one of the most amusing and credulous of men and one of the biggest liars ever known, so the phrase may have picked up some of its meaning from being associated with him.

✳ What have *grapefruit* to do with grapes?

THE WORD *grapefruit* bothers a number of exact and earnest souls who do not see sufficient resemblance between the genus *Vitis* and the fruit of *Citrus paradisi* to warrant the similarity in name.

A grapefruit certainly doesn't look much like a grape on our plates at breakfast, especially if—as is usually the case—it's only half a grapefruit. But it grows in grapelike bunches on the tree and it was named before it was picked, packed, and shipped.

For that matter, a grape doesn't look anything like a grape, either. *Grape* was originally not the name of the berry but of the small hook by which the bunches were gathered in France: a *grape* (or, as we would say, a *grapple*). It is ultimately related to the word *grab*. The old English word for grape was *wineberry*, a far more sensible word. The French word was probably used because grapes were more a thing of France than of England and also because the Norman overlord kept his grapes for himself and used his word for them—and left wholesome Saxon *mead*, *beer*, and *water* for his Saxon servants.

✳ Why a *grass widow*?

IN AMERICA *grass widow* is often used as a synonym for a divorcee. Some have tried to derive the expression from "grace widow," that is, a widow by courtesy. But no etymology supports this and no one has ever been able to find the phrase *grace widow* in use.

Formerly the term designated an unmarried mother and here parallels in German (*Strohwittwe,* "straw widow") and other Teutonic languages show that "grass" is intended, in a significant contrast to "bed," as the place of the child's begetting. We have a slang phrase, "a roll in the hay," that has the same idea.

✻ *groom* or *bridegroom?*

MANY people object to calling the secondary figure at a wedding the *groom.* They say he should always be called the *bridegroom* because *groom* means a stable boy. Awkward in his rented finery, he often looks like a stable boy (especially to the bride's parents), but that only makes it the more imperative to give him his full title.

Those who so protest are confusing two words. But since the entire language has confused them for more than 600 years, they can hardly be blamed.

The word *groom* appeared in our speech about the year 1200 and meant a boy. Then it came to mean a manservant (as the French call a waiter *garçon,* which means "boy," and as all black male servants in South Africa are addressed as "Boy," a term which they furiously resent). But it was not until the seventeenth century that it became fixed in its present specialized sense of a servant who attends to horses.

The other *groom,* a shortening of *bridegroom,* was originally *guma,* the Anglo-Saxon word for man (compare the modern German for bridegroom, *Bräutigam*). The *r* got in *guma* to make it *groom* through the influence of the other *groom.*

Purists condemn the use of *groom* for *bridegroom.* But Shakespeare so used it. So did Dryden and Browning and Tennyson. And so do millions of Americans, every day, especially during June. And every modern dictionary accepts it.

✻ to *grouse*

THE WORD *grouse* for the English game bird (*Lagopus scoticus*) has been in the language for 500 years. Its origin is unknown.

185 · *guts*

There is no connection between it and the slang word for grumbling or complaining. This latter was added to the general language very recently—in 1892, by Rudyard Kipling. It was a common term, apparently, in the British Army. Some think it may be related to *grouch* or *grudge,* perhaps from an Old French word *grousser,* "to murmur."

In the phrase in which the word first appeared, Kipling has a character say, "Don't grouse like a woman." But today *grousing* is confined almost entirely to masculine complaining. Perhaps *grouch* affected it.

※ *gumption*

Though it sounds as though it were slang and something "made up," *gumption* is a perfectly acceptable word. One hears it all the time and it has been in print for more than 250 years. It's humorous and colloquial, but Henry James puts it into the vocabulary of Lambert Strether, the dignified central figure of *The Ambassadors.*

It's one of the many words that came into American speech from Scotland. The dialect which we know as Scotch (and which the people who speak it prefer to call "Scots") is in many respects merely very old English. *Gumption,* meaning common sense, initiative, quick-wittedness, probably derives from an obsolete Middle English word *gome,* meaning "care" or "heed."

※ Is *guts* a proper word for "courage"?

It is certainly not decorous, which is one meaning of "proper." But it is often appropriate, which is another meaning of "proper." It's a coarse but effective word used almost universally by American men in informal talk. It was once used in serious, even lofty writing: a fourteenth-century psalter beseeches God to renew a holy spirit in our "guttes." But the use of this word from the pulpit would startle most congregations today.

The connection of fortitude with the intestines is as old as speech, perhaps because we feel fear in the solar plexus. In recent years, especially in England (whence some Americans have borrowed it), the word *pluck* has been substituted for *guts.* But *pluck* once meant exactly what guts means: the internal organs.

And it, too, was once indecorous. Sir Walter Scott called it a "blackguardly" word.

In American slang *guts* is widely used for *impudence* ("He's got his guts, coming in here without being asked!"). This is not surprising, because whether an act is courageous or impudent is often a matter of viewpoint.

✷ Why does *to gyp* mean to cheat?

THE VERB *to gyp,* meaning "to cheat," is a shortening of *gypsy.* The gypsies were, or were thought to be, great cheats and rascals.

They were called *'gypcians* when they first appeared in England, about the beginning of the sixteenth century, because it was thought that they came from Egypt. Cleopatra is called a gypsy in Shakespeare's *Antony and Cleopatra* because since she was queen of Egypt it was assumed she was an Egyptian (actually she was Greek) and because "like a right gipsy" she had deceived Antony.

We know now that the gypsies came originally not from Egypt but from India. Their language is a debased Hindi dialect with a great many Persian, Armenian, and European words—which they had picked up in their wanderings—added. They call themselves *Romany,* from their word *rom* which mean "a man."

✷ Is it "I *had rather*" or "I *would rather*"?

OF THE expression as a whole, there is no doubt that *had rather* is historically correct. It's the old literary form ("I had rather be a doorkeeper in the house of my God, than to dwell in the tents of wickedness"—*Psalm* lxxxiv:10). Shakespeare uses *had rather* fifty times, *would rather* not at all.

But the nineteenth-century grammarians were bothered because they couldn't parse *had rather* and decided, with the innocent egotism of the learned, that if they couldn't parse it no one ought to use it. Their trouble was that they believed *had* to be an auxiliary verb without a main verb and that, despite the *Psalms* and Shakespeare's fifty uses of it, couldn't be.

The trouble with the grammarians was that they didn't know

that *had* in *had rather* is the past subjunctive of *have*, with the meaning of *hold* ("I would hold it to be better"). The grammarians felt that *would*, the subjunctive of the verb *to will*, fit their rules better and declared it to be what Shakespeare and the Bible and everyone who had ever spoken English up to that time really meant to say. And so solemnly did they pronounce this that "I would rather" is now equally correct, an error so solidly established as to be standard.

Not that it matters much. We say "I'd" and let grammarians worry about what the " 'd" sound would be if it were written out.

※ Can anything be *half empty*?

WE CAN'T say that something is *half empty*, we are told. It's an impossibility. It's like being "half dead."

Well, we not only can say that something is *half empty*, we do say it, all the time. And a listener who sincerely does not understand what we mean must have a half-empty head.

If you wanted to be rigidly exact, you could say that half the container was empty. But all you would get for your trouble would be your own admiration and everyone else's derision. We say we were scared "half to death" and only the most desperate wit would ask which half. We even go further and say that we're dead with the heat or with exhaustion.

※ Just what is a *handsome* man or woman?

ORIGINALLY *handsome* meant "easy or pleasant to handle," just as *toothsome* means "pleasant to bite." An early narrative speaks of a knight who, unarmed, picked up cobblestones that were "good and handsome" to throw at his opponent. And another work warned knights that their long lances were not "handsome" among trees and shrubs.

From "pleasant to handle" the meaning broadened out until the word became a term of general commendation (like *smooth* in modern teen-age slang), meaning "appropriate," "apt," "decent," "dextrous," "suitable," "graceful." These are attractive qualities and it was a short and almost inevitable extension for the word to mean "attractive."

However, *handsome* does not mean merely "good-looking." It designates beauty that is combined with dignity. There is always a suggestion of stateliness in it.

✷ the *handwriting on the wall*

As a metaphorical term for a prophetic warning of certain doom, a definite indication of retribution and destruction, *the handwriting on the wall* is taken from the fifth chapter of the *Book of Daniel*. There we are told that Belshazzar, the son of Nebuchadnezzar, made a great feast in the course of which he and his courtiers desecrated the sacred vessels which his father had brought from the Temple at Jerusalem.

Punishment came swiftly: "And in the same hour came forth fingers of a man's hand and wrote over against the candlestick upon the plaster of the wall" the enigmatic words MENE, MENE, TEKEL, UPHARSIN. The king's soothsayers were unable to guess the meaning of the mysterious message. But the prophet Daniel interpreted the words to mean: "God hath numberd thy kingdom and finished it. Thou art weighed in the balances and art found wanting. Thy kingdom is divided and given to the Medes and Persians."

Daniel exercised a prophet's insight in arriving at this translation. Scholars are agreed that the words literally mean either "numbered, numbered, weighed, and divisions" or "a mina, a mina, a shekel, and a half-mina."

✷ the origin of *hangar*

MRS. JONAS LANG, a friend of the Wright Brothers, interviewed on her eightieth birthday, had many recollections

189 · *hangar*

of the famous aviators. In particular, she remembered that she had "had a part in coining the word 'hangar'—a place for storage of aircraft."

> "The place where the Wrights kept their biplane, she said, was known simply as 'the shed.' The brothers thought they should come up with a more dignified appellation.
> "Because the wheelless biplane was hung up in a small tent adjacent to a large building which housed a dirigible [in Washington, D. C.], they thought first of 'hanging garage.'
> " 'That was too long; we wanted something shorter,' Lady Jack [Mrs. Lang] said.
> "Next 'hanging-garage' was shortened to 'hang-gar.'
> "But, when Wilbur started to paint 'hang-gar' on the end of an apple box to make a sign for the tent, he found he had room for only one 'g' in the word. Hence the place to store aircraft became 'hangar.'"
> —*Monterey Peninsula Herald* August 3, 1960. Fourth Section, p. 35.

There you have it, as fine a sample of homespun etymological recollection as you will meet with, carrying conviction in every syllable. That little touch about the apple box and the great inventor who could conquer space but couldn't plan ahead to fit seven letters where they had to go. One can just see Wilbur (as I feel urged to call him) smiling wryly at his own ineptitude while Orville, or Orv, laughed outright and Mrs. Lang tactfully concealed her amusement.

What a charming scene, and what could be more boorish than to question it? Yet what boors linguists are, as devoid of respect for the dead as of chivalry for the living (see *a gentleman and a scholar*), tactless, meddlesome, concerned solely with their own base, grubbing interest in facts.

Only such a one would point out that *hangar*, meaning a covered space, shed, or shelter, especially for vehicles, had been in use at least fifty-seven years before the incident Mrs. Lang describes. "Mademoiselle," said Prince Charles to Beatrix, in Thackeray's *Henry Esmond* (1852), "may we take your coach to town? I saw it in the hangar." "The people gathered . . . under an immense hangar or covered space," says the English translation of DuChaillu's *Equatorial Africa* (1861). And there are other instances.

It may all have happened as described, but it was a remarkable coincidence that the suspension of the plane, the size of the apple box, and Wilbur's limited abilities all combined to produce the exact word that was already in use.

✻ a *hangdog* look

A *hangdog look* is either the look characteristic of a base fellow whose office was to hang dogs or the craven look of some wretched dog about to be hanged.

In former days the great English country houses were infested (or enlivened, depending on how you feel about dogs) with dogs. They were allowed in the dining halls and fought and snatched at food and otherwise misbehaved under the table. There was a regular functionary who quelled their riots and kept some sort of order among them. Special misdoers got special whippings and incorrigible miscreants were hanged, like their human counterparts.

Shakespeare (a dog-loather) refers to the hanging of dogs five times in the course of the plays. And there is a great scene of horseplay, or dogplay, in *Two Gentlemen of Verona* (IV.iv.1-42) in which Launce, the clown, reminds his dog, Crab, that he has saved him from being hanged only by taking on himself the guilt for one of Crab's grossest social misdemeanors.

✻ Is a criminal *hanged* or *hung?*

A CRIMINAL is generally *hanged*, but if he is *hung* the effect is the same, linguistically as well as physiologically.

For involved reasons, the verb *to hang* developed both as a weak (*hang, hanged, hanged*) and as a strong (*hang, hung, hung*) verb. By the sixteenth century the strong inflection had displaced the weak in all general senses except for the particular sense of being put to death by hanging. Here the old weak form was widely retained, possibly because the judges (legal language is strongly conservative) used the old form in pronouncing sentence. And certainly in all phrases based on the idea, the old form alone is acceptable ("I'll be hanged if I do"). But in reference to the actual fact, *hung* gained ground in the speech and writing of Southern England while *hanged* was more common in the North.

In the United States today *hanged* is by far the commoner form, possibly because of the strong influence of the Scotch emigrants on our speech, reinforced by the fact that *hung* in some contexts has an indecent meaning.

None the less it is not incorrect to say that a man was *hung*, meaning that he was killed by hanging.

✳ Is there such a word as *hassle?*

This is one of those "Is-there-such-a-word?" words. Certainly there is! We hear it all the time and are beginning to see it in print. Dictionaries compiled more than twenty-five years ago don't seem to know of its existence. So it is obviously a new word, or at least a word that has only recently come to the attention of people who write dictionaries. Recent dictionaries list it but classify it as slang.

It was originally a Southern dialect word, meaning to pant or breathe noisily like a dog. In Caroline Miller's *Lamb in His Bosom* (1933) we read: "He ran straight in front of the dog that was hassling foam like soap water."

It is a good word to describe emotionally charged situations, usually quarrels, in which the contestants are breathing noisily and panting with excitement. It suggests both *wrastle* and *hustle*. And since the modern world is increasingly full of such situations, the word is increasing in use. It isn't a formal word yet, but it is an effective one in speech and says something that *squabble* and *quarrel* don't quite say.

✳ the pronunciation of *hazard* and the hazard of its pronunciation

Hazard was originally the name of a game played with dice in which there were many chances to lose. The word was a French corruption [*hasart*] of an Arabic name [*'Ain Zarba*] of a castle in Palestine. The castle stood a long siege and during the siege, to while away the time, the game was invented.

There are people who feel that foreign names should be pronounced as "they" pronounce them. These are the people who took the perfectly good and established *Mon ac' o* and hastily changed it to *Mon' uh co* when they learned that was what

Prince Rainier called his casino. The word *hazard* offers them a glorious opportunity. Instead of an English mispronunciation of a French corruption, they can go directly to the Arabic, and not modern Arabic, which is probably corrupt, but right back to the medieval Arabic. They will be "correct," but they will not be understood and after they have explained themselves they will simply be regarded as fools.

✻ heaping coals of fire

WHEN we do a favor for someone who has done us a dirty trick we say that we are *heaping coals of fire on his head*. In so saying we are quoting St. Paul (*Romans* xii:20) who was quoting *Proverbs* (xxv:21-22): "If your enemy is hungry, give him bread to eat; and if he is thirsty, give him water to drink; for you will heap coals of fire on his head, and the Lord will reward you."

The emphasis of the Biblical passages, it need not be said, is on the hot shame of the enemy as he realizes what a heel he is and what a wonderful person we are. But cynicism has shifted the emphasis for many to their own enjoyment of the enemy's burning self-reproach.

In most cases, however, this flaming remorse is more imagined than actual. There seems to be a larger amount of asbestos in the human skull than St. Paul or the author of *Proverbs* was aware of. Most ingrates remain comfortably cool.

✻ hearse and rehearse

A STRIKING example of the extent to which different meanings can derive from the same word is furnished by *hearse* and *rehearse* which are linguistic second cousins.

A *hearse* was originally a large rake or harrow. Then the name was borrowed to designate a framework which resembled a harrow but was used to support tapers and other decorations over a coffin at elaborate funerals. The body of Henry VIII, we are told, was "set under a goodly Herce of wax, garnished with banners." This in time was enlarged to a sort of canopy and from that the name was easily transferred (in the seventeenth century) to the carriage or car which bore the coffin to the grave. It, at first, was a canopy over the coffin, which was on a cart. It was usually ornate and decorated with banners.

Rehearse goes back to the rake. To rehearse is to rake over, break up the lumps, smooth off. It is a harrowing procedure.

✳ *heart-rending* or *heart-rendering?*

"I HEARD on television 'heart-rendering.' Shouldn't it have been 'heart-rending'?"

It all depends on the context.

To rend is to tear violently. Though the heart is an incredibly tough muscle, there is an ancient and intrenched belief that it can be lacerated, rent, and even broken by sorrow, pathos, pity, love, and other dismal emotions. Situations or narratives likely to effect such damage are all-too-often described by the cliché "heart-rending." And since television is addicted to clichés, this is most likely what was meant.

But *render* has several meanings that might have been intended. One meaning of *render* is "to give" ("Render unto Caesar") and the incident on TV may have been someone giving his heart away. Another meaning of *render* is "to melt the fat out of." As children in Sunday school we used to have an irreverent joke about the organ pealing potatoes while the choir rendered lard. Now it is possible that the situation alluded to in the program was such as to melt the fat out of a sensitive heart—make one blubber, so to speak. If so, *rendering* would have been the word.

There's always the chance, of course, that the speaker was a cornball humorist and the confusion of the two words was deliberate.

✳ a *hectic* day

MANY people object to *hectic* being used to mean "exhausting because of a multiplicity of stresses," but they are opposing a perfectly natural development.

Hectic is derived, ultimately, from a Greek word meaning "habitual" and once in a great while it is used to mean habitual. Milton so used it when he referred to mankind's "hectic disposition to evil." In common use, however, it was soon restricted to habitual symptoms of certain diseases, especially of the disease that we now call tuberculosis. People spoke of the hectic cough, the hectic fever and the hectic flush of that disease.

The flush and the fever got connected with the flush and fever of excitement. And with good reason. For the feverish are often excited, fitful, and restless, and the excited, fitful, and restless are often feverish. When, for instance, Hazlitt said that Shelley "had a maggot in his brain [and] a hectic flutter in his speech," he may have been alluding to the consumption which Shelley was thought to have or he may have been alluding merely to his excitable and impetuous nature.

So that the extension of *hectic* to mean "characterized by emotion and excitement" was thoroughly natural. But since prolonged emotion and excitement was tiring, its further extension to mean "exhausted" is equally natural ("The Christmas vacation was just too hectic. I'm done in"). Then some of its present-day popular meaning may be due to its resemblance to the word *heck* which is widely used as a polite substitute for *hell*. That is, *hectic* suggests *hellish*.

This last meaning of *hectic*—exhausting beyond endurance—is still colloquial. But thousands of words have developed in such a way and there is no reason why this particular one should be singled out for protest.

❋ **Is there such a word as *heighth*?**

Is THERE such a word as *heighth*? One hears it every day but most dictionaries either ignore it or insist that it is a corruption.

But isn't it, rather, a permissible variant? The *t* and the *th* sounds are often interchanged in English. Some men are called Anthony and some Antony. Everybody pronounces *Thomas* and *Thames* as though they were spelled *Tommus* and *Temz*. Many are uncertain about *drought* and *drouth*.

Since the beginning of the language the quality of being high has been represented (and apparently pronounced) with either a *t* sound or a *th* sound at the end. Boswell frequently wrote it *highth* and so did Milton ("He from Heaven's highth/All these our motions vain sees . . .") and so do millions today.

All other qualities of space measurements have settled on

the *th* ending (*breadth, length, width, depth*) so that, actually, it is the *t* ending of *height* (which many insist is the only permissible pronunciation) that is unusual. These same people, by the way, crow with righteous and truculent superiority when they hear some uneducated person apply the *t* ending to any of the other words—as "lengt'," "widt'," or "breadt'."

✳ *heist*

Heist, a widely used colloquialism, meaning "to steal," is merely an archaic or dialectal pronunciation of *hoist*, "to lift." The sound *oi* was frequently pronounced in earlier days like the *i* in *line*. When Alexander Pope wrote in 1711, that: "Good nature and good sense must ever join;/To err is human, to forgive divine" his rime (and hundreds of supporting rimes) make it plain that "jine" was then the pronunciation of *join*. And, what's more, it was the pronunciation heard in rural America up until fifty years ago.

So also with *hoist*. Mark Twain's famous jumping frog, Dan'l, with his belly full of buckshot, only "hysted up his shoulders" (1865). Cows were ordered to "hist," meaning to lift their hind leg out of the milker's way. A *hip-hist* was a throw in wrestling. In central Pennsylvania a *heister* is a jack for lifting wagons and in the deep South to "hist the rhyme" is, or until recently was, to lead the singing.

To *lift* (or *hoist* or *hist*) is a common term for stealing. One has only to think of *shoplifting*.

✻ *hell bent* for election

One meaning of *bent* is "forced into a curve, as a bent bow." Things bent in this way have a tension, an inherent force to thrust themselves out of the bent condition. Hence *bent* also meant "braced or wound up for action, crouched as for a spring, full of force and not to be turned aside, determined and resolute."

Hell bent is an American expression of the early nineteenth century, meaning so energetically bent on a course of action as to be heedless of all consequences, even of hell itself, and hence determined to proceed towards a desired end with reckless fury and speed.

The full phrase came into our speech in the campaign of 1840 when Edward Kent put up such a vigorous fight for the governorship of Maine that he was said to be "Hell-bent for election." He won and his party, the Whigs, celebrated in a song: "Oh have you heard how old Maine went?/She went hell-bent for Governor Kent,/And Tippecanoe and Tyler, too!"

✻ *"here's mud in your eye"*

This lugubrious incitement to conviviality is of recent invention. It is thought to come from Australia where, among the virile set, it is apparently deemed better to be firm than finicky in your drinking. The meaning seems to be an adjuration to raise your glass so high and drain it so completely that all that will be left will be a drop of muddy lees to fall in your eye. Since you are, presumably, proceeding to get blind, this will facilitate the process.

✻ are *high* and *tall* interchangeable?

High and *tall* agree in referring to some height above the average. We may refer to high buildings or to tall buildings.

High is the more general term. It indicates either extension upward or an elevated position (a high mountain, a high ceiling, a high ledge). The opposite of *high* is *low.*

Tall designates either something which is high in proportion to its breadth (as *a tall glass*) or to something higher than the average of its kind (as "He's a tall boy for his age"). We think of Lincoln, for instance, as a tall man because, though muscular, he was thin. Washington, who was almost as tall as Lincoln, was more massive and we think of him rather as a big man than as a tall man. The opposite of *tall* is *short*.

Each word has, in addition, become fixed in certain contexts: prices, lively spirits, and dead fish are always *high;* exaggerated stories are always *tall*.

※ **highfaluting**

Highfaluting or *highfalutin* is a vague word of good-humored mockery whose very lack of exact meaning is part of its expressiveness, reflecting what it describes. It was originally applied to oratory. Nineteenth-century America was severely afflicted with rhetoric, a sort of hangover hiccups of the noble inebriation of the Revolution. Public speakers would rant, bellow, and soar for hours, and the rhythm and sentimentality of their talk was as high as its thought was low. Mr. Dooley said of Senator Beveridge's prose that "you could waltz to it." Some word was needed to describe this sort of thing and our ingenious ancestors coined *highfalutin(g)*.

It's a good word because, like the speeches, it seems to make sense but somehow doesn't. *High* is plain enough, and suitable. In *faluting* there are echoes of *fluting* and *saluting* and *flying*, all characteristic of patriotic oratory. It would be hard to suggest all this in any other word.

※ **eating *high on the hog***

WHEN you're eating *high on the hog*, you're eating well. The finest meat on a hog is the meat high on its body—

pork chops, spare ribs, and tenderloin. If you cannot afford these cuts, you must eat low on the hog—pigs feet or knuckles, hog jowl, and sow belly. It is probably no accident that the names of the choicest cuts—tenderloin and pork chops—come from French words, while the inferior cuts have Saxon names. The Normans, who came from France and conquered England when our language was beginning a period of very active development, apparently named and ate the high part of the hog and left the rest to the Saxon laborers.

The Saxon laborer, by the way, was called a *ceorl* or *churl*—which shows how he felt about it.

✳ *hob and nob*

Hobnob is a condensation of the phrase *hob and nob* which, in turn, was a corruption or change of *hab* (have) *and nab* (not have). By Shakespeare's time the expression meant "give or take." Sir Toby Belch (in *Twelfth Night*) tells Viola that Sir Andrew Aguecheek is so angry with her that he will accept no satisfaction "but by pangs of death and sepulchre. 'Hob, nob' is his word; 'give't or take't.'"

A hundred years later it had become a drinking term. The transition seems to have been "Give a drink or take one." To drink *hob nob* or *hob a nob* was for two cronies to drink alternately to each other, usually clinking their glasses together before each drink. Such drinking required a certain amount of friendship and goodwill to begin with and no doubt increased both as it progressed. Hence the term came to mean, as it now does, to be on intimate terms of good fellowship.

The idea of drinking has faded out of *hobnob*, but the atmosphere of drinking remains.

✳ Is a *hobby* noble or contemptible?

COMPLETE changes in the meanings of words—such as the change of *talent* from a weight or monetary unit to a special ability, of *fiasco* from a bottle to an ignominious failure, of *junket* from a reed to a trip at someone else's expense—are interesting but there is sometimes an even greater interest in more subtle changes, changes in which the meaning is kept but the attitude of the speaker towards the meaning is changed.

The word *hobby* illustrates this sort of change.

Originally a hobby was a middle-sized horse. Robin and Dobbin are related names. A hobby was an ambling or a pacing horse. Very early the name was extended to a horse's head on a stick which a little child bestrode and pretended he was riding. And it was from this (extended to and including rocking horses), and especially from the absorption and obsession with which a child will ride one of these things, soothing himself almost to a bliss of unconsciousness by its motion, that the modern meaning of *hobby* came.

Until very recently—merely a generation or so ago—*hobby* was disparaging. Connotations of childishness and futility clustered thick about it. It denoted an obsession, a trifling occupation pursued (in the speaker's opinion) out of all proportion to its real importance. Men were always spoken of as "riding" their hobbies. Typical hobbies would have been Uncle Toby's infatuation (in *Tristram Shandy*) with the science of fortification or Mr. Dick's concern (in *David Copperfield*) with King Charles's head.

But, in a twinkling of a Rotarian's eye, all this has changed. A hobby is now felt to be so virtuous that (one suspects) many businessmen assume one who actually have it not. Reporters, interviewing celebrities, resent the Great One if he says he doesn't have a hobby. It's un-American. Who is he to be so much better than other people as to pretend that he is interested in his work and has no great longing for some childish diversion?

What does it all mean? That we have more leisure than we know what to do with? That most work is hateful? That in our society most men remain children and that there is no necessary connection between success in business and maturity?

※ **What is *Hobson's choice*?**

Hobson's choice, which means no choice at all, alludes to the rule of Thomas Hobson, a carrier at Cambridge, England, in the seventeenth century, that his customers could not select the horse they wanted to hire but had to take the next in line. It was that or nothing—like the choice that Henry Ford offered the purchasers of his Model T automobile: any color so long as it was black.

Hobson's requirement was humane and just. But it was so opposed to the spirit of the age, in which special treatment for the gentry was taken for granted, that it attracted great attention.

One of the streets of Cambridge is named after the man. Steele wrote an essay about him (*Spectator* No. 509) and Milton wrote two poems about him. When we add to this the fact that his name has become a proverb, we must concede that few kings or philosophers have gained as much fame as this obscure carrier.

✻ What does *"hoist with his own petard"* mean?

WHEN someone is *hoist with his own petard* he is caught in a trap he has set for someone else, he is destroyed by some device that he has prepared for the destruction of another.

The expression comes from *Hamlet.* The sycophants, Rosenkrantz and Guildenstern, feigning friendship to Hamlet are actually part of a conspiracy to have him killed. They are to accompany him to England, bearing secret letters in which the King of Denmark asks the King of England to have Hamlet executed immediately. Hamlet has got hold of the letters and so changed the wording that Rosenkrantz and Guildenstern are designated as the ones to be executed. In telling his mother of his plans he admits that it would be "knavery," but adds that it is "sport to have the enginer [what we would call a sapper] hoist [i.e., hoisted, blown up into the air] with his own petard [bomb]."

It is.

✻ What do we mean when we say that someone "can't *hold a candle*" to someone else?

WHEN we say that someone *can't hold a candle to* someone else, we mean that the person spoken of is unworthy even to serve the other in a menial capacity.

The reference—once quite plain—has been obscured by changes in our way of living. We no longer have servants and our candles are paraffin and ornamental, with romantic associations of intimate dinners and Christmas trees.

But when candles were used as the main source of illumination, they were usually made of tallow. They spluttered and smoked, dripped hot fat, and smelled abominably. So that the job of holding a candle was unpleasant and very likely painful. In addition it was tedious and probably a task that brought a lot of nagging and scolding, since the candle-holder would be expected to stand still for a long period of time. Then it put the holder in a special awareness of his social inferiority, since he was compelled to stand very near to the gentry—who might be reading or playing cards—and yet was not regarded as one of the party but simply as a piece of animated furniture.

※ *"hold no brief"*

A *brief* is a lawyer's summing up of the facts of the case he is to defend, with the relevant points of law, suggestions of points to be taken up with witnesses, and so on. *To hold a brief* is to be retained as a lawyer. So that when someone says "I hold no brief for so-and-so," he is saying "I am not a lawyer paid to defend him." He then usually goes on to say, "But there are certain things to be said in his defense," that in at least some details the case against him is being exaggerated or misrepresented.

※ *holp*

A CORRESPONDENT writing from eastern Mississippi is puzzled by "a very peculiar thing" in the speech of the people there: "They say *hope* instead of *helped*. Such things as 'She hope her sister when she was sick.'"

This is the sort of letter a linguist likes to get. The correspondent is not hearing *hope* but *holp*, an archaic past of the verb *to help*. Since she says she's lived there all her life and heard this strange thing all her life, it's apparent that the old preterit is still vigorously alive in eastern Mississippi. It's also apparent that its use is restricted to some particular social class, since it doesn't seem natural to the correspondent, even though she's heard it for many years.

Had she not misspelled it as *hope*, I might have thought she was trying a little joke, like someone who steals a dinosaur bone from a museum and with feigned innocence asks the local butcher what it is. But the misspelling is pretty good evidence that she had no idea she was dealing with a fossil. Many *l*'s that we now pronounce were formerly not pronounced. The name we pronounce *Ralph*, for instance, was formerly *Raph*, and Shakespeare (who uses *holp* many times, by the way—"Three times today I holp him to his horse," etc.) rimes *halter* with *daughter*.

✱ Holy Smoke!

THERE doesn't seem to be any specific meaning in the exclamation *Holy Smoke!* It's just one more piece of pseudo-profanity.

Some claim that it is a reference to the pillar of cloud that preceded the fleeing Israelites by day (*Exodus* xiii:21) or the smoke that "ascended as the smoke of a furnace" when the Lord descended upon Mount Sinai. But people who know their Bibles that well rarely use imitation profanity.

Partridge in his *Dictionary of Slang and Unconventional English* lists more than a dozen of these irreverent but presumably safe exclamations that begin with *holy*. Berrey and Van den Bark in their *American Thesaurus of Slang* list sixteen. Not listed by either, however, is the common but shocking *Holy Mackerel*, one of the most dreadful pieces of impiety ever framed by the foul and foolish mouth of man. Many an ignorant user of this harmless-seeming exclamation is going to be dismayed on Judgment Day to find out what a reckoning he has coming!

✱ Robin Hood no *hood*!

"Is A CRIMINAL called a *hood* because of Robin Hood?" I am asked. And I'm saddened at even being asked, to think that anyone, anywhere, could have such doubts about one of my boyhood heroes.

Hood, in the sense of a criminal, is a shortening of *hoodlum*, a name applied to youthful gangsters in San Francisco in the 1870's. Some think the word was a reversal of the Irish name *Muldoon*, with an initial *h* substituted for the *n*. But it is more probably the Bavarian dialect word *hodalum*, which means exactly what we mean by *hoodlum*. (Incidentally, anyone who is greatly upset over modern juvenile delinquents should read about the San Francisco hoodlums and other gangs of youthful cutthroats that terrorized our cities a century ago. Our monsters are extraordinarily mild compared to their forerunners.)

Robin Hood was not a hoodlum. He was not thought of as a criminal but as a champion of the downtrodden, taking from the rich only to give to the poor, living a wholesome life in Sherwood Forest, supported by his Merry Men, diverted by Friar Tuck and soothed by Maid Marian. In earlier times he was known as Robin o' the Woods. Robin was a common name for a certain type of spook or pixie (Robin Goodfellow) and some scholars believe that Robin Hood was the last dim, sad appearance of the once-great god Woden.

✳ by *hook or crook*

WHEN this phrase first appeared in print (in the writings of John Wyclif, 1380), it meant just what it means now—"by fair means or foul." The best guesses are that it originated in the early English forest laws governing the right of the poor to secure firewood. They were not allowed to use axes or saws, but were entitled to pull off whatever they could *by hook* (a hooked pole, like a shepherd's curved staff) or hack off *by crook* (a sickle). A passage in the *Bodmin Register* (1525) says that a certain wood was open to the inhabitants of Bodmin "to bear away upon their backs a burden of *lop, hook, crook and bag wood*." The peasants probably hacked and slashed, with hook and crook, as furiously as they could.

✻ horrific

A CORRESPONDENT saw a Boris Karloff movie advertised as "horrific" and writes to ask "Is there such a word?"

I am unable to find it listed in any dictionary, but that's beside the marquee. The owner of a movie has the same right that anyone else has to coin any word that suits his purpose.

And *horrific* may have suited his purposes. He couldn't advertise Mr. Karloff as *horrid* because that suggests personal disagreeableness and Mr. Karloff, in his most monstrous moments, is never disagreeable. He couldn't say that he was *horrible*, because that might be interpreted to mean that in this particular film he was not up to his usual delightful gruesomeness. There is an established word *horrific* ("horror inspiring") and that might have been meant but misspelled. And there are also *horrorous* and *horrorsome*, but they verge on the comic.

The chances are that the marquee meant just what it said: *horrific*. Movies of this kind have become a recognized genre, known as "horror films," and the *-ific* suffix hoped to convey to passing devotees of gooseflesh that this picture had all the qualities desired in a horror film to a highly satisfactory degree.

✻ pronunciation of *hors d'oeuvres*

Hors d'oeuvre(s) is one of those borrowed words on which the American people, by common consent, have fixed their own pronunciation: *or derv'* in the singular and *or dervz'* in the plural. In the French pronunciation the final *s* of the plural form is silent, but not in the American. The French pronunciation, by the way, is something close to *awr duhr' vruh*, but that no more concerns an American at a cocktail party than the manner in which the Turks pronounce *Istamboul*.

✻ just plain *horse sense*

A HORSE isn't very intelligent—compared to a pig or an elephant or a porpoise or some people—but it has certain instinctive awarenesses. Within limits, it has some knowledge of the way home. It won't eat food utterly unsuited to it. It attempts to escape from its enemies. And so on. These are not breathtaking demonstrations of brilliance, but they are more than some members of the human species, especially young members, always show.

The expression is usually employed in a negative context (as, "Anybody with plain horse sense would have known better than that!"), marking a sort of irreducible minimum of sense. In positive contexts, the term is more likely to be *common sense* ("He may not be very learned, but he's got a lot of common sense").

✳ hostages to fortune

A *hostage* is a person held as security. In former times a conqueror would sometimes compel those whom he had defeated to send him their sons as surety for their good behavior. Then if they revolted, their sons were put to death.

"Hostages to fortune" came into the language in the opening sentence of Francis Bacon's essay *Of Marriage and Single Life* where he says: "He that hath wife and children hath given hostages to fortune; for they are impediments to great enterprises, either of virtue or of mischief." *Mischief* was then a much stronger word than it now is. It meant harm or evil wrought by a particular person. Bacon's meaning is that our loved ones are sureties that we will behave, because *they* will suffer if *we* do wrong. But this very fact tames us; we hesitate, for their sake, to take risks, either of good or evil.

The thought was common among the Romans who often referred to children as *pledges*.

✳ "Mr. X *hosted* a party"

SOCIETY columns frequently state that "Mr. X hosted a party." This agitates a number of their readers but it is grammatically justified. A host has as much right to *host* a party as a pilot, say, has to pilot a ship or a lord has to lord it over his inferiors.

Up until 300 years ago the word was frequently used as a verb. Spenser in *The Faerie Queene* (1596) says of a hag who entertained her betters that she was "unmeet to host such guests." Shakespeare used it as a verb to mean "being a guest." And there was a proverb: "Great boast and a small roast/Make unsavory mouths, wherever men host."

But though grammatically warranted, *host* as a verb seems stylistically wrong today. It suggests that the society columnist is reaching hard to relieve the tedium of what must be one of the most boring chores on the face of the earth. *To host* had better be left in the oblivion to which time had relegated it.

※ a *hot cup of coffee*

HALF a dozen correspondents have written to ask why in the name of everything sacred some people insist on asking for "a hot cup of coffee" when they obviously want "a cup of hot coffee." The tone of the inquiries ranges from the stern to the hysterical but all suggest that if grammarians can't do something about it the police ought to be called in.

It seems to me the writers must have been drinking something a great deal more disturbing than coffee. If someone asks for "a hot cup of coffee," surely his meaning is clear. He is not talking about the container but about its contents, treating the word *cup* as a term of measure. Nobody assumes, for instance, that when a recipe calls for two cups of flour that the cups are to be thrown in too.

※ *housewife* and *homebody; housework* and *homework*

NOWHERE must the foreigner learning English be more bewildered than in the maze of words connected with *house* and *home.* Most women want to be married and to have a house of their own, yet many resent being called *housewives. Hussy* once merely meant housewife but now it is downright libelous. And what's a *homebody?* and why does a woman do *housework* while her high-school daughter does *homework?* We sell houses, but on homesites, and with increasing humanity have changed the Poorhouse to the Old Folks Home.

The meanings associated with *house* and *home* are various and complex, but the rough outlines of their division are still marked by Edgar Guest's assurance that "It takes a heap o' livin' and some love to make a home."

The word *wife* originally meant "woman," not necessarily (as now) a married woman. So a woman is a housewife or housewoman when she's doing the work around the place. She has no great love for much of it which, by its nature, is repetitious and drudging. When at such work she feels the place to be a *house* and the work *housework*. But in her emotional attachment to it, it's a *home,* and if she is that rare female creature who would rather stay in the house than go out, she's a *homebody.*

The schoolwork done in the house after school hours by the child is *homework* if only to distinguish it from the even-more-loathed housework. But it may also reflect the fact that, at least when contrasted with the school, the house is a place of warmth and affection, a home, something more than a mere structure.

※ **Why is a tomboy sometimes called a *hoyden?***

THE BEST-GROUNDED assumption is that it is related to the German word for heath (*Heide*). That is, a *hoyden* was probably a roaring, romping, mannerless critter fresh in from the briar patches. She would have lots of vitality, but little polish. If she had no more religion than culture, she was a *heathen* as well.

※ **What is the literal meaning of *humbug?***

No ONE knows just what *humbug* means. It came into the language (1751) from the lingo of the underworld. It became a vogue word and was very smart, but even at the time no one had any idea what it meant. It was a sort of humbug in itself.

The original meaning of *bug* is "bogey," and *humbug* may have meant simply a bug that hums and frightens us even though it is in reality harmless. There is oblique support for this in the fact that the Spanish word for humbug is *abejón,* literally "drone."

But it may not be this at all. Formerly people expressed approbation—as we do by clapping hands—by humming, and the word may have had some suggestion of false encouragement, leading a fool on by false approval.

Or it may have had a darker meaning. *Bug* is a dirty word in British speech. The English are always startled to hear Americans refer to insects as "bugs." DeQuincey, in 1828, called *humbug* "a coarse word" and there may have been some indecent meaning in it that we no longer perceive.

✳ *hurry* and *hustle* and *bustle*

THE WORD *hurry* is cognate with the word *hurl*. It designates not merely hasty action, but excited, impetuous action, with a suggestion that the emotional pressures which distinguish it from mere haste are excessive and that the haste may not be absolutely necessary.

Hustle, a colloquialism which seems to combine *hurry* and *jostle,* suggests not only hurrying but pushing others aside in one's aggressive haste. George Ade defined a *hustler* as "one who is busy, persistent, resourceful and combative, usually that he may accumulate money (*Doc Horne,* 1899)." Sinclair Lewis drew a hustler in "Honest Jim" Blausser in *Main Street. Babbitt* opens with a minor symphony on the word *hustle.*

Bustling is a sort of mock hustling. It is simply making an obtrusive show of energy, usually with much noise and agitation, in order to seem important and busy.

Hurry is colored by fear, *hustle* by greed, *bustle* by vanity. They are all good names for bad things.

✳ "There's *husbandry* in heaven"

A husband was originally a peasant who owned his own house and land. *To husband* was to manage. In managing his small estate the husbandman had to be prudent and waste nothing. Hence *husbandry* came to mean thrifty management. When Banquo, in *Macbeth,* sees that it is a dark and starless night, he says, "There's husbandry in heaven; their candles are all out." Then as now, apparently, it was Father who went around putting out unneeded lights to save expense.

Husband is often used in connection with our natural resources and is well chosen. It implies that we must cherish them, be thrifty with them, and make provision for their replenishment—as the head of a family manages his estate so that his children and grandchildren may have something.

It is significant—and to a male a little depressing—that the word which once meant "general manager" has come to be merely the correlative of *wife*.

※ **What has *hysteria* to do with *hysterectomy*?**

Hysteria and *hysterectomy* (the surgical removal of the womb) both derive from the Greek *hystera*, "womb."

Hysteria reflects the curious ancient belief that the womb was an unfixed organ which, moving about in the abdomen, tickled and upset a woman and produced hysteria.

Since hysteria was caused by the womb, it followed that men could not be *hysterical*. When men had tantrums and smashed things and shrieked and wept, they were merely displaying force of character. Nothing was more bitterly resented in Freud's early teaching than his insistence that men, too, were subject to hysteria.

The womb was sometimes called *the mother* and hysteria was called "a fit of the mother." From this use of mother (*matrix*) derive such expressions as "mother of pearl" and "mother of vinegar."

※ ***I*, i**

THE NOMINATIVE for the person speaking, used to be written either as a small "i" or as a capital. It was standardized on the introduction of printing to its present capitalized form. This was probably a matter of convenience rather than of egotism, since *me, mine,* and *my* are not capitalized. So small a letter standing alone was possibly easily lost among the type or dropped inadvertently from lines.

The older form of the nominative of the first personal pronoun was *ik* or *ich*. The vowel was pronounced like the *i* in *his*. Our "I" (not pronounced *ai*, as we pronounce it, until much later) was merely a shortened form of *ich*. This old word lingered on in English dialects until only a few centuries ago. Shakespeare's hayseeds sometimes use it. When, for instance, Edgar, in *King Lear,* assumes the speech of a rustic, he says "chill" [(i)ch (w)ill] for "I will" and "chud" [(i)ch (wo)u(l)d] for "I would."

The dot over the small *i*, by the way, was not originally a part of the letter. It was introduced by scribes about the eleventh century when two *i*'s came together (as in *filii*) to distinguish them from the letter *u*.

❋ "He gave it to John and *I*"

WE OFTEN hear "He gave it to John and I." The grossness of the error is made clear if the recipients are put into separate sentences. "He gave it to I" would surely grate on any ear.

The construction, which is common among the half educated but is never heard among the educated or the uneducated, seems to have had its origin in a fear of the word *me* in combination with another pronoun. Possibly those who use the "gave it to John and I" construction had been furiously rebuked or savagely derided in their childhood for saying "John and me did this-or-that." Someone shouted "John and *I*" at them or made them stay after school and write "John and I" on the blackboard two hundred times, and "John and I" it thereupon became in all circumstances.

Certainly many middle-class Americans seem afraid of the word *me*. Some, panicstricken, say "He gave it to John and I." Others use the equally ghastly—less incorrect but more affected and self-conscious—"He gave it to John and myself."

❋ *idiomatic* English

Idiom comes from a Greek word meaning "peculiar." An idiom is an expression fixed by usage in a language although it is opposed to the regular grammar of the language or the regular meanings of the words which compose it. *Who did you give it to?* is, for example, good idiomatic English although, in the strictest sense, it is ungrammatical. *So long* is fully understood as an expression of goodwill at parting, but there is no meaning of *so* or *long* that explains the phrase. Pink is a shade of red, but there's a difference between being "in the pink" and being "in the red." When freight goes by car, it is a *shipment;* when it goes by ship, it is a *cargo.* You can order calf's liver and veal chops, but you would be stared at if you ordered veal liver or calf's chops. We take *to* people, take them *up,* take them *in,* take them *off* and, if they resent it, take them *down.* The French *hors* means "out," *de* means "of," and *oeuvre* means "work"; but *hors d'oeuvre* does not mean "out of work." It makes a world of difference to a ball team whether a valuable player *resigns* or *re-signs* and even more difference to a condemned man whether his reprieve is *upheld* or *held up.*

It is idiomatic to say that wounded or civilians were *evacuated* from a city, though strictly it was the city that was evacuated of them. Or we may say that we *enjoyed ourselves,* when we mean, and are clearly understood to mean, that we enjoyed the company of others. Or a woman may weep at the death of her husband, as the greatest evil that could befall her, sobbing that he's gone *for good.* Or we say that we clean a spot off the floor when, actually, it is the floor not the spot that is cleaned.

Many worthy people, who lack windmills to tilt at or mops with which to turn back the tide, expend a great deal of energy trying to "correct" such idioms. If they succeeded we wouldn't have a language, because English is highly idiomatic. But there is little chance of their succeeding. They are almost all people of a little learning (not "little learning"—that's an entirely different thing in English idiom) who have merely dampened their lips at the Pierian Spring. But if among their little learning is by chance some acquaintance with a foreign language, they usually exult in their familiarity with the idiom of *that* tongue and are loud in their derision of anyone who ignores it.

✳ *if* and *though*

"Is THERE any difference between *if* and *though?* Does *as if* imply any different condition or concession than *as though?*"

When introducing a clause that concedes something, *if* and *though* have slightly different shades of meaning. *Though* makes lighter of the concession. It suggests that what follows may be true but has no bearing on the point at issue ("Though he slay me, yet will I trust Him"). The concession implied in *if,* however, may be central ("If he's not on time, I won't wait a minute").

Despite this distinction, however, there is no difference at all between the phrases *as if* and *as though*. They mean exactly the same and are completely interchangeable.

✷ an *ill wind* and a *silver lining*

LOST in a maze of proverbs, a correspondent wants to know if "It's an ill wind that blows nobody good" and "Every cloud has a silver lining" mean the same thing.

They are poles apart.

That every cloud has a silver lining was first stated by a nineteenth-century professional optimist by the improbable name of Samuel Smiles whose *Self-Help* (1859) had all the success that the do-it-yourself spiritual books have had in our time. Mr. Smiles, drawing for a metaphor on the bright edging of a storm cloud, was simply urging the dejected to buck up by assuring them that things are bound to get better and there's a good time coming by-and-by.

"It's an ill wind that blows nobody good" was proverbial when it first appeared five hundred years ago. It says, in effect, that someone profits from almost any disaster and that in the infinite variety of fortunes good and evil are often merely different aspects of the same thing. The ice, for instance, that fills the aged with fear of slipping, fills the young with hope of sliding. The epidemic is tough on the victims, but a windfall for their residuary legatees. The sixty-car smash on the superhighway brings remunerative employment to wreckers, mortuary cosmeticians, photographers, reporters, and other assorted ghouls—and makes exciting reading at a million otherwise-dull breakfast tables.

✷ Is one *immune to* or *immune from*?

ONE MAY be either. And in addition one may be *immune against* or *immune of*.

Immune originally meant "exempt from certain services or duties." This meaning is now archaic, at least in the United States, and would sound strange to us ("If a man has served on a jury in a murder trial he is [in England] thereafter immune from jury duty").

Immune may also mean "free of" and in this sense may be followed by *of*. But this would sound even stranger.

Whether one is immune *to, from,* or *against* a disease probably depends on how the speaker regards the relationship of man and disease. If one thinks of the disease as attacking, then one is immune *to* or *against* the attack. If one thinks of the immunity as an impregnability, natural or acquired, then the attacked organism is immune *from* the attack.

Certainly the most common current American preference is for "immune *to.*"

※ an *impending* bride

A CORRESPONDENT sends a clipping from a society column which refers to a woman about to be married as "an impending bride."

To impend is to hang over, and since things that hang over us make us uneasy, it has acquired an overtone of menace. It can also mean "to be imminent, to be about to happen"—and here again, though not invariably, there is a suggestion that that which is about to happen will be unpleasant when it does happen.

Now, unless a pun was intended, the bride-to-be is not hung over, and politeness compels us to assume that neither she nor the event constitutes a menace. As for the idea of imminence, impending, in this sense, is never used of persons. Events may *impend,* but people don't. The wedding may be *impending* but the bride—presumably—is eager. And even in respect to the wedding, it would certainly have been more delicate to have found some word to indicate its approach that doesn't have the idea of something hanging over those involved.

※ Do you go *in* the house or *into* the house?

EITHER is correct, though contemporary American usage inclines increasingly to *into* where the motion is to be emphasized.

Some grammarians would like to see *in* restricted to the idea of inwardness or remaining and *into* employed solely where motion or direction is to be expressed. And it might be an addition to the language to make this distinction. But it would be a change. That is, it isn't that way now; these grammarians are hoping or suggesting, not stating what is done. *In* formerly carried all the meanings of *into;* and although *in* is definitely weakened, it is not yet improper with a verb of motion.

※ Does one live *in a street* or *on a street?*

AMERICANS say that so-and-so lives *on* such-and-such a street. The British say that he lives *in* such-and-such a street. Each regards the other as an idiot for speaking so absurdly. "To say he lives *in* the street," says the American, "is to assert that he has pitched a tent or set up a cot and a stove right in the middle of the street." "To say he lives *on* the street," snorts the Briton, "is to state that the blighter exists, somehow, on the very surface of the macadam. Really!" And so they huff and puff and with increasing acrimony shove and jostle each other toward(s) Bunker Hill.

※ shot down *in cold blood*

MANY viewers of TV Westerns seem to be puzzled by the expression *in cold blood,* the condition in which the villains frequently shoot their victims. There is something touching in the thought of a TV viewer trying to make out the exact meaning of a Western and I hasten to clarify this, the smallest of their confusions.

The *cold blood* belongs to the shooter. The blood of the man shot is presumably, 98.6° Fahrenheit.

Many figures of speech associate heat with strong emotions—fiery temper, burning desire, seething rage, fuming impatience, and so on, down to and including a red-hot mama. And all this heat, whether real or metaphorical, is thought to be carried by the blood. So that *in hot blood* means "under the stress of a strong emotion" and *in cold blood* means "unmoved, calm, indifferent." And not only unmoved, of course, but unmoved where a normal person would be moved. After all blood is naturally fairly warm.

To kill someone in the heat of emotion has always been regarded as less reprehensible than to kill with careful, unemotional deliberation and planning. To kill when your blood is "cold" is dastardly. Or it is so regarded by those who disapprove of the killing or the killer. Where they approve, it is called "coolness." The handsome sheriff is always "cool" as he mows down the cold-blooded killer.

※ *in line* or *on line?*

CERTAINLY the standard expression is *in line*. Ships have sailed in line, men have stood in line or been forced to get in line, trees have been planted in line, and so on, for centuries. But increasingly we are hearing *on line*. Is this simply a misinterpretation of the "'n line" that we generally speak? I don't think so. "On line" is too common and is reported by too many correspondents from all parts of the country.

It may be a regional variation that is suddenly spreading. Unusual expressions, words, and pronunciations often lie dormant in dialects for hundreds of years and then suddenly spread through the entire speech and become standard. No one knows why. Possibly because the term was natural to someone who suddenly became prominent and whose way of speaking was imitated.

An old woman writes to say that when she went to school *in line* meant one behind the other, facing the back of the one ahead; whereas *on line* meant shoulder to shoulder facing the teacher, as for a spelling bee. It would be interesting to know if this distinction was made in many schools—and if the teachers making it had any idea that they were monkeying with the language.

※ Is there any difference between getting somewhere *in time* and *on time?*

THE TIME of getting there might be the same, but the attitude toward the arrival is plainly different. *Just in time* implies that a moment, or even a second, later would have been too late. The phrase often carries a sense of emergency and either reproach for having caused it or relief that something unpleasant had been averted.

Just on time implies that the arrival was at the exact, stipulated time. It lacks the urgency of "in time" and more often expresses satisfaction than reproach.

Punctual people are always *on* time. Careless people, if they get there at all, manage to do so only *in* time.

✻ Indian giver

"Why *Indian* giver?" a little girl wants to know. "Did Indians want their gifts back more than anyone else?"

They probably did. Or at least they were probably more open about it.

The term is an Americanism and goes back to our very beginnings. Most primitive people, we now know, exchange gifts. So that when an Indian gave a gift he expected its equivalent in return. Perhaps a great deal more than a mere equivalent, since your prestige was enhanced if you gave more than you got and the white man was strong on prestige. The Indians who hopefully gave our forefathers a swatch of wampum or some porcupine quills expected in return, most likely, some beads or a mirror or even a knife. And when they just got "Thank you," as apparently they sometimes did, they were indignant and demanded their gift back.

It seems naive, but is it? Doesn't everyone, really, expect something in return for a gift? If not the material equivalent then, at least, affection or loyalty or service or an acknowledgment of the giver's magnificence? And if we don't get any of these things, aren't *we* indignant? And wouldn't *we* take our gifts back if we could?

✸ *initiate* and *instigate*

To *initiate* is to start something. To *instigate* is to incite someone else to start something. Instigate, quite understandably, has picked up a slightly sneaky connotation.

✸ Can a good thing be *insinuated?*

A WOMAN who had said that we "should insinuate good taste" later overheard her phrase quoted in derision. She asks, "Has the word come to express only the unpleasant or the downright bad? Can nothing good be *insinuated?*"

To insinuate comes from a Latin word meaning "to bring something in imperceptibly, by windings and turnings." Now good things may be so brought in. Good taste, in particular, is best so brought in, so slyly and artfully suggested, so cunningly introduced, that the hearer thinks the ideas his own. Dryden says that Horace "insinuates virtue." Isak Dinesen speaks of a mother as "insinuating and enticing" in her manner of leading her daughter to honor and courage. *Insinuation* was often used as a synonym for "subtly charming."

But all indirection is suspect and *insinuation* (like *artful*) has acquired a strong suggestion of slyness and evil purpose. So much so that in general use now it means cunning or underhand action for a bad purpose. To *make insinuations* always implies something bad. *An insinuation* usually means an evil suggestion. Perhaps the word has been affected by an association of the sound of *sin* or *insidious*.

The basic meaning is still current, however, and it is certainly not incorrect to use it in a favorable sense. The correspondent's annoying experience of being snickered at, however, stresses one of the basic realities of language: it's a two-way business. It's not enough that we know what we're saying; we have to wonder what the listener thinks we're saying. If we insist on using words in their less common senses, we will be admired by the knowing and despised by the ignorant. We must, therefore, pick our company or our words.

※ the *s* in *island*

ONE OF the more admirable actions of the English-speaking peoples is their stubborn refusal to pronounce the *s* in *island*. It doesn't belong there. For 900 years the word was properly *iland*. Then some overlearned pedant decided that it was a misspelling of *isle-land* and stuck the *s* in. By 1700 his bumptious ignorance had overawed the feeble minority that knew how to write and they all put it in when writing. But the common people, happily unable to read or write and determined not to be bullied by self-appointed oracles, kept right on pronouncing the old word in the old way. But now that everybody has learned to read, they'll probably be bluffed into pronouncing it one of these timid days.

※ *italics* in the Bible

EVERY reader of the King James or Authorized Version of the Bible should be warned that it has a punctuation of its own. One detail, in particular, can be very misleading: italics in the King James Version are not, as with us, for emphasis but to indicate that the italicized words were inserted by the translators in order to make the meaning clearer. The text was, properly, so sacred to them that they felt it impious to add a single word without making it plain that the word was not a part of the original.

Some extraordinary misreadings are possible if the reader is not aware of this fact. Thus *I Kings* xiii:27 reads: "And he spake to his sons, saying, Saddle me the ass. And they saddled *him*." Now to give *him* in this sentence the emphasis that the italics would suggest to a modern reader is to distort the meaning ludicrously. All its italicization means is that it was not in the original text and was supplied by the translators to round out the sentence.

Nor is it merely a matter of whimsical absurdity, like the above. The whole question of who killed Goliath, for example, David or Elhanan, is dependent entirely on the adroit use of italics. Compare *I Samuel* xvii:49-51 with *II Samuel* xxi:19.

✷ an *ivory tower*

THE EXPRESSION *tower of ivory* first appeared in the *Canticles* or *Song of Solomon* (vii:4) where the beloved is told, "Thy neck is as a tower of ivory." In one of the most popular of all prayers to the Virgin Mary, in the Litany of Loretto, Mary is called "thou Ivory Tower" where the phrase refers to her immaculate inviolability.

The modern use of the expression to signify the lofty detachment of pure theorizing comes from the nineteenth-century French critic Sainte Beuve who in a certain passage (1837) praised Victor Hugo as a feudal knight armed for battle but complained that Alfred de Vigny (a romantic poet who laid great stress on "the inner life") had retreated, before the heat of the day, into his *ivory tower*.

The phrase, probably more echoed than drawn directly from the litany, was a fine poetic image. *Tower* suggested the detached observer, lofty, smug, unassailable, withdrawn from the dust and heat of the battle, feeling "above it all." Ivory added connotations of coolness, luxury, and elegance, and implied an almost voluptuous concern with smoothness and form.

Like many good phrases, it has been overworked. It was even used, a year or two ago, in a popular song ("Come down, come down from your Ivoree tower"), in which occupation of the ivory tower meant nothing more than a reluctance to respond instantly to a caterwauling lover's frenetic demands.

✷ the profane *jackass*

THE *Louisville Courier Journal* ran a story (Feb. 19, 1958) stating that a teacher in Knoxville, Tennessee, had called a student "a jackass." The teacher's dismissal was demanded on the ground that she had used profanity. The sender of the clipping from the *Courier Journal* wanted to know if *jackass* was profanity.

The word *profane* means "before or outside of the temple." Rites and words which were sacred in the temple were profane outside of the temple. In one sense anything is profane which is not sacred, as we speak of profane virtues and profane history when we mean nonreligious virtues or nonreligious history.

In the widest interpretation of its commonly accepted meaning *profanity* is the use of sacred things (especially sacred names) in an irreverent or blasphemous manner.

Now neither a *jackass* nor a student is a sacred object. Which is more insulted by the comparison depends on the particular student and the particular jackass, but the comparison can hardly be regarded as profanity. The teacher may have been insulting, abusive, or bad mannered. Or she may have been brilliantly accurate. But in this particular, she wasn't profane.

✻ *just* and *fair*

IN THEIR common meaning of "being free from improper pressures and considerations in making a decision," *fair* and *just* have different shades of implication which, in practical application, may be far-reaching.

Just is a stern word. We think of a just man as equitable and impartial but we also think of him as implacable. One is just who without fear or favor, and firmly restraining all personal inclinations, makes a decision which adheres strictly to the rules or terms that have been established. In Shakespeare's *Merchant of Venice*, Portia was a just judge when she ruled that Shylock was entitled to his pound of flesh.

Fair is a gentler, milder word. Fairness is justice tempered with every conceivable concession to every reasonable claim of one's opponent—concessions made by one with the power to deny them but who has generously taken no advantage of his power. Despite his cruel intent, we all feel that Shylock was not treated fairly.

Just is usually applied to grim things: a just rebuke, a just punishment. *Fair* is usually applied to pleasing things: a fair reward, a fair division of the spoils, a fair exchange.

✻ "the *Kaffee Klatsch*" is "the coffee break"

A HOUSEWIFE voices a complaint. Why is it, she asks, that when business people stop working and drink coffee, it's called "a coffee break," whereas when housewives do the same it's called "a coffee clatch."

I think she has a point.

Klatsch is a German word. It means "a gossip, a good gabfest." It assumes that the talk will be of a personal nature and interestingly spiced with malice and enriched with scandal (children *klatschen* when they "tell on" other children to the teacher). It's a humorous word and a frank and honest word.

Break, in this context, is, on the other hand, a sly word. It suggests an unavoidable interruption. It implies that unrelieved continuance of toil would have been unendurable; the work *had* to be interrupted. If this caffeinated interval were called, for instance, a "coffee dawdle" or a "coffee escape" or a "coffee loaf"— any one of which would merely parallel the frankness of *Kaffee Klatsch*—its true nature would be more accurately described.

Kaffee Klatsch, however spelled, has a simple, good-humored heartiness about it. *Coffee break* has a whine of self-pity about it, muttered mutiny at the water cooler.

✱ kidnap

THE WORD for a young goat, *kid*, was used in thieves' lingo as early as the sixteenth century to mean a child and it is interesting that although it has been in common use now for almost 400 years, it has never been accepted as standard. It is still slang or colloquial. Perhaps the continuance of the animal meaning prevented its acceptance in serious use.

The second part of the word *kidnap* is an obsolete form of *nab*, "to grab hold of." It, too, was thieves' lingo, meaning "to steal." In a dictionary of underworld jargon published in 1700 "to nab a wiper" was defined as "to steal a handkerchief."

✱ pronunciation of kiln

MOST people who work professionally with kilns call them "kills." That is, they omit the final *-n* in their pronunciation.

This is startling to the layman, however accustomed he may be to the vagaries of English spelling and pronunciation. But that's probably because few layman ever have an occasion to say *kiln*. We omit some other final *n*'s, but since we have left them silent so long that we don't include them in the spelling any more, we're not aware that they're no longer there. *Ell*, in "Give him an inch and he'll take an ell," was formerly *elln*. And our common word *mill* (from the Latin *molina*—as kiln is from the Latin *culina*, "cookstove") had a final *n* up until a few centuries ago. Caxton spelled the plural *myllenes*.

It is just one more reminder of how natural slurring and other speech processes are and how cheerfully we accept those we don't know enough to recognize and how absurd is most indignation at the language for going right on the same paths it has always traveled.

❋ kittycornered

Kittycornered is a playful variation of cattycornered. By using the diminutive of *cat*, the word may intend to suggest that the offense was slighter, the risk less great, or the jaywalker so young as to be irresponsible.

Cattycornered is a mispronunciation of *catercornered* and the first element, *cater-*, is a development (or a further mispronunciation if you will) of the Latin *quatre*, meaning "four." *Cater*, in this sense, was used as a verb, meaning to place or set rhomboidally, or to cut, move, or go diagonally. So that *catercornered* meant cutting diagonally from corner to corner. The word was dialectal and even now, however pronounced or spelled, is colloquial; no one would use it in a formal document.

There are other combinations: *catercross, caterways,* and *caterwise*. But they have fallen into disuse.

❋ klang association

THERE is a mental quirk that affects our use of words. It is called *klang association*—or the hearing of one word in the sound of another and being affected in our use and understanding of words by these irrelevant echoes.

Thus *fakir* which is derived from an Arabic word meaning "poor" suggests an impostor because in it we hear the word *fake*, though the two words are unrelated. The meaning of *belfry* has been shaped by the wholly accidental sound of *bell*; originally a belfry had nothing to do with bells but was a defensive tower. The persistent misspelling of *sacrilegious* is undoubtedly due to the feeling that *religious* is in the word someway. People of delicate racial sensitivities would hesitate to use the word *niggardly* if a Negro were present and few ministers stress in their sermons that the Ark of the Covenant was made of shittim wood. When Senator Lehman (in 1951) referred on the floor of the United States Senate to Senator McCarthy's conduct as "dastardly," a fellow senator rose at once to protest and Senator Lehman changed the adjective to "cowardly." Dr. C. S. Blumel relates that a schizophrenic patient under his care when charged before a committee of doctors with a fault—by a doctor he particularly disliked—said: "I grant the allegation, but I defy the alligator."

✷ Should we say "He *kneeled* down" or "He *knelt* down"?

There are a number of verbs in English that change a long *ee* sound in the present-tense form to a short *e* and add a *d* or a *t* sound to form the past (*sleep–slept, creep–crept, weep–wept*, etc.)

In almost all of these the short *e* and the *-t* are now required. There are, however, four verbs in common use today which are exceptions to this rule. They are *dream, kneel, lean,* and *leap*. These four may form the past tense by either keeping the long *ee* sound and adding *-ed* or by shortening the sound to *ĕ* and adding *–t* (i.e., *dreamed* or *dreamt, kneeled* or *knelt, leaned* or *leant, leaped* or *leapt*).

Where both forms are permissible, the *-ed* form is generally preferred in the United States and the *t* forms in Great Britain. *Leapt* as the past of *leap* and *leant* as the past of *lean* (pronounced "lept" and "lent") would sound a little strange to American ears.

Therefore we may say either "He kneeled down" or "He knelt down." The dictionaries give the preference to knelt but I think *kneeled* would sound more natural to most Americans.

✷ *knowing* and *knowledgeable*

The *knowing* are shrewd and sharp, secret and cunning in their wisdom, hence to be resented and feared.

The *knowledgeable* are perceptive, intelligent, discriminating. They buy the right kind of whiskey, know the proper night-clubs, dress in easy taste, are psychiatrically literate. They are urbane, urban, and suburban.

Knowledgeable is enjoying a vogue. A remarkable thing about it is that although it is generally labeled "colloquial" in the dictionaries, it is used only by the educated.

* kudos

Kudos is merely our form of the Greek *kýdos*, "glory." It entered English as a piece of university slang and is now used almost exclusively to designate honorary degrees at colleges and applause at athletic events. Sometimes one sees a false singular, *kudo* ("Chicago's Ben Heineman . . . gets a well-deserved kudo in the current *Time*"). From this it is simply best to avert the gaze.

If you want to be very highfalutin (and in using such a word you might as well be), you will pronounce it *kyoo' doss*. However, if you prefer your Greek with a homely, folksy flavor, you are within your rights if you pronounce it *koo' doss*. It's downright vulgar, though, to say *koo' dose*.

It's an excellent word not to use at all. To paraphrase Mark Twain, a man could start building a very expressive vocabulary just by leaving *kudos* out.

* lagniappe

Lagniappe (pronounced either *lan yap'* or *lan' yap*) is a Louisiana-French version of the American-Spanish *la napa*, meaning "the gift." It is properly applied to something given with a purchase to a customer over and beyond what was bargained for. Lollipops to children in barber shops are true lagniappe. Tips are not.

* land on the moon

"CAN A ROCKET *land* on the moon?" a youthful astro-linguist wants to know. "We don't know that there *is* any *land* there!"

To land was originally "to put ashore, to put on land from the sea." But it was quite natural for it to mean to touch land

("The ship landed at New York") or to come to rest on land ("The plane landed at LaGuardia airport"). Even though it's paradoxical, no one who speaks English would be puzzled if he were told that a seaplane landed on the water.

One of the derivative meanings of *to land* is "to come to rest on" ("He landed on his feet"). It doesn't matter what the moving object comes to rest on. So far as grammar is concerned, a rocket could *land* on the moon if it were made of green cheese.

※ the gay *lark*

IT CERTAINLY seems natural that a spree should be called a *lark*, after the bird. The lark is a gay bird and the excitement of its song and the vigor of its soaring may have influenced the word. But in its origins it is a wholly different word, deriving from a Saxon word meaning "sport." Like many other words, it disappeared from standard usage but continued in the dialects of northern England. In the sense of a frolic, *lark* was a common term among North Country jockeys and from them it came back into upper-class smart chat at the beginning of the nineteenth century. Byron used it in a letter (in 1813) and called it a poetic term of "flash dialect." By "flash" he meant gaudy, showy, smart, in-the-vogue.

The Saxon word (*lac*), by the way, had no *r* in it. It's the same word as the second element of *wedlock*.

※ Is *latch on to* acceptable English?

Latch on to is listed as slang, but *latch*, meaning "to take hold of, to grasp, to seize," is a good old English word ("I have words/That would be howl'd out in the desert air,/ Where hearing should not latch them"—*Macbeth* IV.iii.194). By itself *latch* seems to have become obsolete, but *latch on to* is heard everywhere every day in the United States.

It must have fallen out of standard use but been retained in a dialect, possibly Northern English or Lowland Scots. Some group in whose vocabulary it was an accepted word brought it over here and in some manner it came back into general use. But it's been away a long time and most people feel there's something a little funny about it and hesitate to use it in formal writing. We are beginning, though, to see it even there ("Examples are always dangerous, as they invite one to latch on to conditions peculiar to the case in point . . ."—Charles Siepman, *TV and Our School Crisis*, p. 124. "There was a great stirring of trade within the realm, and more and more of the lowly found profitable means of latching on to coin . . ."—R. W. Ferguson, *Naked to Mine Enemies*, p. 49).

✳ the *late Mr. X*

THE WORD *late* once meant "slow, sluggish." And since if you were slow enough you were certain not to be on time, it came to mean "tardy." This meaning we still keep ("Hurry up, or we'll be late!").

Then it came to mean an advanced period of the day—a time at which the slow and sluggish always seem to find themselves, with their work unfinished.

Finally it reached its ultimate (still expressed in the adverb *lately*) meaning of something which existed up until a little while ago but now doesn't exist at all. That is tardiness carried to perfection!

This meaning, taken over by the adjective *late* from the adverb *lately*, got attached to persons recently deceased. It was probably a euphemism, an attempt to say an unpleasant thing as pleasantly as possible. There is a dignity in "the late Mr. X" that is lacking from a reference to his corpse as "lately Mr. X." Then *late* in this sense was a useful word. The dead live on in affairs for a brief while and there must be some way of alluding to them and acknowledging their status.

"Widow of the late Mr. X" is a redundancy. She wouldn't be a widow if he weren't late.

✳ Why *lazy Susan?*

A REVOLVING stand in the center of a table, by "handing" pickles, muffins, and such like around the table, takes the place of a maid. And *Susan* was once a general name for a maid, as "George" used to be for Pullman porters ("Brisk Susan whips her linen from the rope"—Swift, *Description of a City Shower*).

The *lazy* part of the term could apply to the "maid," implying that she's too lazy to get up and hand the food around, or to the people at the table, implying it's a "Susan" for folks too lazy to pass things.

The homely nature of the term leads one to assume that it must be old. There's a colonial flavor to it. But the earliest quotation given in Mathews' *Dictionary of Americanisms* is 1934 and none of the older dictionaries list it. Nor is it in the *American Dialect Dictionary*. All of which suggests that it may have been the creation of some mute, inglorious Milton of a copy writer. The present Duke of Bedford in his autobiography (*A Silver-Plated Spoon*, p. 22) describes just such a device which his grandfather used forty years ago, but it was called "a dumb waiter."

Lazy Susan has been extended to a revolving hatrack and a small sewing kit is dispensed under the name of *Sewing Susan*.

✻ What is a *lead-pipe cinch*?

THE *cinch* part's a cinch. It comes from the Spanish word for a saddle girth. When the *cinch* was well fastened, it held securely. Hence a cinch, in slang, was something made sure of, and a sure thing, by a natural psychological extension, became an easy thing. For at least sixty years *a cinch* has been something sure and easy.

But what's a *lead-pipe cinch*? Some have suggested that it means a cinch made double sure by being made out of lead pipe. But equestrians and plumbers both reject this as ludicrous, absurd from the viewpoint of either cinches or lead pipes.

A more likely explanation is that a short section of lead pipe made an effective blackjack. For disposing of an unwary victim, it was a cinch. Furthermore, a man caught carrying a piece of lead pipe could not be arrested for carrying weapons.

✻ Should we be leery of *leery*?

Leery is not standard; it shouldn't be used in a formal speech or document. But it is used so widely and so naturally, with almost none of the archness that so frequently marks the use of slang, that I would classify it as colloquial.

Leer was an old English word for "cheek." Tears ran down leers for six hundred years, easing the task of poets as much as *moon* and *June* in our own day. Our modern verb *to leer* means to glance over the cheek and a leer was a sidelong glance. It once conveyed malice but has become restricted to conveying only lasciviousness.

A *leery* person is one who is continually glancing sidelong with apprehension. He is suspicious, uneasy, alarmed, but afraid to face directly whatever it is that he's scared of.

✻ What's *left*?

To say that someone left, meaning that he departed, when the basic meaning of the verb *to leave* is "to allow to remain," does seem a little absurd at first thought. But it's really a matter of point of view. The person who has gone has left the person speaking behind, and the person speaking says, "He left [me here]" or "He left the house [to remain here, while he went elsewhere]". It's a very old idiom, being recorded as early as 1225 and used continuously ever since.

Leave in the sense of "permission" ("Do I have your leave to leave?") is an entirely different word. It is related to *lief*, meaning "dear" ("I'd just as lief") and, ultimately, to the word *love*. The idea was that the approval resulted from pleasure.

✻ Why are radicals referred to as *left-wing*?

In 1789 France's financial condition was so desperate (in part because of her assistance to us in our Revolution) that the king convened the States General, a deliberative and advisory body that had not met for 175 years. It consisted of three "estates": the Clergy, the Nobility, and the Third Estate or common people. In their seating, the nobles took the position of honor on the President's right and the Third Estate sat on his left.

The members of the Third Estate wanted sweeping reforms. They wanted to get at the root of the country's troubles. They were *radicals* (Latin *radix*, "root") and they soon precipitated the French Revolution.

The seating had at first been a matter of ceremony, but it became a political symbol and as, through the first half of the nineteenth century, other revolutions gained representation for other peoples, their representatives always sat on the speaker's left, to mark their sympathy with and kinship to the famous Third Estate.

Left-wing seems to be an adoption of military terminology, as an assertion or a charge that the political conflict was class war.

✷ *Let's* wash the dishes and *Let us* wash the dishes

ALTHOUGH there is no grammatical reason for it, although but for a slight elision both sentences have the same words with the same meanings in the same order and both would parse exactly alike, usage has established a clear distinction between "Let's wash the dishes" and "Let us wash the dishes."

If there is a slight emphasis on *us*, "Let us wash the dishes" is a request to the person spoken to to allow the speaker and a third person to wash the dishes. Whereas "Let's wash the dishes" is a suggestion that the speaker and the person spoken to should wash the dishes.

So that if you are the person spoken to, the difference between the two sentences is whether you are to help with the dishes or not. And if you don't like to wash dishes, that's a lot of difference.

The two sentences remind us that speech, with its elisions and infinite variations of emphasis, is incredibly more fluent and subtle than writing. It reminds us also that there are many situations in the language which formal grammar simply cannot explain.

✷ *lighted* or *lit*

A DETERMINED mother writes that whenever her wayward children had used *lit* instead of *lighted*, she had "corrected" them. Her fourteen-year-old son, however, plainly a lad of mettle, had shown her *lit* where she would have insisted on *lighted* in the magazine *Life*. Broken and bewildered, she stretches lame hands and gropes for guidance: "Is *lit* now acceptable in place of *lighted*?"

Let her drain the bitter chalice to the last drop: it is not only now acceptable but always has been. From the beginnings of the language, ages before Henry Luce said "Let there be *Life!*" the two forms *lit* and *lighted* have been interchangeable.

About two hundred years ago some self-appointed oracle decided that *lit* was "low and vulgar" and millions, of whom this poor mother is one, have become afraid of it. Maybe the original worrier thought that since *fit* was an improper past for fight (though it was in common use then among the uneducated), *lit* belonged in the same class. But it doesn't.

Lighted seems much commoner when the past participle is used as an adjective. It would seem more "natural" to most Americans to refer to "a lighted match" rather than to "a lit match." But Christmas trees are more often "lit up" than "lighted up."

Eager faces seem divided between being "lighted up" and "lit up." A drunk, however, is invariably *lit*.

* the origin of *limerick?*

Limerick, as the name for a special kind of five-line humorous verse, is a mystery word, the more mysterious in that it is a recent addition to the language, its earliest recorded use being 1898.

The conjecture that has most approval is that the making up of humorous (and often indecent) rimes in this form and meter was once a game at convivial and ribald parties. Each man present was required, in his turn, to extemporize one of these short verses and between efforts—to give the next man time to drink and think—a chorus was sung which contained the words "Will you come up to Limerick?"

The invention—or at least the perfection—of the form is attributed to Edward Lear in his *Book of Nonsense* (1846), but he was dead long before the word *limerick* was applied to the form. In the ravings of Mad Tom in Shakespeare's *King Lear* (about 1605) there is an imperfect limerick.

* *literature* or *"advertiture"*

AN INNOVATOR writes: "I don't like calling advertising matter *literature*. I've been using a new word—*advertiture*. Is this good or bad?"

He is assuming that *literature* has only one legitimate meaning. But it has many. Most dictionaries list seven or eight. They all stem from the Latin word for *letter* and, apparently, anything that employs the letters of the alphabet has a just claim to be called *literature*. Among the definitions all dictionaries include "printed matter used for advertising."

Advertiture (which, by the way, relies on an echo of *literature* for its meaning) is, at the moment at least, a bad word because it fails in the fundamental obligation of a word: it isn't understood by anyone but its author. And one simply can't use words that have meaning only for himself. Schizophrenics do it all the time, to be sure, but we lock them up.

Of course, if the innovator has an enormous fortune and his feeling about the matter is strong enough, he might, by public relations, the use of radio and TV spots, advertiture and so on, persuade the public to use his word. Then it would be all right. But it seems easier to use the language other people use.

※ **Was a *livery stable* a place to which horses were delivered?**

It wasn't the horse that was delivered to the stable, but the provender which was delivered to the horse at the stable. *Livery* is related to *delivery*. It originally meant food and clothing delivered by the master to his servants as an agreed part of their wages. Hence a footman's or a chauffeur's livery was the suit delivered to him. The horse was as much a part of the great household as the groom—and far likelier to be better treated. *Livery* also meant an allowance of provender for horses. A horse *at livery* was kept for the owner and fed and groomed at a fixed charge. This is the meaning of the word in *livery* stable which, but for this one use, is now obsolete.

✱ livid and vivid

Livid and *vivid* are almost exact opposites, yet they are frequently confused.

Livid is a particularly gruesome shade of blue, a leaden gray tinged with blue. It is the color of corpses, bruises, and other ghastly things. Etymologically it is related to *lavender* and its synonyms are *pale, wan, ashen*.

Vivid means vigorous, intense, brilliant, bright-colored. It comes from the Latin word meaning "to live." It is related to *vivacious,* and its synonyms are *clear, lucid, bright*.

The confusion is due primarily to the similarity of their sound. But it may also be due in part to the fact that *livid* is now used chiefly in the worn phrase "livid with anger." In mild, or comparatively mild, anger people often get red in the face. Hence their color is, for the moment, more vivid. Furthermore, *they* are more vivid—more intense, more violent, more picturesque. But in extreme anger, as in extreme fear, the complexion may become *livid,* or bluish pale.

✱ "*loan* me your ears"

The use of *loan* as a verb is condemned by the British as an Americanism and many intimidated Americans who assume that in linguistic matters the British must always be right have foolishly and ignorantly repeated the condemnation.

But *loan* is a fully respectable verb and has been in use for almost eight hundred years. In 1542 it was used in an Act of Parliament. The early settlers brought the form to America and continued to use it after the people in England had dropped it and adopted *lend*. A British visitor to the United States in the last century noted that "the lower classes" here used *loan* instead of *lend*. This probably meant that ordinary people used it but that the wealthy and traveled minority (which then aped British ways assiduously) had heard and taken over the British *lend*. But now that the use of British English has waned as an upper-class ideal in the United States, ordinary speech has asserted itself and one hears *loan* as a verb in America today from all classes, especially when used in regard to money.

Even without the historical justification, of course, it would be acceptable. One hundred and eighty million people have the right to speak as they choose.

Lend is quite all right too. But it no longer has even a touch of superiority.

✷ lock, stock, and barrel

THE EXPRESSION refers to a gun. The *stock* is the wooden or metal piece to which the barrel and the firing mechanism are attached. The b*arrel* is the tube through which the bullet is discharged. And the *lock* is the mechanism by means of which the charge is exploded. There are many kinds of these—flintlocks, matchlocks, firelocks—but they are all locks.

The full phrase *lock, stock, and barrel,* meaning "the entirely of something" came into general use through Sir Walter Scott, who was a sportsman as well as a student of language, a poet, a novelist, and a lawyer. The expression occurs—ascribed to Scott himself—in his son-in-law's life of him. It seems to have been an allusion (echoed in a passage in Carlyle) to a joke about a highlander's gun that needed only a lock, a stock, and a barrel to be in good shape.

✷ lodge a complaint

To lodge was, originally, "to place in tents, to provide with a habitation." From this it developed the meaning of putting in a specified place of custody or security. When something is *lodged* somewhere—as a kite in a tree, for instance— it is fixed there securely and will be difficult to remove or *dislodge.*

From this meaning it acquired a special legal meaning of depositing in court, as a formal statement, with some appointed official. This was far more certain than merely placing or making a complaint. It has something of the same relation to merely complaining that making an affidavit has to merely saying or that swearing out a warrant has to merely protesting. And it is this use that we employ in the common expression.

✷ at loggerheads

FOR AT least four hundred years *loggerhead* has meant a thick-headed, stupid person, a blockhead. For three hundred years the word has had the additional acquired meaning of an iron instrument with a long handle and a ball or bulb at the end. The bulb was heated in the fire and when hot was used for melting pitch. Such a device, hot or cold, would be a murderous instrument in the hands of an angry man.

At *loggerheads,* meaning "engaged in a quarrel," was originally "gone to loggerheads" (or, as we would say, "Taken to loggerheads"). The suggestion was that the animosity had reached such a pitch that the opponents were belaboring each other with these devices. However, there is still in the expression an echo of the earlier idea of stupidity. One feels that when men are said to be at loggerheads, the excess of their resentment has made them stupid. They are block-headed, impervious to reason or compromise.

✤ "look and see"

AMONG our verbal vigilantes none are more active than those who have devoted their lives to ferreting out all unnecessary repetitions in speech. One can only imagine the splendid economy, the pithy brevity, and terse laconism of their own communications.

Among the phrases which they have under suspicious scrutiny is the common *Look and see.* "When a person looks," one of the brotherhood demands, "can it not be taken for granted that he will also see?"

I suspect him of being a bachelor, someone who has never sent a child to look for something and had him report back that he couldn't find it, even though it was out in the open and as plain as day.

To look is to fix the eyes upon something or to turn them in some direction in order to see ("Don't look now"; "Look for the silver lining"). It implies a desire to see but not necessarily the fulfilment of that desire ("I did look for it, Mother, but I can't see it anywhere!") *See* may be used to indicate little more than a use of the organs of vision ("He can't see with his hat pulled down over his eyes"). But more commonly it implies a recognition or appreciation of what is before one's eyes ("None so blind as they who will not see"). *Look* bears to this use of *see* (and this is the use in *Look and see*) the same relation that *listen* bears to *hear:* in each case the first term suggests a preparation for the second.

✷ *loose* and *unloose*

The verbs *to loose* and *to loosen* are derived from the adjective *loose*. They overlap in one of their meanings but have acquired other meanings where they cannot be used interchangeably and are now listed in all dictionaries as separate words.

To *loose* now means "to set entirely free," the meaning more commonly expressed in *to let loose* or *to set loose*. *Loosen* used also to mean this but today it means "to make looser" or "to free from binding." One can loosen the rope that binds a tethered animal without loosing the animal. That the two words, once alike, have become different is shown by the fact that the opposite of *to loose* is *to bind* while the opposite of *to loosen* is *to tighten*.

Logically *unloose* ought to mean "tie up." The reason it does not is that when a negative meaning is already in a word (as the negative of *tie up* is already in *to loose*), the prefix *un-* is merely an intensive.

✷ the ludicrous *lude*

We have *preludes* and *interludes* and *postludes* but no *ludes*.

Ludus was the Latin word for "a play or diversion." An *interlude* was, originally, a light and humorous short performance introduced between the acts of the mystery and morality plays. When the Duke of Albany, in *King Lear* (V.iii) arrests Edmund on the charge of treason and says with caustic wit to Regan that he must forbid her to marry Edmund because his own wife, Goneril, is already "subcontracted" to him, Goneril sneers "An interlude!" By which she says, in effect: "Ah, amid all this tedious moralizing my witty husband is going to divert us with one of his famous comic performances!" It is a magnificent piece of dramatic condensation, one of the last glimpses we have into her hate-tortured heart.

By the seventeenth century *interlude* had come to have its modern meaning of mere interval between the acts of a play,

Prelude is younger than interlude by several centuries, but it still goes back to at least the sixteenth century, when it meant a preliminary performance or action. *Postlude* is very recent, being hardly more than a hundred years old.

There was once a *lude*, "a play," but it was rarely used and soon died out, though *ludo* remains as the name of a game and *ludicrous* means "amusing." And we once had *ludent*, "a player," and *ludible*, "playful," and *ludibry*, "derision," and *ludificate* and *ludify* and *ludicrosity*—and several other words based on *lude*. It's hard to feel that their disappearance was a great loss.

※ *lukewarm* Luke

THE FIRST syllable of lukewarm has nothing to do with the given name *Luke*. *Lukewarm* is one of those words in which there is a hidden repetition, because *luke* (or *lewk*) meant "tepid." This is made clear in Wyclif's translation (1388) of *Revelation* iii:16: "Thou art lewk, neither cold, neither hot." The Authorized Version (1611) and the Revised Standard Version (1957) have "lukewarm."

Luke, in this sense, persisted alongside of *lukewarm* down into the nineteenth century. Sam Weller in Dickens' *Pickwick Papers* (1837) asks for "nine penn'orth o' brandy and water luke."

※ *mad* and *angry*

Mad is certainly the common everyday, spoken American word for *angry*. Except for the fact that it has been a target of special attack by purists, it would have been standard long ago. If an American says "I'm mad," no other American assumes that he is making a public declaration of mental incompetence.

Mad in the sense of *insane* has had a revival in American speech, but it's been a borrowing from the British and has loud overtones of shrill amusement ("He's mad!, The man is utterly mad!"—*Mad Comics*). It's forced and a little affected.

The use of *mad* to mean *angry* is a natural extension, for the similarity of anger and insanity has always been perceived. It is not a corruption. Hotspur, in Shakespeare's *I Henry IV*, says that the haughty demands of a mincing, perfumed dandy made him "mad," and the passage leaves no doubt that by "mad" he meant angry, just as any modern American would. And St. Paul told Agrippa (*Acts* xxvi:11) that before he was converted he hated Christians and was "exceedingly mad against them" and persecuted them. In the Revised Standard Version this is changed to "raging in fury against them."

One cannot use *mad* this way any more in a formal document. The attacks on it have made us too self-conscious. But all people, educated and uneducated, use it in their everyday speech.

❋ "mad as a hatter"

EXCEPT for the strain that contemplating some women's hats must put him under, a hatter probably isn't any madder today than anyone else. But he used to be, or at least he seemed to be. Hatters were poisoned by the mercurial compounds formerly used in making hats. Their gait was lurching, their speech often incoherent, and their minds confused. Tenniel's famous drawing of the Mad Hatter in *Alice in Wonderland* is said to be a good clinical representation of the appearance of these unfortunate men. Lewis Carroll didn't invent the *Mad Hatter*. He simply included him in *Alice*, along with the March Hare, because he was proverbially mad. The expression "as mad as a hatter" antedates *Alice in Wonderland* by at least thirty years.

❋ magazine

Magazine was originally an Arabic word meaning "a storehouse." It was brought into English in the late sixteenth century by the merchant adventurers who had journeyed to Turkey. It could designate a storehouse of anything. Ben Jonson spoke of a certain woman as "a magazine of bliss." Well into the nineteenth century what we call *department stores* were called *magazines*.

One of the special applications of the word was to a military storehouse. But it included stores of every kind. Those that stored only gunpower—and, naturally, they were kept apart from the others—were called *powder magazines*. Military terminology, by the way, like ecclesiastical terminology, is very conservative and will hold a meaning centuries after it has been abandoned elsewhere.

The application of *magazine* to a periodical publication (to indicate that it was a storehouse of essays, stories, poems, etc.), now the most common meaning of the word, took place in the eighteenth century when *The Gentleman's Magazine* first appeared (1731).

✷ the *main* thing

ONE OF the older meanings of the word *main* was "physical strength, force, power." Several hundred years ago writers spoke of a hero's "mighty main" and an old man, lamenting the loss of his vigor, could say "marred is my main." But this meaning is now obsolete except in the expression "might and main."

One of the interesting things about the word is that it is related to the verb *may* whose basic meaning is to have power or might in the matter, to be physically able. A fourteenth-century encyclopedia says that the kite (a small hawk) "is a bird that may well with travel." By which it meant that the kite, though small, had the strength to fly great distances.

This is something to bear in mind when some amateur grammarian is laying down the law that *may* means "by permission" and *can* means "ability to do."

✷ Just what do we mean by *many happy returns?*

WE ARE expressing the hope that the birthday of the person spoken to will recur many times and that each recurrence will be a happy time for him. In other words, we are wishing him a long and happy life.

The phrase has become fixed with us solely as a birthday greeting. Until recently, however, it was applied on other occasions. Dr. Johnson wished his friends many happy returns of New Year's Day and Charles Lamb wished his friends many happy returns of April Fools' Day.

Everyone has a recollection of having misapprehended the simplest phrase in his childrood and, being ashamed to ask the meaning of what appeared obvious to everyone else or so sure of a wrong meaning that no elucidation seemed necessary, having entertained the most ludicrous error for years. Birthday presents played a large part in my childhood speculations and I thought *returns* in this phrase meant profit, like "returns" on an investment. So I assumed that when you met a friend on his birthday you expressed the rational hope that he had received—or would receive—many valuable presents.

✳ What is a *mare's nest?*

"THE ONLY way I see out of our mares' nest," Mr. John Keats writes of the automobile and traffic problem (*The Insolent Chariots*, p. 217) "is for everyone to seriously ask himself, Why do I live where I live? What must be done about the shape of our towns, suburbs, and cities?"

I think Mr. Keats has mistaken a *mare's nest* (a curiously inept figure for the automobile problem) for the general untidy mess often called a *rat's nest* or, for some mysterious reason, a *hurrah's nest*.

"Finding a mare's nest" was an old humorous expression for making an illusory discovery, for finding out something that seemed extraordinarily important to the finder but was, actually, nonexistent. When simpletons laughed without cause, someone would ask them if they were laughing at the eggs in a *mare's nest*. Swift listed this as a cliché in 1738.

✳ margarine

THE WORD *margarine* is the product of two mistakes.

A French chemist, Chevreul, in the early nineteenth century thought that there were three fatty acids—oleic, stearic, and margaric. He gave the name *margaric* to the third because it had a pearly luster and *margarités* is the Greek word for "pearl" (whence, also, the name Margery and, ultimately, Marguerite, Margaret, and Marjory).

Subsequently another chemist showed that Chevreul's margaric acid was really a combination of the other two, but by that time the term *Margarin* had been applied to the glyceride of the assumed acid and this, through a misapplication of the chemical term, was transferred to the substitute for butter (which in some margarine advertisements is known, rather greasily, as "the high-priced spread"). In 1888, after trying *oleomargarine* and *butterine,* Parliament made *margarine* the legal name of the substance and it has stuck to our language and our bread ever since.

It is pronounced *marr' juh rin,* despite the vigorous efforts of some to force us to retain the hard *g*.

❋ **Since *matinee* is French for "morning," why do we use it to designate an afternoon performance?**

THE SIMPLEST answer is that part of the period which we call *afternoon* used to be morning.

The mystery lies, really, in the much stranger word *noon,* which comes from the Latin *nona,* meaning "nine." The day used to be computed from sunup (not, as we compute it, from midnight—what owls we have become!) and the ninth hour, noon, was three hours after midday. Anything before that was morning.

The heavy meal of the day was eaten (as until quite recently with us) at noon. In great houses minstrels, jugglers, and strolling players put on their performances in the great hall for the gentry just before this meal was served and, therefore, in the morning.

By the fourteenth century noon had shifted to midday, leaving various fragments of the morning (such as *matinees*) stranded in the afternoon. [There may be some confused recollection—or recollection of confusion—concerning this in the old nursery rime: "A diller, a dollar, a ten o'clock scholar,/What makes you come so soon?/You used to come at ten o'clock/But now you come at noon."]

✳ Mary *Maudlin*

Maudlin (*Maud* for short) is the old pronunciation of Magdalen (in which the g was not pronounced and the a was pronounced *aw,* as in *caught*). Magdalen College at Oxford is still pronounced "Maudlin."

In medieval illustrations and in the old folk plays based on the Bible stories, Mary Magdalen, the repentant sinner, was depicted as weeping ceaselessly for her sins. Her name, with its old pronunciation, got transferred to any weeping penitent and then, slightly colored by cynicism, became a term for weak sentimentality and excessive and lachrymose self-reproach. Since an excess of alcohol seems to stimulate these conditions in many, the word today is usually linked with drunkenness.

✳ How does the *mawkish* differ from the sentimental?

Mawkish originally meant "maggotty." Thence—as it well might—it came to mean nauseous, disgusting, loathsome. Until recently the word could be used literally. As late as 1876 there was a reference to "a mawkish wine."

But today the word can only be used figuratively and even then it must be confined to matters of taste.

If *sentiment* is feeling and *sentimentality* is affected or excessive feeling, *mawkishness* is one step further—sentimentality so strained and affected as to induce nausea.

As a poem of sentiment, one might instance Byron's "She Walks in Beauty like the Night." Of sentimentality, "Little Boy Blue." Of mawkishness, Joyce Kilmer's "Trees."

✳ *may* and *might*

May and *might* belong to a special small group of verbs called subjunctive or modal auxiliaries. They introduce a note of uncertainty into a statement. *Might* is grammatically the past tense of *may.* But neither ever refers to the past. Both always refer indefinitely to the present or the future. With these verbs the difference between what is called the present and the past

othing to do with time but with the amount of un-
[t]he past tense form expresses more uncertainty, more
[than] the present tense. *He may come* represents the event
[as possibl]e. *He might come* represents it as possible but not
[likely. Bo]th forms carry the idea of *perhaps,* but *might* carries
more [of i]t than *may.*

Note that this use of *may* and *might,* which is firmly established, has no foundation in either grammar or logic. It just is. That's the way usage has made it. Yet it is correct.

In asking a question *might* is more diffident than *may*. It expresses more doubt of a favorable answer and hence is more humble, more placating. If someone says "May I come in?" he is merely asking permission to be admitted. If he says "Might I come in?" he is suggesting that he doesn't expect to be allowed to come in and won't be surprised by a refusal. That doesn't mean, of course, that if he is told to stay out, he won't break the door down. Words serve to conceal as well as to express our true feelings and intentions.

✷ *Mayday!*

Mayday, the radio telephonic distress signal, seems unsuitably gay for a despairing cry in desperate circumstances until one learns that it isn't the English *May Day,* suggesting spring and gaiety, but the French *m'aidez,* meaning "Help me!" It was adopted as a distress signal for ships and aircraft as a part of International Radio Regulations. It has the same advantage that S.O.S. has in telegraphy: it is brief, yet clear and unmistakable.

✷ *"Me too!"*

Purists insist that where we assent to some statement by using the first personal pronoun, we must use the form of the pronoun that we would use if we were completing the sentence we are echoing. That is, if someone says "He saw her yesterday" and you say "Me too," you will mean "He saw me also." Whereas if you say "I too," you will mean "I also saw her."

If this distinction were always felt, then it would be wise to observe it. But it isn't felt. All uneducated people say "Me too" when they mean "I also saw her" and most educated people say it a great deal more often than they say "I too." Actually, only a few people say "I too" and then—probably—when they "think of it," when, that is, the idea of form or correctness or making an impression is more important than the answer or agreement to the previous statement.

"I too" just doesn't sound right, and euphony is as much a part of speech as theoretical grammar. There was a popular song some years ago in which the singer expressed his eager desire to do whatever his beloved did. Part of the chorus went: "Who? Who? Who? Who?/Me too!" Can anyone imagine it being "I too"?

❋ Just what are we when we are *mealy-mouthed?*

Mealy-mouthed may mean just what it seems to mean—that is, speaking so softly that the mouth seems to be filled with powdered wheat meal. (One has to emphasize *wheat* meal because to an American *meal* alone is more likely to mean *corn meal*. But corn meal was unknown when the phrase came into the language. And corn meal is coarse and gritty, wholly unsuited to the metaphor.)

Mealy-mouthed usually means something more than speaking softly or in a muffled mumble. The expression is used chiefly of someone who did not "speak up" when it was expected of him or who flattered or cajoled when he had led others to expect that he would be blunt or defiant. This has led many students of language to believe that the expression was originally *meal-mouthed* and that its first element was the Latin *mel* (French *miel*), "honey." So that a *mealy-mouthed* person was a *honey-mouthed* person ("sweet talk" is a Southern colloquialism for flattery and cajolery). And, of course, a mealy-mouthed person does have honeyed words for those he fears or fawns on. It's only the resentful bystander who scorns him as mealy-mouthed because he won't voice the bystander's own resentments.

❋ the meanness of *meaning*

"U<small>SE WORDS</small> correctly to mean what they mean and half the difficulties of life will be solved," roars Thunderbore

Absolute. But, alas, how do you do it? Words have many meanings, often contradictory meanings, and their meanings change. The most one can say is, "This is what these particular people thought this word meant in that context at that time." And, of course, some of them disagreed or the question would never have been raised.

If any words have an absolute meaning, terms for weights and measurements should, yet everyone knows that they do not. A gallon and a ton have one meaning in Detroit but may have an appreciably different meaning in Windsor, Ontario, less than a mile away. Nor is this difference solely international. The courts have held (*Smith v. Wilson, 3 Barn. & Adol. 728*) that in the rabbit industry the word *thousand* means 1200 and may in the shingle trade (*Bragg v. Bletz, 7. D.C. 105, 110*) mean only 800, while in the brick trade, under some circumstances a thousand "may be ascertained, not by actual count, but by the measurement of the walls in which the bricks are laid" (*Lowe v. Lehman, 15 Ohio St. 179, 182*).

In archery a *pair* of arrows is three and in stairsteps it may be a dozen. *Barrel* may mean fifty gallons by definition, but in the oil industry it normally means 40 gallons and in the beer industry it may mean 31. In scores of cases the courts have ruled that terms of measurement will be interpreted to mean whatever they are used in the particular trade to mean, regardless of what they mean in plain English. [See *run*.]

✶ Can a man be a *midwife?*

THE FIRST element of *midwife* is an Old English word meaning "with." It's the same word that appears in modern German as *mit*. *Wife* originally meant "woman." So that a *midwife* was one who was with a woman when she needed help. A man can be a midwife. The German is *Beifrau*, that is one who is "by the Frau."

An *obstetrician* sounds more important, and will probably cost $100 more than a midwife. But there's no linguistic gain; it's the same word in another language. *Obstetrician* comes from a Latin word meaning "to stand by."

✻ "I don't *mind* if I do"

"I DO NOT permit my children to say 'I don't mind' doing this or that," a spartan mother writes, "nor would my mother permit any of us to say it."

Imagine a family that for two generations has had children willing to do things and has acknowledged its good fortune merely by suggesting that the agreeableness be expressed in other words! It takes the breath away, and the more so because "I don't mind" is perfectly good English.

As a verb, *mind* has grown by a natural extension to mean many things. It can mean "to remember" ("Do you mind how we used to . . . ?"); "to obey" ("You must mind your mother"); "to have the oversight of" ("We have a sitter minding the children"); "to heed" ("Mind your *p*'s and *q*'s"). It can also mean what the correspondent's dutiful children meant it to mean: "to object to." When someone says he doesn't mind doing something, he means "I am not so opposed to it that it bothers me in my mind." "If you don't mind" is often used as an elaborate or ironical substitute for "Please."

✻ *mixed metaphors*

A *mixed metaphor* is one whose several parts are incongruous. They have a common likeness but there are irreconcilable further aspects. Or a metaphor sound in itself is employed in an unsuitable context.

DIXIE HARD CORE EBBS IN INTEGRATION BATTLE, shouts a headline. But cores don't ebb and flow. "Moscow stokes up cold war," says a news story. Mr. Ed Murrow will travel abroad, we are told, "to refresh his perspective." The reader hears the rattle of the ice cubes on the Soviet shovel and feels the dew on Mr. Murrow's transit.

There is a peculiar kind of absurdity in metaphors that is caused by the inappropriateness of the figure's literal meaning in a context where its metaphorical meaning is all right. The application of the figure conflicts with its original sense. You can't, for instance, say that an association of dry cleaners will press their suit—meaning that they vigorously seek legal redress for some wrong—unless you intend to be funny. But I read that the police compelled a suspect to admit his identity by "confronting him with a bullet hole in his back." I read of a "king-sized tyrant" and of a frisky dog "feeling his oats," and I am told that "Rome is the Mecca of all good Catholics." "Dear Dr. Molner," an inquirer writes to a medical adviser, "Would you give your opinion on 'natural' childbirth? There seems to be a lot of misconception about it."

✻ modesty and prudery

Modesty is freedom from vanity or boastfulness, a becoming shyness, sobriety, and proper behavior. Proper behavior, especially in such matters as dress and deportment, consists of conformance to custom. The deportment, dress, and even speech of modest men and women of one age could very well seem immodest—or grossly indecent—to those of another age.

Prudery designates an exaggerated modesty, a self-conscious adherence to, even a flaunting of, propriety; a conformity to respectability so marked as to suggest affectation. *Prudery* is an unfriendly word, usually applied with contempt. Its adjective is *prudish*—though the closely related *prudent* is laudatory.

✻ What is a *mollycoddle*?

Molly is an affectionate diminutive of *Mary*. It became a general name for a girl and in some uses, as in "a gangster's *moll*," acquired a tinge of contempt. Among its contemptuous uses was its application to an effeminate boy.

To coddle is "to boil gently," hence to treat tenderly, to nurse or tend indulgently. Coddling differs from pampering in that one pampers the healthy but coddles the sickly.

Hence a *mollycoddle* is an effeminate, sickly boy who has been overindulged with tender care. It's a sneering term used by he-men of those who do not measure up to their standards. It came into use as an upper-class term in England in the middle of the nineteenth century, along with the spartan regime of outdoor sports, cold baths, open windows and underheated houses whereby such of the empire builders as survived lived in perpetual gooseflesh and self-laudation.

✷ "a *more perfect* knowledge"

No BASTION of linguistic purity has been more fiercely defended than the incomparable absolute. We are told, for instance, that we cannot say "more perfect" because if something is perfect neither it nor anything else can be more so.

Yet in *Acts* xxiv:22 we are told that Felix, the Procurator of Judaea, had a "more perfect knowledge" of certain matters than some other men, and the Preamble to the Constitution of the United States tells us that it was ordained and established by the people "in order to form a more perfect union." The termites have gotten to the Bible and in the Revised Standard Version Felix's knowledge has been woman's-club-chairman-Englished up to "rather more accurate." But the Constitution, up to the time of going to press, remains unbemerded by any such improvements.

It is true that there are certain concepts or qualities which do not admit of degrees, either more or less, such as *round, square, empty*. Theoretically, and logically, if something is round, nothing else can be rounder. If something is empty, nothing can be emptier. If something is straight, nothing can be straighter. And people who ride theories instead of listening to what other people say or noticing what they write, have had a debauch of snobbery out of this idea. Mr. Eric Partridge, for example, has drawn up a whole list of such words and solemnly tells us that we can't say something is *more essential* or *more obvious* or *more worthless* or *surer* than something else.

But the fact is, if one insists on dragging logic into it, that you can't logically go beyond the positive of any adjective. Nothing is blacker than black or whiter than white. Since this is absurd, it is plain that the comparative and the superlative do not represent higher degrees of the same quality but are forms used in making comparisons in respect to that quality and frequently represent very low degrees, as when we say that "the oldest child is only five." We continually compare individuals in respect to qualities which, logically, they cannot possess at all unless they possess them in perfect—and therefore equal—

degrees. All who speak the language, educated and uneducated alike, those who now speak it and those who spoke and wrote it in times past, said and have said *fuller* and *purer* and *surer* and *emptier* and speak and have spoken of "more equal share" and "a more perfect union" and "the most extreme position."

There are some words we do not use in making comparisons. We don't say *more double* or *more daily* or *more previous*. But no one argues about this, because no one ever hears it. When we begin to hear that we "can't do" this or that in speech, it usually means that we are doing it. And it often means that we have been doing it for the past five hundred years.

✻ "*more than one woman have changed her mind*"

A CORRESPONDENT poses a question which I happily pass on to those who try to make English grammar conform to logic. In the sentence "More than one woman has changed her mind," he points out, the subject is, by its own statement, plural. Yet not only is the verb singular but the "proper" plural verb ("More than one woman have changed her mind") doesn't sound right.

He's right on both assertions: the subject ("more than one") is avowedly more than one and yet the singular verb is demanded. It is demanded for the wholly illogical reason that the extremely singular *one* stands close to the verb. To be logical and "grammatical" and say "More than one woman have changed her mind" would simply be wrong. It would offend any ear attuned to English idiom. One has to be illogical and ungrammatical here, to follow custom in direct opposition to theory, in order to be right.

✻ "There is *more than one way to skin a cat*"

TO SAY "There is more than one way to skin a cat" is to state no more than is usually obvious—that there are other ways of going about whatever it is that has been undertaken, that the same ends may be accomplished by other means. It is ordinarily said when some course of action has failed, and it's hard to see what it says that a plain statement wouldn't say better. It's annoying, too, because it has an oracular sound and is often delivered with a knowing smirk, as though there were a deep meaning behind it, when, actually, it is neither profound nor mysterious.

The older form of the saying, however, made more sense. It was: "There are more ways of killing a cat than choking it with cream." Since cream is particularly unsuitable as a chokant and since cats love cream and grow fat on it, it was a humorous way of saying to someone that he had chosen an especially expensive, foolish, and unlikely way of going about whatever it was he hoped to accomplish.

※ *mosaic* and *Mosaic*

THERE ARE two words: *mosaic*, which means a design or picture made of small pieces of glass or stone, and *Mosaic*, which refers to the prophet Moses.

The first of these two words is connected with the muses. It came into English, through French, from Italian *mosaico*, which was a form of the Vulgar Latin *musaicum opus* (a "work of the muse" or, as we would say, a work of art). It has always meant just what it means now: a picture or decoration composed of small colored stones.

Since Moses's name is particularly connected with the ten commandments and since one of these forbids (by Jewish and Mohammedan interpretation at least) the making of any likeness of anything whatever, whether it be a thing of heaven, earth, or water, the preservation of the distinction between *Mosaic* and *mosaic* is obilgatory. Few capital letters have more significance than this *M*.

※ *mother(s)-in-law(s)*

COMPOUNDS made up of a noun, a preposition, and a second noun traditionally form the plural in English by making the first noun, which is the principal word, plural. This would make the plural of mother-in-law *mothers-in-law*—which many insist it should be.

And the rule is usually observed with words that are not often used in the plural, as *commanders-in-chief*. But although this is technically correct, it often sounds a little strained and overprecise—as in *courts martial, attorneys criminal,* and *Lieutenants-General.*

So that the plurals of familiar compounds are more often than not, in contemporary American usage, formed by putting the *s* at the end. This offends many people. Or at least it affords them an opportunity of seeming to be offended in order, one suspects, to demonstrate their greater sensitivity. But it is likely to become the standard form if only because it is regular and there is a strong tendency in English to replace all irregular plurals. It is hard to conceive of the most precise person asking for two "whiskeys-and-soda" or alluding to the "last three Fourths-of-July."

Phrases of this kind, by the way, always form the possessive by adding *'s* to the final word: as his *mother-in-law's* house. It makes no difference whether the words are written with hyphens or not.

※ **How do you write out "Mrs." in full?**

You can't do it. *Mrs.* was originally an abbreviation of *mistress,* but *mistress* has so changed its meaning that it cannot be used today as an equivalent of *Mrs.* If the standard American pronunciation of *Mrs.* were written out, it would be *Missus* or *Missis,* but since these spellings (and *Mizziz*) have become literary indications of illiteracy, they won't do either.

Therefore *Mrs.* can't be written out in full without affecting its meaning. It is simply the symbol of the title of respect we give to a married woman. It has achieved the status of a word by itself.

The problem is not new. Queen Elizabeth I, writing a letter of thanks almost four hundred years ago to Archbishop Parker's wife, wrote: "And you—*Madam,* I may not call you, and *Mrs.* I am ashamed to call you, so as I know not what to call you, but yet I do thank you." So that, even then, it would seem, *Mrs.* equalled *mistress* and *mistress* was not the proper word for an archbishop's wife. And he would be a bold man who would suggest a solution to a problem in relation to the English language that Queen Elizabeth couldn't solve!

✷ heap big *mugwump*

THE USE of *mugwump* to designate an individualist serves today chiefly to call attention to the old-fashioned, backwoodsy humor of the speaker, for the word is now a piece of outmoded drollery.

It began, so far as English is concerned, in 1663, when the Reverend John Eliot, who was translating the Bible into the Indian languages, translated the word *duke* (*Genesis* xxxvi) by the Algonquin *mugquomp* which, apparently, meant "heap big chief."

The word was picked up by backwoods humorists and applied to local big shots. Then in the Blaine-Cleveland presidential contest of 1884 it was applied in derision, by the New York *Evening Post*, to certain conspicuous Republicans who bolted The Grand Old Party and refused to vote for Blaine but supported Cleveland, the Democratic candidate. The idea in the use of the word was to sneer at the defectors for being too important, in their own opinion, to vote the party ticket. However, the public chose to admire them for their independence and the word intended in scorn was adopted, at least in part, as a term of approval.

But, whether it expresses contempt or admiration, it's pretty forced today.

✷ " 'Tis worse than *murder*"

WHY ARE ordinary people *murdered* but great ones *assassinated*? Isn't this undemocratic?

Assassination and *murder* have different shades of meaning. A murder is committed for some personal advantage. An assassination is usually a disinterested killing of a public figure by one who hopes thereby to forward some political or other ideal. Because of the greatness of the one to be attacked, an assassination must be carefully planned and the approach to the victim carried out with stealth. So that *assassination* has connotations of cold bloodedness and treachery.

The word *assassin* is one of the most curious in our language.

It derives from the narcotic *hashish*. The Sheikh al-Jabal (better known as "The Old Man of the Mountain," which is simply an English translation of his Arabic title), a Moslem fanatic of the eleventh century, trained young men to commit ruthless murder at his bidding. To encourage them he admitted them to a luxurious retreat he had and fed them hashish. They were told that the voluptuous visions which the drug induced were a foreglimpse of the true Paradise to which they would be translated immediately should they be killed in carrying out their mission.

King Edward I of England was stabbed by one of these zealots, in 1272, while on a crusade. He managed to kill his assailant and survived the wound inflicted on him.

❋ Who's a *nag*?

Nag in this sense has nothing to do with the word for an old horse. It's related rather to the word *gnaw*. In northern England they would say, until quite recently, "Give the child a crust to *nag* on." It's the endlessness of the complaining that makes it nagging. This sense didn't come into the word until the nineteenth century, when women were beginning to assert themselves.

❋ *namby-pamby*

THE SNEERING term *namby-pamby*, used of something which the speaker regards as insipidly sentimental, is a leftover from a long-forgotten literary squabble.

Alexander Pope (1688-1744), a brilliant but waspish little

man, was enraged because the public preferred the pastorals of Ambrose Philips to his. Philips was a feeble writer and outdid himself in feebleness in a number of insipid verses that he wrote to the children of some of his friends. They were parodied by another poet, Henry Carey (author of "Sally in Our Alley"), who entitled his parody *Namby-Pamby* in mockery of "Amby" Philips.

Pope, whose ear was the most delicately attuned to malice of all who have ever used the English language, immediately sensed the genius of the phrase and used it in his enormously popular poem *The Dunciad* (1733). It struck the popular fancy and stays on in our speech long after Philips, Carey, pastorals and even *The Dunciad* have been forgotten.

A sample of Philips:
>Timely blossom, Infant fair,
>Fondling of a happy pair,
>Little gossip, blithe and hale,
>Tattling many a broken tale,
>Simple maiden, void of art,
>Babbling out the very heart . . .

And so on *ad nauseam*. Well done, Master Carey!

✳ "His *name is mud*"

It is often asserted that the common humorous expression to indicate that someone is in disfavor—*His name is mud*—is a reference to Dr. John Mudd, the physician who unfortunately treated John Wilkes Booth after the assassination of Abraham Lincoln and was, in consequence, regarded as an accomplice after the fact. That is, it is alleged that the expression means, "He is as detested as Dr. Mudd was."

But there is no evidence to support this. The earliest known use of the expression is 1891 (in J. C. Goodwin's *Wang: Elephant Song*) and by that time Dr. Mudd (who had died in 1882) was more an object of pity than detestation.

The real origin is as plain as mud. With our sidewalks and asphalt drives and concrete roads, we scarcely know mud any more, but until forty years or so ago it was one of *the* burdens of life. In Mitford Mathews's *Dictionary of Americanisms* seven columns of fine print are devoted to the word *mud*. Mud played a ghastly part in the lives of the pioneers and the farmers and the villagers. It held them prisoners for months on end. It made every step a struggle. It oozed up through every crack and caked on to every object. It swallowed up anything that was dropped. It required endlessly to be shoveled, scraped, and washed away. If your name was MUD, you were loathed, hated, detested, with dreary, sick revulsion, with tired, heartbroken, utterly beaten aversion.

✻ "very *naughty* figs"

Naught and *nought* were once simply variant spellings and *naughty* meant *nought-y,* or "worthless." The transition from meaning worthless to meaning bad is illustrated in the twenty-fourth chapter of the *Book of Jeremiah* where it says, speaking of two baskets of figs: "One basket had very good figs, even like the figs that are first ripe: and the other basket had very naughty figs, which could not be eaten, they were so bad."

Among the numberless badnesses of which children are capable, disobedience ranks high in the estimation of harassed parents. And hence in its application to children (and the word is now rarely used in any other application) *naughty* means "disobedient," especially the wilful doing of something that was expressly forbidden.

In the course of changing from "worthless" to "disobedient," *naughty* was for several centuries a word of strong disapprobation. It has been so weakened by its particular restriction to children (whom, unfortunately, we can't really hate, try as we may) that we are startled to come on it in its earlier strength. When Regan helps to blind the aged Gloster, for instance (in Shakespeare's *King Lear*), he calls her a "naughty lady," a reproach which seems ludicrously inadequate to us. A house of prostitution was a "naughty house," a vicious ox was a "naughty beast," and a good deed shone far "in a naughty world."

✻ *nauseous* or *nauseated?*

OF THE two unpleasant possibilities, sensitive people prefer to be *nauseated* rather than *nauseous.* That is, they would rather suffer nausea than make others suffer it.

The two words are frequently confused. "Most asthma is a form of allergy. Some people get hives, some swell up, some itch, some become nauseous, some have hay fever." So writes a learned physician. And he may have meant it. Sometimes people with allergies are so persistent and tedious in discussing them that you just want to throw up. But I think he meant that *they*, those afflicted with allergies, sometimes threw up. If so, *nauseated* was the word he wanted.

That which causes nausea is *nauseous*. To be affected with nausea is to be *nauseated*.

Nausea is the Latin form of the Greek word for "seasickness." It derives from the Greek word for *ship* and is related to *nautical*. The ancient Greeks were poor sailors; seasickness was synonymous with ship, so far as they were concerned.

✳ neatsfoot oil

Neat- in *neatsfoot oil* isn't the common word *neat*, meaning orderly, even though the oil, a preservative of leather, does make the boots look neater. It is an obsolete word meaning "cattle." A passage in Shakespeare's *A Winter's Tale* makes the old meaning plain: "The steer, the heifer, and the calf,/Are all called neat."

Neatsfoot oil is oil obtained from the feet of neat, or cattle.

✳ What is my *neighbor?*

Your neighbor is a *boor* who lives *nigh* you.

But however much humor (or one's neighbor) may encourage one to accept the old meaning, it's only fair to point out that at the time it had this meaning *boor* merely meant *farmer*.

✳ news for amateur etymologists

Let the President set aside one day (April the first would be an excellent choice) on which every year in every newspaper and on every TV show and over every radio station it shall be stated emphatically that the word *news* does *not* derive from N(orth) E(ast) W(est) S(outh). The saving in postage of those who write to editors to insist that it does will more than defray all costs involved.

Since at least 1362 the word has meant "new things, novelties," and since at least 1500 it has meant tidings of new things and events—those things that are new. Until quite recently it could be treated as a plural ("The amazing news of Charles at once were spread"—Dryden; "There are bad news from Palermo" —Shelley).

※ *nickname*

A *nickname* is a corruption, a slurring, or a development of *an eke name*. *Eke* means "also," "in addition to" ("The king himself did eat thereof/And eke the court beside"). When we speak of someone "eking out an existence," we mean that he is reduced to adding various makeshifts in order to get along. A man might be a high-school teacher, for instance, and eke out a living by collecting garbage on Saturdays.

So that *an eke name* was an extra name given to you in addition to your proper name.

The adherence of an initial *n* to a preceding indefinite article (*a*), so that it becomes *a(n)*, is fairly common in English. *An orange, an apron, an adder,* and *an umpire*, for instance, were once "properly" a *norange*, a *napron*, a *nadder*, and a *numpire*. People who work mightily to stay the "corruption" of the language might try to revive these old "correct" pronunciations. Then they would really have something to feel superior about.

※ "the *nightmare* and her nine fold"

THE SECOND part of the word *nightmare* is an Anglo-Saxon word for a demon which oppressed his victims in the night, causing them to have terrible dreams. It goes back to a root word meaning "to crush."

The other word *mare*, "a female horse," has been mixed up with the Saxon word for as long as we have any record. The mix-up was probably a natural consequence of assuming that the incubus rode on his victims. The nightmare is referred to in folklore as a demon of either sex, though usually female. In Shakespeare's *King Lear* there is a charm against bad dreams in which there is a reference to "the Night-Mare and her Nine Fold." Scholars have assumed that "Fold" here means "foals." In the charm the Night-Mare is compelled to "alight." So she's been riding on something. It's all wonderfully confusing.

✳ a *nip* in time

THE *nip* in "a nip of whiskey" is an abbreviation of *nipperkin* and a nipperkin was a vessel containing a little less than half a pint. Our fathers were mighty men for this to represent merely a nip. A *nip* today would suggest a much smaller quantity. Perhaps it has been weakened by its resemblance to and association with *sip*.

Two other meanings of *nip*—"to bite" and "to move nimbly"—color the present use. When a man says he'll take a nip of whiskey, he implies that he'll take a quick sip, just enough to savor the bite of it.

What he will actually do, of course, is another matter; he may take a whole nipperkin.

✳ "No soap!"

RESTRICTED now to being a wrily humorous way of announcing the failure of some mission or plea, *no soap* is a curious linguistic trifle.

It's a part of some gibberish that the comic actor Samuel Foote made up impromptu, in 1755, when a fellow actor, Charles Macklin ("Old Macklin," he lived to be a hundred), boasted that he could repeat anything after hearing it once. Never the man to decline a challenge of that sort, Foote immediately improvised the following nonsense: "So she went into the garden to cut a cabbage leaf to make an apple pie; and, at the same time, a great she-bear coming up the street pops its head into the shop—What! no soap? So he died; and she very imprudently married the barber; and there were present the picninnies, and the Jobilies, and the Garyulies, and the great Panjandrum himself, with the little round button at top."

I don't know whether Macklin was able to repeat it or not, but I do know that forty years ago in Ohio the phrase was always "What! no soap?" and that when I first heard it, it was a part of a rigamarole, meaningless story and the actual words were attributed to a bear! How strange that this fragment should get fixed in our speech! Perhaps it was used as a mnemonic exercise in some schools.

This Foote, by the way, and despite this sample of his wit, was a very funny man. Dr. Johnson disliked him ("Sir . . . he never lets truth stand between him and a jest") but confessed that Foote once compelled him to laugh against his will. However, he redressed the balance by checking Foote's laughter on another occasion. Foote had announced that he was going to do a comic imitation of Johnson in a public performance. Johnson ordered an oaken cudgel of unusual thickness and sent Foote word that he would himself come onto the stage and "correct" any faults in the impersonation. The skit was cancelled.

※ a *nominal* charge

A *nominal* charge does not mean, or should not mean, merely a small charge. An advertisement which states that "there will be a nominal charge for handling and mailing" and then charges a sum which, though small, is quite commensurate with the service rendered, is abusing either the language or the purchaser. Because *nominal* means "in name only" and should not be used to mean "trifling" or "inconsiderable" when referring to something trifling or inconsiderable. A nominal fee is not merely a low fee, but one so low, compared to what might be expected, that it can be regarded merely as a token payment. If a charge, however small, is a reasonable charge for what is done or given, it is not nominal.

※ "but *notwithstanding*"

THE SLIGHT strangeness that we feel in the word *notwithstanding* has made it the basis of a number of jokes ("the boy wore out the seat of his pants, but notwithstanding").

It's all due to the fact that *with* used to mean "in opposition to." This old meaning is kept in *withhold* and *withdraw*, in the archaic *withsay*, "to deny, refuse, contradict" and in *withstand*, "to oppose". So that *notwithstanding* means "despite the opposing of."

The commoner meanings of *with* ("accompanying, in association with, in regard to") were acquired when it took over the function of the Anglo-Saxon *mid* ("with"). These meanings have now become its chief meanings, and when we encounter the old meaning we are a little puzzled. This is especially true in *notwithstanding* where the old and modern meanings of *with* seem opposed. There's a difference between *standing with* a man and *withstanding* him.

✻ "Here we go gathering *nuts in May*"

Brewer's *Dictionary of Phrase and Fable* says that "nuts in May" is a corruption of "knots of May" and refers to bunches of flowers. Elizabeth Burton in *The Pageant of Elizabethan England* describes Elizabethan knot gardens, gardens laid out in intricate designs of crossing lines. They were mainly shrub gardens, she says, because flowers in Elizabethan England were mostly spring flowers. Of the song she says: "Knots of May were clusters of Spring flowers gathered from the fields by an old custom on May Day." Queen Elizabeth herself went gathering knots of May the year before she died.

The Oxford English Dictionary, unfortunately, doesn't recognize this particular meaning of *knot*, though it does have a number of quotations to show that *knot* meant "a bud." That doesn't mean that Brewer's and Miss Burton's explanation is wrong, but it would be more convincing if it were supported by texts.

Nursery songs aren't always logical or meant to be. The interest in the song for children could have been the very fact that there are no nuts in May.

✻ the *oboe*

There's a "slurred" word for you—*oboe!*

We took the word from the Italians. It's their form of the French *hautbois* or "high wood." That is, a wooden instrument with a high tone.

Formerly English used the French spelling, with many variations. Shakespeare commonly spells it *hautboys*, though once in a while *hoeboy*. Other Elizabethans spelled it *oboy, hau'boy, hobois, hoboie, hoboy*.

✻ *obsolete* and *obsolescent*

THE PREFIX *ob-* has the meaning of "inversely" or "reversely." The rest of *obsolete* comes ultimately from the Latin *solere,* meaning "to be accustomed" (*insolent* people are not accustomed to the ways of good manners). So that *obsolete* means "something we are no longer accustomed to"—because it doesn't exist any more or isn't used. *Obsolescent* means "some thing that we are gradually using less and less."

The word *wode,* meaning "insane," to give an illustration, is now obsolete. We don't use it at all any more. The word *perchance* is obsolescent. One might use it, just to be funny, but it isn't used very often, though it was once as common as *perhaps.* Sailing ships are now obsolete in naval warfare. Propellor-driven airplanes are obsolescent in combat.

A clear line cannot always be drawn between *obsolete* and *obsolescent* because there are many things about whose complete lack of usefulness there is argument. Middle-aged scholars, for instance.

✻ some *obsolete words*

HERE is a list of some obsolete English words. There's nothing wrong with them except that men simply don't use them any more and hence they are meaningless. Except in context one couldn't even guess the meaning of most of them. Yet men once spoke them in anger and greed and fear and hate and love and, most of all, just matter-of-factly because they wanted to get on with the business in hand. They were no more strange to those who used them than "bread" or "hotdog" or "competition" or any other word that we use is to us. There's an "Englishness" about most of them. One feels that he ought to know their meaning, that it lies only a little beyond immediate recollection and will come to mind in a moment.

These are only a sample. There are hundreds upon hundreds of such words and they do not prove that the language is dying but that it is living. Many of them are strikingly vivid and it is a tribute to the vitality of English that it could cast them aside so prodigally. They are good, strong words and when one becomes familiar with them he acquires a sense of the living-ness of the time that produced them. The matter is charmingly summed up by Chaucer (from whose writing most of them are taken): "You know," he says, in one of his poems,

> ... in form of speech there is great change
> Within a thousand years, and some words then
> That had great value, now seem queer and strange
> To us; and yet they spake them so
> And sped as well in love as men do now.

1 adawed	16 derne	31 leer	46 threep
2 agryse	17 deynous	32 lemes	47 thring
3 algates	18 drovy	33 lich	48 tretys
4 anlas	19 eme	34 losel	49 twiewifing
5 ayel	20 ei	35 lyart	50 wanhope
6 barm	21 fremde	36 mette	51 wem
7 bisemare	22 gargat	37 nouthe	52 wlatsom
8 blent	23 gipser	38 pile	53 wonger
9 blyve	24 gnof	39 rath	54 wode
10 boun	25 gome	40 reve	55 undern
11 breme	26 grame	41 scathe	56 unnethe
12 chimb	27 gruf	42 smoterlich	57 yerne
13 contek	28 halke	43 swevenes	58 cantle
14 courtepy	29 holour	44 swink	59 swap
15 daswen	30 inwit	45 thole	60 herie

[key:

1 awake	10 prepared	17 arrogant	26 anger
2 to terrify	11 furiously	18 turbid	27 grovelling
3 anyway(s)	12 rim of a barrel	19 uncle	28 nook, corner
4 a dagger		20 egg	
5 grandfather	13 strife	21 foreign	29 adulterer
6 lap	14 short, rough jacket	22 throat	30 conscience
7 scorn		23 purse	31 cheek
8 deceived	15 to be dim	24 churl	32 flames
9 quickly	16 secret	25 man	33 body

34 scamp	42 disreputable	48 neat	55 9 A.M. to noon
35 gray	43 dreams	49 bigamy	56 scarcely
36 dreamed	44 labor, drudgery	50 despair	57 eagerly
37 at present	45 to endure	51 spot, blemish	58 portion
38 to plunder	46 scold	52 disgusting	59 strike
39 early, soon	47 push	53 pillow	60 praise
40 steward		54 mad, insane	
41 harm, pity			

✸ occasional poems

THE MODERN meaning of *occasional*, "now and then," has made the use of the word in the title of collections of poems—*Occasional Poems*—seem like a ludicrously frank admission on the part of the poet that his inspiration was feeble and intermittent.

However, were this the case, the poet would be the last to admit or even perceive it. *Occasional* in this context has an older meaning of "written on specific occasions."

✸ October

A LITTLE learning, as Alexander Pope observed, is a dangerous thing. For instance, you learn to count up to ten in Latin and immediately you notice that our tenth month is called the eighth month, our ninth the seventh, our eleventh the ninth and our twelfth the tenth and at once you get into a terrible swivet that might have serious consequences for a delicate constitution.

The explanation is that in the old calendar the year began with March. In many ways this was more sensible than beginning it as we do in January, but it's too late to change back now.

August used to be called *sextilis* because it was the sixth month from March, and September, October, November, and December made sense in that sequence. Then *sextilis* was changed to *August* in honor of Augustus, the first of the Roman emperors. He had already changed *quintilis*, the fifth month from March, to *July*, in honor of Julius Caesar. June was named after the great Junius gens. May was named after the goddess of increase. April is from a Latin verb meaning "to unfold." March is named after

263 · Old Nick

Mars, the patron god of Rome. February (Latin *februo*, "to purify") was the month of purification and January was named after Janus, the two-faced god who looked before and after.

[July, by the way, was until very recently pronounced to rime with *duly*. Suckling (1646) rimed it with *dewly* and Wordsworth (1798) rimed it with *truly*.]

✻ Old Nick

It's a fundamental rule in demonology that the mention of a demon's name may evoke the demon himself. It's also a rule that evil things had better be alluded to playfully under fair or harmless names. This is partly to fool them, so they won't know they're being talked about, and partly to flatter them so they won't do any harm.

The Devil's real name has been a matter of much dispute among the learned, and attempts to ascertain it were regarded very much as we regard attempts to perfect a cobalt bomb. Although given honorable preeminence as *the* Devil, there are millions of devils. *Satan* isn't a name but a sobriquet or epithet; it means "the adversary." *Beelzebub* was a god of flies, worshipped in Ekron. He was a prince of devils, to be sure, but authorities (Milton among them) rated him only as second in command. Lactantius, a writer of the fourth century, announced that he had finally discovered Satan's real name and that it was *Demogorgon*, but since he was not immediately vaporized, oxidized, and atomized, he was probably mistaken.

Nickel was a Germanic name for a mischievous elf and a *nixie* was a water sprite. "Old" has long been a term of affectionate respect ("Old Blue Light" was the first nickname the soldiers gave Stonewall Jackson). So that "Old Nick," as a name for the Devil had the value of suggesting a spook and the safety of pretending that you were only shortening *Nicholas*. Sometimes, just for added insurance, the Devil was humorously called Saint Nicholas, which was a bit hard on the real Saint Nicholas and sometimes confusing to the kiddies at Christmas.

The metal *nickel* and the latter part of *pumpernickel* are the same Germanic word, meaning a devil. The first was so called because the ore looked like silver but wasn't, so the devil was in it. The second was so called because that particular kind of black bread was esteemed capable of producing flatulence in the Devil himself.

✻ the *on* of disadvantage

MANY people are puzzled by the use of *on* in such expressions as "The motor went dead on me."

One of the uses of *on* is to emphasize that an action is, or was, continuing and not completed. When we say, "I am working on an idea," we suggest a continuing process.

From this may have derived another meaning of *on*, and that is the meaning of "against." Perhaps in the idea of unendingness, of never being completed, we feel a hostility. At any rate, for almost 600 years *on* has been used to indicate a person or thing against which hostile action is directed ("an attempt on his life"; "I'll tell on you").

And this is the *on* of "The motor went dead *on* me." It is sometimes called "the *on* of disadvantage." Its meaning is plain in such sentences as "They played a trick on me" and "They shut the door on me." Here *on* is used in contrast with *for* which means "in favor of." Compare "They played a trick on me"; "They shut the door on me," with "They played a trick for me"; "They shut the door for me."

✻ once removed

WHILE *removed* is sometimes used vaguely to suggest a distant relationship ("He's my cousin several times removed"), the proper use of the word in this sense refers to a degree of relationship in descent. Your first cousin *once removed* is your first cousin's child. Your first cousin twice removed is your first cousin's grandchild. And so on. The term isn't used much any more because the breakup of the old family unit has made almost any relationship outside of the immediate family too remote to be considered.

✻ "At *one fell swoop*"

THE *swoop* is the fierce, hurtling descent of a hawk as it strikes. *Fell* in this expression is not related to the past of *fall* but to the noun *felon;* it means "savage, cruel, appallingly destructive."

The expression *at one fell swoop* comes from *Macbeth*. Macduff, the Thane of Fife, almost alone among the Scottish nobles, has refused to bow to Macbeth's tyranny and has fled to England. Macbeth, furious at his enemy's escape, has had Lady Macduff and all Macduff's children murdered. News of this dreadful event is brought to Macduff in England and he sees the tragic event in the metaphore of a hawk striking defenseless prey: "Did you say all? O hell-kite! All?/What, all my pretty chickens and their dam/At one fell swoop?"

A kite was a fierce but ignoble hawk, or falcon, that preyed on small quarry.

✳ Is there only one place for *only?*

There is a group of mortals so fortunate, so free from the burdens that occupy the thoughts and consume the energies of most people, that they are able to devote themselves to a campaign to fix the word *only* immediately before whatever word it is intended to modify.

One of them solicits my support. He had read, he says, of something that "could only happen once" and wants to know if it should not have been "could happen only once."

It could be either. It all depends on where and how the speaker wants the emphasis to fall. The correspondent feels that *only* is bound solely to the word it precedes and that "could only happen once" can only mean (mean only) that the event can happen—that is, take place by accident—only once, that on all subsequent occasions it must take place by design.

Whereas anyone who speaks English knows that in ordinary use the phrase conveys the idea that the event was of a nature that it could occur one time and no more. *It could only happen once* is more "natural" and more literary than *It could happen only once.* That is, not only would it come more spontaneously to the lips of those who speak English but it has come more spontaneously to the pens of those who have written it. The second of the two sentences would require a moment's thought and a little conscious rearrangement of the words.

If the speaker intended the meaning that the correspondent

feels is implicit in *It could only happen once,* he would have to emphasize *happen* and even then, the chances are, he'd have to do a lot of additional explaining to get such an involved idea across.

✣ operated (on)

"She was operated last Tuesday" said the lady behind me on the bus. She wasn't talking to me and we hadn't been introduced, so I couldn't shout "operated on" as all my expensive education demanded that I should.

Yet I knew that I was being linguistically provincial, that many intransitive verbs have become transitive and that *operate on* doesn't really make much sense when you lay it right on the table. Surgeons and other educated people say *operated on,* but these things change and the increasing frequency of merely *operated* indicates that many must find the *on* unnecessary or puzzling. After all, except for skin graftings, most operations are *in,* not *on,* but nobody uses *in.* If enough people find *on* superfluous —and increasing numbers seem to—it will probably disappear. Many such words have. Not long ago educated people used to say *taste of the soup.* Now everybody says *taste the soup.*

✣ opt and choose

"Confronted with a choice between the two, most intelligent people will opt for Prendergast"—Martin Mayer, *Madison Avenue, U.S.A.,* p. 305. And "Either you dieted and exercised, the woman said, and kept your behind slender and allowed your face to grow haggard and lined, or you opted for your face and let your behind spread. Carlotta had clearly opted for her face."—Irwin Shaw, *Two Weeks in Another Town,* p. 312.

Confronted with a choice between *choose* and *opt,* my impulse is to opt for *choose. Opt* is a nineteenth-century coinage based on the Latin *optare,* "to choose." In the common word *adopt,* "to choose for oneself," it has become thoroughly a part of the language. It suggests *optimum,* "the best," and that is good in some circumstances and it provides for variety if you wish to avoid repeating *choose.* I feel that Mr. Mayer simply didn't wish to say *choose* so soon after *choice,* but I think he would have done better to have done so. Repetition isn't a serious stylistic fault, whereas the straining for an equivalent (what Theodore Bernstein calls *synonomania*) can be. Opt may have another advantage. It may avoid the suggestion in *choose* of an advantageous selecting, of a careful sorting out of the one best. It merely means taking one of two. This, I feel, is Shaw's reason for using it. Carlotta had to take one of two alternatives, neither wholly desirable.

✻ the proliferating *-orama*

To FUTURE times we may be known as the age of the *-orama*.

It all began when Patent No. 1612 was granted in 1787 to Mr. Robert Barker for the invention of a continuous landscape or other scene on the inside of a cylindrical surface (the spectator to be the center) or to be unrolled, from one cylinder to another, before the spectator's ravished eyes. Two years after its invention Mr. Barker had a second inspiration and named his creation *Panorama*, from the ancient Greek *pan*, "all" + the modern Greek *hórāma*, "view."

Panoramas became very popular. They lent themselves to vast spectacles, such as the Thames from London to Richmond, Custer's Last Stand, and so on. Strange as it may seem, there didn't seem to be a good English word for the comprehensive view and this one caught on and passed almost at once into standard English as a term for an unbroken view of a region or a complete and comprehensive survey or presentation of a subject.

And so it lay dormant for a hundred and fifty years and then the rear end suddenly broke loose and exploded. God, or more likely the Devil, only knows why. Probably in the frenetic competition for attention and the dollar the idea of something's being spectacular underlay it. At any rate, I myself have seen a Food-o-rama (grocery) and have read notices of a Weld-o-Rama (a demonstration of welding equipment and methods) and a Save-o-rama (a used car lot). To these Mr. Stanford W. Berman, of Washington, D.C., has added a letter (supported by detailed addresses, pages and dates of advertisements): Art-o-Rama (artists supplies), Videorama (a style of television set), Bulge-O-Rama (humorous name for fictitious slenderizing salon on a TV show), Futurama (lipstick), Motorama (exhibition of automobiles), Cinerama (large-screen movie), Pizzarama (restaurant specializing in pizzas), Figurama (slenderizing services), Lightorama (lighting fixtures), and Powderama (face power).

✳ an *ornery* tendency in language

Ornery was simply an American dialectal pronunciation of *ordinary*. It's a frequent word in Huck Finn's vocabulary, where it means low-down, vulgar-common, mean, contemptible.

So many words that once meant just the common man now have a tinge of contempt or are downright disparaging: common, ordinary, mean, vulgar, lewd, rascal. Is the ordinary person such a heel? Or is the language shaped by people who feel themselves to be above the ordinary?

✳ Do you say "He *ought* to be hanged" or "He *should* be hanged"?

Should and *ought* are very close synonyms, so close that in most sentences it wouldn't make any difference which was used. Both imply obligation, conformance to some expectation or principle. There's very little difference, for instance, between "Children should be seen and not heard," and "Children ought to be seen and not heard."

Yet *ought* seems, somehow, the stronger verb ("We have left undone those things which we ought to have done; and we have done those things which we ought not have done; And there is no health in us." *Should* would be weaker here). It is used particularly in regard to matters of moral obligation.

So that if one wanted to insist on a distinction, he might say "He ought to be hanged" if he meant that because of the enormity of the crime committed, hanging was the proper punishment and "He should be hanged" if some other form of executing him were proposed and the speaker felt that hanging was more suitable.

But it is hard to feel that the ordinary intelligent man or woman would have the opportunity or the impulse to make such distinctions.

✽ the complaisant *ouija*

WHOEVER invented or named the *ouija* board must have been a cynical wit. The word is simply a combination of the French word for "yes" (*oui*) and the German word for "yes" (*ja*). Apparently the device was expected to stress the positive, to respond favorably to most questions put to it. The obvious meaning of its name is slightly obscured by the usual pronunciation: *wee' jee.*

✽ *oust; out* and *outrage*

SINCE the word *oust* means "to put out" and since it sounds much like *out*, it would not be unreasonable to assume that the two words were in some way related. But they aren't. *Out* is a pure Germanic word. *Oust* was an Anglo-French word. The *s* has been lost in French and the word, meaning "to take away or deprive," appears in modern French as *ôter*. *Oust* may derive from the Latin *obstare*, "to be in the way," or from *absitus*, "out of the way, remote."

Outrage would seem to be related, too—something done openly in a fit of rage. But it isn't. The *-age* ending is a noun suffix that denotes condition (as in *bondage*, "the condition of being in bonds"). It is attached not to the word *out*, as it so obviously seems to be, but to an English form of the Latin word *ultra*, meaning "beyond." The *l* was lost, as in the related form *utter* ("utter foolishness" is foolishness beyond all folly or limits).

So that an outrage is a condition of *u(l)tra-age*—that is, something that has gone beyond established or reasonable limits. Outrages are often committed in rage and they certainly provoke rage in their victims and it is highly likely that our ears hear the word *rage* in outrage and that this affects our use of it (see *klang association*).

✽ legislative *oversight*

THE PUBLIC was a little startled when events a few years ago brought the Congressional Subcommittee on Legislative Oversight into the news. While a certain amount of carelessness (especially in relation to their expense accounts) was assumed in the legislators, it was not thought to have reached the place where a special committee had to be appointed to deal with it.

But it was all a mistake. The word *oversight* has two meanings, almost diametrically opposed. The commonest meaning today is "a careless omission, an error due to inadvertence or a failure to see something that should have been noticed." However, the word can also mean "supervision, inspection, watchful care," and it is this, the older meaning, that is in the committee's title.

Overlook has the same two meanings. There's an old joke that combines them by referring to the summer resort that overlooked everything but the bill.

✳ mind your *p*'s and *q*'s

Mind means "be careful of." Beyond that all is conjecture.

Some say it means that you are to watch your *p*(int)s, and *q*(uart)s at the alehouse.

Some say it's advice from a French dancing instructor to his pupils to be careful with the *p*(ied)s [feet] and their *q*(ueue)s [pigtails]. It is said that when making a formal bow in dancing—which required one foot to be advanced—an awkward fellow would cause his pigtail to fall forward ludicrously. This would put the expression back into the eighteenth century, when gentlemen wore their hair in a queue. But it's a doubtful explanation.

Some say it's advice from sailors' wives to their husbands warning them to be careful not to get the tar from their *queues* onto their *pea*-jackets. Sailors did tar their hair and they wore it in queues long after it was stylish to do so elsewhere. A quotation from a play by Thomas Dekker (1602) lends considerable support to this possible origin of the phrase. "Now," says one character to another, "are thou in thy pee and cue" and the context makes it plain that *pee* here means a pea jacket and *cue* means a queue. But the passage is probably a joking allusion to an already established expression, for in another play, only ten years later, a character orders a quart of wine and insists that "it be Pee and Kew."

Some say it's an admonition to a typesetter not to confuse the two closely-similar letters *p* and *q*.

Some say it's a warning from a schoolteacher to his students to make the proper distinction in their writing between the *p*'s and the *q*'s—which are alike except for the direction of the vertical loop. And whether this was the original meaning or not, it is what has been presumed to be the meaning by most people for the past 200 years.

※ a *pair of twins*

"Isn't the common expression 'a pair of twins' repetitious?" demand the redundancy hunters.

And in the strictest sense, they are right. *Twin* is related to *two*. It means "two at a time." *Pair* originally meant a matched set. Chaucer refers to "a paire of beads" in a way that shows he meant what we would call a strand or set. The English still refer to what we call a flight of stairs as "a pair of stairs," and a deck of cards used to be called "a pair of cards."

So that "a pair of twins" is repetitious. But, then, twins

themselves are repetitious and the idea of their living redundancy gives the phrase a sort of poetic justification. At any rate, it's an established term and must be accepted as standard.

Of course if a Smith twin were dancing with a Jones twin, the most uncompromising purist would have to admit they constituted a true pair of twins. Or would you have to have each Smith twin dancing with a Jones twin to make it a pair of twins?

✻ beyond the *pale*

Pale here doesn't mean "pallor." It is, rather, a fence or "paling," as we now express it. "The Pale" was formerly applied to certain territories (presumably originally enclosed by a fence) under special jurisdiction. When England owned Calais, the district immediately around that city was known as the English Pale. The most famous of these regions, sometimes called the English Pale but more often simply the Pale, was the territory around Dublin over which England had power (for Ireland was never completely subjugated).

So that when we say someone is *beyond the pale* we mean that, so far as we are concerned, he's outside our values, laws, and customs. We have no jurisdiction over him. He's not one of us.

✻ *Pall Mall*

"What is the meaning of 'Pall Mall'?" a correspondent asks, thereby offering an opportunity for one more lesson in the nature of language.

Because it all depends on where and when. The meaning in the United States at the present moment is the trade name of a brand of cigarettes. The meaning in England at the moment is the same cigarettes and a street in London.

The cigarette was named after the street because the street was distinguished by a number of fashionable clubs. The manufacturers of the cigarette hoped, no doubt, that some of the prestige of the clubs which had tinctured the name of the street (as Wall Street, Park Avenue, and Madison Avenue have acquired certain social connotations) would be associated with their product, that the purchaser would feel, in smoking Pall Malls that he, too, was a clubman about London.

The street was named *Pall Mall* in the seventeenth century because it occupied the site of the royal *pall-mall* alley. And a pall-mall alley was a place where you played pall-mall, which was a game, popular in Italy, France, and England in the sixteenth and seventeenth centuries. In the game a boxwood ball was driven by a mallet through an iron ring suspended some distance above the ground. It was a sort of mixture of golf, croquet, and mayhem. It was so called from the Italian *palla-maglio* which means, literally, "ball-mallet."

※ **the great god *Pan***

Panic derives from one of the most profoundly imagined of all man's gods, the Greek god *Pan,* who, half-god, half-beast, ruled those deep impulses beyond the reach of conscious intelligence. To the Greeks he was one of the most terrible of supernatural forces, sometimes, in an instant, driving whole armies into frenzied rout.

He is a god of folk music, of jazz and rock-and-roll, of the delight in our animal being, of lust and perversion. In the sultry afternoons he slept and it was most dangerous to wake him.

※ ***pandemonium,* or perfect Hell**

Pan- means "all" (as in Pan-American). *Pandemonium,* a word which John Milton made up to designate Hell, means "the place of all demons." Tired parents and exhausted commuters have simply assumed that Hell would be full of noise and confusion.

✻ panel

THE WORD *panel* derives from the Latin word *pannus*, "a piece of cloth." It is the diminutive of *pane*, as in a pane (or strip) of glass. It is related to *counterpane* which is a corruption of *coverpane*—that which covers the pane, or cloth, on the bed.

Panel was applied to small strips of cloth and especially to the small strips of parchment on which the sheriff listed the names of jurors. From this it was tranferred to the jury itself and from a jury, in recent times, to two or three people assembled to decide some problem and often merely to discuss it.

Panel shows, on radio and TV, are cheap to produce and are therefore plentiful, especially on nonsponsored programs where the budget is low and the thought high. On the whole, the ordinary viewer finds panel shows more admirable than interesting; he dials them out with great respect. The participants are inclined to be stately, deferential, noncommital—and dull, and these facts are adding a new shade of meaning to the word *panel* on its long journey from a little strip of cloth.

✻ "Pardon me!"

"PARDON ME" is definitely regarded as non-U in England where "Sorry!" coldly or angrily sneered, is preferred by the strictly U to even the middle-class "Excuse me." But in the United States "Pardon me" is accepted and even gratefully received. However, it is a little stilted. Pardon is usually asked of God, governors, rulers, and other superiors who have the power to remit punishment. And it must usually be *begged*, not merely asked. "Excuse me" is the better term as a polite request to overlook some accidental or unavoidable breach of etiquette.

The single word "Pardon!" meaning either "Excuse me" or "I'm sorry" or, often, simply "I didn't hear you," is regarded by some as even more reprehensible than "Pardon me." But there is no reason why this should be so. Its condemnation is really very hoity-toity towards many genuinely meek and humble people.

✷ What are *parlous* times?

THE POLITICAL machines of our great cities, so the editors of *Fortune* tell us, "have fallen on parlous times."
  Parlous is simply an archaic dialectal pronunciation and spelling of *perilous*. Snout the Tinker felt that in *The most Lamentable Comedy of Pyramus and Thisby* it would be "a parlous fear" to the ladies in the audience were he to follow the script and kill himself. But this pronunciation (it is one of the *derby-darby, clerk-clark* parallels) has been banished from general standard use for almost three hundred years. It is restricted to one or two hackneyed expressions, such as *parlous state* and *parlous times* and even there its use is parlous if one expects to be taken seriously. To use it anywhere else (as to say on an icy night, "The expressway is parlous") would be ludicrous.

✷ passing the buck

COMMON and clear as the expression *pass the buck* is, no one knows for sure what it is that is being passed. The *buck* was plainly a counter used in poker, but just what it was is uncertain and disputed, though it is agreed that it first appeared about the time of the Civil War. A book of rules for card games, published seventy years ago, says that a pocket knife, known as "the buck," was passed around from person to person to indicate who was to deal. Herbert Asbury, in *Sucker's Progress* (1938), a history of gambling, says that the knives then usually had buckhorn handles and that fact shaped the phrase. It may be so, but there is no known quotation that makes it clear.

✷ the patient *patient*

Patient, in all its uses, stems from a Latin verb meaning "to suffer." *Patience* meant "enduring pain," and he who endured pain came under medical care and was a patient.
  But much of what we have to suffer in life (even at the hands of the best physicians) is hope deferred, nonfulfillment,

pain without remedy, evils that must be endured and are best endured without complaint. So that *patience* has come to mean not only suffering but uncomplaining endurance, quiet resignation.

The fantastic and interminable length of time that one who now goes to see a doctor is compelled to wait in the reception room, before being admitted to the Presence, is adding a new dimension to the word.

✱ pecking order

"THE CHICAGO *Tribune*'s Sandy Smith, who knows the mob's pecking order better than most hoods."—*Time* (April 20, 1959, p. 53).

Pecking order (sometimes *peck order*) is a scientific term based on a study of the social life of chickens made by a Norwegian, Schjelderup-Ebbe, in 1922. He found that in every flock of chickens there was a system of social precedence based on pecking and that once a chicken had pecked or been pecked into a certain status in the flock, it and others accepted that position. Schjelderup-Ebbe's researches suggest that all hierarchies in social animals (including human beings) are based on force.

Time's phrase is a good one since it implies that gangsters, like chickens, establish their position in relation to each other by ceaseless ferocity and intimidation.

It is interesting that the editors of the magazine assumed that this fact about animals was so well known as to need no explanation. Maybe they were just showing off, attempting to establish a dominant pecking order in relation to the reader so that, intimidated, he wouldn't dare not to resubscribe.

✱ Are one's *peers* one's equals or one's superiors?

THEY are one's equals in the eyes of the law. *Peer* is, ultimately, the same word as *pair* and *par*.

Confusion about the word's exact meaning, which is fairly widespread, is caused by the fact that the English nobles are called peers. But this originally meant that they were each other's peers or equals at Court. Legally, however, they were superior to the common people and, in some minor respects, still are. The law in England, as in America, assures an accused man the right of a trial by a jury of his peers. This means that a lord may insist on being tried by a jury of lords (usually the House of Lords), not commoners, and in several notorious cases the lords seem to have been lenient with their own.

An English lord has several other legal perquisites. If he has to be hanged, for instance, he can insist on being hanged with a silk rope rather than with a common hemp rope. (One of the arguments that influenced the French National Assembly to adopt the guillotine was that it was egalitarian and brought decapitation, theretofore a privilege of the aristocrats, within the reach of the masses.)

✳ ten-*penny* nails

"WHY ARE nails measured in terms of 'penny'—that is, eight-penny nails, ten-penny nails, and so on? And why is this abbreviated as 'd'?"

There's a question that takes us, hop-skip-and-jump, right into the Middle Ages and then back into the Roman Empire.

Penny, applied to nails, is a survival of the way they were priced in England in the fifteenth century. That is, nails of a certain length were priced at fivepence a hundred, nails of a greater length at tenpence a hundred, and so on. These terms persisted after better manufacturing methods had reduced the prices and they now designate sizes, not cost.

The term *d* is used as a symbol for *penny* because the English used their own word *penny* as the equivalent of the Latin *denarius.* In writing, that is. There was an old English word *pening,* which was probably the spoken word, but anyone who could write in the Middle Ages would be far more used to writing in Latin than in English and the Latin symbol was selected—possibly because the writers (mostly monks and priests) found *denarius* in their version of the Bible.

Denarius means "every ten." The Latin coin was the *denarius numus,* denary coin, worth ten asses (a small copper coin). It was named, exactly as our dime was, because it had a unit value of ten.

✻ the stormy *petrel*

THE LITTLE birds often seen in mid-ocean are called *petrels* (or *stormy petrels* since they were thought to foretell and were sometimes seen in storms) because *petrel* (formerly *peterel*) is a diminutive of *Peter*. And the birds are called after St. Peter because, like him, they seem to walk on the sea (See *Matthew* xiv:29).

They are also called Mother Carey's chickens and this is an even more curious corruption because *Mother Carey* is a sailors' corruption of *Mata cara* ("dear mother," or the Virgin Mary). The French call them "birds of our Lady" or "birds of St. Mary."

✻ *Piccadilly Circus*

THE *Circus* part is easy: Piccadilly Circus was originally a *circle* where several streets came together.

But *Piccadilly* is a dilly. Scholars have beat their brains against their dictionaries for centuries in vain efforts to solve the problem of its origin.

Deriving from the Spanish word *picado* meaning "cut or slashed," a *pickadill* was an elaborate border to a collar or belt or the hem of a skirt. The word got attached, particularly, to the elaborate ruffs or pleated collars which, starched and supported (as they had to be) with wire and pasteboard, were one of the most striking features of early seventeenth-century European costume.

At the place where Piccadilly Circus now stands there was a large house called Pickadilly Hall. But no one is certain why it was so called. Even three hundred years ago nobody knew. Possibly because it was something frilly on the very outskirts of the city. Or possibly because the Mr. Higgins who built it was a tailor and had made his fortune in pickadills.

✱ Why when a bill has been set aside by Congress is it said to have been *pigeonholed?*

BECAUSE of the similarity of the rows of little compartments, used for filing, in the old roll-top desks to the openings in a dovecote or pigeon house. These, now rare, were once to be seen on every barn.

Originally (about the middle of the nineteenth century) *to pigeonhole* meant merely "to file." The present meaning—to put aside with the intention of forgetting—is an understandable extension of the older meaning, enriched or embittered by long experience of things getting lost by being filed away for future reference.

✱ *pinched hit*

"ALL SPORTS ANNOUNCERS SAY QUOTE PINCHED HIT UNQUOTE STOP," cried the telegram marked "urgent," "PLEASE DO SOMETHING ABOUT IT."

I won't even try. I would expect the past to be *pinch hit* or *pinch hitted.* But if people in the baseball world have decided it is *pinched hit,* there is nothing I or any other grammarian can or should do except to record that towards the close of the sixth decade of the twentieth century this particular form was adopted for this particular use.

✳ *"Pipe down!"*

Pipe down was a nautical term. The piping in it was the sound of the bosun's pipe or whistle by which various commands were transmitted from the officers to the crew. *Pipe down* was the dismissal of the men from the deck after a duty had been performed. The slang use of the phrase, meaning "make less noise" or "shut up," may have been based on the assumption that the crew could be heard less when they were below decks. But more probably it is simply the idea of *down*, of a lowering of the volume of noise.

Piping in *piping hot* refers also to the whistling or piping sound that is made through a pipe. The term is a reference to the whistling of steaming liquids, as from the spout of a kettle.

✳ *playwright, -write, -right*

STUDENTS who misspell *playwright* as *playwrite* have no idea of the sympathy for their error the professor feels despite the red-pencilled correction that he is reluctantly compelled to make. For certainly *playwrite* seems more natural and *playwriter* would probably have to be accepted, though it appears in no dictionary.

The second element of *playwright* derives from the Anglo-Saxon *wyrcan*, "to work." A playwright, therefore, is one who works or fashions plays as a wheelwright fashioned wheels and a shipwright fashioned ships. A plain *wright* was a carpenter, whence our very common surname.

Just to complicate matters further, there is still another word—*playright*. It means the legal right of presentation which a playwright has in the play he writes.

✳ *"please reply"*

WHAT part of speech is *please?* all dictionaries and grammars list it as a verb, and in such a sentence as "It pleases me," it is plainly a verb. But what is it in such common use as "Please reply"? In an analysis of this statement according to the principles of formal historical grammar, *please* is the verb and (*to*) *reply* is its object. But a modern feels *reply* to be the verb, in the imperative, and *please* to be an adverb—an adverb of mollification or what-you-will, but an adverb. The only difficulty is that no book recognizes this, though many grammarians feel the need for its recognition. The moral may be to write a new grammar.

✻ Potter's *ploy*

There are several words *ploy*. One means to form a column from a line of soldiers so as to give the enemy less to shoot at. One means to bend. One means a pastime or sport.

Stephen Potter, the English humorist, has blended all of these meanings, and it is his use of the word *ploy* that has made it a vogue word at the moment. Potter is the founder of the art of one-up-manship, which consists of getting the better of aggressive bores. And the first move in the game of doing this is what Potter calls the ploy.

An example will illustrate. Suppose that some insufferable acquaintance is condescending and superior in regard to music. He knows, let's say, that you like *The Blue Danube* or *Tea for Two*, so he's always talking about Hindemith or atonal disharmonies or interpolated fifths or something else that he knows you don't understand. Now, Potter says, it's wrong to cringe or apologize for your musical likings. You're simply handing the cad the victory. The proper response is to outdo him in sneering, to assume knowledge not only equal to that he assumes but infinitely greater. He suggests a splendid ploy: "What, you stayed for the Debussy!"

✻ just *plum(b)* crazy

Though pronounced *plum*, the intensive ("He's just plumb crazy") is spelled *plumb*. It's not related to the fruit but to a carpenter's plumb line, a piece of lead on a string, used to mark perpendicularity. The device gets its name from the Latin *plumbum*, "lead." A *plumber* is one who works with lead.

In the sense of marking a true perpendicular ("The house is out of plumb," "The car fell plumb into the creek"), the word is not only correct but very old. Satan, in Milton's *Paradise Lost*, flying through chaos, "meets a vast vacuity" and "plumb-down he drops, Ten thousand fadom deep." But except in its strictly technical sense, the word with this meaning is now rustic or facetious.

From the idea of a perpendicular descent, it was a natural extension for the word to mean downright, sheer, or thorough, and from these to become a mere intensive ("I'm plumb tuckered out!"). But this last use remains colloquial. We hear it occasionally in easy, humorous talk but never in formal speech. Nor do we see it in serious writing.

✷ come out *plump*

THE CANDIDATE said that he would "come out plump" for the measure.

That doesn't mean that he would put on weight and then declare himself. *Plump* in the sense of downright, unequivocally, emphatically, was originally one of those words that echo the sound they refer to. Akin to *bump*, it first conveyed the hollow sound of a solid body dropping into water (but with far less splash and vigor than *plunge*). Then it came to mean to go into something with an abruptly checked movement and then to go into something all at once and with a sudden finality. John Adams wrote, in 1776, that he thought the delegates to the Continental Congress would, early in July, "vote plump" on the question of American independence.

And he was right. They did!

✷ Was a *poached* egg once a stolen egg?

No. Here's one place where we can definitely say which came first, the stolen chicken or the egg. And it's the egg, by at least three hundred years.

The *k* sound and the *ch* sound are interchangeable in many English words. Thus *dike* and *ditch* were once the same word. Everyone knows that the word we pronounce *church* is *kirk* in the Scotch dialect. And *deck* and *thatch* are simply variants.

Among such words is *poke,* meaning a bag or sack ("a pig in a poke"), of which our *pocket* is a diminutive. Now a poached egg is merely one that has been *poached* or *pouched* or *pocketed* in its own congealed white. Whereas a *poached* hen or rabbit is one that has been *pouched* in the *poacher's* pouch or *poke.* This use is the much later one, not appearing until the end of the seventeenth century. But there are references to poached eggs as far back as 1390.

✳ *polka dots*

Polka is the Polish feminine of *Polak,* "a Pole." From about 1835 to 1845 a lively, hopping dance called the polka swept over Europe and was the rage. As often when something is wildly fashionable, various garments and designs were named after it. A polka-dot pattern is not merely a collection of dots but a design of dots of uniform size and arrangement. And it may have been this mechanical uniformity reflecting the mechanical uniformity of the dance—which suggested the name. Or it may have been merely the clothmaker's desire to cash in on the vogue.

A more interesting part of the puzzle is that the dance was not Polish in origin, but Bohemian, and was originally called the *Nimra.* Some scholars think that *polka* may be a corruption of Czech *pulka,* meaning "half," and the dance may have been so called because of its short half-steps. Others think the Czechs may have called it *polka* out of compliment to the Poles. But the Czechs weren't given much to complimenting the Poles.

The *Polonaise,* a genuine Polish dance, is a stately dance in three-quarter time.

✳ *pollyanna*

As A TERM of contempt for anyone incorrigibly cheerful, *pollyanna* derives from Pollyanna Whittier, the eleven-year-old orphan daughter of a minister, the child heroine of Eleanor H. Porter's *Pollyanna* (1914) and its interminable sequels.

Pollyanna carries the unhomeric epithet of "the glad girl," because she plays "the glad game," a psychopathic diversion which consists of finding something to be glad about in any circumstances. Thus once when she wanted a doll someone sent her a pair of crutches. She was glad because she didn't *need* the crutches. She is run over and her back is broken. She is glad because she *used* to be able to walk. And so on.

For a generation the Pollyanna books, vastly admired by parents, took joy out of birthdays and Christmases and when the generation upon which they had been inflicted grew up their revenge was to make *pollyanna* a word of scorn. Now one almost weeps at its naivete and for the dear, dead days beyond recall when parents were still able to hope that children might be docile, obedient, clean, cheerful and, above all, grateful for small favors.

Children, of course, preferred books like *Huckleberry Finn* where in imagination they could get away from home and, maybe, if luck held, find Pap dead floating down the river.

* *"poor as Job's turkey"*

MANY people have worried because they are unable to find any reference to a turkey in the *Book of Job.*

They have been shaking the wrong roost. *Job's turkey* seems to have been invented by Judge Thomas Chandler Haliburton, a Canadian humorist of the early nineteenth century. He was the first Canadian writer to attain an international reputation and greatly influenced Mark Twain and other U. S. humorists by his use of homely, down-East speech. One of his books (*An Historical and Statistical Account of Nova Scotia,* 1829, not a humorous work) was the source of Longfellow's *Evangeline.*

Among the inventions of Haliburton's humor was Sam Slick, a Yankee clock-mender and a great teller of yarns. In one of his stories Sam wanted to improve on the established simile "as poor as Job" and made it "as poor as Job's turkey."

This would have been funnier to our grandfathers than to us. Our turkeys are reared with avaricious tenderness and fed special mashes laced with antibiotics. But a century ago a turkey was simply a half-wild scavenger, eating whatever scraps it could find around the place until it was eaten in its turn. Now Job was so poor—after Satan was through with him—that he hadn't even scraps. So his turkey would be even poorer.

285 · *practical joke*

And by "poor" Sam Slick meant not only impoverished but scrawny, sickly, and feeble. He said that Job's turkey was so poor that he had only one feather in his tail and had to lean up against the barn to gobble.

✳ *portmanteau words*

HUMPTY DUMPTY, explaining to Alice (in Wonderland) the meaning of some of the odd words in the poem *Jabberwocky*, said they were "portmanteau words" with "two meanings packed up into one word." *Chortle*, for instance, was a combination of *chuckle* and *snort*.

Called *blending* by linguists, this process has produced many words in the language. *Porridge* is probably *pottage* and *porrets*. To *don* (a garment) is to *do on* and to *doff* to *do off*.

Blending is very stylish today. Walter Winchell is obsessed by it (*Reno-vated* marriages, *infanticipating*). *Time* loves it (*cinemorsel, sexhibition*). And the advertising profession labors mightily at it (*exercycle, triscuit*).

Among noteworthy coinages may be mentioned *Convair* (conveyer by air) and *contrails* (condensation trails). On the gayer side, Leila Hadley's reporting that in Ratnapura, Ceylon, there was only one taxi in town, an automobile of ancient vintage called a *quickshaw*; James Thurber's reference to the "self-conscious *urbanality*" of the early issues of *The New Yorker*; and Garson Kanin's designation of the expression of democratic sentiments by those who oppose democracy in action as *democrapic*.

✳ What's practical about a *practical joke?*

A *practical joke* is practically certain to be stupid and dangerous and to injure or at least to infuriate the victim. *Practical* in this use means "applied in action" (as *"Practice what you preach"*). It distinguishes a joke involving action from one of mere wit or words.

Once in a while one hears of a practical joke that has some wit in it. Such as that perpetrated by a wealthy humorist who bought up hundreds of copies of a dull, thick book that had been warehoused. These he mailed to acquaintances with this brief, unsigned note: "I think you'll find the reference to yourself in this book sufficiently amusing to compel you to overlook its malice." Vanity probably led most of the recipients to drudge through the dreary tome several times.

✳ the present meaning of *presently*

Presently used to mean "immediately, in the very present moment of speaking." When an Elizabethan said that he would do something presently, he meant that he would do it at once. This meaning is made plain in a reference to a reward which was "to be rendered hereafter, not presently."

But procrastination is as fixed in human nature as larceny and lying and almost all words and phrases that began by meaning "instantly" come in time to mean "soon" or "after a while" or "when I get around to it." *Presently* was no exception and for the past two hundred years or so, in general use, it has meant "in a little while." In military affairs, however, where language is conservative and where no procrastination is allowed in trifles, the old meaning has been retained. Orders beginning "You will proceed presently . . ." do not mean that you are to proceed some vague time after lunch or the day after tomorrow.

Recently the obsolete sense of *presently* has been revived and has become fashionable, to the confusion and irritation of many honest citizens who feel the word means "by and by," not "now." The contact of millions of civilians with the military may have had something to do with its revival and it may spread into general use. If it does, it will be a fairly rare linguistic phenomenon—a word that has changed its meaning and then, centuries later, changed back to its earlier meaning. But its old meaning hasn't spread into general use yet and at present is slightly affected.

✳ Can *pretty* be used as a mild form of *very*, as in *pretty nice* and *pretty soon?*

Pretty, in this sense, doesn't exactly serve as a mild form of *very*. It doesn't intensify at all, but weakens. To be "pretty certain," for example, is not to be as certain as being "certain."

Originally *pretty* meant "cunning or crafty." Then this was softened to meaning "roguish or artful," in the appealing way that a child is roguish. From this it became a general epithet of admiration (as with so many words that have had a particular application to children). Even in the common meaning of "good looking," *pretty* retains some of its former application to children: it doesn't mean beautiful but beautiful in a slight or diminutive way, possessing beauty without dignity. That is, it designates the beauty of children and of childish women. A man would be offended at being called pretty.

From this it followed the same path as *fair*, which also can mean "pretty" and also can serve as a weakening term. To be fairly certain is, again, to be less than certain. This usage, in regard to both words, is very old, though some dictionaries list it as colloquial even yet.

✻ Why do people say *preventative* when they mean *preventive?*

ALL PEOPLE don't, of course, and those who do might ask, "Why do people use *preventive* when they mean *preventative?*" For both forms are acceptable. Both came into the language at approximately the same time (mid-seventeenth century) and both have been used by distinguished authors. John Milton, Sir Thomas Browne, and Sir William Blackstone seemed to have preferred *preventive*. But Adam Smith, George Washington, the Duke of Wellington, and Cardinal Newman seemed to have preferred *preventative*. Defoe, Southey, and Bulwer-Lytton were impartial and used both forms.

Of the two forms of the noun, *preventive* is now regarded as preferable, but all dictionaries list the longer form and there is certainly nothing wrong with it.

There are, to be sure, many words in which we do occasionally stick an improper extra syllable, just to give them rhythm, I suppose. John Crosby records coming across *commercialicisation*. I have heard *rotisserator* for *rotisserie* and I remember when the Kaiser abdicated, in 1918, hearing an excited newsboy shouting that he had *abdidicated*.

※ **Why is a common soldier called a *private*?**

No one who has experienced the public indignities of induction into the army can fail to wonder what humorist ever thought of calling the common soldier a *private*. No one has less privacy. Even goldfish are left alone part of the time.

It all becomes brilliantly clear, however, when one is reminded of the word's cousins: *privation* and *deprivation*. Latin *privatus* meant bereaved, set apart (from others), hence single, without (public) office (as "a private citizen").

The word *soldier* is an old French word derived from a word meaning "pay." It's the same root word that appears in the modern French *sou*, the small coin. Ordinary soldiers used to be called common soldiers, but they didn't like this and wanted to be called something fancier. So "private soldier" was substituted in the sixteenth and seventeenth centuries, on the analogy of "a private gentleman." By the twentieth century, however, *private* had become undesirable. The United States Air Force has abolished the rank.

But it doesn't matter what you call him. The low man on the military totem pole will always (and with good reason) feel that it's a harsh designation.

※ **England's *public* schools**

"Why do the English call private schools *public* schools?" a matron demands, and in demanding echoes a query that has been in thousands of American minds.

When I was in a country grade school, we were taught that the Chinese did everything upside down, inside out, and the wrong way round. They lived on the other side of the earth, with their feet opposed to ours. Their men wore skirts, their women trousers. They used logs for pillows, chopsticks for forks, and ate rice instead of wholesome potatoes. The father went to bed when a child was born. And so on, and so on, in endless, whimsical perversity.

One is sometimes tempted to explain the English in this way. But to this particular question there is an answer. And the answer is that the meaning of *public* varies in time and place. In the sixteenth century, when the first of the great public schools were founded in England, they were so called because they were founded for the benefit of at least a limited section of the public and publicly administered. This distinguished them from the private tutoring that most young noblemen then received. And it also distinguished them from private schools, schools run solely for profit by private individuals.

※ *pulling a leg*

THE EXPRESSION *pulling his leg* for a humorous deception—now wholly facetious and more British than American—seems to have its origin in the gruesome fact that before the days of the long drop and the hangman's knot, the friends of the condemned, at an execution, were allowed to pull on his legs in order to end his suffering as soon as possible.

To our more humane, or at least more squeamish, times, this would be incredible were it not supported by scores of contemporary references. Hangings were great public spectacles, well into the nineteenth century, and drew crowds of spectators from all walks of life. Charles Dickens, for instance, rented rooms with a good view of the gallows at a famous hanging and invited his friends. Hanging parties of this kind were common. James Boswell was very fond of them.

The sheer horror of it, the ghastliness of showing a man kindness by hastening his death, especially in such an undignified fashion (plus the fact that hanging, granted that one was not directly involved, was a subject of endless rough humor) may have led to the present idea.

※ *pumps*

NOBODY knows for sure why a certain kind of low shoe is called a *pump*. It may be the Javanese *pampoes*, borrowed into English by way of Dutch. Or it may merely echo the soft flopping sound such shoes make as we scuffle along in them, slipshod.

The other *pump*, the device for raising water or forcing liquids or gases through a tube, is equally mysterious. Although water pumps were known in antiquity and, one assumes, used at all times, the word did not come into English until the fifteenth century. And when it did appear, it was applied, at first, only to the pumps used on ships to pump out the bilges. It may originally have been a word for a pipe or tube. But most likely it too is echoic, echoing the hollow sound of the plunger striking the water.

※ **the learned *pundit***

Pundit is the British spelling of the Hindu word *pandit* which means a learned man or teacher, especially a Brahmin versed in Sanskrit and in the laws and religion of the Hindus. It has much the meaning in India that *rabbi* and *rabboni* have in the Bible.

The word was applied humorously and ironically to various mighty thinkers in Victorian England. As a joke it was soon played out and its use subsided towards the end of the nineteenth century. However in the late 1920's and early 1930's it was revived in America, especially by the magazine *Time* which, in its early days, sought attention by inverted word order and strange words. *Pundit* was a sort of an accolade which *Time* bestowed upon certain political prophets whose outlook corresponded with its own. The prophets no doubt winced, but they were helpless.

Pundit is not applied to the merely knowing. No one would call Benjamin Franklin a pundit, or Edison or Franklin P. Adams. The word carries a suggestion of the mysterious wisdom of the East and applied to prognosticators and such like, men who are often uncertain about what is but are quite clear about what is to be.

※ **a *purist***

A Purist is one who applauds a female performer by shouting "Brava! Brava!" while leering with contempt upon the vulgar mob ignorantly shouting "Bravo!"

※ ***Q***

Q is an unreasonable letter. It can't stand alone and other letters express its sound. It's totally unnecessary.

The only purpose it serves is to remind us that nothing connected with language is reasonable and that the alphabet didn't grow on the basis of *our* needs.

Q came into the Latin alphabet from the Greek which had borrowed it from the Phoenician and Hebrew in which it expressed the more guttural of two *k* sounds. The Romans put a *v* after the *q* to represent the sound *kw* (as in *equus*) and we're still putting it there in the form of a *u*.

Cw and *kw* express the sound represented by *qu* and as late as four hundred years ago they were so used in many parts of England. *Qu* didn't get firmly established in English spelling until about the thirteenth century.

Unnecessary as *q* is, however, we'll not get rid of it easily. Major spelling reform is almost an impossibility. There are several intelligent proposals for minor spelling reform that include the elimination of *q*, but even they are not likely to get very far. There is so much else in the world that has priority on anybody's list of things that ought to be eliminated.

※ **Why when soldiers offer to surrender are they said to beg for** *quarter*?

PRISONERS of war were formerly often held to ransom. This strange use of *quarter* was long supposed to derive from an agreement between the Spaniards and the Dutch, in the sixteenth century, that a man's ransom should not exceed one quarter of his pay.

This explanation is doubtful, however. The most valuable prizes would have been young noblemen, who either served without pay or received pay wholly incommensurate with their worth. Then there is no record of any such agreement between the Spaniards and the Dutch, or between any warring nations. And even if there were, it would still not explain the fact that it was the vanquished who begged for quarter.

The more probable explanation lies in the fact that a prisoner had to be maintained by his conqueror until the ransom was paid. And this could run into a lot of money. Gentlemen and nobles—the only ones likely to be ransomed—expected to live like gentlemen and nobles even if prisoners. So the defeated man was asking for maintenance, what we would call "living quarters." And it sometimes took a lot of generosity to grant his request; not cutting a man's throat could be an expensive gesture.

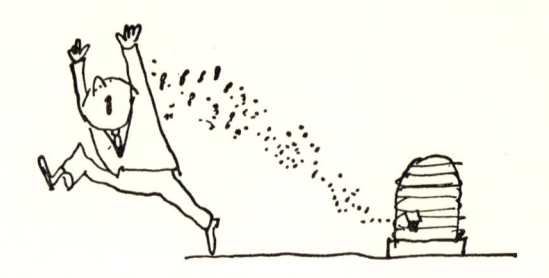

※ **What do we mean when we say that someone is "stung to the quick"?**

THE ORIGINAL meaning of *quick* is "living." Modern traffic has given a double meaning to *the quick and the dead* which at first meant simply the living and the dead. Pregnant women used to be said to be *quick with child* when the movements of the foetus could be perceived. *Quicksilver*, the old name for mercury, was so called because in its liquid form it seems alive. A *quickset* hedge is one grown from live cuttings set in the ground. We refer to the sensitive area under the fingernail as the *quick*. When we say that someone is *stung to the quick*, we mean that he is stung deeply, into the living tissue where it hurts—and where the hurt usually produces some vigorous action.

The ordinary contemporary meaning of *quick*—swift, speedy—is derived from one aspect of certain forms of living things.

※ **The pronunciation of *Quincy***

QUINCY is *Kwinsi* in California and Illinois but *Kwinzi* in Massachusetts. This minor distinction—for a *z* is only a voiced *s*—is one of those elegant trifles that mark the knowing (but only to the knowing, of course).

✳ quiver

NOBODY knows why a portable case for arrows is called a *quiver*. And probably nobody ever will know.

We can only know the meaning of a word by hearing it or seeing it in use. And we have to hear or see it in many different contexts to be absolutely certain what is its basic meaning, what are its extended meanings, what are its metaphorical meanings, and so on.

When we speak of a word's "original" meaning and attempt to explain "why" it means what it now means, all we have to go on are its past and present meanings. And the only way we can know past meanings is to find them in a piece of writing used in such a way that they are absolutely clear.

But some things are older than writing. Man had them before he learned to write. And among the things that our unlettered ancestors had when they emerged from the mists of prehistory were arrows in a quiver.

✳ Why is an illegal activity called a *racket*?

A RACKET originally meant, as it still means, "a disturbing noise." It came to mean an illegal activity or a dishonest business from the practice of pickpockets in the seventeenth and eighteenth centuries. They would have their confederates explode firecrackers or make a noisy disturbance in the street to draw a crowd and distract their attention so that their pockets could be more conveniently picked.

In 1697 a statute was enacted in London forbidding the

throwing of squibs, rockets, and other distracting devices with this felonious intent.

It is an interesting illustration of the ways of words that while *racket* in the sense of a dishonest scheme is still listed by all dictionaries as slang (even though it has appeared in print, and in the works of the most respectable writers, for seventy years), *racketeer,* a derivative, is accepted as standard English.

✳ **A "*ragamuffin*" is ragged, but what has he to do with "muffins"?**

NOTHING whatever, no doubt to his own sorrow. Ragamoffyn first appeared in Langland's *Piers Plowman* (1362-1399) where he was a devil and devils had strange names. Devils were notoriously dirty and the ideas of dirty, raggedness and deviltry that were associated in the word led it to be transferred, apparently, to any ragged, dirty, or disreputable boy. The -muffin ending may be the same as the second element of curmudgeon, also a mysterious word. The muffin that we eat is probably the second part of *pain mofflet* meaning soft bread. (The modern French form is *pain mollet.*)

✳ **Is *ransack* a good word?**

Ransack is one of the oldest words in all known human speech. Men apparently have been losing things or having them stolen and then hunting for them furiously ever since—and probably long before—the Old Stone Age. *Ran* originally meant "dwelling" and *sack* is related to *seek.* So to ransack is to seek through the house. Nothing is more infuriating than to seek and not find and as our fury grows, so does the violence of the search, until *ransack* has acquired the associated image of open drawers and strewn clothes and papers and a wake of disorder.

This worthy word, after serving us faithfully for several millennia, now seems to be withdrawing into country and small-town speech. Maybe city apartments are too cramped and bare to allow much ransacking.

✻ a *real* warm question

A VISITING Northerner, growing irritable under Dixie's torrid skies, blows his stack at being assured for the tenth time in one day that it is "real warm." "Is not the use of *real* as an adverb," he demands, "incorrect, reprehensible, and senseless?"

Incorrect? For formal use, yes.

Reprehensible? No. It is spoken by far too many Americans of all regions and levels of education to be considered blameworthy, deserving of rebuke, censure, or reproof.

Senseless? Certainly not. Its meaning is quite clear.

Real is recognized as an adverb by the *Oxford English Dictionary* and the unabridged *Merriam-Webster*, though the latter labels it "loose and uncultivated." It is used chiefly as an adverb to qualify adjectives and other adverbs. I have never heard it used to qualify a verb. And we must remember the saying of the Latin grammarians: *All words gravitate towards being adverbs.*

We must also remember that the word *very* (which those who object to *real* find fully acceptable as an intensive—*very hot, very funny*, etc.) meant originally "true" or "real" ("Art thou my very son Esau?"—*Genesis* xxvii:24; "this is the very Christ"—*John* vii:26).

✻ dragging a *red herring* across the trail

A *red herring* is merely a smoked herring. When a herring is smoked it turns a brownish-red but, more to the point of the phrase, it develops a very pungent odor—as anyone knows who has ever been within thirty feet of an Englishman enjoying his morning kipper.

So strong is the smell that a red herring on a string was formerly used to train hunting dogs to follow a scent. And sometimes it would be drawn across the natural trail they were following in order to throw them off. Foxes and rabbits give off a pretty gamy odor but not enough to stand out against a smoked herring.

It's from this that the modern expression derives. An investigation will be going along fine and then someone will draw something fishy across the trail in the hope that it will break up the pursuit.

✷ *redding* up the house

"SHE DIDN'T like to disturb Cadwallader . . . with . . . her casual dustings and, as she called it, 'redding up.'"—Russell Lynes, *Cadwallader*, p. 21.

Mr. Lynes ducks behind quotation marks with *redding*. Many correspondents have heard the word and are puzzled about it. The usual form of their questions is "Is there such a word?"

Variously pronounced and spelled as *rid, red, redd, redd up* and *ridd up, redd*, meaning "to put in order, to make neat," or "to clear or clean out," is an old English word that survives in many parts of the United States. It was once a standard, even a literary, word but it is now colloquial. Like many such words, it may have come into our speech by way of Scotch emigrants since it lingered in Northern English speech and appeared in Northern writing long after it had fallen into disuse in Southern England.

✷ *refrain*

IN THE old comic strip "Bringing Up Father," Maggie, a culture seeker, would compel her lowbrow husband, Jiggs, to attend a highbrow musicale. Jiggs would ask the soprano if she knew anything with a *refrain* and when she said she did, he would ask her to refrain.

Refrain seems to have two opposed meanings: "to stop doing something" and "something that is sung over and over again." And the heart of the mystery is that the verb and the noun are wholly different words.

The verb *refrain* does not really mean "to stop." It means, rather, "don't begin" (which would have suited Jiggs even better). It comes from the Latin *refrēnare* which means to rein in or check by pulling back on a bridle (Latin *fraenum*).

The *refrain* of a song is from the Latin *refrangere,* meaning "break back." It was a direction to a singer to break off and go back to the chorus. Its meaning is shown by another term used for the same thing: *Ritornello.*

※ *rely* and *depend*

Though the general meaning of *rely* and *depend* is the same, there are many subtle variations in their use.

To *depend* is to hang from. When, in *The Beggar's Opera,* Polly Peachum, lamenting the imminent execution of her highwayman lover, sings "From the rope that hangs my dear depends poor Polly's life," she makes a good pun.

To *rely* is to bind together. When we say, "You can rely on it," we are saying "You can bind your fortunes to the assurance and be certain it will be made good."

Dependence is the general condition, reliance the more particular. We depend on persons or things. We rely only on persons or their promises. We say, "That depends," meaning "it is contingent upon." We never say "That relies." *Depend* is applied to basic expectations of long standing. Children depend on their parents and the aged on their children; they are called *dependents.* But we rely on certain persons to keep their word, to be punctual, etc. Dependence implies the greater need and the greater trust. Reliance applies almost entirely to the future.

※ *rendezvous*

Pronounced *rahn' d'voo* (though *ron' di voo* is heard so frequently that it must be accepted as a permissible variant), *rendezvous* means, strictly, "betake yourselves to." It is used in military terminology to designate the spot to which a detachment of soldiers is to go. There, often, they will meet with other detachments.

In common use *rendezvous* means "a meeting spot." And because it is used so frequently of the meeting spot of lovers, it has acquired a suggestion of secrecy and even a shade of the illicit. It's sentimental and hackneyed.

A curious parallel to this meaning of *rendezvous*, a place of illicit meetings, is furnished by *joint* (i.e., "a place where things come together").

✳ hats in the *ring*

THE METAPHOR is from a custom in the early days of boxing. The champion stood in the ring and challenged all comers; anyone inclined to accept the challenge flung his hat into the ring and leaped in after it. Although he may not have been the first to apply the phrase to a candidacy for the Presidency, Theodore Roosevelt's use of it in the 1912 election tickled the nation's fancy and did much to make it the cliché it now is. "Teddy," a gentleman boxer in his youth, plugged the metaphor for all its pugnacious worth: "My hat's in the ring," he announced. "The fight is on and I'm stripped to the buff." After the election he was stripped down even a little further; Wilson had taken off a bite of the hide as well.

✳ *rocket* and *missile*

A *missile* is the whole vehicle, ready for launching. It includes the shell, the fuel, the control devices, and the payload.

A *rocket* is one of several types of engines used to power a missile. A ramjet missile, for example, is not a rocket missile.

✳ a *Roman holiday*

"Chief of Detectives James Leggett . . . charged that thrill seekers [who had swarmed to Idlewild airport on hearing that a damaged airliner was going to have to make an emergency landing] created 'a Roman holiday' of the ordeal of the 102 passengers and 11 crew members aboard the plane."—UPI dispatch, July 13, 1959.

"Warned Justice Tom Clark in his dissent [from the ruling in the Jenks case, that a defendant in a federal criminal case had a legal right to examine pretrial statements of government witnesses]: the decision granted criminals a 'Roman holiday for rummaging' in FBI files."—*Time*, July 6, 1959.

Detective Leggett's use of *Roman* holiday is correct; Justice Clark's is not.

A Roman holiday is a holiday the pleasure of which is obtained at the cost of someone else's suffering, or a holiday of which the cost in pain far exceeds the pleasure gained.

The expression is taken from Byron's *Childe Harold* (Canto iv, st. 141). The poet had seen the famous antique statue called "The Dying Gaul" which represents—or was thought to represent—a prisoner of war taken in some Roman victory, carried to Rome and forced to fight in the arena where he had been mortally wounded. Byron imagined "the inhuman shout" of the brutal spectators as the prisoner fell, a shout which the dying man disregarded as his last thoughts turned to his "rude hut by the Danube": "*There* were his young barbarians all at play,/*There* was their Dacian mother—he, their sire,/Butcher'd to make a Roman holiday."

With the traffic fatalities, the maimings and mutilations of *our* holiday weekends, and, above all, with the public's gloating over the mounting tally and the newspapers and the newscasters, under an unctuous film of seeming to deplore, eagerly listing the exciting tally, hour by hour, the expression ought to be changed to "butcher'd to make an *American* holiday."

✳ "root" for the home team

OVER 100 years ago root was college slang for studying hard. And here one can see some relevance, whether one thinks of getting into the root of things or just rooting into the books like a pig rooting with its snout. It's a good term for hard digging. This slang meaning became obsolete, however; and about 1890, when intercollegiate athletics were getting into their first raucous rapture, the word root suddenly appeared in its present slang meaning of "shouting for" or "supporting vigorously." It may have been an adoption of the earlier collegiate slang —simply hard work in another branch of college activities. Or it may have been based on some yell, such as the old "Root de toot, root de toot/We're the girls from the Institute."

✳ *roots* and meanings

MANY words have come so far from their root meanings that it is astonishing to learn their origins. I have heard a pompous fellow say that he never used a word without first considering its root meaning. What pretentious nonsense, as a few examples will show:

Clinical, basically, means "pertaining to a bed." *Silly* means "blessed or happy." To *tell* is "to count," to *prevent* is "to go before," to *abscond* is "to conceal." The root of *protocol* is the Greek *kolla*, "glue." The word *animal* derives from *anima*, "the soul," the one thing we deny animals. *Money* is so called because the Roman mint was attached to the temple of Juno Moneta, Juno the Admonisher. *Vogue* goes back to a word meaning "to row a boat" and *canapé* to the Greek *Konops*, "mosquito."

These things are curious and interesting to know, but a knowledge of them has no bearing whatever on the words' modern meanings.

✻ rule the roost

To say of someone who is not merely the boss in his own house but rather likes to make a display of it, that he *rules the roost* is to employ a very old expression, one that goes back to the fourteenth century and was a proverb even then.

The chief drawback to using it is that no one seems certain whether it is ruling the *roost* or the *roast*. The modern American version plainly has it *roost*, with the meaning being absolute master, as a cock is among the hens—with a suggestion of slightly amused contempt for the pettiness of the authority exercised.

The Oxford English Dictionary lists the saying under *roast*, as a roast piece of meat, and—together with other dictionaries—regards *roost* as a corruption. Yet it can assign no exact meaning to *ruling the roast* other than the obvious one of being master of the house. And the matter is further complicated by the fact that *roost* was formerly pronounced as we now pronounce *roast*.

Perhaps the British version once had a meaning that became lost and the Americans, by a sort of pun, infused a specific meaning into it.

✻ run, run, run

The Oxford English Dictionary lists 72 meanings of *run* as a noun and 265 meanings of *run* as a verb. This last figure includes special idiomatic combinations with prepositions. The list is not complete, however, if only because several generations have passed since this great work was compiled and many new meanings have been added to the word. The OED does not, for instance, include the common American euphemism for diarrhea, *the runs*.

Among the nounal meanings are: a landing of smuggled

goods, a shoal of fish, a drove, a tramway, a measure of yarn, a mole's path, a pipe, a laugh, and a set of millstones. Among the verbal meanings are: to curdle, to have legal power, to tout for a boarding house, to sew lightly, to form a cornice, to tease, to smelt, and to send a ferret down a rathole.

Let those earnest individuals who insist that a word can have only one "correct" meaning ponder these things. And let us all spend a moment in silent commiseration for the bewildered foreigner trying to learn English.

❋ *run* or *stand* for office

A CANDIDATE for public office in Great Britain *stands* for the office. In the United States he *runs* for it.

The British term has been in use since 1551. It seems to be related to standing trial. The American term first appeared in 1844, after Andrew Jackson had introduced the spoils system.

The different words reflect different points of view. The British see the election from the point of view of society; the candidate is, as it were, on trial before the bar of public opinion. Like an accused man, he stands until judgment has been passed on him. The Americans see it from the Candidate's point of view—as a race for a prize. To speak of *running* for office reflects unabashed, functioning democracy.

❋ *"that he who runs may read"*

THE COMMON expression "that he who runs may read" is not so clear and simple as most speakers of it assume it is.

In the second chapter of the *Book of Habakkuk*, in the Bible, God commands the prophet Habakkuk to write an account of a vision. "Write the vision," the King James Version reads, "and make it plain upon tables [tablets], so that he may run that readeth it." The Greek version of the Old Testament says "so that he that reads may make haste to escape," implying that the account of the vision would inspire terror.

St. Jerome, however, interpreted the passage to mean that the writing was to be so plain that even a man who ran by could read it. And so he translated it into the Vulgate.

The Revised Standard Version follows the King James here

and has: "make it plain upon tablets, so he may run who reads it." The New American Catholic Edition reads: "Write the vision and make it plain upon tables: that he that readeth it may run over it."

The popular phrase, detached from the Bible, simply means: "Make it so plain that a running man can read it as he hurries by."

✷ the *sabbatical* year

A PROFESSOR's year of leave is called a *sabbatical* because, in theory, it is a year of rest and because—in even more tenuous theory—it is supposed to come every seventh year. It took its name from the Hebrew *Sabbath,* the seventh day of the week (Saturday), set aside as the day of rest and religious observance. The Hebrew word is *shabbāth*. It comes from the verb *shābhath,* meaning "to desist" or "to break off."

There was also among the ancient Hebrews a sabbatical year, in which fields were to be left untilled and debtors were to be released. This last custom may have had much to do with naming the academic sabbatical.

✷ a *sad iron*

A WOMAN writes to ask why an old flatiron which she inherited from her mother is marked "Sad Iron."

One of the meanings of *sad* is "solid" or "heavy." The commonest use of this meaning is its application to cakes that are heavy or soggy after failing to rise. So a *sad iron* is not a regretful iron but a heavy iron.

The word *sad* originally meant "sated." The commoner meaning grew from this; after you'd eaten too much you felt heavy and depressed.

✷ "my *salad days*"

THE EXPRESSION *salad days* originated in a joke of Cleopatra's in Shakespeare's *Antony and Cleopatra* (1.v). She says that when she was young she loved unskillfully. Those were her "salad days" because she was like a salad, green and cold.

✶ Why *saltcellar* but never "peppercellar"?

Saltcellar is a reduplicated word. Its second element, which used to be spelled *seller* and *saler* simply means "salter." So it's a salt-salter. It was fixed as a word long before pepper was in general use.

✶ the parson's *saw*

WHEN in his little song about winter Shakespeare says (*Love's Labour's Lost*, V.2) that "coughing drowns the parson's saw," he doesn't mean that the parson is overwhelmed with bronchitis while working at the woodpile, but that his sententious saying goes unheard because everybody has a cold.

The *saw* with which we cut wood is related to *scythe* and *section*. The *saw* meaning a proverb ("an old saw") is related to *saga* and, ultimately, to *say* and *saying*.

✶ pronunciation of *says*

A MEEK and intimidated poor soul writes: "A very learned relative of mine insists that *says* should be pronounced to rime with "days." Is this true?"

Against such advice I can only urge the correspondent to set the testimony of her own ears: everyone who speaks English, of every estate and condition of learning—bishops and bookies, governors and garbage men, cab drivers and college presidents—*everybody* pronounces *says* as if it were spelled *sez*. And if she's afraid to believe her ears, let her try her eyes: every dictionary of the English language that bothers with the matter at all gives the pronunciation *sez* and only the pronunciation *sez*.

In the spelling of *says* there is often a peculiar touch of snobbery. In the quoted speech of an educated person or someone whom the writer admires, it is always *says*. But in the speech of an uneducated person, or someone whose lack of culture the writer wishes to emphasize, it is often represented as *sez*. Dickens has his lower-class, humorous characters use "sez," and in newspaper accounts of Congressional investigations, labor leaders, racketeers, and others whom editors dislike, are made to say "sez." Yet all—upper-class English, investigators as well as investigated, and even editors—say *sez*.

✱ **"the *scales fell from his eyes*"**

WE ARE told in the Bible (*Acts* ix:18) that Saul of Tarsus, on his way to Damascus to persecute the Christians, was blinded by a dazzling light. Later the disciple Ananias touched him, calling him by the name Paul, by which he is now known, and "there fell from his eyes as it had been scales: and he received sight forthwith . . . and was baptized."

The Revised Standard Version says "something like scales" fell from his eyes. Whatever they were, the phrase's origin still colors its meaning, because we always use it of someone who has been in mental or spiritual darkness and suddenly has seen the light—one who has been freed from an illusion that held him in darkness.

✱ *scanning* **the headlines**

THE BASIC meaning of *scan* was "to analyze verse." From this it came to mean "to examine with great care." And this was its meaning for centuries.

Within the past forty years, however, in the United States, it has taken on almost the opposite meaning—i.e., merely to glance at lightly and hastily. And this is now its dominant meaning to most Americans. That is, if any American gave someone an important document which he wanted him to read thoroughly and the other person returned it with the remark that he had *scanned* it, the American would be annoyed. Because to him *scan* means to glance over with superficial haste.

In some literary phrases *scan* retains its older meaning. When we read of an Indian, or an officer on the bridge, scanning the horizon, we still think of him as regarding it with searching care. But only in special contexts do we feel this, the older meaning.

And so one more word that has two opposite meanings is added to the language.

❋ Just what is a *scapegoat?*

IN THE sixteenth chapter of *Leviticus* occurs one of the most puzzling passages in the Bible. Part of the ritual for the Day of Atonement required the high priest to bring two goats before the altar of the tabernacle. By casting lots he selected one of them as an offering for Jehovah. The other was "for Azazel." We don't know just who or what Azazel was, but most scholars believe that he was a demon that lived in the wilderness. At any rate, the high priest transferred the sins of the people to this goat and then allowed it to escape and go to Azazel.

In 1525 William Tyndale translated this: "To let him go for a scapegoat into the wilderness." We would say *escapegoat*. The Authorized Version adopted Tyndale's translation. The revised Standard Version has "that it may be sent away into the wilderness to Azazel." The New American Catholic edition calls it "the emissary goat" and merely says that the high priest shall "let him go into the wilderness."

So we owe *scapegoat* to William Tyndale's pronunciation of *escape* and his interpretation of the Azazel problem.

❋ Why is twenty *score?*

Score is a Norse word that English borrowed sometime before the year 1400. It meant "to cut or slash" (as it still does) and was related to the Anglo-Saxon word *shear*. [*Sh-* and *sk-* are often merely variants. Thus *shirt* and *skirt* originally designated the same thing, until we applied one form to the upper and one to the lower garment.]

Score, as a noun, meant "a cut or notch" and then a special cut or notch on a stick that served as a tally and, in a particular application, a cut or notch signifying the number 20. In thinking about language we must always bear in mind that up until a couple of centuries ago most people couldn't read and very few, even among those who could read, had anything but the most elementary knowledge of figures. A shepherd was likely to be totally illiterate, yet he had to know exactly how many sheep he had. So he had to count them and twenty (twice over his fingers) was, apparently, as high as he could count (or maybe he fell asleep if he counted too many sheep at one time). So he counted twenty and then made a notch, or *score*, on a stick and then counted another twenty and notched another score.

※ **Why *scot free*?**

The *scot* of *scot free* has nothing to do with Scots or Scotland. The word was originally Scandanavian and it meant "a payment or reckoning," especially a payment for entertainment. It may have been affected by *scotch* meaning a mark (as in *hopscotch*) which the landlord drew on a slate to indicate the pints consumed and hence the amount to be paid. To get off *scot free*, then, was to get off without having to pay the *scot* or reckoning.

In modern usage this *scot* serves merely as an intensive to mean "absolutely free, unconditionally free."

※ **two *scruples***

Scruple has two widely different meanings: (1) one twenty-fourth of an ounce and (2) a conscientious reluctance.

Some scholars think there are two unrelated words here. Those who think them related trace them back to the Latin *scrupus*, "a sharp stone," whose diminutive, scrupulus, a teeny-weeny little stone, may have been used for a small measure of weight. The other meaning, they aver, comes from the idea of such a tiny pebble in your shoe. As a figure of speech for a nagging cause of uneasiness, it was first used by Cicero. The aptness of it appealed and it was adopted into general speech. Certainly everyone knows how exasperating and insistent a grain of sand in one's shoe can be. One tries to go on and ignore it, but he knows from the very first awareness of it that, sooner or later, he's going to have to do something about it. And there are those (Man be praised!) who feel about right and wrong the way others feel about gravel in their shoes.

✳ Can a majority *secede* from a minority?

"THERE has been talk of New York City *seceding* from New York State. But the city has a majority of the state's population. Can a majority *secede* from a minority?"

Secede means "to withdraw" and the withdrawal alluded to is not from the minority but from a political union. It is true that almost all known applications of the verb *secede* refer to the action of a minority, but heretofore conditions have not arisen in which a majority of the population found itself in a political minority. Where the majority is a voting majority, as well as a numerical majority, it doesn't need to secede, since it has in its power through the vote a remedy for its discontents.

The word *secede* in this context is unfortunate, not because of logic but because of its associations. It is not proposed that the city leave the federal union but merely that it form new political and geographical boundaries within the union—as has been done peacefully several times in our history. Therefore those who advocate such a change are unwise to designate it with a word that connotes treason and civil war. What words suggest is sometimes more important than what they say.

✳ *secure* and *security*

ALTHOUGH almost all dictionaries give "to obtain possession of, to get" as one of the recognized meanings of *to secure*, the getting ought, in some way, to be connected with security. Thus when we read of someone securing a seat on a plane, we feel that he not merely got it but made sure he had it or that his getting it gave him a sense of security or made secure some plan or purpose. When Prescott says that Philip II by his cordial manners "secured the sympathy of all with whom he came in contact," we feel that he did not merely get their sympathy but made his possession of it secure.

However, if we are told that someone secured an egg and a

strip of bacon from the refrigerator, at a time when there was no competition for however much was there, we feel that *got* would have been more suitable.

❋ serendipity

Serendip or *Serendib* was the Arabic name for Ceylon. Horace Walpole wrote a story (1745) called *The Three Princes of Serendip*. The young gentlemen of the title were always accidentally making the most delightful discoveries and Walpole coined the word *serendipity* to describe this remarkable ability of theirs: an aptitude for making fortunate discoveries accidentally.

For almost two hundred years the word—an improbable name for an improbable talent—slumbered in desuetude (or, as one might say, lay doggo). But it has recently become part of the esoterica of the esoteric and is now lisped and jabbered freely in the tearooms and espresso bars. The official name of Ceylon is now *Lanka* and another old name was *Taprobane*. So anyone who is annoyed by the use of *serendipity* may get one up on the user by asking him if he doesn't mean *lankasity* or *taprobanality*?

❋ Does one say "The coat *sits well* on you" or "*sets well*"?

HISTORICALLY, it is *sets*. But a flock of nervous, half-educated schoolteachers got our grandfathers so hot and bothered about the difference between *sit* and *set* that the ordinary American is now completely buffaloed and just won't use *set* except in sentences (such as "The sun sets") where it is plain that *sit* can't be *meant*. The teachers even tried to get our grandfathers to refer to a "sitting hen" but in those days most people were farmers and were busy and there was some gumption left in them and they just kept on saying the old "setting hen." Tailors, who like all craftsmen are conservative in the terms of their craft, say "the coat sets well."

✻ Seventh Heaven

IT IS man's glory and shame to be insatiable. Nothing will content him. Heaven is supposed to be a place of utmost bliss, of happiness such as only God himself could conceive or devise. Yet men are always suggesting improvements in it. Swift once wrote in a letter: "If I were to write a Utopia for Heaven . . ." So he obviously expected it to be a place that could stand a little bettering.

Many accounts of heaven—Jewish, Christian, and Mohammedan—conceive of gradations within it, and *seven* has always been a particularly sacred and mystical number.

The Mohammedans seem to have given most thought to—or to have had the most detailed revelations concerning—the various heavens. The Seventh Heaven, in their account of it, is a region of pure light. Each of its inhabitants is bigger than the whole earth and has 70,000 heads. Each head has 70,000 mouths and each mouth 70,000 tongues and each tongue speaks 70,000 languages—all forever chanting the praises of Allah.

It certainly sounds like Hell (see *Pandemonium*).

✻ making a *shambles* of a good word

"ROARING into the shambles [a dip in the ratings] came the CBS board chairman, William Paley, with a 'crash meeting' attended by top brass."—TV column.

A *shamble* was originally a stone or a footstool. The earth was called "the shamble of God's feet" in allusion to Isaiah lvi:1 ("the earth is my footstool"). Then it came to mean "stools or low tables on which goods were exposed for sale," especially the benches or stalls in the public markets on which the butchers set out their meat. This meaning is still retained in Northern

England and all tourists who have visited the town of York have seen the quaint section there known as the Shambles.

From this the word came to be used to describe any scene of carnage reminiscent of the butchers' stalls. Today it is being used more and more, especially in the breathless prose of journalists when they really haven't anything to say, to mean any short of disorder. We read of a ransacked desk being left "a shambles" or, as above, a committee meeting at which there is presumed to be some differences of opinion.

✳ Is the man with the aces up his sleeve a card *sharp* or *shark?*

He's a card *shark*, though there is a standard word *sharper* and a slang word *sharpie*.

One would naturally assume that the social parasite was named after the greedy fish, but the reverse seems more likely. The first shark (fish) that the English people knew much about was exhibited in London in 1569 and aroused great interest. It had been brought home from a voyage by some sailors who called it a shark after card sharks because, presumably, that was the only thing they knew equally hungry for suckers.

Rogues, such as dice- and card-sharpers, usually have a marked aversion to work and *shark* is probably related to *shirk*.

✳ "Wipe out the *shibboleth*"

"The average Catholic voter . . . would like to see a Catholic run, and win, mainly to wipe out the shibboleth that no Catholic can be elected President of the U. S." (*Newsweek*, Dec. 21, 1959, p. 27.)

A shibboleth is not a slogan or a pronouncement or a conviction; it is a way of pronouncing a certain word in order to show that you belong to a certain group.

The word comes from the Bible. The Ephraimites had been defeated in battle (*Judges* xii:4-6) and in their flight came to the passages of the Jordan which were held by the victorious Gileadites. They begged to be allowed to pass over the river, denying that they were Ephraimites. To test them, the Gileadites demanded that they speak the word *shibboleth* (Hebrew for "stream in flood") which the Ephraimites pronounced *sibboleth*. All who so pronounced it—42,000 men—were killed.

History has repeated this sort of grim word test several times. The Sicilians slew a French garrison in 1282 for being unable to pronounce a given word. And in 1381 an English mob hunted down Flemings and killed them when they could not pronounce "bread and cheese."

We don't kill them today. But we exclude them from our clubs if their pronunciation is lowbrow and from public office if it's highbrow.

✳ "I wish I could *shimmy* like my sister Kate"

THE NAME for the vibrating action which sometimes seizes the front wheels of a car is a form of *chemise*, a woman's undershirt—widely pronounced, in the days when they wore them, *shimmy*.

Among the various manifestations of rebellion and general hell-raising that accompanied and immediately followed World War I was a ragtime dance marked by the female partner's stepping back from the male and violently waggling her shoulders and all adjacent parts. This astonishing act—which was meant to induce interest in the partner and apoplexy in the chaperones—was called "shaking the shimmy." (There was a popular song: "I wish I Could Shimmy Like My Sister Kate.")

When the bushings on the front axle of the Model T Ford became worn (which they frequently did), the whole front of the car shook in a wild wobble reminiscent of the motions of the dance—and the word passed to the car.

313 · *shivaree*

✽ -*ship* shape

SEE YOUR AUTHORIZED CHEVROLET DEALER urged the billboard. SEE IT AT YOUR AUTHORIZED CADILLAC DEALERSHIP urged the next billboard. A *dealer* we know; we've buzzed into his web several times. But a *dealership*—what's that? Something august and intimidating, with triple headlights and enormous fins? We drew back uneasily and began to think of a Volkswagen.

The suffix -*ship*, related far off, probably, to *shape*—is used to denote (1) a state or condition of being (*hardship*); (2) dignity or rank (*lordship, worship*—and, I suspect, Cadillac *dealership*); state of life, occupation, or behavior (*courtship, penmanship*); or to indicate a sense of collectiveness (*township*).

The other word *ship*, a vessel, is a part of some compounded words, such as *troopship* or *airship*. But it is unrelated to -*ship*. *Seamanship*, though, is related to -*ship*, not to *ship*.

✽ What's a *shivaree*?

Shivaree is the American form of the French word *charivari*. It was introduced into American English and modified to its present form by the French of Canada and Louisiana. The original meaning is unknown. Possibly it merely sought to imitate the shrill racket it designates.

A *shivaree* or *charivari* is a mock serenade given to a newly-married couple, consisting of discordant blowings of horns off key, beatings on tin pans, and the like. Originally charivaris seemed to have been actuated by malice and confined to marriages of which the community did not approve, such as that of a widow too soon after her husband's death or of a couple between whose ages there was an unseemly disparity. Today they are just a part of the slightly forced boisterous fun that many think ought to accompany a marriage. They have degenerated into caravans of horn-honking automobiles and tin cans tied behind the car of the bridal couple.

Shivaree is merely one name. The custom is widespread and has different names in different regions: *horning* in Rhode

Island, *skimmelton* in the Hudson Valley, *belling* in Western Pennsylvania.

✳ Short shrift

IN FORMER times those condemned to death, especially political offenders, military captives, and traitors, were executed almost out of hand. Since their crimes were not assassinations or murders, however, there was a pretense of justice and the prisoner was usually allowed *shrift;* that is, he was allowed to confess his sins to a priest and prepare his soul for death. But those who had him in their power were usually impatient and the condemned man was thus allowed only a little time for his confession. This, in its literal sense, was short shrift. The term is used today for short notice before some unpleasant event or making short work of something disagreeable.

✳ Who are *siblings*, what are they?

"Is IT correct to refer to one's brothers and sisters as *siblings* in an informal conversation?" a correspondent asks. I felt she really whispered, overawed but still sane and resentful.

All I can say is, it wouldn't be *my* idea of an informal conversation, but if all present were either Anglo-Saxons or social scientists, it might be mistaken for English and get by.

Sibling, in its modern use, is an anthropological term meaning "a comember of a sib," and a *sib* is an anthropological term for a unilateral descent group or what people who speak English call "brothers and sisters." The anthropologists may have made up the word from *sib*, an old word meaning "related by blood," or they may have picked up an actual Anglo-Saxon word *sibling* meaning "those related by blood." If they picked it up, they were either very lucky or very well read, because it was a rare word nine hundred years ago. Aelfric used it in the year 1000 in his translation of *Genesis* and four hundred years later it popped up again in a history of Ireland. But after that, so far as it known, it dropped out of use until it reappeared, all scientificated up, in Anthropology A.

Today it is in wide use in all the behavioral sciences—it's a space-saver for psychologists who otherwise would have to use 3 words ("brother and sister") every time they talk about "sibling" rivalry, "sibling" relationships—and they talk about them plenty.

✻ the *silver cord*

THE PHRASE *the silver cord* comes from the Bible. The sixth verse of the twelfth chapter of *Ecclesiastes* speaks of the last days of life, just before death: "Or ever the silver cord be loosed or the golden bowl be broken." Most scholars think this is a reference to a lamp; it is by a silver cord that the golden bowl of the lamp of life is suspended, and when the cord is loosed the lamp falls and is shattered and the light extinguished.

The transference to the idea of a mother-son attachment, its modern meaning, was due to Sidney Howard's adopting the biblical phrase as the title for a play (1926) in which a widowed mother's love for her sons leads her to interfere with their marriages and almost destroy them. Mr. Howard may have had in mind the common birth tragedy in which a child is strangled by the umbilical cord and, fusing this thought with the biblical metaphor, have seen the cord which gives us life and sustains it as, at the same time, an instrument of death.

✻ the real *simon pure*

SIMON PURE was a character in a comedy called *A Bold Stroke for a Wife*, written by Mrs. Susan Centlivre in 1718. The play concerns a Pennsylvania Quaker called Simon Pure. He has a letter of introduction to Obadiah Prim, the guardian of Ann Lovely, an heiress. This letter is stolen by Colonel Feignwell who pretends to be the Quaker and marries the heiress. Simon appears and after various misunderstandings manages to prove that he is "the real Simon Pure."

The phrase passed into the language, and so completely has the play been forgotten that most people who use the phrase have no idea whether "Simon" is a person or a thing. Except in the vocabularies of older people, the expression has been pretty well supplanted by "the real McCoy."

✳ the *sincere* approach

No word is more frequently used in popular praise than *sincere*. If a man or woman, especially one in the public eye, is thought to be "sincere," nothing else matters. Lack of intelligence, of skill, of responsibility—all are unimportant if there is "sincerity."

Yet no dictionary definition of *sincere* covers what is plainly meant by the popular use of *sincere*. Dictionaries define *sincere* as "free from deceit," "straightforward," "honest," "plain," "open," "genuine," and give *hypocritical* as its antonym.

But this does not meet the word's current popular meaning. It does not recognize, for example, that the word is never applied to anyone who is *dis*liked, however frank he may be and however honestly he may believe in his profession. In popular usage *sincere* means "friendly," "warm," one who arouses and, above all, shares, pleasant emotions—the easiest thing in the world, by the way, for hypocrisy to affect. It really means *sympatico*, *gemütlich* and its true antonym is not *hypocritical* but *cynical*. The cynic is not a hypocrite. Quite the contrary. He is a churlish, snarling fellow, contemptuous of other men, especially of their pretensions to sincerity. He is skeptical, mistrustful, scornful, a misanthrope, with an avowed *dis*like of his fellowmen.

David Riesman thinks this use of *sincere* is an expression of the desire of the members of the lonely crowd "to personalize their relationship to their heroes of consumption." It shifts the basis of judgment from the merits of the performance (which few of them are competent to judge) to the personality of the performer, especially in regard to his attitude towards his audience. That is, they cannot judge a performer's ability but they can judge (or, poor things, they *think* they can judge) whether or not the performer likes them. It is this, of course, that makes the occasional expression of scorn of the public by some performer (who, alas, thought he was off the air when he wasn't) the supreme crime of the entertainment industry.

※ *siren*

THE *sirens* were mythological figures in Homer's *Odyssey*. Half-women, half-birds, they perched on rocks in the sea and by the sweetness of their song lured passing sailors to their death. Odysseus filled his men's ears with beeswax and had himself tied to the mast so that he might hear them and yet live. From the Homeric story, *siren* became a jocular term for a dangerously alluring woman.

The ululant whistle on ambulances, fire engines, and police cars, with its terrifying rise and fall, was named for their song: a frightening and arresting sound. Today, with its further application to air-raid warnings, its horror has increased.

An interesting illustration of the way words change their meanings is afforded by the *siren-suit*, a one-piece garment developed in England during World War II. It was so called because it could be slipped on quickly at the sound of the air-raid siren. Note that *siren* maintained a definite meaning for almost 3000 years and then suddenly, within fifty years, acquired two new meanings, one of which, as far as popular knowledge goes, has completely replaced the age-old meaning.

※ the *skeleton* at the feast

HERODOTUS says that it was a custom of the ancient Egyptians to have the image of a corpse shown at their banquets to remind the guests of the brevity of life. Whether this would add to or detract from the merriment would depend, no doubt, upon the temperament of the individual viewer. Some might be moved to amend their ways and in particular to avoid banquets. Others might regard it as a reminder to get on with the whoopee while the going was good.

Sometimes expressed as "a death's head at the feast," the term today refers to some reminder of care or grief in the midst of pleasure and is often used humorously of dismal people who displace the mirth by wanting to go home or otherwise acting sensibly ("party-poopers" is the slang for them).

The *skeleton at the feast* is not to be confused with his brother corpse, the *skeleton in the closet*. This, a much later cadaver, refers to a secret shame or hidden disgrace, such as is concealed in almost all, even the most respectable-seeming, families. Thackeray was very fond of shaking closet doors and listening for the rattle of bones within.

✶ skid road or skid row?

THE ROAD or track along which logs are hauled to the *skidway* is *skid road*. The term was also used in the West to designate certain streets of saloons and flophouses frequented by loggers. Either the loggers felt it was tough going in such streets, or the term was applied humorously because so many of them were "rolled" on it or dragged along it while "stiff."

Further east, where the loggers' term was not so familiar, it was changed to *skid row*. The idea there seems to be that it is a row where men are on the skids, plunging into the abyss of misery.

✶ "the skin of my teeth"

THOUGH in common use it means "a hair's breadth," "the narrowest conceivable margin of safety," the exact meaning of *the skin of my teeth* is one of the most disputed in all literature.

In the King James Version of the Bible, Job, lamenting the evil plight into which he has fallen, says (xix:20): "my bone cleaveth to my skin and to my flesh, and I am escaped with the skin of my teeth." The Revised Standard Version has: "by the skin of my teeth." The New American Catholic edition has: "my bone hath cleaved to my skin, and nothing but lips are left about my teeth."

Some scholars say it means that his teeth had fallen out. Some say it means he was so lean he could gnaw his own bones. Some say it means that he had only the power of speech left. Some (extraordinarily learned) believe that it is a reference to Nasmyth's membrane, a cutaneous covering of the teeth of a foetus ("Glosinge is a glorious thing, certeyn"—Chaucer) and that it means: "I have lost everything except my youthful integrity."

The Interpreter's Bible sums the matter up perfectly: "No certain interpretation seems to be possible."

✳ slipshoddy

A *slipshoe* was what we call a *slipper,* and since at all times people seem to run slippers down at the heels and to slop around in them long after they should have been dropped gingerly into the garbage can, *slipshod* came to mean not merely "shod in slippers" but "slovenly."

Poe invented a nice portmanteau word, *slipshoddiness,* combining the shabby carelessness of *slipshod* with the worthless pretending to be superior material of *shoddy. Slipshoddiness* in a man's style would be vulgar elegance and absurd intellectual pretension expressed—as it so often is—in loose grammar and bad spelling.

✳ slurvian catechism

To THOSE who profess to be agitated by the slurred speech of others, which they call "slurvian," I address this little catechism:

Do you pronounce

the	a	in	*again, woman,* or *said* with a long *u* sound? And how do you pronounce the first *a* in *Sault Ste. Marie?*
the	b	in	*debt* or *thumb?*
the	c	in	*indict, scythe, victuals?*
the	d	in	*knowledge,* or the old *d* in *godspell* or the first *d* in *Wednesday?*
the	e	in	*gone* or *one* or the first *e* in *forehead* or the second *e* in *respite?*
the	g	in	*caught* or *reign?*
the	h	in	*hour, honor,* or *heir?*
the	i	in	*meringue* with an *i* sound?
the	k	in	*know* or *knot?*
the	l	in	*solder* or *alms?*

the	m	in	*comptroller?* or the *p* either?
the	n	in	*damn?*
the	o	in	*women,* as an *o?*
the	p	in	*pneumonia, receipt, psalm, cupboard?*
the	q	in	any word whatsoever? And, if so, how do you pronounce it except *qu* as *kw?*
the	r	in	*worsted* (the flannel). And if you do pronounce the second *r* in *trousers,* are you aware that it is an error of pronunciation, like *garn,* the cockney slurring of "go on"?
the	s	in	*island* or *demesne?*
the	t	in	*fasten, glisten?* And what about *often?*
the	u	in	*catalogue?* It's no answer to say "I don't even write it." That just shows how far slurvianism has gone with you.
the	v		that used to be in *launder* (lavender) but was slurred out?
the	w	in	*write, two, sword,* or *wreck?*
the	y	in	*Pepys* or *mayor?*
the	z	in	*rendezvous?*

And I would further ask them if they pronounce *mortgage* as *mort gage* or *mor' gij?* And if they used the slurred *instead* or the unslurred *in his stead?* And do they speak the horribly slurred forms *sexton, bosun, sassafras,* and *isinglass* or do they employ only the unslurred *sacristan, boatswain, saxifrage,* and *huisenblas?* And do they say *mob, bus,* and *varsity,* like other people, or do they give the words their full enunciation as *mobile vulgus, omnibus,* and *university?* And do they say *sample* or the "proper" form *example? dropsy* or *hydropsie? gin* or *Geneva? gossip* or *godsib?* And where do they stop short of Latin or Gothic? And do they insist on the same fulness of pronunciation in speaking French and Italian? And, if so, who understands them? Indeed, I am mean enough to go further and ask them, if they do speak French, aren't they rather proud of pronouncing it the way it *is* pronounced, with its thousands of slurrings and elisions (just as English has them) and not the way some theorists think French ought to be pronounced? And why this discrimination against their native tongue?

And I would ask them one last question: Aren't you ashamed?

✳ all to *smithereens*

Smithereens are little *smithers*, little Irish smithers, to be exact, because *-eens* is an Irish suffix indicating diminutiveness.

But what are *smithers?* Other than small pieces, nobody knows. They may have something to do with a *smithy*, a blacksmith's shop, once a part of every village. They may simply be the fragments which the smith, smithing his smithery in his smithy, left around the anvil, or *stithy*.

✳ *snide*

THE WORD *snide* has been in English for at least a hundred and fifteen years. Some dictionaries regard it as slang. Others accept it as standard.

Originally a part of thieves' lingo, it meant "counterfeit." "Snide jewelry" was imitation jewelry—since dignified as "costume jewelry"—so flashy as to be obviously not the real thing. From this, *snide* came to mean "base, tricky, mean," and so reached its present meaning of "derogatory in a sly, nasty, insinuating manner."

The meaning of a word is often affected by hearing in it the echo of another word [see *klang association*]; in *snide* many people probably hear echoes of *sneer* and *sly*.

✳ *so long*

THERE have been attempts to trace *so long*, as a formula of farewell, to the Arabic *salaam* and the Hebrew *sholom*. But the best explanation seems to be that it is merely a shortening of "So long as we're apart, good luck." Walt Whitman used it as early as 1860, but it is probably not of American origin. Olive Schreiner used it in South Africa sometime before 1878.

It's colloquial. That is, it's proper in speech among friends—

even the most highly educated use it—but it would be improper in a formal, written document or in a solemn public address.

Convention seems to demand that on parting we make some cheerful noise, however idiotic, probably to show that we're not going away mad. The British go in for "ta-ta," "toodle-oo," and "cheerio." Of these the American stomach has been able to accept only the last. They are all useful sounds, however, for they permit us to break off chance conversations and get on with our business.

✳ a very *sophisticated* word

WHEN in a TV interview, Mr. Henry Cabot Lodge described certain actions being taken in the Congo as "the most *sophisticated* operation ever undertaken by the United Nations," he may have given all the push that was needed to send this, one of our most erratic words, careering off into still wilder and remoter meanings.

Sophisticated is a protean word. Originally it meant "wise." Then, through its association with the Sophists, it came to mean "oversubtle," "marked by specious but fallacious reasoning," "able to make the worse appear the better reason."

While retaining this meaning, it acquired the additional, derivative sense of "adulterated." A tobacconist in Ben Jonson's *Alchemist* is said to sell good tobacco: "he doesn't sophisticate it," they say, with other materials. Montaigne had the idea of adulteration in mind when he said that philosophy was nothing but "sophisticated poetry." And so did the eleventh edition of *The Encyclopaedia Britannica* when it said (1913) that ground rice was "one of the chief sophistications" of ginger powder. This meaning is no longer heard in general application but it is retained in special, technical applications. We can read of "sophisticated oil," "sophisticated steel," or "sophisticated texts."

From "adulteration" to "corruption" is a short step and the meaning of corruption ran side by side with that of adulteration. Coryat (1611) called dyed hair "sophisticated." King Lear, going mad in the storm starts to strip off his clothes because they are trappings of civilization and civilized man is "sophisticated." Judge Walter J. LaBuy, of the Federal District Court in Chicago, in sentencing an enterprising young woman who was married to twelve sailors and drawing a dependent's allotment from each of them, told her, with stern disapproval, that she was "thoroughly sophisticated" (*Chicago Tribune*, Nov. 18, 1960). Judge LaBuy may have been blending both meanings and punning into the bargain.

Up until about thirty years ago, the most common meaning conveyed by *sophisticated* was of a particular kind of corruption, the corruption of idealism by worldly experience. And this is still given as its principal meaning in most dictionaries.

Then suddenly the attitude implicit in the word was reversed; it ceased to mean unpleasantly worldly-wise and came to mean admirably worldly-wise. Something—possibly depression-begotten cynicism, urbanization, army experiences, the perfume ads, or the glamorous pornography of the picture magazines—had led the populace to revise its estimate of worldly wisdom. For the past fifteen years *sophistication* has been definitely a term of praise.

And even more. "Sophistication," writes Mr. Earl Wilson, "means the ability to do almost anything without feeling guilty." Blum's, the celebrated San Francisco candy manufacturers, on opening a branch store in New York, wooed their new clientele by advising them that their "old-fashioned, home-made-type candies" had been "sophisticated" by their master candymaker. Mr. Lloyd Shearer informed the readers of *Parade* (Nov. 6, 1960) that a famous movie actress's husband "seemed sophisticatedly impervious to jealousy," losing his wife "graciously, understandingly and philosophically . . . to another man." It is no wonder that— gog-eyed with awe and envy—a sophomore English class at New Trier High School, in Winnetka, Illinois, defined *sophistication* as "a grace acquired with maturity."

The beginnings of this reversal can be seen in the words of Duke Ellington's "Sophisticated Lady" (1933). The lady of the title had "grown wise." Disillusion was "deep in her eyes." She was "nonchalant . . . smoking, drinking . . . dining with some man in a restaurant." She missed "the love of long ago" but, plainly, had no intention of returning to its meager ecstasies. She had lost innocence but had acquired polish and when she dined out some man picked up the tab. In the minds of many rustic maidens this— one gathers from the change in *sophisticated*'s meaning—was to be preferred to dewy freshness that dined alone at home on leftovers or carried lunch in a paper bag. And by 1958, in the world of Mr. John O'Hara's characters, *sophistication* had come to signify not corruption but almost the irreducible minimum of good manners ("You're much too sophisticated to goose an airline hostess"— *From the Terrace,* p. 814).

Not content with such audacious change, about three years ago *sophisticated* went hog wild and started to mean "delicately responsive to electronic stimuli," "highly complex mechanically," "requiring skilled control," "extraordinarily sensitive in receiving, interpreting and transmitting signals." Or at least that is what one must guess it means in such statements as "Modern radar is vastly more sophisticated" than quaint, old-fashioned radar (*Time,* Aug. 10, 1959); Vanguard I "may be small but it is wondrously sophisticated" (March 31, 1958); "the Il-18 is aeronautically more sophisticated than the giant TU-114 (Sept. 5, 1960); "Pioneer V is exceedingly sophisticated" (*Chicago Sun-Times,* March 16, 1960); and "The Antikythera mechanism is far more sophisticated than any described in classical scientific texts" (*Scientific American*).

The connection between these and any previously established meanings of the word are not clear, but since they are definitely favorable, they must spring some way from the post-Ellington uses. My own guess would be this: the sophisticated are not unperceiving, insensitive clods; on the contrary, they are particularly aware of nuances, act on the merest hints, are moved by delicate impulses and respond to subtle stimuli. They don't have to be shoved. They know their way around and move with ease in their allotted orbits.

But what did Mr. Lodge mean? He is too staunch a supporter of the U.N. to have meant that the action in the Congo was specious or corrupt—and too much of a diplomat to have said so even if he had thought it. He could have meant that its effectiveness was adulterated by Russian participation, but this—relying, as it must, on an archaic or technical meaning—would have been obscure and Mr. Lodge is always lucid. And the sheer facts of the operation would hardly support the interpretation that it was marked by an excess of worldly wisdom, reprehensible *or* admirable.

So we are forced to assume that he had the very latest meaning in mind: that the operation was a highly complex mechanism, requiring great skill for its direction and delicately responsive to the impulses of world opinion. Or he may have agreed with the high-school students and meant that our tame endurance of insults and violence and our patience in the face of provocation indicated not timidity or cowardice or even confusion but a grace that comes with maturity.

Whatever he meant, he may have started something. Words acquire meanings from the situations in which they are used. And who can say what meaning *sophisticated* may pick up in the Congo?

* sophomore

SOME say that *Sophomore* is a combination of two Greek words, one meaning "wise" and the other meaning a "fool." But tempting as this explanation is (especially to Juniors and Seniors), it must be rejected. The word seems to come, rather, from *sophom*, an obsolete variant of *sophism*, and the agent suffix *-or*. This is the same suffix that we have in actor, "one who acts." So that a *sophomore* was one who was active in the dialectic exercises which used to make up a large part of college activities. The word formerly appeared in several forms that now seem strange to us, as *Sophy Moors, Sophumer,* and *Soph Mor*.

The application of the word to a student in his second year originated at Cambridge University, in England, but it is now used only in America. It is intriguing to think that John Harvard, a Cambridge man (hence Cambridge, Massachusetts), brought it to us, along with his books and the £800 that served to establish the university that bears his name.

* "a *sorry* excuse"

A CORRESPONDENT is disturbed by the use of *sorry* in such expressions as "a sorry excuse." As usual, he feels that it is a "corruption," that it is "spreading," and wonders if it is "likely to be accepted."

The answer, also as usual, is that it is not a corruption, it is not spreading, and it has been accepted as long as we have any record of the language.

Sorry and *sorrow* are in no way related. When someone says,

"I'm sorry," he is not saying, "I have sorrow for what I have done" but "I am sore—that is, I am in pain—for what I have done."

The extension of *sorry* to mean "vile, wretched, mean, of little account" (the meaning that the correspondent, and many others, regard as a corruption that is spreading) dates back to at least 1250. Shakespeare so used it. Macbeth looking on his bloody hands after killing Duncan says "This is a sorry sight" and in another play we are told that certain bad news will provide "a sorry breakfast" for one of the characters.

Sorry came to be used particularly of lean or feeble horses ("a sorry nag"). Here, perhaps the idea of saddle sores or harness galls or the wounds of blows and spurs may have reinforced the idea of pain and wretchedness.

✻ sound sense

SOME of the simplest but most effective words in the language consist of nothing more than an echo of the sound of the thing they designate—such as *boom, bang, burp*. But, at best, words can only approximate a sound and different ears sometimes hear different sounds in the same thing. The splash of water has been represented as such different sounds as *bil-bil* and *glut-glut* and *boop-beep*. The Elizabethans used *bounce* to render the sound of the discharge of a cannon and it has much to recommend it over our *bang*.

Conscious attempts at onomatopoeia are not much in fashion at present, but every now and then some old virtuoso will unlimber the alphabet and have a go at it. Worthy of honorable mention is P. G. Wodehouse's description of the sound a pig makes when eating (*Blandings Castle*, Chapter 3): "a sort of gulpy, gurgly, plobby, squishy, wofflesome sound."

All echoic words are impressionistic and there are more impressions than the purely aural. It has often been pointed out, for example, that *cock-a-doodle-do* is a very poor representation of the actual sound of a cock's crow. The French *coqerico*, Italian *chic-chirichi* and the Danish *Kykeliki* (Jacobs, *Naming-Day in Eden*, p. 93) are thought by many to be more accurate. But *cock-a-doodle-do* has more rhythm and rhythm suggests the dancing strut which conveys more idea of the bird, perhaps, than the mere sound of its cry.

✱ sour grapes

Sour grapes is drawn from one of Aesop's fables. A fox seeing some luscious-looking grapes tried every way in his power to get some of them to eat. But they hung out of the reach of his highest leap and when, after great exertion, he found he couldn't get them, he said he didn't want them anyway because they were sour.

The phrase is used by us only to indicate that some belittling remark is, at bottom, an expression of envy. But LaFontaine, the greatest fabulist next to Aesop, regarded the attitude of the fox as admirable. "Wasn't it better," he asks, after repeating the remark about the sour grapes, "than complaining?"

✱ Do you say "I'll *speak* to him" or "I'll *talk* to him"?

IT DEPENDS on the nature of the intended communication. *Speak* implies that you have something specific to say or ask. *Talk* implies that the other person will also have something to say.

Where a rebuke or a command is to be given, *speak* is harsher. Where a request is to be made, *speak* is more diffident. Because in both cases it doesn't convey the idea of reciprocity latent in *talk*.

Talk is generally the more familiar, easy term ("We talked by the hour but I don't remember a thing that was said"). It implies listeners who joined in ("Sir, we had good talk"). *Speak* can mean anything from a word or a disjointed utterance ("Speak of the Devil"; "He tried to speak but was too frightened") to a prolonged and stately oration ("The minister spoke to an attentive House for three hours"). *Speak* can refer to volume ("Speak softly"). *Talk* can refer to content or general import ("Talk sense").

✻ Why were "liquor joints" during prohibition called *speakeasies?*

A PLACE dedicated to violating the law is not one in which bibulous bellowing is desired. One good chorus of *Sweet A-del-ine* and you might all be in the clink. The name "speakeasy," however, far antedates Prohibition, just as the illicit manufacture and sale of liquor does. It was in use in America as early as 1889 and far before that English smugglers called the places where they dispensed illegal liquor "speak-softly-shops."

✻ Isn't *spendthrift* a contradiction?

THERE is not the contradiction in *spendthrift* that there seems at first glance. The older meaning was "one who wasted an inheritance," that is, one who spent the accumulation of someone else's thrift. Sometimes he was called a *wastethrift*. The archetype was the Prodigal Son.

The word was applied solely to young men. Maybe they are more inclined, and more compelled, to spend freely than young women but, most probably, until quite recently young women rarely had the chance. An old spendthrift is inconceivable. If it were inherited money, he'd have spent it long ago. If it were his own that he'd saved, he'd not be eager to throw it away. And, anyway, old men are inclined to the drab vice of avarice rather than to the splendid wickedness of living it up.

✵ more than one *sphinx*

THE PLURAL of *sphinx* perplexes many, though there are very few plurals that an English-speaking person is likely to need less. But if on a trip to Egypt one has had a drink too many and happens to see several of them, he may refer to them as *sphinxes*—although in that condition *sphinxes* would be a very difficult word to pronounce. If he wants to be absolutely correct, however, he will say *sphinges*. The only drawback will be that no one will have the faintest idea of what he's talking about.

✵ *spic and span*

THE FULL expression was *spick and span new* (or *speck and span new*). And before that it was merely *span new*, the *spick* being tacked on just for the cadence and alliteration.

So the question is, what's a *span*? Why should something freshly new be *span-new*? And the answer is that a span was a chip of wood (a *spick* was a spike or splinter). *Span* is related to *spoon*, chips of wood, apparently, being once used as we use spoons.

So that *spic and span* means as new and fresh and clean as a fresh chip of wood. And anyone who has split kindling knows just what that means: there isn't anything cleaner and fresher and *newer* than a freshly split chip of wood.

※ the *split infinitive*

"THE PRINCETON PRESIDENT [*Harold Willis Dodds*] is not a distinguished speaker. He splits infinitives but his utterances are clear and . . . vivid."—*The New York Times,* April 13, 1957, p. 22.

Any man whose utterances are clear and vivid is a distinguished speaker, if only distinguished from people whose utterances are enfeebled by the fear of splitting an infinitive.

It is always proper to split an infinitive when the alternative is to be ambiguous or cumbrous.

One of the characteristics of contemporary American English is a marked increase in the use of the infinitive. Road signs, for example, that only ten years ago read KEEP TO THE RIGHT EXCEPT WHEN PASSING now read KEEP TO THE RIGHT EXCEPT TO PASS. An English woman was quoted in the papers recently as saying sarcastically of another woman, "It's very nice of her giving me advice." An American would have said, "It's very nice of her to give me advice."

Now there are many occasions in using this increasingly popular grammatical construction in which one can express one's exact meaning only by putting an adverb between the verb and the *to*. "He hoped to at least double his income" is not expressed in "He hoped at least to double his income" because in the second sentence "at least" may modify *hoped*, not *double*. And people whose "utterances are clear . . . and vivid" never hesitate for a second to split an infinitive rather than run the slightest risk of being misunderstood.

President Dodds may console himself with the reflection that as an infinitive-splitter he is not only in the company of a

331 · *stadium(s)*

hundred million or so of his lesser fellow Americans but also in the company of Ben Franklin, Abraham Lincoln, Henry James, Theodore Roosevelt, his predecessor Woodrow Wilson, and Herbert Hoover.

✶ a *square meal*

THE HOMELY, simple, common expression *a square meal* takes us deep into the psychology of speech. It's a transference of the sense of satisfying completeness that somehow we derive from a square's having four equal sides and four right angles. It's solid, neat, balanced; it's full.

✶ *stadium(s)*

IF YOU are referring to a football *stadium,* the plural is *stadiums.* It's hard to imagine the expression on a coach's face if he were told that "six new stadia" have been built.

If, however, you are referring to the ancient Greek and Roman measurement of distance, the plural is *stadia.*

The modern word makes its plural in the regular English way, by adding *s,* because it is a regular English (American) word, merely based on a Latin word. It's a very recent word, by the way, and, in the sense in which we use it, an American coinage. Dictionaries forty years ago did not recognize what is now, to most Americans, the word's only meaning: the place where football games and other athletic events take place before large audiences.

✳ Why is a *stogie*?

Stogies, now a generic name for cheap cigars, were originally *conestogies* and so called because they were smoked by the drivers of the heavy covered wagons made in the Conestoga Valley of Lancaster County, Pennsylvania. These were the "covered wagons" of the Western migrations. The drivers were big, hearty, bearded men and, apparently, part of their picturesqueness was their long homemade cigars. They wore a characteristic heavy boot which was also called a *stogie*. Maybe the smell of the cigars and the boots intermingled.

✳ a *stool pigeon*

ORIGINALLY a *stool pigeon* was a decoy, a pigeon—possibly fastened to a stool—used to lure other pigeons within range of the hunter's gun or the fowler's net. The expression *stool pigeon* is an American term and the metaphorical application of it to a police informer was made almost simultaneously with the expression's appearance.

Sometimes the decoy bird was merely called a *stool*. This would seem to be a shortening of *stool pigeon* were it not that there is a very old English word (going back to the ninth century) *stale* that means a decoy ("Like unto fowlers that by their stales draw other birds into their nets"—1595). And this, too, was extended by metaphor to designate police informers and criminals' decoys. In this last sense it got attached particularly to prostitutes and this may have driven it out of respectable speech.

✳ the old, old *story*

LEARNED men have puzzled for centuries over the use of the word *story* to designate the "layers" of a house ("The second story is reached by an outside staircase"). Some think it was used because goods may have been *stored* at different levels. Or there may have been the thought of rooms furnished with *stores* of *furniture*.

But the oldest form of the word is not *story* but *historia*, the Latin word meaning "a narrative" which we also use in the word *history*.

The houses of the poor were just huts. But the mansions of the rich (the only ones that would have several "layers") were often very ornate, elaborately painted and sculptured, inside and out. So that the *stories* of a house were probably tiers, or "layers," of paintings or sculpturings each of which told some famous story. One still sees such representations on many German houses, especially in Bavaria. This theory of the origin of *story*, in relation to a building, is supported by the fact that we use *story* when thinking of the *outside* of a building, *floor* when thinking of the inside. There are fantastically subtle memories in our speech!

✳ the *strai(gh)t* and narrow path

THE PHRASE the *straight and narrow path* is based on a passage in the Bible (*Matthew* vii:14). The King James Version has: "Because strait is the gate and narrow is the way, which leadeth unto life." The Revised Standard Version has: "For the gate is narrow and the way is hard." The New American Catholic edition has: "How narrow the gate and close the way that leads to life."

Althought *strait* in the King James Version applies to the gate, *narrow* in that version and *close* in the New American Catholic version apply to the way or path. With these two words *strait* is synonymous and *straight* is not. So it is properly *the strait and narrow path*.

However, since *strait* as an adjective is archaic and since straightness has become fixed in our speech as a term for moral rectitude, and since the phrase is not a direct quotation anyway, it would be almost ostentatious to insist on *strait*. Certainly it is now popularly conceived to be the *straight* and narrow path.

※ *strait-laced*

Though often spelled "straight-laced," the proper expression for someone who is morally rigid is *strait-laced*. Strait means narrow—geographic straits are narrows—coming from the Latin *strictus* which we have also in *constriction*.

The expression *strait-laced* is drawn from the lacing of a bodice or corset. When the laces are drawn tight, so as to narrow the opening, the body of the wearer is compressed and held rigid and upright. So when our moral bonds are drawn tight, we are likely to be repressed and severe. Furthermore, an unlaced person, especially a young woman, was more voluptuous and enticing. And here again we draw a moral parallel in the word *loose*.

Strait-laced is used today almost exclusively to refer to moral attributes. But formerly it was used of many things that were cramped and narrow. People spoke of strait-laced interpretations and referred to obstinate or moody people as *strait-laced*, that is, bound within themselves. People who hated to let go of money were called strait-laced. We call them *tight*.

※ the *struthious* bird

Struthious, the adjective for *ostrich*, has the charm of being one of the least practical words that one can add to his vocabulary. So few things are like an ostrich that occasions for its use rarely present themselves. And even as "ostrich-like" or "ostrich-ean," it's limited. You can't say "My mother had a struthious feather in her hat," though the statement would doubtless attract gratifying attention. However, it can be applied to the head-hiding ostrich of folklore just as validly as to *Struthio camelus* itself. You can say, "He struthiously hid his head in the sand."

Ostrich is simply a slurring of *avis struthio*, a late Latin form (*avis*, "bird") of the Greek *strouthion* which meant "ostrich." The Spaniards have left it almost as they found it, *avestruz;* but the Germans have denuded the poor fowl down to the almost unrecognizable *Strauss*.

✻ stummick

No DICTIONARY recognizes the pronunciation *stummick* for *stomach*, yet one certainly hears it with increasing frequency and from people of some education and social position.

To those who pronounce *stomach* as *stummuk*, *stummik* is often highly offensive, yet there is no reason why *-ach* should be pronounced *-uk* rather than *-ik*. Far greater changes than that have taken place in the pronunciation of thousands of words and have been accepted and used by the most highly educated.

What is interesting is the warmth of our resentment against this particular pronunciation, even though we know that it is widespread. I share the resentment, but I suspect that to a large extent it's snobbery — or, if it softens the charge to put it in sociological jargon, it is a group-defensive response. *Stummick* is the pronunciation of the poor and the uneducated (what our grandparents would have more courageously called a "common" or "vulgar" pronunciation) and we want to be sure that no one thinks we are one of them.

✻ sudsy

SUDSY NOVEL, the *Chicago Sun-Times* heads a book review, while the *New York Times* in the course of a review refers to a similar novel as "soapy."

Did the Chicago paper mean that the novel was frothy, or bubbling or flashing with iridescent color, like soapsuds? Did the New York paper mean that its novel was slippery or evasive (as it would have meant a hundred years ago) or that it in some way cleaned things up or washed out dirt?

Not at all. Both papers meant that the book being reviewed was, in the opinion of the reviewer, improbable, oversentimental, strained in its pathos, jerkily episodic and tedious in its excess of woes and misfortunes. That is, it was like a radio *soap opera*.

Few dictionaries recognize any such meaning for *sudsy* or *soapy*, yet no American would have the least doubt as to what was meant by these words in these contexts. This is living language.

Radio soap opera is now extinct and it is likely that the

meaning with which it irradiated these words will quickly fade. But it is possible that the meaning may stay in them long after the reason for it has been forgotten. It has happened thousands of times in the history of the language.

※ **the *swan song***

UNLIKE ducks, geese, gulls, and other gabby waterfowl, the swan is mute. In anger it will hiss, but otherwise its dignity and beauty are not marred by graceless squawking and chattering. From the time of the ancient Greeks, however, it has been believed that the bird (sacred to Apollo and gifted with prophecy) breaks this lifelong silence just before it dies with one supremely melodious song. From this has come our use of *swan song* to mean a final utterance.

Ornithologists regard this alleged performance with chill incredulity but the poets (who invented it) have embraced it warmly.

❋ the *sword of Damocles*

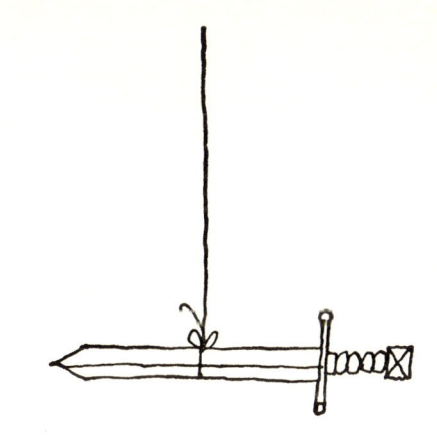

THE *sword of Damocles* is a symbol of the fears and worries that prevent people in seemingly enviable positions from enjoying the pleasures and glories of their state.

The expression is drawn from a Greek story of a flatterer called Damocles who kept telling Dionysius, the Tyrant of Syracuse, how much he admired and envied him. Dionysius said he would be glad to let Damocles have a taste of the felicity he praised so highly. The sycophant was served a sumptuous banquet but over his head a sharp-pointed, heavy sword was suspended by a single hair. Damocles, afraid to move or speak lest the thread break, found the meal an agonizing torment.

❋ *talent*

A *talent*, in ancient times, was a unit of weight and this weight of silver or gold constituted a monetary unit. In one of the parables in the Bible (*Matthew* xxv:14-30) a master gives each of his servants a certain amount of money and tells them to invest it profitably in his absence. The man with only a single talent was afraid of losing it and buried it in the ground that he might, at his master's return, at least show no loss. For this timidity, however, he was cast into outer darkness, to weep and gnash.

The most common modern meaning of *talent*—some special, natural (i.e., God-given) ability or aptitude—is a figurative development from the parable. It is an interesting illustration of one way in which a word can suddenly acquire a totally different meaning. In the TV world *talent* now distinguishes performers from cameramen, cosmeticians, directors, and other of their betters.

✳ *tandem*

Tandem is the Latin word for "at length" (as in "at length he agreed"). It was a measurement of time, not of space. In the late eighteenth century it was very flashy and fashionable to harness two horses, not abreast but one behind the other. And some learned wit called it "driving tandem." Everyone who could afford horses and followed fashions in harnessing them had a smattering of Latin in those days and the absurdity of this application of *tandem*, so suitable to the absurdity of the thing it designated, made the word catch on.

A hundred years later (1884) someone extended the term from horses to the double-seated, double-sprocketed bicycle.

There are several words in the language based on learned jokes. One of them is *mob*, which is a clipping of *mobile vulgus* ("the moving, or fickle, common people")—though this is more of a sneer than a joke. Another is *bus*, a clipping of *omnibus*, the dative of the Latin word for *all*, meaning a conveyance "for all," as distinct from a private carriage.

✳ tarred with the same brush

THE METAPHOR *tarred with the same brush* seems to be drawn from the marking of sheep. Sheep can't be branded. The brand would spoil the fleece and after the first season the wool would conceal the brand. So they are daubed in various distinguishing ways and formerly tar was the commonest substance used. So those "tarred with the same brush" belonged to the same flock.

The expression is usually employed in a derogatory sense. This may be due to the color of tar and the many bad associations with blackness. It may also have been influenced by the popular saying that "He who touches pitch will be defiled."

There was a proverb against false economy that said "The sheep was lost for (i.e., for the lack of) a pennyworth of tar." This became corrupted to "The *ship* was lost. . . ."

✳ two *tattoos*

EXCEPT for being combined in such rare puns as that in the old song about the tattooed man ("It's perfectly true, you can beat a tattoo,/But you can't beat a tattooed man"), the two *tattoos* have nothing in common.

The *tattoo* which designates designs made by puncturing the skin and inserting pigment is a Polynesian word (*ta·tu*). It appeared in English in Captain Cook's *Journal* of his first voyage to the South Seas (1769).

The drumbeat *tattoo* was borrowed by Cromwell's soldiers from the Dutch in the middle of the seventeenth century. At that time it was *tap-to* and was the tap of the drum that ordered the men to turn *to* or *in*. Soldiers still call it *taps*, though it is now sounded on a bugle. It was also interpreted as the signal for closing the taps or taverns in communities under martial law.

Just to complicate matters further, there's still another *tattoo* in English—a variant spelling for one of the names of the eight-banded armadillo. Somewhere in all this there must be a challenge to some punster to produce a masterpiece.

✲ Why does an airplane *taxi* out to the runway?

DR. WOODFORD HEFLIN, editor of *The United States Air Force Dictionary*, says, in that work, that an old beat-up monoplane used on the ground to train student pilots, at Brooklands, England, in 1911, was called "the taxi" by the students. The word spread to the trainer plane at other air schools and was extended, as a verb, to any plane in motion on the ground. The noun was soon discarded and forgotten and all idea of humor faded out of the verb. It served a need and did as well as any other word.

Taxi is a shortened form of *taximeter-cab*. And *cab* is short for *cabriolet* which was so called because it bounced around like a jumping goat. It's akin to *caper*. The *taxi-* of *taximeter* is simply *tax*, the amount to be paid. Cabs with meters that registered the amount to be paid were new in 1911.

✲ "tell it to the marines"

THE FULL saying used to be "Tell that to the marines—the sailors won't believe it."

By "the Marines" today an American means members of the United States Marine Corps but formerly *marines* were merely troops assigned to warships, partly to serve as landing forces and partly to keep order on the ship. This last duty would hardly endear them to the sailors who were highly-skilled men and, though rough, far more likely to be intelligent and informed than common soldiers. At any rate, the sailors despised the soldiers and apparently amused themselves by telling them cock-and-bull stories. A sailor would stigmatize a yarn as fantastic by saying, in effect, "You can tell that to the marines, because they're stupid and will believe anything; but don't expect me, a sailor, to believe it."

The use of the word *soldier* as a verb, meaning to shirk or loaf on the job, to "goof off," was originally a seaman's term.

✲ How much should a *teller* tell?

SINCE banks maintain a highly proper reticence about their depositors' affairs, the word *teller* seems, at first thought, a most inappropriate name for the man behind the window.

But, of course, it isn't. The original meaning of the verb *to tell* was "to count." We still say "There were six of us, all told" —that is, all counted. *Untold* wealth is not wealth that you've not told anybody (especially the Director of Internal Revenue) about, but wealth so great that it remains uncounted.

So a bank teller is a counter of money, not a narrator of private affairs.

Tell and *count* blend in the word *recount,* in its sense of narration ("He recounted his adventures"), which has to be distinguished by special punctuation from the word meaning to number over again (*re-count*). The idea underlying *recount* is that in former days (in the old once-upon-a-time days before the flashback) events were narrated in the order of their happening.

The same idea has shaped the equivalent German words. The German word for count is *zahlen.* The word for narrate is *erzahlen.* Just like *count* and *recount.*

✻ *that* and *who*

"The man *that. . . .*" Shouldn't it be "The man *who . . .*"?

Not necessarily.

That is the oldest of our relative pronouns and the most useful. It may certainly be used of persons ("Blessed is the man that walketh not in the counsel of the ungodly") and of animals and inanimate things. In the old nursery rhyme about the House that Jack built, it is used in reference to the house, the malt, the rat, the cow, the priest, and the maiden all forlorn.

Many people prefer *who* to *that* when the reference is to a person, and they are free to make this distinction between themselves and animals and inanimate objects if the necessity of it presses upon them. But earlier generations were confident enough not to feel the need of it.

Many are even concerned about God's identity—or, ignoring certain implications in the *Book of Job,* want to insist that He, too, is a human being. Twentieth-century translations of the Bible are likely to read "Our Father who art in heaven" in place of the old "which art in heaven." The Authorized Revision of 1885 had it "that art in heaven." There is more real piety and humility in the "that" and "which" than the insisters on "who" will ever be able to imagine.

※ "another *think* coming"

"People say 'You have another *think* coming.' Shouldn't it be 'another *thought* coming'?"

Thought wouldn't quite say what was intended because *think* in this colloquial expression usually means a whole course of thinking, not merely a substitute or additional idea.

Thought wouldn't do for another reason. "You have another think coming" is always intended to be pert, flippant, or downright rude. And for this purpose *think* is better. The retort usually follows the use of *think* by the one snubbed. He has said, "I think thus and so" and is answered by being told that he has another think coming. Now the throwing of someone's words in his teeth (as it used to be called) is an act of deliberate provocation. And the using of an ungrammatical form implies that you are so contemptuous of him that you feel no need to speak formally to him, or even correctly. Ludicrously bad grammar is good enough for the likes of him!

So that, all in all, *think* serves a bad purpose well—far better than *thought* would serve it.

※ a *thoughtless* criticism

"People say 'That was a thoughtless act' or 'That was a thoughtful act.' But acts can't think!"

No, but those who perform them can and their thought or lack of it often shows in the act.

When Hamlet asks the gravedigger for what man he is digging a grave, the precise lout says, "for no man, sir." "What woman, then?" the prince asks, with a touch of irritation. For no woman either, the yokel replies in triumph, but for one that was a woman. "How absolute the knave is," Hamlet says to Horatio. "We must speak by the card [the compass card, marked with the points of the compass], or equivocation will undo us."

This insistence on absolute literalness occurs many times in the comic scenes in Shakespeare's plays. Shakespeare was obviously amused and repelled by those who, if they had their way, would reduce language to a signpost.

Anyone who is seriously puzzled by such an expression as *a thoughtful act* needs to join the human race and feel the delight of exercising a little imagination and of perceiving the uses of condensation and ellipsis.

※ a *tinker's damn*

A *tinker's damn* is just what it says, a tinker's curse. Seemingly tinkers swore so much that their oaths had little value.

In the nineteenth century a *Dictionary of Mechanics* said that a tinker erected a small barrier of mud around the area he wanted to solder and that this was his *dam* and that, plainly, nothing could be worth less than this little ridge of mud when he had finished his job. But this suggestion is totally lacking in support. That is, no one has been able to show any statement or passage in print (prior to the publication of this particular dictionary) that bears this meaning out. Whereas there are very many old expressions that mark the profanity and dissoluteness of tinkers: "as drunk as a tinker," "to swear like a tinker," and "not worth a tinker's curse." Some of these expressions are three and four hundred years old.

It is sometimes written "a tinker's dam," but this is probably a mere avoidance of *damn*. In fact, the whole phrase is an avoidance. Instead of saying, "I don't give a damn," some people say "I don't give a tinker's damn." This not only rounds out the rhythm (and rhythm is very important in swearing) but puts the responsibility for the profanity on the tinker.

※ a *tip*

A *tip* is a light *tap*. Gratuities are given with an assumed surreptitiousness. You just brush your hand against the discreetly lowered palm of the head waiter and leave a bill in it and he thanks you with a low fervency that keeps the transaction gratifyingly intimate but is still loud enough to inform others of your magnificence and admonish them to follow your example. So that a tip was, originally, a light tap against the palm of a recipient.

But that is not absolutely certain. It's simply the best guess in the light of the history of the word which came into the language about the year 1700, passing from thieves' cant to upper-class slang (as many words have) at a bound.

One often hears that *tip* derives from a sign over a box in a restaurant, soliciting gratuities: $T(o)$ I(nsure) P(rompt service). But there is no evidence to support this and anonymous, communal giving would defeat the whole purpose of tipping.

✳ the *toast* of the town

Drinking a toast seems to be a contradiction, but the expression grows out of an old custom of adding flavor to a glass of wine by putting a piece of spiced toast in the glass. "Fetch me a quart of sack," Falstaff commands Bardolph (*Merry Wives of Windsor,* III.v.3); "put a toast in't."

Then, about the beginning of the eighteenth century, a figurative application was developed. The company was requested to drink to some lady (often a reigning belle) whose name was supposed to flavor the drink like the spiced toast.

Sir Richard Steele says (*Tatler,* June 4, 1709) that this figurative extension grew out of an incident that happened at Bath in the reign of Charles II (1660-1684). A celebrated beauty of the day, he says, was in the bath (a public, medicinal bath; she would have had some sort of garment on, though no doubt it would have been clinging most voluptuously to her) when one of her admirers scooped up a glass of the water she was in and drank her health in it. "A gay fellow, half-fuddled," Steele adds, said that though "he liked not the liquor, he would have the toast" and would have jumped in after the lady had he not been forcibly restrained.

Linguists—dull fellows—are inclined to doubt the anecdote.

✳ *tolerance* and *understanding*

A CORRESPONDENT, whose dictionary must be printed on pink paper and bound in mother-of-pearl, writes: "Wouldn't it be a step forward if the word *tolerance* were replaced by *understanding?*"

In my opinion it would be a loss because it would blur important distinctions of meaning.

To *tolerate* (in the social sense) is to allow, permit, not to interfere with, to recognize and permit the holding of (and, within limits, the practice of) beliefs and customs *without necessarily agreeing with them or even respecting them*. It is the last part of the definition, which I have *underscored*, that makes toleration a social virtue; because, for the sake of civil order, we must live at peace with people with whom we disagree and whom we do not like. The word *toleration* does not imply that you must be fond of your neighbor or even sympathize with him. It simply says live and let live.

Understanding (in this context) is a condescending word. It implies, first, that you *can* understand your neighbor (which is perhaps more than he can do) and then, even more doubtful, that if you do understand him you will like him. It's a patronizing and fatuous word.

✳ not *too* good

The use of such expressions as "I'm not feeling too well" has led many to ask whether this use of *too* is "good English."

One of the meanings of *too* is "beyond what is desirable, fitting or right" ("No, you've given me too much"). So that when a man says "I don't feel too well," he is employing understatement. Instead of saying, "I feel awful," he is saying, "I don't feel healthy beyond what is desirable, fitting or right." It's a way of minimizing complaint and since we don't like to hear any complaints but our own, it's an attempt not to be disagreeable.

In the sentence "don't be gone too long," the *too* doesn't bother us.

The real trouble with the "I don't feel too well" utterances is that they have become a vogue and are overworked. When it becomes a habit of speech, understatement is as annoying as continual exaggeration.

Some of this overuse of *too* may be due to the fact that millions of Americans have been taught to avoid *very*—which serves the same purpose. I'm afraid that if it were put to a vote more people would object to "not very good" than to "not too good." And they would have the backing of their teachers.

❋ a *towering rage*

ANGER and altitude are curiously associated in English. We say that tempers *rise*. If they rise high enough, they may become a *towering rage*. We say so-and-so will "blow his top" or "hit the roof." King Lear, in more dignified language, cried to his "climbing sorrow."

The association is so common that it may have a physical basis. It may reflect the rush of blood to our head as the adrenalin released by fear stimulates the energy of anger.

Towering is derived from falconry. A falcon was said to *tower* when she hovered at the height of her ascent. When it was fresh, *towering rage* was a fine phrase, because it suggested that—as the falcon's towering would be followed by its strike—the mounting anger would be followed by a sudden, precipitous, murderous attack on its victim.

❋ *trade-lasts*

NOT EVERY compliment is a *trade-last* (or a *T.L.*, as they are often called). A trade-last is a quoted compliment (in the nomenclature of schoolgirls) and is offered only on condition that the person to whom it is given reciprocates by quoting something nice that she has heard about the speaker. It seems to mean just what it says: "I'll trade you compliments, but mine will have to come last—that is, after yours." This probably is to insure that the compliment demanded in exchange will be of high quality. Only the very innocent or the very corrupt could deal in such hypocrisy bait.

✳ **Is is a reproach to say of a man that he *trims his sails*?**

If he is a sailor and the phrase is used literally, it isn't a reproach but praise. To adjust sails advantageously with reference to the direction of the wind and the course of the ship is the essence of good seamanship. But in its figurative use the phrase is disparaging because it suggests that the man referred to is dextrous in pursuit of his own advantage, shifts his principles with the shifting winds, and has no fixed line of conduct. His skill in so doing doesn't recommend him, because a man rarely pursues his own advantage cleverly without detriment to others.

✳ **the singular of *trousers***

The singular of *trousers* is (or was) *trouse*, pronounced as it is spelled in Scotland: *trews*. There's so little occasion for the singular that we've forgotten it, but it was in use and presumably still could be. A seventeenth-century collection of humorous sayings states that a jealous wife "like an Irish trouze" sticks close to her man, and in a surgical work fifty years later a doctor tells of making "a trowze" and seeing that "it" was properly fitted.

The plural was *trouses*. The *r* got into the word by mistake, probably under the influence of *drawers*. The common expression "a pair of trousers" is thus a double plural with an unnecessary *r* thrown in.

The fact that our bodies are composed of symmetrical halves has caused several grammatical confusions of this nature. The Anglo-Saxon equivalent of *trouse*, for example, was *brōc*. The plural was made not by adding an *s* but by changing the vowel (as we change *foot* to *feet* and *goose* to *geese*) to *brēc*. This plural was then doubled to *breeks* (as the Scotch still call them). And since in English the Northern *k* sound often appears as a softer *ch* (as *kirk/church*), *breeks* is *breeches*.

✷ What originally was a *trousseau*?

THE WORD *trousseau* is the French diminutive of truss or bundle. It was the sort of thing that cartoonists represent tramps as carrying tied to a stick over their shoulders. Such burdens have always been a little undignified. A 13th-century homily, in fine alliterative disregard of the double negative, says that noblemen "bear not no packs and don't never go about trussed with trousseaus." Brides today usually have no such reluctance in the matter.

✷ a treasure *trove*

A *trove* is something that is found. There was formerly a verb *to trove*, "to find." And there is in law an action of *trover*, an action to recover goods which another has found and converted to his own uses.

Some people object to anyone's saying "He found a treasure trove," insisting that *find* is implicit in *trove* and the statement is redundant. But since very few people are aware of it, the redundancy can grate on only the most learned ears and one suspects that such objections are raised more to call attention to the objector's knowledge than to relieve his lacerated feelings or to improve the language.

Repetition is commonly used for emphasis and such obviously redundant expressions as "joint partnership," "reported back," "true facts," "consensus of opinion," and "endorse on the back" offend only the hypersensitive. And the chances are that they themselves use many established redundancies which they don't perceive to be repetitive—*salt-cellar, greyhound, ostrich, Sahara Desert, wreak vengeance,* and *downhill.*

✳ no *truck* with trucks

WHEN you refuse to have any *truck* with a man, you won't deal with him in any way. *Truck* in this sense comes from the French *troquer*, "to barter." It was much used by the early voyageurs and explorers who brought *truck*—glass beads and the like—to barter with the Indians. We have the same word in *truck garden*, the garden in which the farmer grew vegetables that he might exchange, or barter, in town.

The other *trucks*—those behemoths piloted by Hoffa's minions that roar past us on the highways, buffeting us with the wash of their wind—had, linguistically at least, a modest beginning. This *truck* is short for *truckle*, "a grooved wheel, the sheave of a pulley." It was at first a small spokeless wheel, as still in the nautical *truck*, the disk of wood at the mast-head. But, Lord, how it has grown!

※ **Why are certain drinking glasses called *tumblers*?**

THE WORD *tumbler* is now applied to a heavy, flat-bottomed drinking glass without a handle or stem. In the seventeenth century the word describing a drinking cup with a round or pointed bottom, made that way so it could not be set down until emptied. Drinking deep was regarded as a virtue and the cup's design was to compel you to keep at it.

※ **the *tune the old cow died of***

The tune the old cow died of is used chiefly today as a humorous expression of distaste or boredom, with a suggestion that the *tune* in the saying was so dreary that even a cow died from hearing it too often.

Formerly, however, the saying referred not to boredom but to disgust or irritation at being given good advice or sound explanations when what you needed was help.

The story, which goes back at least 250 years, concerns a man (sometimes called Jack Whaley) who had a cow but had nothing to feed her.

> So he took up his fiddle and played her a tune:
> "Consider, good cow, consider;
> This isn't the time for the grass to grow;
> Consider, good cow, consider."

But, despite the reasonableness of Mr. Whaley's explanation of why there was no fodder, the old cow, it would seem, was not considerate and selfishly died of hunger.

✷ *turkey* talk

A LADY once asked Dr. Samuel Johnson how he came to define *pastern* in his dictionary as "the knee of a horse." His answer, "Sheer ignorance, Madam!" explains many linguistic mysteries.

In former days people knew very little about geography. Columbus, as everybody knows, thought America was India—and the natives remain "Indians" to this day.

So Turkey was a vague far-off place from which strange creatures might have come. A dictionary published in 1602 says that the German word for the *turkey* was "an Indian hen"; the Dutch, "a Turkish hen"; the Spanish, "an Indian peacock." The French couldn't decide whether it came from India or Africa (it comes from America), but settled for India, calling it a "poulle d'Inde." This in time became *dinde*, whence a new masculine *dindon* has been formed, the present French word for "turkey-cock." But when applied to a person, it means a goose. So the French are even more mixed up than we are.

The colonists, of course, knew from the beginning that the turkey was a native American bird, but the language was then still being shaped in England.

✷ *twilight*

THE *twi-* of *twilight* means "two, double or doubly." *Twilight* is the time of two lights, the fading sunset and the emerging light of the moon and stars.

The prefix *twi-* was once much more widely used than it now is. *Twichild* was second childhood. *Twi-banked* described a ship having two banks of oars. A *twibill* was a double-headed bill or battleaxe. *Twiwifeing* was bigamy.

✷ *typically* and *usually*

THE USE of *typically* for *usually* ("You can typically tell") is bad English. Each word has a distinct meaning and those who interchange them at will are still in so small a minority, happily, that they cannot claim the sanction of usage.

A *type* is a kind or class or group as distinguished by a particular character. That is *typical* which conforms to the type, manifests the distinguishing characteristic or is so in accordance with the other members of the group that it could serve as a representative specimen.

That is *usual* which is habitual or customary or ordinary or commonly met with. Within the group it would, of course, be usual to encounter the typical. But the two words are not the same at all. The synonyms for *usual* are *customary* and *habitual.* The synonyms for *typical* are *representative, similarly distinctive.*

✻ Why is a little boy called an *urchin?*

Urchin was the old name for the hedgehog, a little mammal covered with spines that can roll itself into a tight, bristly ball when threatened. It looks something like a small porcupine, but it is actually related to the mole. Nocturnal in its habits and weird in its movements, it is a solitary and ugly creature, rarely glimpsed. And there is an air of mystery about it; cutting through roots as it burrows underground, it causes plants in its path to wither.

It is not surprising, then, that in former times superstitions gathered about the urchin. It was believed to suck cows dry and sometimes to poison them. Fairies, elves, and goblins were thought to assume its form; and from goblins it seemed logical to apply its name to mischievous little boys. And the word retains a trace of its old meaning: an urchin is just not any little boy; he's a mischievous little boy, a gamin, a goblin-like creature.

✷ pronunciation of *vacuum*

ALL OF the dictionaries say that it is pronounced *vak′ yoo um*. But I don't believe them. It may be so pronounced when used in scientific terminology to designate a space void of matter. But in everyday speech, where it is used almost exclusively to desigate a special kind of carpet sweeper, it is pronounced *vak′ yoom*. At least *I* have never heard anything else, even from the most highly educated cleaning women. The double *u* sound is too rare in English to seem proper. There are only a few words that have it—such as *duumvir*, *residuum*, and *triduum* —and none of these lends itself easily to ordinary conversation.

✷ *varmint*

Varmint, now facetious and affectedly rustic, is simply the word *vermin*. It was applied 150 years or so ago to anything or anyone objectionable, from bedbugs to rustlers. It may once have been used seriously, but it has been a laboredly funny word for generations and is relegated, even at that, to Grade B Westerns.

Its spelling and pronunciation are not as peculiar as they seem. *Er-* and *ar-* sounds are interchangeable in many English words (Derby-Darby; further-farther; 'varsity-university, etc.). The *t* seems to have been added to varmin(t) to correspond with the *t* in *braggart* or the *-d* in such words as *laggard, coward, dullard, drunkard*, expressing contempt.

✷ *very pleased*

"I AM TOLD that I ought to say 'I am very much pleased,' not 'I am very pleased.'"

Don't believe everything you're told. *Very* has been used as an adverb before adjectives and adverbs for more than 500 years. When the past participle of a verb is used as an adjective (as *pleased* is used in your sentence), it may be qualified by *very* or *much* and the contemporary preference is for *very*.

Very much is quite permissible, because *much* is a true adverb and *very* modifies it and not the verb (*am*) itself. "Very much pleased" is stronger than "very pleased" and "much pleased" is archaic. But "very pleased" by itself is all right.

✳ *vittles*

"THE UGLIEST word in the language is—victuals. You can't say it or write it. The best thing is to forget it." Only in America could a word be so maligned. Soon after the appearance of Harry Golden's pronouncement I was deluged with letters, chiefly from the South, belaboring poor old *vittles*. I was informed that it was "low," "unintellectual," "vulgar," and "plain nasty" and there was a suggestion that if the lower orders persisted in using it, the militia must be called out.

Vittles is a very old English word. Chaucer spells it *vytaille*. It is not a corrupt pronunciation of *victuals*. *Victuals* is a pedantic misspelling of *vittles* that took place in the sixteenth century. But the public, fortunately more sensible than many of its self-appointed mentors, went on pronouncing the word as it always had. The few that could write, however, were easily intimidated and put in the extraneous *c*. It is only spelled *vittles* now when the writer wishes to show his own social superiority to the speaker he is quoting (along with *Missis* for "Mrs.," *wimmin* for "women," *woz* for "was," etc.). So that now there is no way of writing the word as it is pronounced without seeming to be either ignorant or condescending.

In regard to providing a ship or an army with food, *to victual* is the standard, formal verb, Mr. Golden notwithstanding. As a noun, in reference to ordinary food, the word was once an elegancy and, like many elegancies, is now rustic or slightly comic, at least to educated city people.

I don't know, but I suspect that in the South (where it is chiefly heard) it is a back-country word, a word one is more likely to hear from poor whites and Negro sharecroppers than from ranch-house suburbanites. And I suspect that the reason it seems "the ugliest word in the language" is that it is a pretty plain group-identification word. Well, enjoy, enjoy, your own status!

✶ void and devoid

Void means empty. *Devoid* means empty, but empty after something has been taken away. *Void* can stand alone, but *devoid* is always followed by *of* and a statement of whatever it is that has been removed. *Void* describes a state or condition. *Devoid* describes a state or condition resulting from some antecedent action of removal. Thus *void* can be substituted for *devoid* because it describes the general condition. But *devoid* cannot be substituted for *void* unless we are told what has been removed.

The second verse of the first chapter of *Genesis*, for instance, says that "the earth was without form and void." *Devoid* could not be substituted here because "In the beginning" the earth, though void, had nothing of which it could have been devoided.

Avoid is related. Originally it meant "to empty." A fifteenth-century book of etiquette tells children always to "avoid" their plates at dinner. The modern meaning came from the idea of emptying some place of one's self by keeping away from it.

✶ vouchsafe

Vouchsafe is one of those words which every educated man understands when he comes across it in his reading but which he never uses in his speech and might not hear in his entire life. It reminds us of what we need to bear in mind, that we have several levels of use and comprehension in our vocabularies.

It means "to give or grant in a gracious and condescending manner." But since we resent condescension, it often has overtones of irony. It was originally *to (a)vouch safe*—that is, to warrant that something which was being given was in good condition. This was a little more than merely giving. It had an extra grace. And this extra grace, in the giving and the manner of giving, came to be the word's meaning.

✶ Why is a humorist called a *wag*?

Wag, meaning "a humorist," is an abbreviation of *waghalter*—that is, one who will end up being hanged or wagging a halter in his death struggles. It seems originally to have been applied to mischievous boys as a term of abusive endearment (like our expression "little devils") and then to older drolls and merry fellows, especially such as kept a youthful impudence.

To us there is nothing very funny in the idea of being executed, but when hanging was common it seems to have been an inexhaustible source of humor.

✻ "The cat *wants out*"

IT WAS at one time a rule in English speech and writing that verbs of motion were omitted after verbs of willing. "I will myself into the pulpit first," says Brutus in Shakespeare's *Julius Caesar* (III.i.236).

It's retained in poetry today, as in Housman's "I'll to the woods" and Masefield's "I must down to the seas again."

This old usage survives in some parts of the United States, especially in the Midwest, but only with the verb *to want*. It would certainly not attract any attention in any Midwestern city if a passenger on a bus said, "I want off here."

So that while you may say "The cat wants to go out," you may with equal propriety say "The cat wants out." If you use the second form you will be speaking good Midwestern English and the sort of language the best poets have used in some of their best poems. Unpoetical, uninformed people from certain parts of the East Coast may think you're speaking Pennsylvania Dutch, but that's their ignorance, not yours.

✻ *watch* the clock

A *clock* was originally a bell—though the earliest clocks were sheets of iron that were struck, rather than cast circular bells. Striking on them told the time.

The reason for *watch* is plain: it was watched. Yet we speak only of "clock watchers," never of "watch watchers" of "watch clockers."

It took centuries (and the mass production of watches) for *watch* and *clock* to be assigned, as they are with us, to small and large timepieces respectively. What we call a *watch* was for a long time called a *pocket watch,* which would imply that *watch* was also used to designate larger instruments. *Clock* was likewise used of the smaller timepieces. Izaak Walton tells of "a striking clock" which John Donne "had long worn in his pocket."

✻ "of the first *water*"

IN THE grading of diamonds the finest are said to be *of the first water*. Gradations of "the second water" and "of the third water" are also recognized among the highest grades, but these terms have not passed over into common speech.

The expression seems to have been borrowed from the Arabian diamond merchants among whom (perhaps because of the great value of water in their desert land) "water" was a term of high commendation, especially to designate luster and transparency.

"Of the first water" was used at first to designate only desirable qualities but was extended ironically to include vices. No one today would be puzzled if told that someone else was "a liar of the first water." He would simply assume that he was a liar of the highest degree of mendacity.

✻ the lock in *wedlock*

THE *lock* in *wedlock* isn't the *lock* of "lock and key." It isn't the sort of lock with which an errant husband is debarred from his house or a contraption to secure the old ball and chain.

It's the word which in other contexts we pronounce *lark* and use to mean a gay minor adventure or innocent hell-raising. Its original meaning was "sport" or "play" and then a gift given in pledge of love and as a token of pleasure. Marriages used to be very festive occasions, with a great deal of horseplay—such as stealing the bride's garters and breaking into the nuptial chamber to get the latest bulletin.

※ **What are "*weasel words*"?**

IN TODAY's usage weasel words are words with several possible meanings, so used that the utterer can weasel out of any commitment. Back of the expression one feels the swift furtiveness of the weasel, its sinuous ability to twist and turn and escape through crevices. According to Theodore Roosevelt (who popularized the expression over 40 years ago), the activity of the weasel referred to in the phrase was its habit of sucking eggs so that the meat is sucked out and just the shell remains. A weasel word was a word that sucked all the meaning out of some other word.

Stewart Chaplin, an American writer who made up the expression about 60 years ago, illustrated by saying that a political party might consider adopting as a plank the statement that "The Public should be protected." Before the plank is adopted, however, the word *duly* will be inserted before *protected*, so that it reads: "The Public should be duly protected. That makes it completely safe and it will be accepted unanimously amid wild cheers."

※ **widows' *weeds***

THE DEEP mourning which a widow formerly wore during the first year of her widowhood was called her *weeds*. It included a long black crepe veil which was called a *weed*. The other garments were always designated by the plural.

Weed, meaning "garment," is a very old word and an entirely different word from the other, or common garden variety, *weed*. It was a general term for any and all garments, men's as well as women's ("For each man's worth is measured by his weed"). Shakespeare, in *A Midsummer Night's Dream*, calls the snake's cast skin "Weed wide enough to wrap a fairy in." By the nineteenth century this general use was restricted to poetry ("In words like weeds I'll wrap me o'er"—Tennyson) and the word continued in popular use only in reference (in the plural) to a widow's mourning apparel. And even that meaning, now that the custom has been pretty well abandoned in English-speaking countries, is rapidly fading.

✳ *well-heeled*

FIGHTING cocks are equipped with razor-sharp metal spurs and a cock so equipped is said to be *well-heeled*. The term was adopted by the underworld to mean "armed" or "heavily armed." A well-heeled man carried a gun or a knife—which were his spurs.

In the modern world money takes the place of all weapons, offensive and defensive, and "well-heeled" in the innocent evil of common speech now indicates one who packs a bundle instead of a rod. It's a very grim phrase, when you think about it.

✳ Do the Welsh *welsh?*

AN INEBRIATED American once asked me the way to the men's room in a restaurant in Madrid and when I told him his face beamed with happiness and he gave me a friendly hug and said, "You ain't no God-damned foreigner; you're an American."

His assumption that all Spaniards were foreigners, even in Madrid, led me to suspect that he was of Anglo-Saxon lineage, because this has always been the Empire-builders' attitude toward the lesser breeds. When the invading Saxons first landed in England they immediately dubbed the native Celts *wealhs*, "foreigners," and drove them into the western mountains (hence called Wales) where, for a thousand years, they maintained their language and customs and waged ceaseless border warfare with the English.

And, in the Anglo-Saxon canon, not only are all strangers foreigners but all foreigners are fools or knaves and probably both. Many terms in English reflect on the Welsh, particularly on their poverty: a Welsh carpet is a painted floor, a Welsh comb is the fingers, Welsh rabbit is toasted cheese, and so on.

In English literature the Welsh have figured as unscrupulous—from Shakespeare to nursery rimes ("Taffy was a Welshman./Taffy was a thief./Taffy came to my house/And stole a leg of beef"). The use of *welsh* as a verb, to mean "reneging," first appeared in the nineteenth century. It was a racetrack term. A great many bookies, seemingly, were Welshmen and were crooked or were thought to be.

* **a whale of a *w(h)aling***

THE BOY who is punished has no doubt about what he has received, but the linguist is most uncertain. A wale is the mark or ridge raised on the flesh by the blow of a rod or lash: and if he is beaten hard enough, the boy will have some of these. They used to be as common on boys as freckles. However, since the word appeared, about 200 years ago, it has had the h in it. The elder Finn, when he was sober enough to catch him, used to whale Huck. So it may have originated in thrashing with a whalebone whip. Most likely the two ideas—the raising of wales with a whalebone whip—were blended.

* **the *wherewithal***

THE *wherewithal* is the means, supplies or necessities by which (wherewith) to accomplish a desired end. And since money will furnish most necessities and seems indispensable to the accomplishment of almost everything, it is often humorously called "the wherewithal."

Wherewithal is simply three common words fused together that (like *notwithstanding*) in their fusion have acquired a meaning they do not have separately. *Withal* is *with all* and its meaning is plain. It means "with, or in addition to, all else" ("Nor lord nor knight was there more tall/Or had a statelier step withal"—Scott). In *wherewithal*, it means "the one thing that is needed, the circumstances being what they are, to suffice." *Where* means place or position or case (as in "Scratch where it itches").

There used to be a word *forthwithal* but it has been lost.

✷ Can you say, "While the top of the car is white, the body is green"?

IF YOU mean that the top is white during the time that the body is green, you can. Otherwise, it's sloppy English.

Used as a conjunction, *while* may mean "during the time that" or "at the same time" ("It snowed while we were sleeping"). This is fully acceptable, standard English. It may also be used to introduce a contrast ("While Jack is a whiz at tennis, he is a dub at golf"). But this use can lead to ambiguity, because we are not always certain whether *while* in such a sentence means "although" or "as long as." *While* may also have the force of "but" or "whereas" ("Jack Sprat could eat no fat/While his wife could eat no lean").

In all these uses there is an intention of contrast and all are acceptable. Sometimes, however, *while* is used where no contrast or no reference to time is intended. Here it simply has the meaning of *and* ("Sam comes from New York, while Pete comes from Chicago") and this (which is like "While the top of the car is white, the body is green") is not good English.

✷ Does one *while* or *wile away* the time?

While means a space of time. When we say that something is worth while, we mean that it's worth the time it takes. Coleridge speaks of a tedious guest "who hath outstayed his welcome while." So that to "*while* away time" is repetitious. Yet that is the proper form and, perhaps, since the act itself is wearying and repetitious, the form is highly suitable. There is often a poetry in our speech that those who would sacrifice everything for "correctness" cannot reach to and often, apparently, can't perceive.

Wile is the same word as *guile*, meaning "to deceive or induce by cunning." Now when one is very bored one does employ wiles to make the time pass. And it is possible that the similarity in sound of the two words, with their overlapping meanings, led to an association. This possibility is supported by the fact that the French phrase for whiling away time is *tromper l'heure* which literally means "to deceive the hour."

✷ white hope

THE EXPRESSION *a white hope*, still regarded as slang, came into the language about 1910. It was used at first in pugilistic circles to designate a hoped-for white prizefighter who would be skillful enough to defeat Jack Johnson. Johnson, an American Negro, had defeated Tommy Burns at Sydney, Australia, in 1908 and vociferously claimed to be the world's heavyweight champion. The man who then held the championship, Jim Jeffries, was finally persuaded to fight Johnson and was knocked out at Reno, Nevada, in 1910. This left Johnson indisputably the champion. Boxing fans made a racial as well as a sporting issue of the matter and Johnson tossed them a little moral lagniappe by violating the Mann Act. His defeat, therefore, in the opinion of many, was necessary to restore White Supremacy and the purity of womanhood, and, with so much at stake, a Galahad of fisticuffs was eagerly sought and much discussed. Johnson, however, evaded both the police and left hooks with equal success until he was knocked out by Jess Willard in Havana, in 1915.

✷ "sowing *wild oats*"

THE *wild oat* (*Avena fatua*) is a common European weed. It infests meadows and is hard to get rid of once it has a foothold. To go out and sow it deliberately is not only to expend energy fruitlessly but to make unnecessary trouble for yourself for years to come.

The aptness of the simile to that extent is plain. The puzzle is why it is always used leniently with a suggestion of later reform. Perhaps because sowing wild oats, though a foolish thing to do, need not be disastrous. With great labor the wild oats could later be eradicated. Possibly because the exuberance of youth is at once appealing and pathetic and the charm and harm of the young are inextricably mixed.

The expression is very old. It was used by Plautus in 194 B.C. Once in a great while it is used, usually humorously, in the singular ("The King . . . having already sown his one wild oat"—E. S. Turner; "A wild oat or two won't hurt him"—Mary McCarthy).

✳ Why a *wiseacre?*

THE WORD *wiseacre* has nothing to do with acreage. It is an alteration of the Dutch *wijssegher*, a wise-sayer or soothsayer or prophet. The *-acre* in our word was an attempt to reproduce in English the sound of the Dutch *gg*.

Since the word first appeared in English it has been a term of contempt. Apparently the Britons didn't think much of Dutch soothsayers.

✳ pronunciation of *won't*

WE SAY *won't* instead of *willn't* because 500 years ago the word which now has only the one pronunciation *will* had several different pronunciations: *wille, wull,* and *wole*. The *o* pronunciation became fixed in the negative form. We do the same thing with *ain't*. Apparently a different vowel serves to stress the negation.

✳ "Don't take any *wooden nickels!*"

THE ADJURATION not to *take any wooden nickels* appeared in the language about 1915.

One of the main facts of American life for the past sixty years has been the moving to the city of people bred in the country or in small towns. Of the many fears that beset the yokel setting out on this adventure, not the least was of being "played for a sucker" and one of the commonest ways of being played for a sucker was having counterfeit money foisted on you.

Now a wooden nickel would be so obvious (and so improbable) a counterfeit that only the most stupid hick, the most unknowing lout, would be deceived by it. So that in warning a friend departing for the city not to take any wooden nickels, one was implying that in his case such a warning was necessary.

That it might occasionally be necessary, even to city slickers, is borne out by the fact that a few years ago authorities in Chicago found it necessary to warn the public against some counterfeit bills drawn in pencil on ordinary bond paper!

※ **Why is absent-minded inattention called *woolgathering*?**

IN ITS literal sense, *woolgathering* is the act of gathering bits of wool torn from sheep by bushes and other natural obstructions. Since these were scattered over the fields, woolgathering could not be done systematically. Furthermore it was an occupation for children and often attended with frolicking and the magnificent inattention to an assigned task that children are capable of. These things combined to make it a good metaphor for wandering fancies and purposeless thinking.

※ **"This is the dog that *worried* the cat"**

To MANY moderns the use of *worry* in such a sentence as "The terrier worried the rat" seems ludicrously inadequate. They feel that the rat was a great deal more than worried.

But this is the original meaning of *worry*—"to kill by strangling." Thus in a fourteenth-century document we read of one who "worried" another man "with his hands" and we read of thieves "worried on the gallows." Stewart in his *Croniclis of Scotland* says that a piece of bread stuck in Earl Godwin's throat and he "worried to death." This would make meaning to a modern reader, but not the intended meaning.

The interesting thing is how weak the word *worry* has become. It is now merely a synonym for anticipatory fear and often-unwarranted concern. The wonderful, strong, older idea of choking to death with fear has almost completely faded.

✱ *worsen*

Worsen was standard literary English until about 300 years ago ("Times are changed and men are worsened"— 1450). Then the word fell into disuse among the educated, though the uneducated kept on using it. It might well have disappeared, however, had not the romantic poets, seeking for effective, homely words, revived it.

But they were too successful. The public, reminded of what a fine old word it was (compared to *deteriorate*, which had replaced it), took it up again. It served as a good opposite to *bettered* and soon lost its quaint earthiness and became a sensible, everyday word again. Today it is listed as standard by all dictionaries.

Many people—I among them—find "get worse" more natural English. But *worsen* may make "get worse" seem quaint or awkward within a few years.

✱ "*I wouldn't know*"

One of the articles of the ordinary educated person's faith concerning the English language is that the subjunctive is disappearing. But in some places it is, on the contrary, increasing. There has been in the past few years, for instance, a widespread substitution of "I wouldn't know" for "I don't know."

The difference between these two statements is easier to see in the third person. "He doesn't know" is a statement of fact.

"He wouldn't know" suggests that there is no reason to think that he would know.

The substitution is made chiefly in answer to a question. Now a man can always say "I don't know." It often takes courage and intelligence and sometimes a great deal of knowledge, but it can be done. But when he says "I wouldn't know," he seems to be implying "There was no reason to think I knew" or "Whatever made you expect me to know?" And this is irritating because it accuses the questioner of being unreasonable.

However, such implications may not be intended. For some reason many people think "I wouldn't know" is more elegant and many others think it is more modest. They are creating what I would call the diffident subjunctive. This doesn't make "I wouldn't know" any better, but it puts the speaker's motive in a different light and makes irritation unwarranted.

✻ ye, you, you-all and yous

"You WHO is so much dearer than all the world beside to me"—John Churchill to Sarah Jennings.

"But seeing you was so far from it . . ."—Queen Mary II to the Princess Anne.

"I *thou* thee, thou traitor!"—Sir Edward Coke, reviling Sir Walter Raleigh.

"Taunt him . . . If thou thou'st him some thrice, it shall not be amiss."—Sir Toby Belch, instructing Sir Andrew Aguecheek in the art of writing an insulting letter.

"Do not they speak false English . . . that doth not speak *thou* to *one* . . . and is he not a Novice and Unmannerly, and an Ideot and a Fool, that speaks *You* to *One*, which is not to be spoken to a *singular*, but to many?"—George Fox, the Quaker, in a humble, Christian discourse on pronouns.

* * *

Historically *you* is plural and the accusative. The nominative is *ye*. To say "You are" is, grammatically, the exact equivalent of saying "Me am," and if you say "You are" to a single individual person you are, in the opinion of those who want to keep the language free from "corruption," not only corrupt but "an Ideot and a Fool."

The singular was *thou,* but *thou* became restricted to (1) God and (2) one's social inferiors, children and servants. This soon made it impolite, even insulting, to use to one's equals. Sir Edward Coke was doing the next best thing to spitting on Raleigh when he *thee'd* and *thou'd* him in court and was mightily pleased with himself for having thought of it and interrupted his attack to point out that he did it deliberately to show contempt.

But this polite use of *you,* with the disuse of *thou,* has left a gap in our speech, because there are many times when we want to make it plain whether we are speaking to one person present or to several. And we no longer have a standard word that makes this desirable distinction. In the South *you-all* has been invented as a new plural (though many are already using it as a singular) and among the uneducated (who are fully aware of distinctions they want to make and not, in this instance, so much ungrammatical as uninhibited) the country over we hear increasingly a new plural *yous.* This may be a Hibernianism. Fifty years ago comic Irishmen (and the Irish being then poor were all regarded as comic) were always represented as saying *yez* for *you.*

✻ **"Oh *yeah!*"**

Yeah has come to stand, to those who get excited about such matters, as the most slovenly of all "corruptions" of our speech. Choked with emotion, they ask of us only that we make the slight, the infinitesimal, effort to pronounce the simple little three-letter word *yes.* "Surely you can do this much," they plead, "to sustain common decency, to keep human communication going, to prevent the language of Shakespeare and the Bible from crumbling into brutish babble and grunting."

But I doubt very much that *yeah* is a corruption of *yes.* No one, however careless in his speech, omits the final *-s* from any other monosyllable ending in *-s.* No one ever says "gla" for "glass" or "hou" for "house."

Since the beginning there have been two words of affirmation in English. One ends in *-s.* It is variously spelled *yis* or *yes* and is always used when the speaker wants the affirming to be emphatic. And this, by the way, is the peculiar word; no other

Germanic language has it. Then there is an affirmation without a final *s*, the affirmation that is common to every Germanic language. And writers and speakers of English use them both and have ever since we have had any record of the tongue we speak. Chaucer uses *yis* and *ye*. The Bible uses *yea* (which we sonorously pronounce *yay*) 321 times but *yes* only 4 times. Shakespeare uses *yea* 16 times, *yes* 10 times. And our own ears will tell us that all Americans, of all walks of life and degrees of education, use *yea(h)* rather than *yes* in everyday speech to mark a simple, unstressed affirmation. Just as their fathers did before them for at least 1200 years.

The British use *yes* for light affirmation and meet the needs of emphasis with "rather!" (pronounced, for this purpose, *rah' thurr'*) and "quite!" The old and honorable *yea(h)* and *yes* seem preferable.

✻ yeast, leaven and sourdough

Yeast is now the common name for the material substance of the micro-organisms that cause the fermentation used in various processes and especially in the raising of bread. *Leaven*, a mass of fermenting dough reserved for producing fermentation in a new batch of dough, has, perhaps because of its Biblical associations, a dignity that has led to its being used almost exclusively in all metaphorical extensions of the idea of fermentation ("When this revelation had had time to leaven the city"; "The world was seething with the leaven of Christianity").

Sourdough, which means exactly the same thing as *leaven*, is now a slightly comic word. It was used in the pioneering days in our own West and in Western Canada and in Alaska during the Gold Rush days to designate fermented dough kept from one baking to start the next, then to biscuits and pancakes, and then to the pioneers themselves. The word became a term of praise and all Alaskans now call themselves sourdoughs.

So strongly does our feeling about the associations a word has acquired condition its meaning, that it is almost inconceivable to us that *sourdough* could be used in lofty seriousness. Yet *Matthew* xiii:33 which in the Authorized Version compares the Kingdom of Heaven "unto leaven, which a woman took, and hid in three measures of meal, till the whole was leavened," appeared in Wyclif's Version (1362) as "like to sour dough, the which taken, a woman hid in three measures of meal, till it were all sourdoughed."

✻ "doing *yeoman's* service"

Yeoman is merely a shortening of *young man*. It was applied formerly to a servant or attendant, as "Boy" is still a common term for a servant even though he may be a grown man. So *maid* originally meant merely a young woman ("the hired girl"). And it is the same in other languages: the French *garçon*, "waiter," literally means "boy."

Soldiers, being of necessity young men, are often called boys ("the boys in blue," "doughboys," "infantry"). So it is not surprising that *yeoman* became a term for a soldier and was then fixed as a definite army rank or the name for a special cadre.

Yeoman's service means good, useful service, the sort that one would get from a faithful, young, and energetic servant, one willing to work hard on the grubby, unromantic, unrewarding aspects of the task. Enough to make any employer's mouth water!

Index

(This index does not repeat the main entries, which are in alphabetical order. If an entry occurs here which duplicates one of the main entries, it means that supplemental information will be found on the designated page.)

abdidicated, 287
Abraham, 60
"accentuate the positive," 75, 269
Acts, 237, 247, 305
Adams, Franklin P., 290
Adams, John, 282
Ade, George, 208
adverb, 129, 132, 295
advertising, language of, 119, 143, 230, 240, 267, 285
Aelfric, 315
Aesop, 78, 327
Agrippa, 237
ain't, 363
'Ain Zarba, 191
Albany, Duke of, 235
Alcatraz, 23
Alchemist, The, 322
Alice in Wonderland, 125, 237, 285
alligator, 223
alphabet, hidden tyranny of, 72
Ambassadors, The, 185
Americanisms, 118, 144, 166, 176, 181, 204, 208, 214, 216, 232
American College Dictionary, 109, 155
American Dialect Dictionary (Wentworth), 227
American Pronouncing Dictionary (Colby), 145

American Thesaurus of Slang (Berrey and Van den Bark), 202
Ananias, 305
Antony and Cleopatra, 186, 303
any more, 12
apostrophe, 106
Aquinas, Thomas, 134
arcticus, 33
Arnold, Matthew, 36
Asbury, Herbert, 275
ascot, 162
Ash, Dr. John, 111
assassin, 251
assimilation, 153
audience, 79
Austen, Jane, 36, 52
Australia, 31, 196
Azazel, 306

Babbitt, 208
Bacon, Francis, 205
back formation, 71, 118, 144
Banquo, 208
Barham, Richard Harris, 165
barrister, 48
Bartholomew Anglicus, 31
Bath, 344
Beatty, Jerome, Jr., 155

371

Index · 372

Bedford, Duke of, 227
bedizen, 122
Beebe, Lucius, 83
Beelzebub, 263
Beggar's Opera, The, 297
Behrman, S. N., 75
Belch, Sir Toby, 198, 366
belfry, 222
Bell, Adam, 113
belling, 314
Belshazzar, 188
Bentley, 120
Berman, Stanford W., 267
Bernstein, Theodore, 29, 164, 178, 267
better half, 122
Beveridge, Senator Albert Jeremiah, 197
Bible, 28, 33, 39, 43, 45, 48, 50, 51, 61, 62, 81, 87, 96, 115, 130, 134, 218, 277, 315, 368
—*Authorized Revision* (1885), 341
—*Interpreter's Bible*, 319
—*King James Version*, 134, 218, 236, 302, 306, 318, 333, 368
—*New American Catholic Edition*, 303, 306, 318, 333
—*Revised Standard Version*, 134, 177, 236, 237, 247, 302, 305, 306, 318, 333
—*Wyclif's* translation, 96, 236, 369
Blackstone, Sir William, 137, 287
Blaine, James G., 251
Blandings Castle, 326
blending, 285, 319
blimp, 121
"Blue Danube, The," 281
Blumel, Dr. C. S., 223
bobby, 103
Bodmin Register, 203
Bold Stroke for a Wife, A, 315
Book of Common Prayer, The, 124
Book of Martyrs, The, 92
Book of Nonsense, The, 230
Booth, John Wilkes, 253
Boswell, James, 18, 194, 289
bored, 159
Borgia, Cesare, 173
bounce, 326
Braine, John, 35, 147
breeches, 318
bride, 122
Brown, John Mason, 53, 174
Browne, Sir Thomas, 287

Browning, Robert, 184
Bryan, William Cullen, 110
Bulwer-Lytton, Baron Edward, 287
Burke, Edmund, 98, 162
Burns, Robert, 6, 81
Burton, Elizabeth, 164, 259
bus, 174, 339
Butler, Samuel, 101
Byron, Lord George Gordon, 49, 56, 132, 225, 241, 299

cellar, 43
Centlivre, Mrs. Susan, 315
Ceylon, 309
cab, 340
Cadwallader, 296
Caesar, Julius, 356
calefacient, 102
"Camptown Races, The," 42
canapé, 301
Carey, Henry, 253
Carlyle, Thomas, 162, 233
Carroll, Lewis, 237
Catton, Bruce, 21, 77
"cat wants out," 11
Cavendish, Henry, 172
Caxton, William, 38, 138, 222
Chambers's Twentieth Century Dictionary, 156
Chaplin, Stewart, 358
Charing Cross, 84
Charles I, 86, 199
Charles the Simple, 55
Chaucer, Geoffrey, 27, 40, 76, 110, 112, 261, 271, 318, 354, 368
chemise, 312
Chesterfield, Philip Dormer Stanhope, 170
Chevreul, Michel, 239
Chicago Sun-Times, 324, 335
Chicago Tribune, 323
Childe Harold, 299
childer, 138
Chinese, 288
Christmas Carol, A, 88
II Chronicles, 139
Cicero, 307
Clark, Justice Tom, 299
clean, 5
Clegg, Charles, 84
Cleopatra, 186, 303
Cleveland, Grover, 251

clock, 356
Clooney, Rosemary, 112
cockatrice, 92
cockney, 35, 133
coddle, 246
Cohen, Mickey, 47
cohere, 20
Coke, Sir Edward, 366
Coleridge, Samuel Taylor, 127, 361
colloquialism, 144, 151, 194, 195, 221, 227, 282, 296, 321
Colly Weston, 168
Columbus, Christopher, 75, 351
comfort, 96
Congo, 322, 325
Constitution of the United States, 8, 104, 247
Cook, Captain James, 339
"corruption of the language," 40, 80, 145, 256
Crimean War, 26
Cromwell, Oliver, 117
Crosby, John, 100, 287

Daly, John, 144
d'Amboise, Georges, 172
Damocles, 337
Dampier, William, 105
Dana, Richard, 105
Daniel, 154, 188
Dan'l, the Jumping Frog, 195
dastardly, 223
Daughters of the American Revolution, 173
David, 218
David Copperfield, 199
dealership, 313
Dean, Dizzy, 160
dearth, 115
debase, 116
Defoe, Daniel, 142, 287
Dekker, Thomas, 271
Demogorgon, 263
denarius, 277
DeQuincey, Thomas, 52, 159, 208
"Description of a City Shower," 226
destruct, 11
de Vigny, Alfred, 219
devil, 53, 117, 119, 263, 294
devoid, 355
devoutly, 103

dialect, 95, 113, 120, 144, 150, 185, 215, 222, 225, 268
Dickens, Charles, 88, 115, 121, 236, 289, 304
dictionaries, 146, 156
Dictionary of Americanisms (ed. Mitford Mathews), 227, 253
Dictionary of American Slang, 133
Dictionary of Phrase and Fable (Brewer), 259
Dictionary of Slang and Unconventional English (Partridge), 202
Dido, 59
Dietrich, Marlene, 112
dilapidated, 79
Dimond, William, 83
Dinesen, Isak, 217
dissimilation, 95
dizzy, 5
dodder, 122
Dodds, Harold Willis, 330
Dombey and Son, 121
Don Juan, 56
Donne, John, 357
Dooley, Mr. (Finley Peter Dunne), 197
drinked, 131
Dryden, John, 184, 217, 256
Dublin, 128, 272
DuChaillu, Paul, 189
Dunciad, The, 253
Dunmow, 40
Duns Scotus, John, 134
"The Dying Gaul," 299

Ecclesiastes, 315
Edgeworth, Maria, 68
Edison, Thomas Alva, 290
Edward I, 252
Edwards, Douglas, 164
eggheads, 57
ei, 138
eke, 256
Eliot, John, 251
Elizabeth I, 250
Ellington, Duke, 323
Emerson, Ralph Waldo, 47, 170
Emmet, Daniel Decatur, 123
Encyclopaedia Britannica, The, 322
Ephraimites, 311
epidemic, 145
Eric the Mad, 180

euphemism, 9, 107, 117, 119, 171
Evelyn, John, 44
Exodus, 202

Fabius Maximus, Quintus, 149
Faerie Queene, The, 205
fakir, 222
Falstaff, 119, 344
Faulkner, William, 16
Felix, Procurator of Judaea, 247
Ferguson, R. W., 226
Festus, 51
fetch, 66
fiancé, 63
fiasco, 198
Fielding, Henry, 162
flounder, 161
folk etymology, 25, 29, 94, 168, 189
Foote, Samuel, 257
Forbush, Nellie, 122
Ford, Henry, 199
Ford, Model T, 312
Fortune, 275
Fowler, H. W., 24, 84
Fox, George, 366
Foxe, John, 92
Franco, General Francisco, 156
Franklin, Benjamin, 290, 331
Fratantonio, Bernadette and Venita, 128
Freud, Sigmund, 209
From the Terrace, 324
Funk & Wagnalls Standard Dictionary of the English Language, 155, 157

gallon, 244
Genesis, 147, 164, 251, 295, 315, 355
Gentleman's Magazine, The, 238
Gibbon, Edward, 62
Gilbert, W. S., 134
Gilbert and Sullivan, 71
Gileadites, 311
Gloster, Duke of, 254
gobbledygook, 157
God, 92, 150, 154, 176, 202, 274, 310, 367
Godden, Rumer, 27
Golden, Harry, 354
Goldsmith, Oliver, 76, 161
Goliath, 218
Goneril, 235
gossips, 5
Graham, Billy, 10

gratulate, 99
Gray, Thomas, 36
Great Wall of China, 100
guillotine, 277
gypsy, 58, 186

Habakkuk, 302
Hadley, Leila, 285
Haliburton, Judge Thomas Chandler, 284
Hamlet, Prince of Denmark, 200, 342
Hamlet, 58, 62, 200
Hannibal, 103, 149
Hakluyt's *Voyages*, 108
Handlin, Oscar, 21
Harris, Jed, 17
Harvard, John, 325
hasart, 191
Hayes, Helen, 17
Hazlitt, William, 140, 194
heathen, 207
heck, 194
Heflin, Dr. Woodford, 117n., 340
Hell, 273, 310
Hells Canyon, 32
helicopter, 141
Hemingway, Ernest, 29, 156
I Henry IV, 51, 122, 236
Henry VIII, 192
Henry Esmond, 189
Herodotus, 317
Hippolyta, 25
hire-purchase, 73
Hobbes, Thomas, 142
hobby, 5
Hoffa, James, 349
Holland, Philemon, 21
Holy Mackerel, 202
hoodlum, 202
Hoover, Herbert, 331
Hoover, J. Edgar, 102
hopscotch, 307
horning, 313
Hotspur, 122, 236
Householder, Professor, 24
"House that Jack Built, The," 341
Housman, A. E., 356
Howard, Sidney, 315
Howells, William Dean, 42
Huckleberry Finn, 168, 268, 284, 360
Hudibras, 101
Hugo, Victor, 219

Index

Humpty Dumpty, 5, 285
hussy, 206
Huxley, Aldous, 113
hydrophobia, 126

Iago, 151
Ickes, Harold, 84
incomparable absolutes, 247
indicated, 11
Ingoldsby Legends, The, 165
Insolent Chariots, The, 239
interloper, 140
Ironside, Field Marshall Lord, 156
irregular verbs becoming regular, 39
Irving, Washington, 93, 104, 162, 181
Isaiah, 310

Jackson, Andrew, 302
Jackson, Stonewall, 263
James, Henry, 22, 185, 331
Janeway, Elizabeth, 93
Jefferson, Thomas, 110
Jeffries, Jim, 362
Jeremiah, 254
Jerome (Saint), 302
Jiggs and Maggie, 296
jihad, 109
Job, 48, 318, 341
John, 295
Johnson, Jack, 362
Johnson, Dr. Samuel, 6, 18, 36, 58, 111, 172, 239, 258, 351
Jonah, 114
Jonson, Ben, 238, 322
Joyce, James, 27, 77, 131, 148
Judges, 311
July, 263
juvenile delinquency, 22, 64, 203

Kanin, Garson, 107, 285
Karloff, Boris, 204
Keats, John, 16
Keats, John (modern prose writer), 239
Kent, Governor Edward, 196
Kerouac, Jack, 46
Kilmer, Joyce, 241
King, Alexander, 107
King Lear, 209, 230, 235, 254, 256, 322, 346
I Kings, 218
Kipling, Rudyard, 185
Kiss the Boys Goodbye, 171

klang association, 269, 321
knowledgeable, 95
Krakatoa, 105

LaBuy, Judge Walter J., 323
Lactantius, 263
"Lady of Shalott, The," 139
LaFontaine, 327
Laine, Frankie, 140
Lamb, Charles, 239
Lamb in His Bosom, 191
lambaste, 44
Landers, Ann, 63, 100
Lang, Mrs. Jonas, 188
lark, 357
Lardner, Ring, 89
Launce, 190
"laws" of grammar, 8
Lear, Edward, 230
Lee, Gypsy Rose, 175
Leggett, James, 299
Lehman, Senator Herbert, 223
Leviticus, 306
Lewis, Sinclair, 208
lief, 228
Life, 129, 164, 229
Lincoln, Abraham, 6, 96, 110, 138, 197, 331
Linguistic Atlas of the United States and Canada, 131
"Little Boy Blue," 241
Lodge, Henry Cabot, 169, 322
logic and language, 52, 89, 235, 243, 247, 248
London Times, The, 140
Lorelei Lee, 10
Los Angeles, 90
Louis XII, 172
Louisville Courier Journal, 219
Love's Labour's Lost, 112, 304
Luce, Clare Booth, 171
Luke, 143, 177
Lynes, Russell, 58, 164, 296

Macaulay, Thomas Babington, 162
Macbeth, 208, 225, 265, 326
Macklin, Charles, 257
Madison Avenue, U.S.A., 266
Madrid, 156, 359
Magdalen, 241
"Maggie Lauder," 82
Mark, 134

Mark Twain, 78, 79, 115, 168, 195, 224, 284
Mary II, 366
Masefield, John, 356
Mason-Dixon Line, 123
Mathews, Mitford, 85, 227
matinee, 79
Matthew, 124, 278, 333, 338, 368
Mauritius, 125
may, 238
Mayer, Martin, 266
McCarthy, Senator Joseph, 223
McCarthy, Mary, 93, 140, 363
meaning, 138, 143, 148, 158, 243, 293, 301, 338
—changes in, 199
—many meanings, 156, 159, 168
mecca, 109, 246
Mencken, H. L., 24, 93, 179
Mene, Mene, Tekel, Upharsin, 188
Merchant of Venice, The, 220
merrythought, 165
Merry Wives of Windsor, The, 119, 344
metathesis, 38
meter maids, 9
Midsummer Night's Dream, A, 275, 358
Millay, Edna St. Vincent, 18
Miller, Arthur, 107
Miller, Caroline, 191
Milton, John, 37, 52, 73, 132, 193, 194, 200, 263, 273, 282, 287
mischief, 205
missile, 298
Mississippi, 201
Missouri Compromise, 69
Mithridates, 183
mob, 173, 338
Mola, General Emilio, 156
Moliere, 170
Molner, Dr., 246
Monaco, 191
money, 301
Montagu, Mrs. Edward, 56
months, origin of the names of, 262
more perfect, 247
mother, 209
mother of pearl, 209
Mudd, Dr. John, 253
Muffett, Little Miss, 68
Murrow, Edward, 245

Naked to Mine Enemies, 226

Nashville, 90
Nasmyth's membrane, 318
National Enquirer, 100
nautical, 255
Nebuchadnezzar, 153
negative and positive, problems in the expression of, 75, 125, 129, 130, 139, 245
New and Complete Dictionary of the English Language, 111
Newcastle, 89
Newman, Cardinal John Henry, 287
Newsweek, 106, 311
New Trier High School, 323
New York City, 308
New Yorker, The, 54, 285
New York Times, The, 28, 29, 93, 141, 164, 169, 174, 178, 330, 335
Nicolson, Harold, 36
no, 125
noon, 240
number, agreement in, 8, 104, 113, 248

O'Brien, Margaret, 164
obstetrician, 244
O'Connor, Frank, 36
O'Hara, John, 107, 324
O. Henry, 112
Old Man of the Mountain, 252
Olmsted, Frederick Law, 131
onomatopoeia, 35, 67, 326
Orpheus C. Kerr, 4
Orwell, George, 108
Osnaburg, Bishop of, 173
ostrich, 334
Othello, 151
"O Western Wind," 62-63
Oxford, 134, 169
Oxford English Dictionary, The, 62, 80, 85, 109, 164, 166, 259, 295, 301

pack, 115
pair, 244, 271, 276
Paley, William, 310
Pall Mall, 30
par, 276
Parade, 323
Paradise Lost, 282
Partridge, Eric, 202, 247
Paul (Saint), 51, 192, 237, 305
Peachum, Polly, 297
Pearl, Jack, 100

Peel, Sir Robert, 103
peeler, 103
Perelman, S. J., 67, 133
persuade, 101
Philip II, 308
Philips, Ambrose, 253
Pickwick Papers, The, 236
Piers Plowman, 73, 78, 294
pilgrim, 34, 95
pineapple, 33
Pirates of Penzance, The, 71
Plautus, 363
Pliny, 183
pluck, 185
plumber, 281
plurals, of compounded words, 249
Pocahontas, 159
policeman, 102
Pope, Alexander, 195, 252, 262
Porter, Eleanor H., 283
Potter, Stephen, 281
preterite, formation of new, 39, 160, 174, 279
produce, 17
Pronouncing Dictionary of American English, A (Kenyon and Knott), 24, 144
Prospects Are Pleasing, The, 151
protocol, 300
Proverbs, 39, 192
prudery, 246
Psalms, 120, 161, 186
pumpernickel, 263
purchase, 73
purism, 118, 137, 142, 143, 184, 242
purple cow, 129
Puttenham, 6
pyrogen, 102

Quakers, 18
quicksilver, 292

Rabelais, François, 162
radicals, 228
Rainier, Prince, 192
Raleigh, Sir Walter, 366
reading "at sight," 27
redd up, 177
redingote, 67
redundancy, 74, 135, 226, 267, 271, 349
Regan, 254
rehearse, 192

Revelation, 236
Richard II, 37, 96
Riesman, David, 316
"Rime of the Ancient Mariner, The," 127
riming slang, 65, 133
ringer, 115
Rollo, Baron, 55
Rolls-Royce, 119
Roman de Favel, 111
Romeo and Juliet, 112
Romans, 192
Romany, 186
Room at the Top, 35, 147
Roosevelt, Theodore, 69, 251, 298, 331, 358
rosbif, 67
Rose, Billy, 175
Rosencrantz and Guildenstern, 200
Ross, Harold, 54
rotisserator, 287

sack, 132, 158
sacrilegious, 222
Sainte Beuve, Charles Augustin, 219
Salmagundi Papers, 181
Sam Slick, 284
I Samuel, 218
II Samuel, 218
Satan, 263, 284
Saturday Review, The, 155
Saul of Tarsus, 305
scan, 5
Schjelderup-Ebbe, 276
Schreiner, Olive, 321
Science News Letter, 137
Scientific American, 324
Scott, Sir Walter, 57, 186, 233, 361
see, 234
Self-Help, 212
serenade, 79
Shakespeare, 52, 53, 60, 61, 62, 64, 69, 112, 115, 132, 133, 134, 184, 186, 202, 206, 342, 368
Shaw, George Bernard, 32
Shaw, Irwin, 266
Shearer, Lloyd, 323
Shelley, Mary, 163
Shelley, Percy Bysshe, 194, 258
should, 268
Shylock, 220
Siepmann, Charles, 226

silly, 300
Silver Plated Spoon, A, 227
skimmelton, 314
slang, 133, 141, 150, 158, 159, 185, 188, 202, 225, 294, 321
slurring, 4, 46, 105, 222, 256, 259, 300, 334
Smiles, Samuel, 212
Smith, Adam, 287
Smith, H. Allen, 179
Smollett, Tobias, 114
Socrates, 109
soldier (verb), 340
Song of Solomon, The, 219
"Sophisticated Lady," 323
S.O.S., 242
Southey, Robert, 287
South Pacific, 122
Spectator, The, 200
Spenser, Edmund, 73, 112, 205
stale, 332
Stalin, Joseph, 170
Standard Rate and Data, 113
States General, The, 228
status, 106
Steele, Sir Richard, 200, 344
Stillingfleet, Benjamin, 57
stithy, 321
Stratton, Mrs. William G., 122
Strether, Lambert, 185
Styron, William, 107
subjunctive, 74, 187, 242, 365
Sucker's Progress, 275
Sun Also Rises, The, 29
superlative with only two, 52
Surfeit of Honey, A, 164
sweetheart, 63
Swift, Jonathan, 226, 239, 310

take, 66
talk, 327
tall, 196
Tatler, The, 344
Tenniel, Sir John, 237
Tennyson, Alfred, Lord, 115, 136, 139, 184, 359
"ten o'clock scholar," 240
Thackeray, William Makepeace, 189, 318
thermant, 102
think, 49
though, 211

thousand, 244
Three Princes of Serendip, The, 309
Thurber, James, 54, 285
Time, 47, 276, 285, 290, 299, 324
Tolstoy, Count Leò, 163
too, 139
Tracy, Honor, 26, 77, 151
"Trees," 241
Trinity, The, 68
Tristram Shandy, 199
Trojan Horse, 175
Tucker, Little Tommy, 51
Twelfth Night, 198
twelve, 140
Two Gentlemen of Verona, 190
Two Weeks in Another Town, 266
Two Years Before the Mast, 105
Tyndale, William, 306

U and non-U, 274
uncouth, 107
understanding, 344
unloose, 235
untold, 341
usage, 17, 105, 142, 177, 229

vantage bread, 42
very, 345
Virgin Mary, 219, 278
Vishinsky, Andrei, 169
vivid, 232
vogue words, 207, 224, 345
vulgar, 96
Vulgate, 96

Walker, Representative Felix, 69
Wallace, Mike, 144
Walpole, Horace, 309
Walton, Izaak, 357
War and Peace, 163
Wardour Street, 122
Warren, Robert Penn, 149
Washington, George, 173, 197, 287
Washington, Martha, 159
weaved, 39
Webster, Noah, 38, 62
Webster's Geographical Dictionary, 127
Webster's New International Dictionary, Second Edition, 109, 142, 155, 295
Webster's New World Dictionary, 109, 155

Weidman, Jerome, 124
Welles, Orson, 106
Weller, Sam, 236
Wellington, Duke of, 287
Wesley, John, 57
West, Nathaniel, 179
West, Rebecca, 26
Whaley, Jack, 350
Whitman, Walt, 321
Whittier, John Greenleaf, 47
whom, 10
Wilde, Oscar, 170
Willard, Jess, 362
Wilson, Earl, 323
Wilson, Woodrow, 84, 331

wineberry, 183
wineskins, 61, 67
Winter's Tale, A, 255
wishbone, 165
Wodehouse, P. G., 326
Woden, 203
"a woman preaching," 18
Woodward, Joanne, 106
wright, 280
Wright, Wilbur and Orville, 189
Wyclif, John, 38, 43, 203

yes, 125

Zephaniah, 177